Love after Auschwitz

On the Myth of Objective Research after Auschwitz

Dedicated to the memory of the murdered
to the survivors
to my parents and brothers and sisters

For Nargess, Maryam and Mira

KURT GRÜNBERG

Love after Auschwitz
The Second Generation in Germany
Jewish Children of Survivors of the Nazi Persecution
in the Federal Republic of Germany
and their Experience with Love Relationships
(translated by Huguette Herrmann)

With a foreword by Eva Fogelman

On the Myth of Objective Research after Auschwitz
Unconscious Entanglements with the National Socialist Past
in the Investigation of Long-term Psychosocial Consequences
of the Shoah in the Federal Republic of Germany
(translated by Nadja Rosental)

Printing kindly supported by ERNST-STRASSMANN-STIFTUNG in the FRIEDRICH-EBERT-STIFTUNG.

Bibliographic information published by Die Deutsche Bibliothek
Die Deutsche Bibliothek lists this publication in the Deutsche Nationalbibliografie; detailed bibliographic data are available on the Internet at http://dnb.ddb.de

© 2006 transcript Verlag, Bielefeld

All rights reserved. No part of this book may be reprinted or reproduced or utilized in any form or by any electronic, mechanical, or other means, now known or hereafter invented, including photocopying and recording, or in any information storage or retrieval system, without permission in writing from the publisher.

Layout by: Kordula Röckenhaus, Bielefeld
Project management: Andreas Hüllinghorst, Bielefeld
Cover illustration: Romain Finke, Dachau-Studie 1986,
   acrylic, tusche, canvas, paper on offset plate, 42 x 37 cm
Printed by: Majuskel Medienproduktion GmbH, Wetzlar
ISBN 3-89942-442-5
The german edition was published by »edition diskord« in the year 2000.

Contents

Foreword by Eva Fogelman 9

Acknowledgements 19

1. Introduction 21

2. The State of Research: Selected Studies 25
   2.1 The Survivors of the Shoah: The First Generation 25
   2.2 The Second Generation 30
       Transference of the Trauma to the Next Generation 31
       Aggression and Guilt 34
       A "Syndrome" of the Second Generation? 36
       Social Relationships 39
       Love Relationships 40

3. Jews in Germany Today 43
   3.1 Paradigmatic Events, Positions, and Interpretations.
       An Attempt to Take Stock of the Situation 43
       "Critical" Jews and "Community Jewishness" 49
       Jews in Germany 52
       This is not my Country 53
       Alien in one's own Country 54
       The "Jewish Group" in Frankfurt/Main 59
       The Prolongation of History: Germans, Jews,
       the Palestine Conflict 61
       Bitburg and beyond 63
       The Historians' Dispute 65

	The 9th of November	67
	Reunification	67
	The Gulf War	68
	A Supermarket on Concentration Camp Grounds	68
	Society for the Sponsoring of the Local History of the Administrative District of Verden	69
	International Encounter in Stadtallendorf	70
	Complicity and Parallel Perpetrator-Victim Structures	75
	The Nazi Past and the German Psychoanalytical Association	77
	The Pact of Silence	79
	The Goldhagen Debate	83
	Collective Guilt	85
	Withholding the Truth, Confusion	86
3.2	Summary and the Formulation of Hypotheses Concerning the Second Generation's Mental Processing of the National Socialist Persecution of Jews	88
4.	**Empirical Analyses**	91
4.1	Method	92
	Research Design and Sampling Frame	92
	The Problem of the "Adequate" Control Group	94
	Access to the Sample and Matching Procedure	96
	The Problem of the Representativeness of the Sample	97
	Characteristics of the Sample	99
	Investigation Methods	106
	Questionnaire Investigation	110
	Evaluation Methods	115
4.2	Results	122
	Rachel G.	123
	Samuel N.	150
	Analyses of Contents	190
5.	**Discussion, Perspectives**	211
6.	**Figures**	223
7.	**Tables**	237
8.	**Bibliography**	261

On the Myth of Objective Research after Auschwitz
Unconscious Entanglements with the National Socialist Past
in the Investigation of Long-term Psychosocial Consequences
of the Shoah in the Federal Republic of Germany 283
Issues of Study Design 286
"Independent" Third-Party Rating? 287
Conflict with the Third-Party Raters 290
Clarity Regarding Parents' main Experiences
during National Socialism 293
Researchers' Entanglement with National Socialism 294
Complicity between Perpetrators and Victims? 296
Bibliography 301

Foreword

EVA FOGELMAN

1985 was a pivotal year for post-war Germany. After struggling towards normalization for forty years, American President Ronald Reagan came to Germany's rescue. Reagan laid a wreath at the Bitburg cemetery, and designated the Waffen-SS, as well as the Wehrmacht soldiers, as "victims of war".[1] Thus, a nation that was faced with the conflict of memorializing its own barbarism was absolved of moral responsibility to the true victims of Nazism.

With this background in mind, it is not surprising that a doctoral dissertation on *Love After Auschwitz: The Second Generation*, which was begun the same year as the Reagan visit, was laden with political backlash. Grünberg's research in Marburg's Phillipps University is the basis for this book. The saga of this research project, which spans a generation – twenty years – illuminates not only the intimate lives of the heirs of the victims and perpetrators, but a glimpse into the ultimate question we yet ask: how was it possible for millions of Jews and other minorities to be murdered?

As a graduate student, Kurt Grünberg, a child of Holocaust survivors who grew up in Germany, set out to understand the intimate relations of German Jews and how these Jews compare to a control group of Germans. This group was chosen because it was impossible to find an ideal control group, namely German Jews whose parents did not undergo persecution during the Third Reich. Grünberg's study of love after Auschwitz was further complicated by the lack of trust he encountered when he approached individuals to volunteer to be interviewed about their personal lives. Grünberg encountered tremendous resistance in finding willing interviewees.

---

1 | Young, J. (1993), *Holocaust Memorials and Meaning*. New Haven: Yale University Press, p. 58

This is not a surprising byproduct of second-generation Jews whose parents survived years of persecution and continued to live next door to their murderers. When Grünberg began seeking out subjects, the common image of a packed suitcase and passport at hand (just in case!) was not a myth. Peter Sichrovsky, in his book *Strangers in their own Land*,[2] reveals a collective portrait of young Jews who remained "victims of their victimized parents" with "spiritually deeply unfree voice", inhibitions and angst.

On a personal note, this was the year that I screened my film *Breaking the Silence: The Generation After the Holocaust* at the Berlin Film Festival, February 1985. In discussions that took place after the showing, I learned first-hand about the inner turmoil of non-Jewish Germans who spoke for the first time about the secrecy at home regarding their parents' Nazi past. These group discussions after the film provided a unique emotional catharsis that helped break the silence and isolation of the second-generation Germans. As young adults, some of these second-generation Germans severed all relations with their parents. While others preferred not to drudge up the family Nazi past. And yet others forgave their parents for doing what they had to do in order to survive a fascist regime.

In August of that same year, an Israeli psychologist from Ben Gurion University, Dan Bar-On, started advertising for children of Nazis to be interviewed through the University of Wuppertal.[3] Journalists Gitta Sereny[4] and Peter Sichrovsky[5] were also interviewing children of Nazis. Some of these initial interviewees were eager to meet others who were also struggling with feelings of guilt and shame when Bar-On invited them to meet each other at a presentation of his research findings. A group of Dutch children of collaborators that had been meeting since 1981 joined some of these sessions. The next phase in this healing process was for children of Holocaust survivors and children of Nazis to meet each other and discuss the potential for reconciliation.[6]

What emerged from Bar-On's work about the children of Nazis is that intimate relations are affected by a past punctuated with secrecy. Knowing

2 | Sichrovsky, P. (1985), *Strangers in their Own Land:* Young Jews in Germany and Austria Today. New York: Basic Books, 1986, A blurb on the book jacket of Peter Sichrovsky's book

3 | Bar-On, D. (1989), *Legacy of Silence: Encounters with the Children of the Third Reich*. Cambridge: Harvard University Press

4 | Sereny, G. (1990), Children of the Reich. In: *Vanity Fair*, July, 76-81, 127-130

5 | Sichrovsky, P. (1987), *Born Guilty:* Children of Nazi Families. New York: Basic Books, 1988

6 | Rosalie Gerut formed One By One

or not knowing about one's parental connection to the mass killings during the Third Reich was not the determining factor in how children of Nazis coped with this family history. Bar-On found that "children of perpetrators have married less and are more often childless than children of survivors in the same age group".[7] Bar-On explains these differences by stressing that the children of Jewish Holocaust survivors were charged with the "task of biological survival" and the children of the perpetrators were afraid of transmitting a "bad seed".[8]

Intimate relationships in families that have experienced historical catastrophes cannot be understood in isolation. Such interactions need to be contextualized intergenerationally as well as within the social milieu of the time. Kurt Grünberg's eloquent introduction lays out a post-liberation historical timeline unique to Germany which influenced the identity of second generation of victims and perpetrators. For example, the 1980 crisis had consequences on the lives of the Jewish second generation. Journalist Henryk M. Broder wrote: "This and no further. Thank you very much." This member of the second generation of Holocaust survivors announced he was leaving. Lea Rosensweig writes: "This is not my country." Gloria Kraft-Sullivan describes the legendary packed suitcase: "But it stands in reserve in the cellar, in case it should be needed. Sometimes I go downstairs and dust it." Simultaneously, left-wing Frankfurt Jews identified with the plight of the Palestinians in order to feel a sense of belonging.

As for the children of perpetrators, in 1983, the Germans expressed solidarity with the Palestinians in order to annul their own historical guilt. Legitimate German historians, known as the German "Historians' Dispute" (Historikerstreit), proclaimed that Hitler's primary goal was to fight a war against Russia. Therefore, the war against the Jews, the Final Solution, was incidental in the Third Reich.

It took an American Jewish delegation to empower their German counterparts not to be passive bystanders to the re-writing of history. In 1985, it was an American delegation led by Menachem Rosensaft of the International Network of Children of Jewish Holocaust Survivors from the United States (this author among them) that mobilized German Jews to join them at Bergen-Belsen to protest the absurd equation of the victimization of Waffen-SS with Wehrmacht soldiers. Henryk M. Broder continued expressing his outrage at the Germans in 1986 by writing: "The Germans will never forgive us for Auschwitz." The unification of East and West Germany in 1989 widened the net of victims in Germany to those who lived under communism. During the Gulf War, in 1991, Jews sitting in sealed rooms in

---

7 | Bar-On, 1989, p. 321
8 | Bar-On, 1989, p. 330

Israel and waiting to be gassed by guided missiles from Iraq, which were technologically improved by the Germans, re-kindled the feelings of victimization of Jews. Not a very secure feeling for German Jews!

While many Jewish children of survivors grappled with decisions about their intimate relationships, the tense atmosphere in Germany added to the complexity and exacerbated their struggle with issues of identity, separation from parents, and trust. The interviews and questionnaires conducted by Grünberg (to which readers will be privy to in detail) reveal the barriers that exist in forming committed relationships for this post-Holocaust generation.

As for the non-Jewish Germans, the idea that they are a product of an evil seed and fear of what they may pass on to a third generation has inhibited many of them from marrying and having children. Members of the generation after the Holocaust in Germany, whether descendents of avid Nazis or of passive bystanders, are often plagued with a lack of trust in the parent generation and distorted self-image. Members of this generation therefore face obstacles in forming an intimate relationship.

In contrast, in the United States the evolution of a second-generation identity developed in a different environment. Continuity for Holocaust survivors also meant ensuring biological continuity. Indeed, in the mid- to late 1970s, young adults in America whose parents had survived Nazi persecution, realized a collective identity of their own. Despite their heterogeneity as a sociological group, they shared the bond of a shattered family heritage. Those born after liberation have diverse religious backgrounds, political attitudes, socio-economic and educational levels. Although the circumstances of their parents' survival varied, they all suffered immeasurable loss of community, family, and identity. Whether survivors talked about their dehumanization and grief, or remained silent, their losses were nevertheless reflected in the socialization of their children.

The emergence of a Second Generation consciousness, and the development of an identifiable group, had their origin in the larger "roots" movement in the United States in the mid-1970s, in the increasingly manifest antisemitism in Europe in the early and mid-1980s, and in the restored dignity of Holocaust survivors in Israel.

It was during the social, religious, and political activism of the late 1960s and early 1970s that a number of Jewish graduate students began exploring what it meant to be children of Holocaust survivors. They shared with each other the dynamics of the relationships with their parents, their worldview as children of survivors, and how their perceptions differed from their Jewish American peers. These early discussions appeared in the *Bergen-Belsen Youth Magazine* (1965) and in *Response* (1975), a forum for alternative Jewish views. These discussions inspired psychiatric social worker

Bella Savran and this author to develop awareness groups for children of Holocaust survivors. Independently, W.A.G.R.O. (Warsaw Ghetto Resistance Organization) persuaded their children to meet and form a Second Generation Organization in New York City. Psychoanalysts in New York formed the Group for the Psychoanalytic Study of the Effects of Second Generation, and after much resistance, the American Psychoanalytic Association agreed to have a study group for this population. These heretofore small and invisible group efforts received national visibility in Helen Epstein's watershed *New York Times Magazine* article, *Heirs to the Holocaust* (June 19, 1977). In the spring of 1979, Epstein's *Children of the Holocaust: Conversations with Sons and Daughters of Survivors*[9] continued to galvanize these young adults to talk to each other. In the late 1970s, with some exceptions, children of survivors in America were not afraid to identify publicly with their parents' persecution as Jews. President's Jimmy Carter's announcement of the Commission on the Holocaust signified a recognition of the need to nationally commemorate the destruction of European Jewry.

Several grassroots efforts facilitated the meetings of children of survivors, which reduced their sense of isolation, and increased their ability to reach political, educational, psychological, commemorative, and creative goals. The inaugural event was the First Conference on Children of Holocaust Survivors under the auspices of Zachor, a unit of the National Jewish Resource Center (later CLAL – the Center for Learning and Leadership). More than 600 children of survivors attended, and the conference resulted in the formation of groups and organizations throughout the United States.

The seeds for the formation of an international second generation movement occurred when more than 1,000 sons and daughters of survivors joined their parents in Jerusalem in 1981 at the World Gathering of Holocaust Survivors. Members of the second generation took a pledge at Jerusalem's Western Wall to commemorate, educate, work towards preventing future genocides, and ensure Jewish continuity. Following the 1981 World Gathering of Holocaust Survivors the children of the survivors established their own umbrella organization, the International Network of Children of Jewish Holocaust Survivors, under the leadership of Menachem Rosensaft, born in the Bergen-Belsen DP camp.

The International Network was involved in confronting the injustice of the Holocaust and the silence or complicity of the peoples of the world. The children of survivors, as a group, became a moral voice in the American Jewish community and in the international political arena. Menachem Rosensaft wanted to ensure that the Second Generation would not be insu-

---

9 | Epstein, H. (1980), *Children of the Holocaust:* Conversations with Sons and Daughters of Survivors. New York: Penguin

lar, but would also recognize human and social issues affecting the community as a whole. Thus the International Network was the first group to organize a New York City-wide rally in 1982 on behalf of persecuted Ethiopian Jewry. Rosensaft also led the opposition to President Reagan's decision to visit the German military cemetery at Bitburg in 1985. The International Network consistently and vocally opposed the President's laying a wreath at the graves of members of the Waffen-SS in Bitburg. On May 5, 1985 Rosensaft led a demonstration of Second Generation members at Bergen-Belsen against what he called Reagan's "obscene package deal" of Bitburg and the mass-graves of Bergen-Belsen. The International Network was also instrumental in ensuring the deportation of Nazi war criminal Karl Linnas to the Soviet Union in 1987. Rosensaft, along with Elie Wiesel, spearheaded a project to collect and publish the memoirs of Holocaust survivors, originally under the auspices of the United States Holocaust Memorial Museum, and subsequently Yad Vashem.

Other children of survivors lend their voices on behalf of a range of causes. The social and literary critic Leon Wieseltier of *The New Republic* has spoken on behalf of the memory of the Holocaust dead. When the issue of the cross at the Carmelite convent at Auschwitz was raised in 1988, Wieseltier wrote, in an op-ed article in the *New York Times*: "It appears that Auschwitz has lost none of its power to derange. Nobody dies there anymore; but decency still does."

Social science research, directly or indirectly related to the destruction of European Jewry, reflects the commitment of Second Generation scholars to remember the past and its consequences. To date, close to 150 doctoral dissertations have been written on the psychological results of growing up with Holocaust survivor parents. Others have written about the Holocaust and its aftermath in fiction, plays, screenplays, poetry, and non-fiction.

Kurt Grünberg's doctoral dissertation on love relationships after Auschwitz among the second generation of Holocaust survivors in Germany is an important topic that has not been explored sufficiently. There are a few other doctoral dissertations on this topic of marital relationships of children of Holocaust survivors in America.[10] In Linda Dubrow-Eichel's research, a sample of 46 children of survivors married to spouses who are not children of survivors and 18 children of survivors married to other chil-

---

10 | Dubrow-Eichel, L. (1992), *Marital relationships of children of Holocaust survivors*. Ann Arbor: UMI; Schecker, S.B. (1996), *Exploring the psychological effects of the Holocaust on the second generation:* A phenomenological inquiry with children of Holocaust survivors and children of parents who served the Third Reich. Ann Arbor: UMI; Schneider, G.K. (1996), *Transgenerational effects of the Holocaust:* Levels of object relatedness and intimacy in adult children of survivors. Ann Arbor: UMI.

dren of survivors showed no significant differences between participants and normative samples of marital adjustment of family relationship characteristics. It was found that children of survivors had lower incomes and higher ratings on a measure of resentment than the other couples. Children of survivors scored higher than their spouses on psychological involvement with the Holocaust, suggesting that the psychological impact of the Holocaust on survivors' children may be discernible and discrete. Males scored higher than females on problematic relations with parents. Females scored higher than males on involvement with the Holocaust and a relative comfort with being emotionally dependent and closer to parents. For women higher education related to higher satisfaction and for males, lower resentment was related to higher satisfaction.

In Germany, Grünberg's study shows that children of survivors have close knit ties to their families of origin. These close relations and loyalty make it difficult to commit to a marital relation to a non-Jewish German. Those children of survivors who get intimately involved with Germans often do not marry or live together nor do they commit to having children. Some wait until after their parents die to commit to a German spouse. Only twenty-five percent of children of survivors are married to others from a similar background. These dyads have more satisfying marital relations than those children of survivors who are married to Germans.

When research is conducted on a unique dynamic such as victim-oppressor, the meta-process of conducting such research often replicates the dynamic. It is almost as if an unconscious re-enactment occurs. When I conducted my social psychological study on why non-Jews risked their lives to save Jews during the Holocaust I needed a rescuer to assist me in getting back some of my data that was taken from me when I collaborated with another researcher.[11] In Grünberg's case, "the third-party raters discontinued their work when it became apparent that the second generation Jews were confronted with their parents' experiences during National Socialism in a much clearer and more authentic way than the non-Jewish German comparison group". The German coders accused the principal investigator of unscientific methods to prove that Germans are not capable of good intimate relations. The coders stopped working from one day to the next. They were almost finished with the work, but they did not complete it. Grünberg had to find new coders. They later sued him to get paid for the full amount, even though they did not finish. A compromise was eventually

---

11 | Fogelman, E. (1987), The rescuers: A socio-psychological study of altruistic behavior during the Nazi era. Ann Arbor: UMI; Fogelman, E. (1994), *Conscience and Courage*: Rescuers of Jews During the Holocaust. New York: Anchor Books, Doubleday

reached. Needless to say, this matter held up the research and new coders were needed in order to complete the study. A victim-oppressor dynamic was re-created between principal investigator and his coders.

And if this was not enough, Grünberg also experienced, first-hand, what it was like for Jews during National Socialism and particularly at a university. He audited a course on psychoanalysis and Nazism at his university in Marburg. To his surprise Professor Pohlen explained that the persecuted Jews were "unconscious accomplices". When Grünberg challenged this assertion the professor declared Grünberg a perpetrator who employs "Nazi methods", "Gestapo like slander" and "Stürmer style". The professor said he would take legal action against Grünberg, threatened him with a large fine and with intention of preventing him from completing his doctoral dissertation. What is all too similar to Nazi Germany in the 1930s, not one out of a class of 40 students stood up to the professor. Only one person, a friend, "timidly" asked Professor Pohlen at the end of the seminar whether it was possible that he, Pohlen, might be misguided. The president of the university phoned Grünberg and apologized but never put anything in writing which could be used in a court of law. Grünberg got a taste of what it must have been like for Jews to feel so alone against the hatred and dehumanization against them during the Third Reich. Most people are passive bystanders. It was not from the common, uneducated, workers that the annihilation of the Jews was initiated. Rather, it started at the universities, in the court system, and in the medical profession. It was indeed the most highly educated who jumped on the bandwagon to persecute the Jews. A few months after Hitler got into power, Jews were not rehired to teach in the new semester at universities. Everyone complied. There were no mass demonstrations to question the firing of Jewish professors.

It took courage for Kurt Grünberg to speak up against the idea that the Jews were complicit in their own annihilation during the Third Reich in German occupied countries. Furthermore, it took perseverance to find a new place to complete his dissertation and to empower himself by getting out of the victim-oppressor bind that he relived at the University of Marburg. In the summer of 1990, Grünberg did manage to get some support in a public forum.

Love after Auschwitz is an important document. Previous writings on the post-Holocaust generations in Germany allude to problems in intimate relationships, but Grünberg has more systematic data. It is amazing that with all the historical catastrophes that the world has experienced, the field of family therapy has not studied the impact that genocide and racism have on the love relationships in subsequent generations.

Grünberg's experiences as a student and researcher also shows the courage that it takes to confront man's inhumanity to man. There is still a tendency to "blame the victim". Three generations after the liberation, the descendents of the victims and perpetrators are still re-enacting their roles. Attitudes towards the victims and their heirs will not change unless costly sanctions are instituted if institutions don't comply with how to treat another human being just like oneself. The Golden Rule needs to prevail if humanity is to survive another century.

Acknowledgements

This study could not have been conducted without the extraordinary support I received. Above all, I would like to thank my interviewees for the trust they placed in me when talking about their life stories and personal experiences with relationships. I am certain that this was often quite daunting.

My research project was generously supported by the Friedrich-Ebert-Foundation, the Ernst-Strassmann-Foundation, the Central Council of Jews in Germany, the Federal Association of Jewish Communities in Lower Saxony, the Fritz Thyssen Foundation and Jan Philipp Reemtsma. Their assistance was instrumental in carrying out this time-consuming and costly study.

I am indebted to Prof. Dr. Franz Wellendorf and Prof. Dr. Marianne Leuzinger-Bohleber for their critical and encouraging comments and to Prof. Dr. Gert Sommer, who supported me in the planning and implementation of the study.

I would also like to thank the following individuals for their help: Ewald Aul, Dan Bar-On, Hans Werner Bierhoff, Yigal Blumenberg, Werner Bohleber, Micha Brumlik, Ignatz Bubis, Hans-Joachim Busch, Michael Fürst, Adrian Gaertner, Heinz Galinski, Hanna Gekle, Hans Jakob Ginsburg, Norbert Groeben, Alfred Jacoby, Gerhard Jahn, Stefan Kaatz, Isidor J. Kaminer, Alexander Karp, Hans Keilson, Judith S. Kestenberg, Ute Kirn, Peter Kutter, Jutta Lange-Quassowski, Philipp Mayring, Martina Morschhäuser, Michaela Müller, Moritz Neumann, Gerd Paar, Gabriele Pauquet, Richard Pippert, Thomas Pollak, Klaus Rehbein, Ludwig Reiter, Willy Sage, Kai Schnabel, Christian Schneider, Sieglinde Schneider, Josef Shaked, Norbert Spangenberg, Lothar Tent, Barbara Wiese, Jürg Willi, and Arnold Wilson.

My special thanks also go to my colleagues Marion Ebert-Saleh, Stephan Hau, and Karola Brede for their often painstaking editing of the manuscript.

I owe particular thanks to Herbert Bareuther, Martin Kumpf, Wolfgang Leuschner, Anand Pant, Gabriele Rosenthal, and Jürgen Straub, who supported me in a very special way. They provided critical comments and analyses. They challenged me. And, above all, they encouraged me to persevere in the face of adverse circumstances and many doubts.

Frankfurt/Main, February 2000

The English version of the project required much stamina and effort. Beyond the original study, it includes an article that was written several years after the initial publication, which deals with the evolution of my study "Love after Auschwitz". I hope the reader will appreciate the interrelatedness of the two pieces of work.

The artist Romain Finke of Ravensburg graciously offered a picture of his "Dachau Zyklus" for use as the cover of the book; I appreciate his generosity. I am particularly thankful to Eva Fogelman for contributing a foreword to my book. She was one of the first experts in the field to consider the effects of the Shoah on the Second Generation an important topic of research.

Once again, my family, my colleagues at the Sigmund-Freud-Institute, and my friends in Frankfurt, Berlin and Chemnitz were highly supportive as they listened to and considered my questions, ideas and wishes. I am very grateful to them.

Above all, I would like to thank Huguette Herrmann, who, over the course of many, many months, persevered in the painstaking task of translating my study. She was tireless in her work and completed it despite much adversity. I extend to her my heartfelt gratitude.

I would also like to thank Nadja Rosental who translated the "Myth" article. She was always available when, over and over again, things had to happen immediately. I am very thankful to Elisabeth Eck and Julia Altenburg for reviewing the manuscript.

I am indebted to Gerd Kimmerle of "Edition diskord" publishing house for being entirely cooperative in supporting the English translation of "Liebe nach Auschwitz". I would like to thank Andreas Hüllinghorst, Kai Reinhardt, Karin Werner, Kordula Röckenhaus and Roswitha Gost of transcript publishing house for being a great team of professionals in dealing with all the difficulties that arose while working on this publication. Finally, I am indebted to a number of sponsors who enabled me to complete this English version of my book. I thank the Ernst-Strassmann-Foundation for their funding and I am thankful to Jacky Endzweig, Nicole and Robert Faktor, Daniel Jammer, Hermann Reich, Diana Schnabel, and Nicholas Teller. Without the support of many others, whom I have not mentioned, I could not have completed this project.

Frankfurt/Main, February 2006

1. Introduction

Germany, the "home of the persecutors" is *also* the "home of the victims" – of those few Jews who at least survived the persecution of the National Socialists and who decided to live in this country after the Shoah and in spite of it, and whose children were born here; most of them were German citizens holding a passport of the Federal Republic of Germany, and were invested with all rights and obligations ... Subjective feelings, on the other hand, the personal awareness of one's own life, need not necessarily correspond with these first external facts. For instance, upon being questioned, a "correction" was certainly frequently made to the effect that one had precisely *not* taken a decision to live in Germany; on the contrary, for years one had kept one's suitcases packed in readiness to leave, but ultimately one had "hung on". But even if one had taken such a decision deliberately – even in "one's own country" one could have a very strong feeling of being a stranger there (cf. Broder and Lang 1979). The use of the juxtaposition "Germans and Jews" already calls attention to a deep-seated conflict: is one to understand that Jews with a German passport, who have grown up in Germany, who have a perfect command of the German language, who are conscientious and punctual persons, who do not attract attention in the street or anywhere else, are *not* Germans? Is it not absolutely right that a President of the Central Council of Jews in Germany should protest against the wishes for peace conveyed to him for *his* country, in view of the fact that the Federal Republic of Germany was not involved in any belligerent dispute with another country?[1] On the other hand, can "Jews *in* Germany" really be con-

---

1 | The President of the Jewish Community of Frankfurt/M., Ignatz Bubis, had received "good wishes for Easter" from the Chief Mayor of Frankfurt, Petra Roth (Christian Democratic Party) and from the deputy chairman of the city councillors, Hans Busch (Social Democratic Party), who in their letter expressed the hope "that the peace process in *your* country" (quoted from the *Frankfurter Allgemeine Zeitung* of

sidered as *"German* Jews"? After the massacre of the Jews committed by the Germans, can there still be "German Jews" at all? Do they even share a common language? Can there really still be any possibilities of mutual understanding between them in view of the rift formed between them by the graves of six million murdered Jews? In which context one may still remark that in most cases there are no real graves to be found.

The view that there are (at least) two different "normalities", a Jewish one and one that must be clearly distinguished from it, namely a non-Jewish German "normality" is probably less controversial. It is very likely that a careful look behind the two façades would result in a feeling that one had entered utterly different worlds. An outsider looking at the life of Jewish families in Germany would probably be startled to find how very "fresh" the memories of the period of persecution still are so many years after the Shoah. On the other hand, an outsider looking at the life of non-Jewish German families would probably be startled to find – at least on the surface of things – how "normal" their life seems to have remained in spite of National Socialism. Only a more thorough investigation might reveal how deeply and significantly the German side also is still entangled with the history of National Socialism (cf. e.g. Bar-On 1989, Bohleber 1998, Eckstaedt 1989, Kaminer 1997, Leuzinger-Bohleber 1998, Moser 1993, 1996, Müller-Hohagen 1988, Richter 1986, Rosenthal 1995, Rüsen and Straub 1998, Schneider, Stillke and Leineweber 1996, Sichrovsky 1987, Westernhagen 1987).

It is not only since the "peace" ceremony conducted over the graves of SS men in Bitburg in 1985 that it has been possible to recognize what non-Jewish German "normality" stands for: the Germans are striving to become a "normal" people again; they do not wish to cut a worse figure than that of other nations; further discussion of the topic of the National Socialist extermination of the Jews should come to an end. This is the background against which the unique character of the Shoah was questioned in the course of the "Historian's Dispute" a few years "after Bitburg" and, following the reunification of Germany a few years later, once again the demand

April 15, 1996; italics by K.G.), which was overshadowed by terrible events, might make progress. Bubis's reaction was an ironic one. He was not aware, he said, of any tensions between the Federal *Lands* of Hessen and Bavaria (in which case Roth and Busch would undoubtedly have spoken of "our" country) and it was just as unlikely that reference had been made to the non-conclusion of a peace treaty beween the Allies of the Second World War and Germany. Moreover, he asked to be informed whether the election for the assembly of town councillors had to be held again, in view of the fact that Micha Brumlik, a member of the Jewish Community, had been elected as a councillor.

to end the debate about the persecution of the Jews which had taken place almost half a century before arose. The end of the division of Germany, frequently regarded as punishment, should at long last entail the end of remembering the criminal acts committed.

However, this attempt to deny what actually happened and to cast a cloak of silence over it is counteracted by a force which one may define as the return of what was repressed. In all the social situations mentioned above, for instance, anti-Semitic clichés about Jews reappear repeatedly, and slips of the tongue frequently occur which impressively demonstrate how very much the Nazi heritage is alive among non-Jewish Germans. Whilst it is "normal" for non-Jewish Germans to deny or play down National Socialism and its persecution of the Jews, it is certainly true that for Jews in Germany it is "normal" to live with the Shoah and its consequences (cf. Funke 1988, Heenen-Wolff 1992, Langer 1991).

The use of concepts to describe the Nazi extermination of the European Jews already raises problems. In this connection, James E. Young comments that in principle "the metaphors and archetypes used to represent the Holocaust ultimately generate knowledge of the events as much as they reflect them, and like every other interpretative element in language they veil as much of the reality as they illuminate" (Young 1988, 140 et seqq.; transl. by H.H.).

Above all, the following aspect seems to be important: if the general preference over here is to use the term "Holocaust" – "which German speakers usually do not pronounce like a word borrowed from the Greek, but in accordance with the rules of English phonemics" (Métraux 1998, 370) – then this is problematic because, in accordance with its literal translation as "burnt offering", it gives the genocide of the Jews the mystical-religious significance of a sacrifice. Although the Hebrew term "Shoah" has the equal – putative – "advantage" of establishing a distance to a certain extent between the Nazi persecution and the Germans by using a foreign term, its meaning of "great calamity, catastrophe, destruction" would seem to be a more appropriate description of the persecution and murder of the Jews. In Yiddish we find, moreover, the term "churban" or "churbn" (destruction, ruins) with reference to the Biblical destruction of the first and second Temples, which is why one speaks of the "dritn churbn" (third churbn) in connection with National Socialism (ibid.). In his remarks, Métraux refers to James Young, who stresses that the clear religious connotations of churbn were "the reason why this word was not able to find favour with the Labour Zionists writing in Palestine about the situation in Europe". Accordingly a conscious choice was apparently made in favour of the alternative expression, namely, in favour of using the word Shoah to designate the most recent, unprecedented murder of the Jews (ibid.). At this point, the fact that the use of the term "Shoah" arose at the same time as the event it describes, would also appear to be significant (ibid.).

The present thesis on the "Jewish children of survivors of Nazi persecution of the Jews in the Federal Republic of Germany and their experience with love relationships", which was begun in the faculty of Psychology at the Philipps University of Marburg and concluded at the Sigmund-Freud-Institute in Frankfurt/Main is an attempt to find out more about Jewish, but also about non-Jewish "normality" in this country. In this connection the following facts and questions have served as a point of departure for this research project: many investigations of the consequences of Nazi persecution for the Second Generation have been conducted in Canada, the United States and Israel. But which special features characterize the life of the Second Generation precisely in Germany? Many publications are based on research conducted on clinically impaired populations. For this reason, this investigation has been based on a "non-clinical" population. Moreover, most studies are either descriptions of individual cases without any control groups, or – in another case – they were carried out on a purely quantitative basis with standardized methods of investigation. This study is, in contrast to these former investigations, a comparative inquiry with an evaluation that is based both on quantitative and qualitative criteria.

A special bond with their parents has frequently been noted as one central complex of the problems of the Second Generation. Separation from the parents and the individuation process are regarded as having been impaired (e.g. Barocas and Barocas 1979, 1980). This can also be seen in aggression problems (e.g. Nadler, Kav-Venaki and Gleitman 1985, Sigal, Silver, Rakoff and Ellin 1973). The ties with one's parents play an essential role in connection with the taking up of love relationships (cf. Blanck and Blanck 1968, 5 et seqq., Reich 1987, Winnicott 1965, 88 et seqq.). In addition, as far as potential partners of the Second Generation in Germany are concerned, we are usually dealing not only with non-Jews, but in fact with *Germans*. This means that in these love relationships the critical question of the Nazi past of the partner's family comes up. This leads to a number of problems which have influenced this investigation decisively.

What part does the Nazi persecution of the Jews play in "German-Jewish" love relationships? What does this imply for the future of such relationships, in particular if one is confronted with the wish to have children or with their education?

Is there a special bond between the Second Generation and their parents? Does this hinder the taking up of love relationships? Do the parents exercise special pressure on the choice of a partner? Does the confrontation between Jewish children of concentration camp survivors in Germany and non-Jewish Germans lead to central conflicts in their relationships?

2. The State of Research: Selected Studies

Since a great many publications dealing with the after-effects of Nazi persecution are meanwhile available (e.g. Bar-On 1995, Bergmann and Jucovy 1982, Epstein 1979, Fogelmann 1998, Francesconi 1983, Grubrich-Simitis 1979, Grünberg 1983, Hardtmann 1992, Hass 1990, Herzka, Schumacher und Tyrangiel 1989, Hogman 1998, Juelich 1991, Kestenberg 1980, Kogan 1995, Laub 1998, Luel and Marcus 1984, Marcus and Rosenberg 1989, Quindeau 1995, Rosenthal 1997, Sichrovsky 1985, Sigal and Weinfeld 1989, Steinitz and Szonyi 1976, Valent 1998, Wardi 1990) reference will be made below above all to works which seem particularly relevant to the problem which is being investigated in our own case. To start with, attention will be paid to the subject of the First Generation of survivors; after this, the Second Generation will be subjected to a more precise scrutiny. Then the transmission of the trauma of persecution to the next generation will be examined. Insights gained about primary relationships within the family as well as social, and in particular, love relationships outside the family, and finally an assessment of the world in which Jews live in today's Germany also based on the author's own experiences, will lead to a definition of the hypotheses on which this study rests.

2.1 The Survivors of the Shoah: The First Generation

"How many murders of one's children must a person be able to bear without evincing any symptoms, in order to claim a normal constitution?" This is the question to which the US-American psychiatrist and psychoanalyst

Kurt R. Eissler (1963) came, based on his expertise concerning victims of National Socialism. He criticised traditional psychiatric opinion according to which every traumatic experience – regardless of how overwhelming it is – will only have an effect upon individuals for a limited period of time. All permanent injuries must, therefore, be regarded as conditioned by heredity; they did not have any causal connection with National Socialist persecution (cf. M. Kestenberg 1982). This is also the attitude which has led in innumerable cases to the refusal of claims for so-called "compensation" payments.[1]

This controversy caused a number of psychiatrists to devote intensive study to the injuries suffered by survivors as a result of National Socialist persecution. Since its publication in 1964, the volume *Psychiatrie der Verfolgten* (Psychiatry of the Persecuted) by Walter Ritter von Baeyer, Heinz Häfner and Karl Peter Kisker, whose investigation was based on about 700 expert opinion reports (cf. also Keilson 1979, Lempp 1979), has remained the "standard study" in German. In the authors' opinion, "the more or less persistent *insecurity in personal relationships*" is the main psycho-dynamic reason for the reaction syndrome of the persecuted (Baeyer, Häfner and Kisker 1964, 370). They note a *"generalization of the mistrusting and embittered attitude to the social environment* [...], which is found in nearly all those who have suffered severe persecution. Real experiences, which decisively and permanently destroy personal relations combined with the conflicts in which persecuted persons are entangled with their social environment *after* their liberation lead to a pathological structure of relations, which is an essential characteristic of the change of personality caused by their experience" (ibid.).

The US-American psychiatrist and psychoanalyst William G. Niederland also submitted results of an investigation which attracted great attention. He introduced the term *survivor syndrome* into medical and psychiatric science, since a great many of the concentration camp survivors whom he examined exhibited a similar clinical structure, which other observers in other countries discovered independently of him. Niederland (1961) describes six psychiatric characteristics, which he has found in survivors:

1. One feature which is characteristic for the survivor syndrome is an all-pervasive *depressive mood* with sullen behaviour and a *tendency to withdraw*; either general apathy or occasional short-lived outbursts of anger; feelings of helplessness and insecurity; a lack of initiative and interest; a predominance of self-rejecting atti-

---

1 | M. Kestenberg (1982) has given the very appropriate title *Discriminatory aspects of the German indemnification policy. A continuation of persecution* to his remarks.

tudes and modes of expression. In extreme cases, these victims looked like a "living corpse".
2. A serious and persistent guilt complex is involved. Niederland (1980) speaks of a "deep-seated *survivor guilt* which centers around the question: Why have I survived the catastrophe, whilst others – parents, children, brothers and sisters, friends – perished? This question which is unanswerable probably involves the heaviest psychological burden which the survivor has to bear and at the same time, it illustrates the macabre irony that it is not so much the culprits and the executors of the Nazi crimes, but rather their victims who seem to suffer from the guilt of survival" (ibid., 232).
3. A partial or complete *somatization*, which ranges from rheumatic or neuralgic complaints and pains in various parts of the body, headaches and trembling, to well-known psychosomatic disorders (stomach ulcers, colitis, respiratory and cardiovascular diseases), usually accompanied by hypochondriacal symptoms.
4. Attacks of *panic and agitation*, which led to insomnia, nightmares, motor restlessness, inner tension, trembling or fear of renewed persecution and which frequently culminated in paranoid ideas and reactions. These survivors appeared to be chronically in a state of anxiety and continuously tormented, they were frequently afraid to be alone; yet at the same time, they seemed unwilling to participate in social activities or even to engage in conversation.
5. Survivors, who had been put into concentration camps at an early age, exhibited *personality changes*, which were characterized by a more or less complete breakdown of the entire process of growing up, of behaviour and appearance. However, such changes of personality might also partly be found among adults, who had been exposed to the strain of protracted persecution.
6. One also finds fully developed *psychoses* or disturbances similar to psychoses accompanied by delusions, paranoid phenomena, morbid brooding, complete lethargy, stupor-like or agitated behaviour. In these cases, depressive phenomena also frequently characterized the clinical picture.

Niederland expressly points out that the above enumeration is not to be considered as a complete classification of the psychiatric consequences of Nazi persecution, but that it represents an overview of some clinical or psychodynamically significant aspects. Moreover, mental symptoms that were the result of organic injuries to the brain or concussion, caused by blows on the head or other forms of ill-treatment, have not been included.

In the volume edited in 1980 by Joel E. Dismdale, *Survivors, Victims, Perpetrators*, the "Nazi Holocaust" is considered from the historical, political, psychological, sociological and psychiatric point of view (cf. also Krystal 1968, Krystal and Niederland 1971). One of the authors writing in this book, Robert Jay Lifton (1980) deals with various traumatic experiences (Nazi persecution, the atomic bomb dropped on Hiroshima, the Vietnam war, the flood catastrophe at Buffalo Creek in 1972). Lifton lists five important psychological problems which survivors have:

1. the *"death imprint* with its related *death anxiety"* (ibid., 117). One is dealing in these cases with *"indelible images* not just of death, but of grotesque and absurd" (ibid., 117 et seqq.) forms of dying;
2. *death guilt,* often also called *survivor guilt,* which is epitomized by the question: "Why did I survive while he, she, or they died?" (ibid., 118) The point at issue is the inability to act in a way which one would normally regard as appropriate, and the inability to feel "appropriate" emotions.
   One must distinguish between psychological guilt and moral or legal guilt. As far as survivors are concerned, we are dealing with a "paradoxical guilt", one of the many and possibly the most ironical of the "undeserved" after-effects of their experience. This irony is the more glaring if one remembers that survivors feel more guilt than their tormentors.
   In this connection, Lifton also calls attention to one aspect of the feeling of guilt which he feels to be positive. It can act as a strong incentive for a feeling of responsibility;
3. *"psychic numbing* or the diminished capacity to feel" (ibid., 120). On the one hand, psychic numbing is a necessary psychic defence against overwhelming impressions and stimuli; however, it can soon outlive its usefulness and lead to retreat, apathy, depression and despair;
4. the sensitivity of the survivors "toward the counterfeit or *suspicion of counterfeit nurturance"* (ibid., 122). One is confronted here with a "moral inversion – the counterfeit universe" (ibid.), which the survivors have experienced. They had been torn to and fro, between an impulse to reject these structures completely, and the necessity of adjusting to them, thus even internalizing parts of them in the course of doing so in order to survive. This may later lead to mistrust in human relationships; on the positive side, it may also lead to a special "sensitivity to falseness" (ibid., 123), as the case may be;
5. the "survivor's *struggle for meaning"* (ibid., 123). This might even be a "mission" ("survivor mission"; ibid.), in which, as a witness, one fights for a better world. For many Jewish survivors, this mission has taken the form of a commitment to the state of Israel.

The Norwegian psychiatrist Leo Eitinger (1980) – also one of the authors represented in the volume edited by Dimsdale – attaches great importance to the cerebral-organic conditions in concentration camp survivors, caused by external action. He has carried through very extensive research with concentration camp survivors in Norway and Israel. In one of his Norwegian studies, Eitinger examined more than 2,500 concentration camp survivors in Oslo's university clinic; 227 of them were subjected to a particularly thorough examination. The existence of a "concentration camp syndrome" was discovered, which exhibited a pronounced correlation with the severity of the torture applied, the existence of head injuries, the loss of weight and the hardness of captivity. Altogether it was found that *somatic traumas* predominated: head injuries, hunger and infections produced organic psychological syndromes involving intellectual impairment and other symptoms of slight dementia. On the other hand, there were predominant *psychic traumas* involving states of panic and other mental disturbances, which resulted in clearly affective and emotional irritations and mood disturbances.

In Eitinger's Israeli study (Nathan, Eitinger and Winnik 1964) the *absence* of a cerebral-organic syndrome had been noted. An investigation involving 157 concentration camp survivors had been carried out in a psychiatric hospital. A control group consisted of 120 patients of similar origin who had been able to flee into Soviet exile during the Nazi period. In comparison with this control group, the concentration camp survivors suffered from numerous chronic depressions, panic reactions and disturbances in social and family skills; they did not, however, exhibit paranoid conditions and very rarely psychotic reactions.

The divergent results (Niederland versus Eitinger or Israel versus Norway) as regards the occurrence of cerebral-organic conditions may possibly be due to the *specific* character of the populations involved in each case. As far as the mostly non-Jewish Norwegian survivors are concerned, these were on the whole resistance fighters who had been exposed to different conditions of captivity. The chances Jewish prisoners had had of surviving had been much smaller; severe head injuries for instance would undoubtedly have resulted in being selected to be killed.

A further divergence in the results of the investigations concerns the question of the occurrence of *survivor guilt*. Whereas, according to Niederland, this is one of the essential components of the survivor syndrome (see above), Eitinger was not able to confirm these findings. Here, too, a reference to the different populations which had been investigated ought to clarify the matter. The Norwegian resistance fighters were imprisoned as a result of political activities in which they had deliberately engaged. After their liberation, they were welcomed with open arms as heroes in their own country. Jews, on the other hand, were persecuted solely on account of their Jewish origin, not because of their personal opinions and actions resulting from their political conviction or critical attitude to society. In contrast to political opponents of Nazism, who were persecuted as individuals, *all* Jews were persecuted, regardless of whether they were babies, children, women, men or old people. Moreover, there can be no question of Jews being "welcomed with open arms as heroes", insofar as they returned at all to their "own country".

The Canadian Robert Krell (1984) not only questions the existence of survivor guilt in concentration camp survivors, which in his opinion is too often taken for granted. In addition, he has doubts as to whether research on the problems of survivors is generally adequate. Thus, one must bear in mind that the components of the concentration camp syndrome are at bottom the logical, "reasonable" aftereffects of an experience of persecution which defies all reason. A survivor, who is not mistrustful, who does not suffer from nightmares, who is not sporadically depressed, must accordingly be regarded as a psycho-pathological case. To be "normal" after undergoing the experience of a concentration camp is sheer insanity.

One must undoubtedly, says Krell, regard the constant fear, the threat of death, the loss of a personal identity, combined with the loss of members of one's family, without having the possibility to mourn for them, as the epitome of the experience of a psychic trauma (cf. in this connection D. Becker 1997, 39 et seqq., Davidson 1987, 26 et seqq., Durst 1994, 1995). What consequently seems to be remarkable and ought to be investigated is the fact that so many survivors were at all able to adapt to post-war life.

In addition, Krell disapproves of the use of an inadequate terminology, which results from the research approaches criticized earlier and from the inability of research workers to comprehend the extent of Nazi sadism. They had thus been led to draw unacceptable parallels. For instance, by applying such constructions as "identification with the aggressor", behaviour "similar to that of the Nazis" had been attributed to survivors. The equating of the aggressiveness of survivors with Nazism is a prolongation of their dehumanization. Thus, a mistaken terminology led to misconceived therapeutic treatments being adopted and also resulted in the fact that the remarkable adjustments and strategies of coping with their life achieved by the majority of survivors and their children have remained unnoticed (concerning the subject of psychotherapy with survivors and their families, cf., M.S. Bergmann 1982, Gampel 1998, Marcus and Rosenberg 1989, Speier 1987).

2.2 The Second Generation

First Publications

The Canadians Rakoff, Sigal and Epstein (1966) are the authors of one of the first publications dealing with the children and families of concentration camp survivors. They had been struck by the disproportionately large number of children of concentration camp survivors – matched against the Jewish population of Montreal – in the psychiatric unit of the "Jewish General Hospital" in Montreal (26 out of 97 Jewish families that had come to the clinic within a period of two years were families of concentration camp survivors).

Rakoff, Sigal and Epstein speak of a deterioration in the familial organization structure. The parents' preoccupation with harrowing memories of persecution meant that they had only slight emotional reserves with which they could satisfy their children's needs. Thus the parents tended to expect that *their* children should help them with their own difficulties rather than the reverse. The setting of limits by the parents was either rigid or chaotically ineffective and was rarely related to the children's needs. The children were either apathetic, depressive and suffered from a feeling of emptiness or they exhibited an agitated hyper-activity, which reflected a strong dissatisfaction with their parents and with society. The parents frequently expected their children to incarnate members of the family who had been murdered. When such idealized wishes were not fulfilled, the parents reacted with reproaches, as if their psychic survival depended upon the children's conformity. A genuine emotional commitment was accordingly missing.

Bernard Trossman (1968) records the observations he made of adolescents in Montreal's "Mc Gill Student Mental Health Clinic". He speaks of parents who used their children as an audience for the mercilessly repeated tales of their terrible experiences of persecution. One possible consequence was a pathology of a depressive character. The adolescent felt guilty because his fate was a better one than that of his parents. Trossman also mentions that some parents, plagued by the fear of enduring losses, were excessively overprotective. They constantly warned their children of impending dangers. Whilst some children developed lighter phobias, others made the attempt in ever recurrent fights to fend off their overprotective parents.

Trossman regards the explicit or tacit message that the child must endow the life of his parents – which would otherwise be empty – with a meaning, that it must justify the suffering endured by his parents, as possibly the most problematical attitude adopted by the parents. This expectation which is almost impossible to fulfil led to many, even good students giving up their studies in despair or it resulted in extreme rebellion on their part.

Transference of the Trauma to the Next Generation

In an attempt to throw light on the transference of the parents' extreme traumatization to the Second Generation, the psychoanalyst Ilse Grubrich-Simitis (1979) refers to the term "cumulative trauma" used by M. Masud R. Khan. At the start, we are dealing with a disturbance in the preverbal mother-child relationship. "During the period of greatest helplessness and dependence, at a time when the earliest psychic structures are beginning to be established, the infant is at the mercy of the mother's capacity for flexible empathy and her ability to function as an auxiliary ego for his anaclitic needs, i.e., as a 'protective shield' against the infant's being overwhelmed by internal and external stimuli" (ibid., 431). This does not, however, imply gross neglect; rather are we dealing here with "externally inconspicuous failures of empathy which, over an extended period of time, silently and at first invisibly, exert a cumulative traumatic effect" (ibid., 431 et seqq.) The child is being constantly overtaxed. Further excessive demands represent the delegating of acts which cannot possibly be carried out, such as for instance the expectation that daughters and sons ought to be for their parents "a bridge to life, thereby, once more in a reversal of the natural order of events, giving psychic birth to them, freeing them from their inner deadness" (ibid., 434). The "survivor guilt" in the parents, says Grubrich-Simitis, returns again in the Second Generation as a "specific form of separation guilt which the children feel toward the parents" (ibid., 436). Hillel Klein (1973) states in this connection that survivors tried above all to restore their "lost" families with the help of their children, to undo the destruction that had been suffered. Nonetheless, an overprotective attitude on the part of the parents resulting from this and the over-emphasizing of "the family" should on no account be confused with pathology; one was rather dealing in such cases with a mechanism enabling one to cope with the situation (cf. also in this connection Krell 1984).

Barocas and Barocas (1979) also study the early symbiotic parent-child relationship in survivors' families. They come to the conclusion that in many families the normal course of the separation and individuation processes (cf. Mahler et al., 1975) represents a threat to the family's equilibrium. This danger is also felt by the child, so that a separation calls forth deep fears of destruction on both sides. Concentration camp survivors tried to secure their own identification through their children. Unconsciously, the survivors endeavoured to perpetuate a symbiotic identification with their children. Frequently, the main responsibility for the family's integrity was assigned to the children; "honour your parents" seemed to be one of the chief moral commandments given to the children. This leads to the children having considerable difficulties in expressing aggression and often to oppressive guilt feelings. On the other hand, it was also possible for survivors to subtly convey to their children that they should act out the parents' aggressive impulses which they were unable to express themselves on account of their own difficulties.

Haydée Faimberg (1987) accords central importance to the grave identification of Second Generation members with their parents, even though her remarks are not restricted to the problem of the consequences of Nazi persecution. Taking the analysis of a survivor's son as a point of departure, she discusses the "genealogy of certain identifications". Faimberg speaks of the "telescoping of generations". She found not only an exceptional psychic emptiness in her patient, but also "the tyrannical intrusion of a history that concerned his father. In that sense there was an 'overfullness', an object that was never absent" (ibid., 104), a subject whose secret has to be understood in the analysis. Ultimately, one is dealing with a "condensation of three generations", the parents also "form part of a family system" (ibid., 107). Faimberg is concerned with the "internal parents" in the psyche of the Second Generation. The parents "consider the child as a part of themselves. [...] If the parents' narcissistic love means snatching away from the child what gives him pleasure, as a consequence, when the child differentiates himself, they hate him" (ibid., 116). A further complication is: "*What the parents hate in the child is also what they hate in themselves*" (ibid.). Identity is "*determined* by what had been excluded from the history of the parents". An identity, that is "organized under the aegis of negation, it can be labeled *negative identity*" (ibid.).

More recently, there has been much more interdisciplinary research in the field of (extreme) traumatization (cf. for instance, Appelbaum, Uyehara and Elin 1997, Bergmann 1996, Fischer and Riedesser 1998, Schlösser and Höhfeld 1998, Streeck-Fischer 1998, van der Kolk, McFarlane and Weisaeth 1996). In this connection, reference must also be made to the latest insights into neurology and into brain biology (van der Kolk 1998, van der Kolk, Burbride and Suzuki 1998) as well as to attempts to understand the concept of trauma as a symptom of the epoch beyond the clinical perspective. Characteristic of the interest in this research is e.g. the foundation of an "International Study Group for Trauma, Violence, and Genocide" (cf. Berens 1996), which brought a network of research institutions for this field of study into being in November 1998. An international congress "Body – Soul – Trauma" was held in Göttingen in March 1999, in which several symposiums and lectures dealt with the consequences of National Socialism. In the collection of essays *Schnelle Eingreiftruppe "Seele". Auf dem Weg in die therapeutische Gesellschaft* (Quick Task Force "Soul". On the Way to the Therapeutic Society) published by *medico international* (1997), one finds, however, critical remarks concerning the fact that in "trauma work", the social and political context of the traumatizations frequently continues to be ignored, for instance in the wording of the concept of "Post Traumatic Stress Disorder" (PTSD). This concept is an attempt to define events by means of their after-effects. In this way, the victims were stigmatized and pathologized as "mentally ill", instead of an attempt being made to understand the circumstances in society that had caused traumatization (cf. in particular on this point D. Becker 1997).

Aggression and Guilt

The findings and theoretical considerations based on clinical practice which showed that the particularly close bonds of survivors' children with the First Generation were essentially expressed by the conspicuous inhibition of aggression and by guilt feelings towards the parents have led to several investigations of this interrelationship (cf. Rakoff, Sigal and Epstein 1966, Trossman 1968).

Russell (1974) reports on family therapies conducted with 34 families of survivors in Montreal, Canada. The reason given for coming for therapy was frequently said to be that the adolescents (the patients identified) could "not be controlled". The family therapeutic treatments had proved to be "difficult, but possible". As far as the prognosis is concerned, Russell on the whole tends to be rather sceptical. The sons or daughters of survivors laboured under a tremendous burden of guilt. They were angry with their parents. But their feelings of guilt hardly allowed them to rebel openly against these very same parents "who had gone through such a lot". Moreover, Russell noted that parents either set limits that were too rigid or none at all. Russell diagnosed more "double binds", "skews" and personality splits, destructive dyads and alliances of three, incongruities, dysfunctional communication models and maladjusted sequences of behaviour than were to be expected. Moreover, the parents often had greatly exaggerated expectations concerning the school performance of their children.

Shamai Davidson (1980) describes his clinical experiences with the children of survivors over 20 years of out-patient and in-patient psychiatric treatment in Israel. He, too, sees aggressive behaviour as a frequent problem in the families of survivors. Davidson refers to the parents' experiences of persecution, when they were forced to suppress their own aggressions under National Socialism. As a result, these parents had difficulties in reacting adequately to their children's aggressive impulses, and this led either to excessive or to insufficient control. On the part of both the parents and the children, aggressive impulses were associated with the actions of the Nazi persecutors, causing strong feelings of guilt. Aggressive impulses were either suppressed or they were projected onto other people outside the family or to one of their own children or siblings.

In contrast to several other research inquiries, the Israeli study of Nadler, Kav-Venaki and Gleitman (1985) did not investigate a clinical population, but a group of "normal" children of survivors. Structured research techniques were used to obtain data. The group that was investigated consisted of 19 children of survivors; the control group consisted of subjects of similar origin, whose parents, however, had emigrated to Palestine before 1939. In addition to using a modified version of the "Rosenzweig Picture

Frustration Test", structured interviews were conducted. It was found that the descendants of survivors reacted differently to frustrating situations than the control group. They directed their aggressions not outwardly, but against themselves. They assumed the guilt themselves. The children of survivors seemed burdened by feelings of obligation and responsibility towards their parents and by the need to fulfil their parents' expectations. In order to protect their vulnerable parents from further suffering, they suppressed aggressive impulses. They also learnt that the expression of such feelings invariably involved feeling guilt. The suppression of aggression resulted later in general passivity. Moreover, one was apparently dealing here with "enmeshed" families (cf. Minuchin 1974, 70 et seqq.). The children had a feeling that their parents restricted their personal freedom. The suppressing of aggression resulted in defensive attitudes, guilt feelings and depression. And finally the feeling of an impending catastrophe which is easily roused in the families of survivors signified that there was a higher level of free-floating anxiety in these families.

In another Israeli study, Bachar, Cale, Eisenberg and Dasberg (1994) dealt with the problem of expressing aggression. This is one of the few publications about the *Third* Generation. They investigated 54 grandchildren of Holocaust survivors and 43 subjects from a control group and used the Israeli version of Petermann and Petermann's "test for the detection of aggressive behaviour in concrete situations" (EAS). The EAS is a projective method, in which 22 pictures showing frustrating experiences are submitted to the subjects. The children must then select one of three possible reactions to the frustrating situations presented.

The authors came to the conclusion that the grandchildren of Holocaust survivors did not differ from the control group as far as the externalization of aggression is concerned. In contrast to the findings of Nadler et al. (1985) regarding the Second Generation, Bachar et al. find a tendency in the Third Generation – statistically defined – to show *more* aggression than the control group. Thus Bacher et al. put forward the assumption that this might possibly be considered as indicating that the transgenerational transmission of trauma has come to an end in the Third Generation.[2]

2 | The study of John J. Sigal and Morton Weinfeld (1989) is also one of the few publications dealing with the Third Generation. Between 1975 and 1985, the authors studied all the admission files in the "Department of Child Psychiatry" of the same clinic in which Rakoff et al. (1966) had conducted their investigation. These comprised the files of 127 children, who had been brought for treatment during this period of time. The group of 69 children with a "Holocaust background", had contrary to the clinical impressions gained as regards their moods, personality or behavioural items, *not* differed from the control group. However – and this is significant –

A "Syndrome" of the Second Generation?

Whereas Barocas and Barocas (1979, 1980) see a conspicuous similarity between the symptomatology of the Second Generation and the survivors' syndrome of their parents – and therefore suggest the existence of a specific syndrome of survivors' children –, Sigal, Silver, Rakoff and Ellin (1973) oppose such a hypothesis of specificity, when they declare that similar aftereffects can also be found among the children of non-survivor families if the parents harbour some excessive preoccupation (e.g. as a result of chronic disease or alcoholism on the part of one of the married partners). In this connection, Ilse Grubrich-Simitis (1979) notes that although a far-reaching parallelism of the mental disturbances of both generations which had been initially expected was not confirmed, still "certain similarities in symptoms, fantasies, and defense structure, based on the children's identification with their parents, are nevertheless discernible" (ibid., 436).[3] Furthermore, she states that – in contrast to the *inner* collapse which occurs in psychosis – "in the concentration camps a psychotic universe was *realized*. [...] The perpetration of atrocities of an unimaginable order of magnitude, worse than the worst imaginable oral-cannibalistic or anal-sadistic fantasies, under conditions in which all highly organized defense structures and mature superego demands had been destroyed, these events must have signified the downfall of the secondary process and the 'seizure of power' by the primary process" (ibid., 437 et seqq.). Therefore, the expectation that the children of survivors might restore the parents' confidence "in the secondary process and its ability to control and delay drive impulses" (ibid.) was one that was bound to overtax them.

The question whether one can indeed speak of a *disorder* in the Second Generation is also a controversial one in specialist literature. Fogelman and Savran (1979) discern a "unique" syndrome in the children of survivors, which is not, however, necessarily pathological. Judith S. Kestenberg (1982b), who stresses this point, speaks of a "survivor's child complex[4] –

they noted that the Third Generation was strongly overrepresented, by more than 300 per cent (Sigal and Weinfeld 1989, 154) in comparison with the proportion of Holocaust families in the population.

3 | Grubrich-Simitis (1979) mentions in this connection that both generations have similar nightmares, that they share a disturbed perception of time, the experience of standing still and of having no future, depressions, feelings of alienation and hypochondriacal fears. In addition, she mentions certain similar "specific defenses, developed by the parents during the catastrophe" (ibid., 436) and problems in differentiation between phantasy and reality (ibid., 439).

4 | In the sense of "constellation" (cf. Kestenberg 1980, 776).

not a syndrome". Kestenberg (1980, 801) remarks that most patients of the Second Generation exhibit an unusually strong ego and an enormous ability to achieve sublimation. The same cause that produces pathological symptoms in the children of survivors may also lead to sublimation in these very persons (cf. also Kestenberg 1982a). It may impel them to care for other persons, to work in social professions, to acquire an awareness of social problems, to be creative or active. The wish to live in the parents' past, to undo the Holocaust, may lead to pathology, but it can also prompt a desire to learn from history how another Holocaust might be prevented.[5]

Savran and Fogelman (1979) see that it is possible for the children of survivors who have stopped rebelling against their Jewish identity to find fulfilment in the expression of their Jewishness in the form of communal, religious, cultural or political commitment. It is possible for them to learn or teach something about National Socialism[6], or to express their feelings about it in writing, in films, in art, in music or in dancing.[7] The greatest impact on many children of survivors was possibly that of their commitment to the State of Israel.[8] Other children of survivors have taken up the cause of oppressed minorities; they have fought the racism both of their own parents as well as that generally prevalent. Finally, the authors stress the importance of the organizations of survivors' children, which have been founded especially in the USA.

Based on the experiences they have had, Bergmann and Jucovy (1982, 312) assume, however, that it is not possible for a child to grow up without fear in a world in which the Holocaust represents the dominant psychic

5 | Here the question arises, however, what is the significance for society of such insights acquired by survivors' children. One might critically argue against Kestenberg that the Holocaust was *not* a consequence of the behaviour of Jews, but that the issue was (and still is) the actions that were taken by *non*-Jewish Germans.

6 | L. Newman (1979) speaks of the feeling of obligation of some survivors' children to tell the story of the Holocaust again; cf. also H. Epstein (1977).

7 | There are, in particular, a great many literary works dealing with the experience of the Nazi extermination of the Jews, for instance the numerous books written by survivors such as Elie Wiesel, Jean Améry, Primo Levi, the poems and other works by Paul Celan, the novels of Jurek Becker (1969, 1986), the poems of Hans Keilson (1986), the stories of Friedrich Torberg (1968), Josef Katz's *Erinnerungen eines Überlebenden* (Memoirs of a survivor, 1973) or Ruth Klüger's *Still Alive* (1992). From the Second Generation, we have such unusual works as the "comic strip" *Maus* by Art Spiegelman (1986), the numerous novels by Leon de Winter (such as *SuperTex* 1991, *Serenade* 1995 or *Zionoco* 1995) or Anne Karpf's autobiography *The War After* (1996). A more detailed study would far exceed the limits of this investigation.

8 | Cf. also R. Krell (1979).

reality. The psychological health of survivors' children is, with few exceptions, in danger. Martin S. Bergmann sums up (1982, 265) that one of the most important insights was the finding that survivors' children were not able to live their own lives. They frequently had the "feeling of having to fill 'someone else's shoes'" (Rustin and Lipsig 1972, 89) or a life located in the past (Kestenberg 1982b). Shared survivor guilt led to the creating of a "double reality", in which the parental past and the child's present would have to be fused in order to adjust to present life (Maria V. Bergmann 1982). Through its identification with the parent as a victim, the child of a survivor also became a "survivor"[9] It might even enter into competition with its parents in its need to suffer (Newman 1979).

A great many investigations describe the difficulties that survivors' children have in acquiring an identity of their own (S. Schneider 1981). Elena Kuperstein (1981) is of the opinion that adolescents have a very strong awareness of being Jewish, regardless of whether they reject Jewishness or not; this feeling is rooted in their parents' experiences and exists almost independently of their religious conviction. Fogelman and Savran (1979) describe how some American descendants of survivors feel torn between an American and a Jewish identity. In Israel, states Stanley Schneider (1981), an adolescent is more likely to find his identity. The country needs everyone; the adolescent is aware of this fact, he is part of the culture and of the national process of identification; one is living in one's "own country". Savran and Fogelman (1979) see a solution in an "identity as the child of survivors". The children of survivors may acquire strength by means of integration and identification.

The Israeli psychiatrist and psychoanalyst Yossi Hadar (1991) notes on the one hand that it is clear that there is "no specific, definable clinical syndrome by which the members of this Second Generation can be distinguished from the others" (ibid., 161). But at the same time he works out how the Second Generation is bound in a specific way to the Holocaust. The "chronological time curve" of the survivors all had the same shape: before the Holocaust a "good enough" family structure – to adopt Winnicott's phrase – had existed, which was abruptly interrupted by the Nazi persecution.[10] In a third phase after the Holocaust, survivors had been involved in attempts to achieve rehabilitation and reconstruction. In a manner of speaking, the survivors had a certain place "to which they could return: they had the ability to create a feeling of inner continuity in their inner world" (ibid., 163). Although the "chronological time" of the Second Generation only be-

---

9 | Cf. also Savran and Fogelman (1976).

10 | Niederland (1980) speaks of "a mostly incurable *break in the lifeline*" of the survivors having occurred (ibid., 229).

gan after the Shoah, the date of birth was felt as being located in the concentration camp. The Second Generation was "born into the Holocaust [...], in contrast to their parents who were born in the normal world that existed before the Holocaust" (ibid.). The "individual time continuum" of the Second Generation started "precisely at the point where their parents' individual curve was interrupted" (ibid., 164). The sons and daughters of survivors had "no possibility whatsoever of fading the Holocaust out of their world, regardless of whether their parents spoke about it or not. Their point of departure was the Holocaust, and they had no place at their disposal to which they could return" (ibid.).

Hadar's remarks have a direct relevance to the Second Generation's relationship with their parents. The survivors, Hadar (1991) says, needed to set off something "absolutely good" (for their children born after the Holocaust) against the "absolute evil" (of the Nazis). The children were accordingly given the unequivocal message that they must always be good. On both sides, every kind of aggression was associated with the Nazis. However, since the aggressive delimitation of children and adolescents is a normal component of a normal separation from the parents, the consequences for the parent-child relationship must be fatal if this process is subjected "to the radical dichotomy between good and evil" (ibid., 171). Daughters and sons involved in detaching themselves from their parents might then feel like Nazis or their parents might see them as such.

Social Relationships

Already in early investigations, some of the researchers were struck by the fact that the children of survivors were not adequately integrated in their environment. They had frequently borrowed their parents' negative outlook on the world, which was described as dangerous or hostile. They were afraid of their social environment and were full of mistrust and suspicion when they encountered other people. Survivors' children often felt that they were "different", even if the other people they were dealing with were Jews. They saw themselves as "outsiders", who felt alien and were not understood by their "non-Jewish" environment. Other children of survivors for whom they immediately felt a certain affinity and with whom they sensed a tacit consent were an exception. Some survivors' children also harboured positive feelings towards the State of Israel; apart from that, they frequently felt that they were not part of a community and were living so to speak in a "social vacuum". They described themselves as lonely or isolated.[11]

11 | Cf. also in this connection cf.: Dominik and Teutsch 1978, Epstein

An attempt has been made by Savran and Fogelman (1976) to explain the difficulties experienced by the Second Generation in entering or in maintaining relationships. Many survivors' children suffered from the loss of relations, of culture etc. and accordingly felt angry. Another pervasive feeling was shame. Many survivors had told their children that "the best" had died, this statement probably being based on the parents' guilt feelings. The more shame a survivors' child felt about his parents' humiliation or about the fact that they had survived, the more the child would try to distance itself from this part of its parents' life. These feelings would inevitably affect its relationships to other persons, for the child could not share this terrible and special bond with its parents with anybody else and it feared that it might be "found out". As a result of the terrible insecurity which the parents had experienced in their lives, it was difficult for their children to assume obligations in their relationships, profession, home or family. They were afraid that they would suffer similar losses as their parents.

Barocas and Barocas (1979, 1980) think that the prolongation of symbiotic parent-child relationships beyond the specific period of this phase is responsible for the fact that survivors' children often strive to achieve a degree of "feeling at one" with other persons, which is inappropriate and thus places a burden on personal relationships. At the same time, they are exceptionally sensitive as regards real or imagined experiences of loss and this leads to great difficulties when they look for close relationships outside the family. The congruence in the mind of some survivors between "separation" and "death" which several authors mention makes this connection clearer (e.g. Slipp 1979).

It is evident that the feelings of guilt which are felt by the Second Generation and which also complicate social relationships play a very important part in their life; their influence is not, however, only limited to every aspect of the separation between the parents and their children. Maria V. Bergmann (1982) calls attention to the feelings of guilt experienced by the survivors' children, if they see a possibility of enjoying their own life.

Love Relationships

The severance or separation from one's own parents plays an important role in love and love relationships. Winnicott has remarked how the family contributes to the emotional maturing of the individual, on the one part by "the continued existence of the opportunity for dependence of a high degree; the other is the provision of the opportunity for the individual to break away

1977, Freyberg 1980, Krell 1979, Oliner 1982, Phillips 1978, Rakoff et al. 1966, Russell 1974, Sigal et al. 1973, Slipp 1979, Trossman 1968.

from the parents" (Winnicott 1965, 93) so that it can become increasingly active in the outside world in extra-familial social fields or groups. "It is very difficult for a child to work out the conflicts of loyalties in moving out and in without satisfactory family management" (ibid., 90 et seqq.). Sexual development is described by Winnicott as a "special case", "both in the establishment of a personal sexual life and in the search for a mate. In marriage there is expected a coincidental breaking out and away from the actual parents and the family, and at the same time a carry-through of the idea of family-building" (ibid., 92).

Blanck and Blanck (1968) describe "the *completion of yet another cycle of psychological separation from the parents*" (ibid., 4) as a potential for development in marriage. It offers an "*increased opportunity for the exercise of autonomy*" (ibid., 5). The great closeness in the marriage relationship "is reminiscent of the infantile dependency upon mother, and yet must not repeat and duplicate this primary relationship" (ibid.).

Erik H. Erikson (1959) emphasizes the special significance of having an identity for starting a love relationship. Frequently "an attempt to engage in intimate fellowship and competition or in sexual intimacy fully reveals the latent weakness of identity" (ibid. 124). The creation of a pair relationship invariably also involves the test of "firm self-delineation" (ibid.). The absence of a sure feeling of identity leads to "desperate attempts at delineating the fuzzy outlines of identity by mutual narcissistic mirroring" (ibid., 125).

In his study of partner selection and marriage crises, Günter Reich (1987) also deals with the importance of their respective families for the love relationships. His observations are based on a multi-generational dynamic family approach.

Reich's central thesis is the influence which "the inner and external separation of the partners from their own families, and their 'related individuation'" have on the development and formation of love relationships (ibid., 15; cf. Stierlin 1978 on the concept of delegation). Essential relationship or conflict patterns, which characterized the conflicts of the parents' marriage, recur as an intra-familial repetitive compulsion in the love relationships of the following generation. "Differences displayed by the families of origin as regards life-style and moral concepts, both of which are closely related to the feeling of family and of individual identity, lead to conflicts in the love relationship" (Reich 1987, 45).

The question of the origin of the partners of the subjects interviewed is of especial relevance to the present study. Whereas Trossman (1968) reports that survivors' children insisted – in order to actively rebel against their parents – on having non-Jewish partners, Russell (1974) relates that the survivors' children whom he studied did not dare to have a non-Jewish boyfriend or girlfriend. Savran and Fogelman (1976), too, describe the conflicts of survivors' children over the issue of "marrying outside the faith". The message conveyed by most parents to their children was: "You will kill me, or I will kill you, if you do it."

This problem appears in a specific form in the Second Generation living in the Federal Republic of Germany (Grünberg 1983). Questions concerning the origin of the partners arise in the "land of the murderers" also: love relationships with non-Jews – and this is particularly so in *Germany* – can be interpreted as a threat to the cultural identity of Jews. Moreover, such love relationships in Germany represent what is probably the most intimate contact between survivors' children and the "persecutors' side"; and this contact takes place not only as an abstract general social phenomenon; on the contrary, the persecutors are present in a very concrete form, e.g. as the parents of friends or partners, whose Nazi past burdens present relationships.

3. Jews in Germany Today

3.1 Paradigmatic Events, Positions, and Interpretations. An Attempt to Take Stock of the Situation

"The more German Germany became or becomes, the more powerfully are Jews confronted with the history in which they are involved with the Germans, or which separates them from them, in such a terrible manner" (Diner 1986, 18). According to Diner, "all attempts to normalize life after and in spite of Auschwitz and to step out of the shadow of this monstrous event are doomed to fail" (ibid., 15; cf. also Diner 1988). Since Auschwitz one can "indeed speak of a 'German-Jewish symbiosis' – albeit of a negative symbiosis – involving both parties, Germans and Jews; the occurrence of a mass extermination has become the point of departure of their feeling of identity; a kind of contradictory common ground – whether they wish it or not. [...] Such a negative symbiosis [...] will for generations shape the relations of both sides inside their own groups, but above all in relation to each other" (Diner 1986, 9).

Diner's thesis of a "negative symbiosis" of Germans and Jews represents the point of departure of the chapter "Jews in Germany Today".[1] Our interest will not be centered on either a discourse on the history of the life of Jews in Germany (cf. in this connection Borries 1962, Elbogen and Sterling 1966, Gidal 1988, Kampmann 1963, Reichmann 1974) or on the history and general significance of anti-Semitism (cf. in this connection, for in-

---

[1] | The following remarks frequently refer to the unpublished dissertation (Grünberg 1983, 5-18) and other publications written by the author (Grünberg 1986, 1987, 1997, 1998a, 2002) and to unpublished lectures (e.g. Grünberg 1993), without specific reference being made to them in each case.

stance Berding 1988, Bergmann and Erb 1991, Bohleber and Kafka 1992, Brainin, Ligeti and Teicher 1993, Ginzel 1991, Greive 1983, Loewenstein 1952, Poliakov 1977, Scheffer 1988, Silbermann and Schoeps 1986, Strauss and Kampe 1985). We are dealing rather with an attempt to translate into concepts the world in which Jews of the Second Generation live in Germany after the "break in civilization" (Diner 1988) caused by Auschwitz, after the "refutation of civilization" (ibid., 7) by a "mass extermination which was bureaucratically organized and carried out as an industrial project" (ibid., cf. also Hilberg 1961). Whereas the preceding chapters were essentially based on a selection of the clinical studies of the after-effects of Nazi persecution on survivors and their children published internationally during the last three decades, the following remarks will deal with the social and cultural events which took place during the same period in Germany. Although it would be natural and desirable to take anti-Semitic attitudes, remarks or actions of Germans which have been personally experienced or observed into consideration, this is a difficult proposition for Jews living in the Federal Republic of Germany. For on the one hand many Jews living here prefer to move in non-Jewish circles. They live in a secluded manner, their attitude when together with non-Jews is a reserved one or they cut themselves off, so that observations in this respect will be limited. On the other hand, one must bear in mind that "the average citizen in Federal Germany" does not as a rule "out" himself as an anti-Semite, at least not *towards Jews*. Slogans bandied between friends meeting regularly in pubs and private "confessions" of this type are not usually made in the presence of Jews. It is more likely that Jews will meet with a hidden anti-Semitism in the form of philo-Semitic remarks. The following account is, for the most part, based on publically accessible material, because anti-Semitism is in this respect conveyed to Jews so to speak through the media. This is the field in which they are *obliged* to make their observations, for the experience of "direct" anti-Semitism is restricted in view of its double limitation. Thus, Jews have to "rely" on "deducing" or inferring the anti-Semitic contents of statements from a certain use of vocabulary or from slips of the tongue. On the other hand, this public discourse is also a "monitor", which makes it possible to answer the question in which manner the public reacts to this anti-Semitism. And this again allows us to clear up in a direct way the question how safe one can feel as a Jew living in Germany.

Therefore, the point at issue in the following remarks will mainly hinge on those events, which are significant from the perspective of precisely this Second Generation, in order to understand the conditions in society that operate in the social relationships of Jews with non-Jewish Germans in post-Nazi Germany. The point of departure of our study is the feeling of identity of Jewish intellectuals of the Second Generation, who adopt a critical atti-

3. JEWS IN GERMANY TODAY | 45

tude both as regards the political situation in the Federal Republic of Germany and the policy of the Jewish communities over here. This necessarily means that individual events and experiences will be described in detail, whereas other occurrences which are presumably just as relevant to the state of society will only be summarily dealt with. To that extent the picture of Germany that is painted will not be a "balanced" one, but one that is extremely "one-sided" and "subjective", being bound to the perspective of a certain group of persons. No claim is made to general validity. The claim is being made, however, that we illustrate in-depth and in an exemplary manner the central conflicts in the world in which Jews live in post-Nazi Germany. As far as possible, the chronological sequence of the events studied will be taken into consideration.

It is possible to read the following description and interpretation of paradigmatic cases, each of which sheds light in its own way on the life of Jews in Germany today, as exemplary hermeneutics as defined by Achim Hahn (Hahn 1994). This applies at least to the rough approach and the essential objective of my remarks.

Exemplary cases illuminate what also applies to other situations; they provide insights into the structures of experience, orientation and expectations which impress their stamp on the thinking, feeling and actions not just of isolated individuals. The examples set forth below refer in a concrete, vivid manner to patterns of interpretation which in the author's opinion frequently mark the relations between Jews and non-Jewish Germans. The fact that it is certainly also possible to adduce counterexamples does not affect the validity of this procedure. This stock-taking does not imply any claims to representativeness whatsoever. The exemplary cases are described and interpreted without making any particular methodological claims.[2] When this is done, these exemplary hermeneutics of attributions, labellings and interpretation "charged with tension", which are based on selected cases and meant to cast light upon the world in which Jews live in Germany today, certainly also set off the position and perspective of the author, and thus his subjective approach to the subject. Such an access is, however, of constitutive importance for an independent comprehension of empirical-

---

2 | The reference to Hahn's approach to sociological exemplary hermeneutics suggests itself not least because this author precisely does not make the scientific character of studies depend on complicated methodical techniques. Rather does he plead in favour of a level-headed use of common-place competences, when he wishes to support the formation of sociological experiences and insights upon "the telling of stories and the giving of examples" (Hahn 1994,14). Hahn wishes to show "that experience forms its own 'method' of acquiring and using knowledge, which does not tally with scientifically usual logical conclusive methods" (ibid., 21).

hermeneutic research in the field of biography. In an intentionally "impressionistic" stocktaking not only are first insights provided into thematic links that are of interest and heuristically useful perspectives opened, but the premises are also laid for further empirical investigations. As a rule, this is done tacitly. Precisely if these premises are partly of a subjective character, it can only be of use to the "objectivity" of the present study if they are openly stated, or if they at least can be easily discerned by recipients. The following interpretations of selected events and positions shall not least contribute to this.

In order to avoid "disturbing" the flow of description of the altogether quite comprehensive remarks on *"Jews in Germany Today"* and yet to give readers a guide to the following contents, a survey of the chapter will be given.

The section *'Critical' Jews and 'Community Jewry'* wishes to show how contradictorily and yet mutually related political attitudes can develop *inside* the "Jewish community". Changes in the attitude of critical Jews correspond to a certain extent with a change on the part of the Central Council of Jews in Germany, even though this does not necessarily mean that the non-Jewish German environment "joins in supporting" such changes. The section *Jews in Germany* provides a first demographic look at the life of the Jews formerly living in Germany and living there today.

The section *This is not my Country* takes a prominent individual case in order to describe the striking changes in the attitude of a Jewess in Germany, who after "sitting on packed suitcases" finds her way to integration, only to finally take the decision to leave the Federal Republic after experiencing serious personal and social disappointments. Under the title *Alien in one's own Country* we look at further biographies of Jews, who at first felt attracted by the German students' movements' critical position towards society, who felt that they were "needed" and wanted to take part in the project of a society that was to be changed. Breaks occur when they are confronted with a left-wing anti-Zionism. Questions intrude whether an anti-Semitic attitude transmitted by the parents of the German "comrades" is not making its appearance here ("You are the children of your parents"). The founding of a *'Jewish Group' in Frankfurt am Main* is also prompted by the critical debate with the German Left on the one hand and by membership in Jewish Communities on the other. In this context, reference is made to different forms of the identity of Jews after National Socialism.

The sub-section *The Prolongation of History: Germans, Jews, The Palestine Conflict* deals with the connection between the critical social and political commitment of Jews in the Federal Republic, their simultaneous criticisms of "Community Judaism" and the situation in the 'Near East', in particular after Israel's invasion of Lebanon in 1982. Latent anti-Semitic resentments of the German Left are mentioned, the roots of which are to be found *not* in the Near East conflict, but in the Nazi persecution of the Jews in Germany. The equating of Israelis and Jews with the Nazis results in a "gigantic exculpation".

The chapter *Bitburg and beyond* refers to the increasing endeavours forty years after the collapse of Nazi Germany to put a conclusion to the "dark chapter" of National Socialism in order to be able to conduct the discussion about the growing strength of the German nation that is not so hampered by feelings of guilt. A demonstration of reconciliation between the US President and the German Federal Chancellor that took place at the soldier's cemetery of Bitburg is of supreme significance in this connection. This turning point was meant to make one regard the National-Socialist genocide as a "sacrifice" to a normal war. In addition, the chapter deals with the controversy about the staging of Fassbinder's play *Der Müll, die Stadt und der Tod* (Garbage, The City and Death) in Frankfurt/Main and with the anti-Semitic utterances made at that time by politicians.

The controversy known as The *Historians' Dispute* about the unique character of the Nazi genocide of the Jews, which involved an attempt to play down the enormity of the event by referring to the "Asiatic deed" of the Soviet dictator Stalin, is the central point of the next chapter. The sub-section *The 9th of November* refers to the fall of "the Wall" in 1989, which above all was to serve "to make one forget" the events of the 9th and 10th of November 1938. The section on *Reunification* refers to the significance of this act as a further attempt to get rid of the burden imposed by the history of National Socialism, for the division of Germany was seen by many as a "punishment" for National Socialism, and reunification was regarded as showing that this had now been expiated. The short section *The Gulf War* sheds light upon the peace movement in the Federal Republic, which ignored both the political and economic causes and conditions of the Second Gulf War as well as the fears prevailing in the Israeli peace movement.

The attempt to erect *A Supermarket on Concentration Camp Grounds* and the controversy which arose as a result is discussed, before a closer look at the initiative of the *Society for the Sponsoring of Local History in the Administrative District of Verden* to invite former slave labourers is taken in the next chapter. A similar project is examined in the following sub-chapter *International Encounter in Stadtallendorf*. The slip made in using a wrongly quoted (falsified) saying of the Ba'al Shem Tov as a motto for the event is studied. The concept of reconciliation replaces the preoccupation with a past with which it is impossible to become reconciled.

The chapter *Complicity and Parallel Perpetrator-Victim Structures* criticizes an academic discourse which aims at blurring the essential distinctions between perpetrator and victim and which denies the reality of the presence of violence in relationships in National Socialism in favour of a debate dealing with fantasies. However, this defence strategy just allows that to persist which the point of departure of the discourse had described: the "fascination" with National Socialism.

The following remarks in the next chapter on *The Nazi Past and the German Psychoanalytical Association* take this association as an example of how the controversy about the Nazi past of one its "founding fathers" splits the organization: on the one hand are the critics who demand truth and clarification, on the other hand are the members who feel that when those were responsible in the past are attacked they are also involved in the attack. These members reverse the prevailing circumstances, when they for instance characterize those who put critical questions as the latest "Nazi persecutors".

Similar mechanisms of defence and denial are emphasized in the section *The Pact of Silence*. The relevant psychoanalytical discourse contains equations which lead to distortions, such as the construction of an "insupportable kinship" between perpetrators and victims of National Socialism. The point of departure for such mistaken interpretations is the surface phenomenon of not-speaking-about-Nazi-experiences on both sides. The alleged silence of the survivors is thoughtlessly equated with the withholding of the truth by Nazi perpetrators and their sympathizers. Such attempts at "coming to terms" with the past are compared with the concept of the "ethnically unconscious" as well as with the working out of different familial reparation strategies to encounter the confrontation with the Nazi past (e.g. the "perpetrator-victim inversion"). In this context, the frequently praised statements made by so-called "contemporary witnesses" are critically analysed.

The reception of the studies submitted by the US political scientist Daniel Johan Goldhagen in an attempt to explain the active participation of "quite normal Germans" in the Holocaust, as well as the mass acquiescence of the Germans, are the central subject of the remarks on *The Goldhagen Debate*. Nearly all the common anti-Semitic clichés are mobilized in reacting to Goldhagen's "exposures", for it appears that his arguments "struck" the lies in the life of many and upon the central nerve of Federal German identity.

In the works of Jean Améry, which are briefly dealt with in the following chapter, we find very weighty remarks on the subject of *collective guilt*. Améry calls for the demythologization and demystification of this term, after which it would represent a "serviceable hypothesis", with which one can find an approach to the mass guilt of the Germans. In this way the guilt of individual persons (guilt due to actions, guilt due to a passive attitude, guilt of not speaking up) adds up to the "overall guilt of a people".

In the final chapter *Withholding the Truth, Confusion* an explanation is offered for a number of the slips and mistakes and for the denial and qualifying of the National Socialist annihilation of the Jews. The events that are being interpreted could *as such* be understood as the effect of National Socialism on the non-Jewish German "side", as the result of a certain way of coping with the past, as the result of withholding the truth on the part of Nazi perpetrators and sympathizers, as the return of collective repression. The collective withholding of the truth by Nazi perpetrators and sympathizers leaves their descendants with a collective confusion on a grand scale. The approach which we have adopted may make it possible to understand the massive hatred between the generations, the fear, but also the admiration and fascination which many daughters and sons of perpetrators and Nazi sympathizers feel towards their parents.

It is only possible to get an appropriate and comprehensive idea of the social relations and love relationships of the descendants of survivors which developed in post-Nazi Germany against the background described in the following. Only these insights – combined with the insights gained in the previous chapter from the specialist international literature on the subject of the impact of National Socialist persecution on the children of survivors – allow one access to the social conditions which are also virulent in the intimate relations in the love relationships of the Second Generation in this country.

"Critical" Jews and "Community Jewishness"

In what a conflicting and yet inter-related manner political attitudes can develop *within* the "Jewish community" may be shown to start with by looking at the example of the Jewish Community of Frankfurt and at the Central Council of Jews in Germany. In the so-called "Frankfurt house battle" the owners of real estate and Jewish squatters came into conflict – in a partly quite violent conflict – with each other. Years later, on the other hand, in connection with the controversy concerning the preventing of the staging of Rainer Werner Fassbinder's play *Der Müll, die Stadt und der Tod* (Garbage, the City and Death) (1981), the title of a publication by Micha Brumlik (1985) is, characteristically, *Why I declare my solidarity with Ignatz Bubis. A Confession* (Warum ich mit Ignatz Bubis solidarisch bin. Ein Bekenntnis). Brumlik writes "the point at issue is not a dispute between the Left and the Right, but we are dealing solely with a dispute about anti-Semitism, and this is taking place in various different forms in *all political camps, right, left and at the centre!*" (ibid., 78).

Indeed, not a few of the "critical" Jews in the Federal Republic of Germany had at first identified themselves with the student movement of "68" or had been part of this protest movement until doubts arose about the credibility of the debate conducted by young Germans concerning the Nazi past of the generation of their parents. Whilst some Jews made the decision to leave Germany, others persevered with their political commitment in this country or observed it "from a critical distance". However, hand in hand with the change in the attitude of "critical" Jews a change also occured in the attitude of the representatives of the Jewish community in the Federal Republic. This is also shown not least by the "personnel policy" of the Central Council of Jews of Germany. Critics accused the former Chairman of the Board of Directors of the Central Council of Jews in Germany, Werner Nachmann, who held this office for 22 years, of undue conformity with the forces supporting the state of the Federal Republic (cf. Brumlik 1980). A few months after he died, the fact that Nachmann had embezzled "compensation funds" granted to the Jews became public. As Joachim Riedl (1988) stated in the weekly periodical *Die Zeit* "The bearer of a decoration (Great Order of the Federal Republic of Germany with Star and Shoulder Sash) who for a time held a diplomatic passport from the Federal Republic of Germany, who advanced, and was a symbol of, the cause of German-Jewish reconciliation after the mass murder committed by the Nazis, simultaneously plunged the Jews into the 'severest crisis since 1945' [as Heinz Galinski described it; K.G.]."[3] No proof could be found that Nachmann's successor in the office of Chairman of the Central Council, Heinz Galinski, had been involved in any financial scandals – even though some of his critics would have liked this to be the case (cf. the preceding footnote). Galinski was always regarded as a person of integrity. Yet at the same time other reproaches were levelled at him: he "gave no rest"; he was forever warning that one should not allow the crimes of the Nazis to be forgotten; he was accused of a "morality of schoolmasterly admonition".[4]

The basis for the policy of Heinz Galinski's successor, Ignatz Bubis,

---

3 | Whereas a commentary in the weekly periodical *Die Zeit* aptly said that "Nachmann is no doubt guilty. This does not diminish the guilt of the Germans." (*Die Zeit* No. 21 of May 20, 1988), the periodical *Der Spiegel* quoted the anti-Semitic statement of Hermann Meyer, who had been a member of the Waffen-SS and troopleader and was then the President of the German Association of War Victims and those who did Military Service, of the Disabled, Social Security Pensioners and Surviving Dependents to the effect that "Galinski is a still greater scoundrel; I think he is capable of embezzling three times 30 millions" (quoted from Funke 1988, 225).

4 | Thus the former leader of the "Republican" party, Franz Schönhuber, received loud applause when he called out to his party friends: "Shalom, Mr Galinski, leave us at last in peace; stop your drivel. We don't want to hear it any more, we cannot hear it any more, we do not let ourselves be humiliated any more" (*Jüdische Allgemeine Zeitung* [General Jewish Weekly] No. 45/3 of January 8, 1990).

was the opinion that he should take up a clear position in which he endeavoured, on the one hand, to counter anti-Semitic and xenophobic manifestations in a vigilant and critical fashion, but on the other hand insisted on seeing himself as being a *part* of this society, not as a Jewish "fellow"-citizen, but as a politically active *citizen* of the Federal Republic of Germany, who committed himself whole-heartedly to further the interests of his Jews and the cause of the Jews represented in his organization. Harking back to the "Central Organization for German Citizens of the Jewish Faith", which existed until September 1935, Bubis' "autobiographical talk with Edith Kohn" (Bubis 1993) consequently bears the title: *I am a German Citizen of the Jewish Faith*. In contrast to his predecessors, despite anti-Semitic hostility Bubis' political standing was quite high. For instance, Bubis' name was suggested several times as a candidate for the office of the President of the Federal Republic of Germany. He was regarded as a moral authority. To what extent Bubis' claim to be recognized as a "real" German really found the social acceptance on a large scale which he wished for, however, must remain an open question.[5] The "Easter greetings" extending wishes for peace in *his* country (Israel) which were sent him and which we mentioned in the introduction speak a different language. The ambivalence shown by the Mayor of Frankfurt, for instance, remains. On the one hand, Petra Roth wished the Jews of Frankfurt "health, luck and success in *your home city* Frankfurt" in an announcement inserted in the "Frankfurt Jewish News" (Frankfurt Jewish News, Rosh Hashanah number 5759, No. 97 of September 1998, 15; italics from K.G.); on the other hand, on another occasion which occurred during the same month, namely when the Theodor W. Adorno prize 1998 was presented to Zygmunt Bauman in St. Paul's Church in Frankfurt/Main on September 13, 1998, she remarked that she had forgotten to properly greet the President of the Central Council of Jews in Germany and city counsellor of Frankfurt, Ignatz Bubis. Bubis himself also was sceptical in an interview given in 1999 to the periodical *Stern* shortly before he died. True, he persisted in designating himself as a German citizen ("as long as this constitution accords with my ideas", ibid., 58). But soon after he expressed the wish to be buried in Israel. He did not want his grave to be blown up – as had happened to Galinski's grave – and he feared that it might be defaced by "graffiti": "unfortunately, the risk that the dignity of the dead may be violated is still very great here" (ibid., 58). Above all, however, Bubis made sceptical remarks about the impact of his work on German society: "I have always pointed out that I am a German citizen of the Jewish faith. I wanted to do away with these exclusions, with Germans

---

5 | The same applies to Prof. Dr. Michael Wolffsohn, who calls himself a "German-Jewish patriot" (Wolffsohn 1993).

being on the one side and Jews on the other. I had imagined that I might perhaps bring people to think differently about each other, to deal with each other in a different manner. But, no, I have achieved almost nothing at all. The majority did not even grasp what I found important. We have remained strangers to each other" (ibid.). "The responsibility for Auschwitz has found no place" in the public consciousness of Germany. "Everybody in Germany feels responsible for Schiller, for Goethe and for Beethoven, but nobody does so for Himmler. A great many people think as Martin Walser does" (Bubis 1999, 58 et seqq.).

The so-called "Walser-Bubis debate" (cf. Brede 2000, Schirrmacher 1999 and footnote 94) had probably been a decisive experience for Bubis, which compelled him to feel as a "Jew *in* Germany" that he was a member of an excluded minority in spite of his attitude and of his commitment.

Jews in Germany

> "If the Federal Republic of Germany is more lucky nowadays, if this building, despite its very fragmentary character, is considered by a majority of Germans as their own home much more so than the Weimar Republic ever was, then this is undoubtedly for a large part due to the fact that there are practically no Jews in the Federal Republic any more."
> Golo Mann 1960 (quoted by Poliakov, Vol. VIII, 213)

In 1900 586,833 Jews lived in Germany; in 1933 the number was still nearly half a million (Kuschner 1977, 26 et seqq.). "Our situation is only desperate", wrote the Jewish historian Ismar Elbogen in the C.-V. Zeitung[6] of April 6, 1933 even after the boycott of "Jewish" shops had taken place, "if we ourselves despair. A community does not go under, unless it gives itself up ... Our ancestors bore their fate with heroic courage, with dignity and with religious dedication. Let us learn from them" (quoted by Sterling 1966, 5). Eleonore Sterling, on the other hand, sums up: "The Jewish religious community did go under. The Jews and their communities were destroyed from outside and with physical force. Nonetheless, Elbogen was partly proved right: they did not give themselves up" (ibid., 6).

After the victory of the Allies over Nazi Germany, only a few of the surviving Jews wanted to return to their countries of origin (Heenen 1983). Many felt drawn to Palestine. The smallest stream of people to return to

---

6 | The *C.-V.-Zeitung* (C.V.-Newspaper) was the accepted newspaper of Jewry; it was the mouthpiece of the Central Association of Jews in Germany (Philo-Lexikon 1982, 140).

their home country were those who went back to Germany and Austria. In 1947, about 21,000 Jews, of whom more than half came from Eastern Europe, lived in the zones of occupation.

"Years still after the end of the war a great many people lived in the refugee camps for so-called 'displaced persons' and they found it difficult to get used to the new German normality. An atmosphere of fear and mistrust characterized the relations of these Jews with the German population" (ibid., 105).

"Once upon a time. Once upon a time – German Jewry existed, but it does not do so any more", as Michael Wolffsohn (1983) also says. German Jewry is really dead. True, in 1980, the Federal Republic of Germany with its approximately 28,000 Jews had not been "purged of Jews" (in contrast to the German Democratic Republic, where approximately 650 Jews still lived at that time). These 28,000 Jews represented 0.2 per cent of "world Jewry". However, after the collapse of the former Eastern bloc, the number of Jews in the Federal Republic of Germany rose steeply.[7] In 1990, the Central Welfare Office of Jews in Germany had 28,468 members. A year later it had 33,630 members (1992: 37,498; 1993: 40,823; 1994: 45,559; 1995: 53,797; 1996: 61,203 members). At the end of 1997, the Central Welfare Office counted 67,471 community members. Of these, 45,620 come from CIS countries.

This is not my Country

Lea Fleischmann was born in 1947 in the DP camp Föhrenwald (cf. in this connection Menke 1960) as the daughter of concentration camp survivors (Fleischmann 1980, 24). Against "the background of the debate which centered about the television film *Holocaust* and the rise in neo-Nazi activities" (*Frankfurter Rundschau* of March 31, 1979), she published an article (under her maiden name Lea Rosenzweig) in which she announced her intention to emigrate. It bore the title: *A Jewess leaves the Federal Republic of Germany – 'You haven't changed!'*. Fleischmann studied Theory of Education and afterwards worked as a teacher in secondary vocational schools until the beginning of 1979. At the end of March 1979, she emigrated to Israel (cf. Fleischmann 1979, 1982). In the Federal Republic of Germany she became principally known by her book *Dies ist nicht mein Land* (This is not my Country) (1980).

7 | The following information is taken from the "Statistics of the members of the Jewish communities and regional associations in Germany as per January 1, 1998" of the Central Welfare Office of the Jews in Germany, Frankfurt/Main.

Fleischmann tries to explain why she turned away from Germany by describing her experiences as the daughter of concentration camp survivors in the Federal Republic. In her diploma thesis on extra-familial education, she wrote that after the economic situation had normalized, it began to be clear that the young Jewish generation had "an absolute right to live" here. "The Jewish communities should at last stop propagating emigration to Israel" (Fleischmann 1979, 138). "The stage of living on packed suitcases was over" (ibid.). But the experiences she had as a teacher had drastically altered this view: "Slowly [I got] the feeling that the German civil service was choking me; [...] it seems to me that the German school system serves to destroy, not to educate, children" (ibid.). Fleischmann speaks of the inability of the Germans to give praise. And everybody tries "to carry out everything quite accurately in order to avoid reproaches that one had somehow acted wrongly" (ibid., 140).

In addition, she critically examines the "ban on employing radical teachers and civil servants" ("Radikalenerlaß") and how the process of facing and coming to terms with the past is shirked. She sees that a "collective fear" (ibid., 142), is the reason why so little individual criticism is voiced. One can, of course, also find critical persons in this country. They were also to be found under National Socialism, "but at that time they were in the concentration camps, and today they find it difficult to enter the civil service. Today I am not willing any more, for the sake of a few Germans who behaved differently, to confirm to the Germans that they have changed. [...] 'The apple does not fall far from the tree'" (ibid., 142 et seqq.).

Alien in one's own Country

The following contributions from authors who live in the Federal Republic of Germany and who were born after 1945 have been taken from the anthology of autobiographical texts *Fremd im eigenen Land. Juden in der Bundesrepublik* (Alien in one's own Country. Jews in the Federal Republic) (1979; cf. in this connection Keval 1983) edited by Henryk M. Broder and Michel R. Lang: Henryk M. Broder ("Why I should prefer not to be a Jew; and if it cannot be avoided – then preferably not in Germany"), Peter, Etty and Silvia Gingold ("The answer is assimilation"), Gloria Kraft-Sullivan ("I have got used to living here as if it were a matter of course") and Hazel Rosenstrauch ("Rooted in Nowhere").

Hazel Rosenstrauch was born in England and grew up in Vienna; at the age of 20, she emigrated to the Federal Republic "decidedly on a voluntary basis, very much in the spirit of 'now more than ever' [...], a bit as a protest against my anti-German education, but even more out of curiosity and because I was attracted by a political alertness, which had something to do with the fact that the children of guilty fathers – my own age group – had begun to reflect" on the past (Rosenstrauch 1979, 340). As the "Jewish-Communist-Viennese child of emigrees" (ibid., 341) she wanted to "fight for a just Socialist society" (ibid.) without being labelled a Jewess. She had, for instance, made an ill-fated attempt to change her surname which sounded Jewish.

Rosenstrauch remarks that the growing political awareness of her then contemporaries had much to do with the attitude of their parents towards the Jews. For the first time, she had met young people who "found it harebrained that I did not wish to mention my surname; [...] what do you actually take us for, for us you are you!" (ibid., 342).

Rosenstrauch thinks she has to be Jewish, whether she wishes to be so or not. Gradually she got the feeling "that they almost needed me" (ibid., 343) because of their guilt feelings and their need for a "Jewess with whom one could show off [...]. They like me to be cultured, well aware of my tradition, an ideal world citizen [...]. The ideal citizen is classless, not rooted socially, an egghead floating around" (ibid.).

She experienced a radical change at the end of the sixties when she wanted to collect signatures from comrades in protest against a bomb discovered before the Jewish Community Centre. They refused to sign; they told her that she was "over-sensitive" about this incident.

Rosenstrauch sees a link between the absolute identification of adherents of the "Left" with "Palestinians, their condemnation of the Israelis and their own complicated world, which seems to be transferred to the Near East". In a previous phase, they had identified with the Jews "up to a point of self-negation" (ibid., 345). Then these very same "left-wing" people had become "Socialists" and "could not, therefore, be anti-Semites any more". "Thus everyone takes what they need from the Jews and Israel, and all of them can be grateful to this country which makes it so easy to experience hate and love and to have feelings of belonging" (ibid.).

Gloria Kraft-Sullivan (1979) was born in Germany in 1946. She describes various philo-Semitic and anti-Semitic events and their strong emotional impact on her. After two longer stays with her grandparents in the USA, she "voluntarily" returned to the Federal Republic.

A pronounced ambivalence towards life in the Federal Republic emerges: on the one hand, Germany is what is familiar, what one is used to, what is more comfortable (in contrast to Israel), what is accepted as a matter of course; with Jewish students in community and social life she had been able to cultivate 'Jewishness' "sometimes to a greater, sometimes to a lesser extent" (ibid., 234) and to uphold certain Jewish traditions; on the other hand, she had never seen herself as being a German: "What does a nationality mean other than that one has certain rights and duties as a citizen" (ibid., 128). She wonders how many anti-Semitic or neo-Nazi "isolated incidents" are needed "before they are recognized as the symptoms of a serious risk for this democracy? Or: how many of the 30,000 Jews over here must again be subjected to hardships until one does not speak of isolated cases any more?" (ibid., 240). In Germany, it was not possible to live much as a matter of course any more; she did not feel threatened, only "sometimes rather uncomfortable. True, I am not as a result sitting on the legendary packed suitcase. But it stands in reserve in the cellar, in case it should be needed. Sometimes I go down and dust it" (ibid., 241).

Silvia Gingold (cf. Etty, Peter and Silvia Gingold 1979), whose parents belonged to the French Résistance during National Socialism, was also born in Germany in 1946. In 1975, she was dismissed as a teacher "after 4 years' successful work in teaching" because she was a member of the German Communist Party (ibid., 162). The Ministry of Education of the Land Hessen personally informed her that the fact that she was Jewish had played no part in her dismissal. "But for me the fact remains that already the third generation of my family is being persecuted and subjected to discrimination because of its origin or its convictions and is being branded as outsiders of society" (ibid., 163). It was only as a result of this dismissal that she became really aware of her Jewish origin, which had never played a role in her family. She had been exposed to anti-Semitic remarks for the first time when she was eleven years old. After being reinstated as a teacher as a result of strong public pressure, she experienced further instances of discrimination. First of all, she could not find a school that was willing to engage her and then the "Communist Gingold", who would "corrupt the children" became the "talk of the town number one" (ibid.). "Two housing agents withdrew promises they had made to let her an apartment, because they 'feared they would have difficulties' – as one of them openly admitted" (ibid., 164).

Like Lea Fleischmann, Henryk M. Broder also became known principally as a result of emigrating to Israel.[8] Broder, who was born in 1946, spent the first nine years of his life in Poland; his family then came to the Federal Republic of Germany (Broder 1979). There were probably two reasons why his parents decided to go to Germany in spite of the persecution that had taken place there: "unbroken Polish anti-Semitism" (ibid., 83) and "above all the opportunity with the help of so-called compensation payments of enabling the children to lead a life 'in the free West'" (ibid.). Moreover, his father had been a "fan of Germany" (ibid.). He had a high opinion of the Germans' reliability and efficiency.

8 | As an author, Henryk M. Broder has been a regular member of the staff of the news periodical *Der Spiegel* since 1995; this can doubtlessly be regarded as marking his return to Germany.

3. Jews in Germany Today | 57

He was not able to resolve his conflict of identity as a Jew like other "passport Germans" (ibid., 84), who refer with pride to their Jewishness. One could only be proud of something "for which one is responsible. [...] And if I think about this honestly: I would prefer not to be a Jew" (ibid.). In the home of Broder's parents no topic had been so much spoken of as National Socialism, and it was only later that he realized "that my parents had survived the concentration camp experience only physically and just barely; that they were emotionally annihilated, and that mentally they had indeed gone though the Final Solution" (ibid., 85). This experience was the Jewish part of his life, "something over which I do not have any control, which dominates me as *it* will. [...] And sometimes I think: were I not to live in Germany, I might perhaps be able to discard it. But – in Germany, I am definitely unable to do so" (ibid.).

He regards many things such as punctuality etc. as "typically German", although he is sure that they can also be found in other countries. Broder mentions numerous events of a political, neo-Nazi nature which occurred in connection with the hunt for terrorists or the way "persons of no fixed abode" were treated; although such events also occurred in other countries, nonetheless "nowhere were they so frequent or occurred in such a pure form as in Germany: it is the correct German formalism, which is on the rampage, and which by passing the Nuremberg *laws* was also responsible for the correct execution of a genocide; it is the joy German citizens feel [...] in a self-decreed submission, in denunciation and in the game which house wardens appointed by the party played" (ibid., 90 et seqq.).

No "other Germany" exists; "there are only other Germans; these other Germans always existed; many of them suffer under the prevailing circumstances, they flog their guts out – and achieve nothing" (ibid., 92).

In his book *Danke schön. Bis hierher und nicht weiter* (Thank you very much. This far and no further), Broder (n.d.) announces that he is going to emigrate. He describes various events, collects some of his reports, e.g. his legal fight against the criminal judge from Cologne Somoskeoy, which should help one to understand this decision. "I am sick of listening to such outrageous statements as 'abortion is equivalent to Auschwitz', and I am also sick of reacting to them. And I do not enjoy analysing monstrosities any more and explaining why they are monstrous" (ibid., 239).

In February 1981, the weekly *Die Zeit* published an open letter by Broder to his "more or less dear left-wing friends" (Broder 1981a, 9) bearing the title *You are still the children of your parents*, written shortly before he emigrated to Israel (cf. *Spiegel Gespräch* with Broder 1981b, a talk cf. with Broder in Leiser [1982]: *Leben nach dem Überleben* [Life after Survival] as well as Leiser's television film bearing the same title which was broadcast on March 10, 1982 in the Second German Television Program).

Broder accuses "left-wing persons" and "those holding alternative views" in the Federal Republic of Germany of lacking historical awareness. They pretend that their history is irrelevant. The persecution of the Jews at the most only comes to their mind when they complain about how badly certain groups in the Federal Republic are treated. Then women, students or homosexuals are called "today's Jews". Like conservative politicians of the Christian Democratic Union, they also misuse "millions of dead for [their; K.G.] current political ends" (Broder 1981a, 9). Their parents' "pathologically bad conscience", those parents who had had no knowledge of anything and at the very most had collaborated only in order to prevent something worse from happening, was also their "starting capital" (ibid.).

Broder attacks the theory that left-wing people cannot as such be anti-Semitic. For instance, Gerhard Zwerenz (1973) has of all things written a novel about a Jewish owner of houses and real estate, "because as is well known this country lacks Aryan members in this profession; in the house squatters' war of Frankfurt, the fact that it was directed against Jewish speculators played a decisive role" (ibid., 10).

The "anti-Semitic syndrome" (ibid.) is totally independent of its subject. "It is not the behaviour of the Jews that counts, but the need of the anti-Semite to regard what a Jew does as something negative" (ibid.) Jews are held responsible for every conceivable thing. The Left ignores the fact that the Enlightenment, the labour movement and assimilation did not prevent Auschwitz. "You do not even notice that you go on like a train that has got stuck in mud and rubble precisely at the spot where your parents had to stop their failed attempt to eliminate world Jewry. You continue today to pursue the final solution with ideological weapons [...]. The Jews should cease being Jews; only then are you willing to accept them" (ibid.).

Broder criticizes anti-Zionism as a form of left-wing anti-Semitism (cf. on this point also Heinsohn 1988b, Keilson 1988). The comparisons "Jews are like Nazis" and the "Palestinians are the Jews of the Israeli" or the statement that the Israelis act in the same way towards the Arabs as the Nazis acted towards the Jews are evidence of this.

Those who have never critically discussed the past with their parents criticise the state of Israel as the sole "trouble-maker" in the Near East. The Soviet occupation of Afghanistan is welcomed, the Pol Pot régime in Cambodia is regarded as the people's revolutionary government, one knows nothing or is silent about the deeds of Idi Amin, Gaddafi, Khomeini or about the persecution of the Kurds in Iran and Iraq, the genocide in Ethiopia or the treatment of gypsies in the Federal Republic etc. There is only one "evergreen topic: Palestine" (ibid., 11). And their interest in the Palestinians is only due to the fact that they are being oppressed by Jews. "No left-wing person was indignant that in Entebbe the persons who carried through a selection of Jewish passengers were young Germans, children born after the war. You only got upset when an Israeli commando liberated the hostages. Then you sent your telegrams of condolence to 'His Excellency Idi Amin' and severely condemned the 'violation of the sovereignty of the state of Uganda'" (ibid.).

The "Jewish Group" in Frankfurt/Main

The positions of a group of mostly German-Jewish left-wing adherents from Frankfurt/Main will now be compared with the publications of Fleischmann and Broder.

Micha Brumlik published an article *A Crisis of Jewish Identity?* in 1980. He distinguishes five ways in which Jews establish their identity after National Socialism:

1. Traditional religion
   For most Jews, the Jewish faith and its rituals are "no more than folklore and that means ornamental accessories" (ibid., 6); this uncomprehended tradition is as such fated to in the end go under; it is, therefore, unfit to serve as a "factor creating a feeling of identity" (ibid.).
2. Zionism
   The creation of a Jewish national state has an important function for the survivors of National Socialism in overcoming fear, feelings of guilt and the diminished feeling of their own worth that had been experienced. "The people without land did not [however,] find a land without people in Palestine" (ibid., 7) so that one had had to accept the expulsion and oppression of the Palestinians. From the political and moral point of view, the "Zionist experiment [...] had already failed" (ibid.).
   The "love for Israel and our Zionism" (ibid., 8) had indeed "only" existed "as a result of the lack of Jewish substance and because of fear and our inability to take the Jewish fate in our own hands" (ibid.). Israel was only the place which one needed in order to be able to flee there in an emergency.
3. Assimilation
   The task of the Jews has "per definition nothing to do with a plan for a robust Jewish identity" (ibid.). The personal decision to assimilate should according to Brumlik be respected as the right of every individual: nonetheless, he regards its appearance as a program "as the continuation of the murder of the Jews by spiritual means" (ibid.).
4. The Judaism of the Jewish communities
   The Jewish communities were "closed societies with a vague ideology of unifica-

tion, which is emotionally somewhat zionistically coloured, and which all those who want to have something to say in their midst must, to start with, share – under penalty of being socially excluded" (ibid.).
Brumlik criticises the undemocratic structure of the communities, in which on the whole "officials and rich people" "call the tune". The essential function of organized community Judaism is to serve as "advertising" another Germany, which has drawn the necessary consequences from National Socialism. In this connection, Brumlik refers to a "whitewashing letter"[9] which Werner Nachmann, the former Chairman of the Central Council of the Jews in Germany, sent to Hans Filbinger, the former prime minister of the Land Baden-Württemberg (ibid., 9).
It is reassuring that there are a few positive developments in the field of youth work and culture.

5. Marxist Socialism
The attempt to "regard" Judaism "as being fulfilled in the struggle for social justice on the basis of Marxist theory" (ibid.) has only been made by a small minority. In spite of its "failure over a hundred years" (ibid.) Brumlik respects this approach. Isaac Deutscher (1977) for instance speaks of "non-Jewish Jews" (ibid., 7 et seqq.).
Seen in this light, Judaism is "in the last resort no more than a theory of social justice and anti-Semitism with its uncounted millions of victims [is] above all an example of what capitalist conditions can produce" (Brumlik 1980, 9). Here, the point at issue is not any more to know or observe Jewish traditions, but to get rid of them.
Brumlik thinks radical changes have taken place in Marxist Socialism. The undogmatic Left is no longer concerned with the basic contradiction between Capital and Labour, but with the problems of the human, social and ecological environment. Here, it endeavours to "maintain an identity of its own, for which it has fought and suffered in history" (ibid., 10) and to take a stand for better conditions for humanity and for the environment on that foundation.
Brumlik regards this commitment inside the undogmatic Left as constituting the sole practical consequence for Jews in today's Federal Republic of Germany. A precondition is the readiness to critically examine "this Germany, its past, and

---

9 | "We shall of course also do everything in future in order to enhance the reputation of German democracy abroad ... I see it as my task to always present the right picture of Germany, its citizens and parties whenever we find tendencies which spotlight the 'bad Germans'" (Werner Nachmann, as Chairman of the Central Council of the Jews in Germany, quoted by Broder 1979, 102). Hans-Karl Filbinger, on the other hand, expressed his fundamental opinion as follows: "What was right in the past, cannot be wrong today" (Filbinger, quoted by Broder 1979, 102)!

the economic, psychological and political causes of its development, as well as the traces and marks which this past has left in us and in our parents" (ibid.).

Another member of the aforementioned Jewish Group, Cilly Kugelmann also describes (1981; cf. also Brumlik 1982, Postone 1981) her experiences as a Jewess who is the daughter of survivors in the Federal Republic of Germany, and in particular, her relationship to the "Left" of the Federal Republic. Kugelmann describes her parents' isolation with respect to Germans, a circumstance which also affected her relations with, for instance, German schoolmates. In addition, she deals with the Jewish communities' relationship to Zionism and with the way in which they reacted to neo-Nazi events.

Kugelmann speaks of a "life resembling gymnastic splits [...]: one leg still being within the Jewish community, the other in the left milieu" (ibid., 237). She criticises, above all, that the German post-war generation has not critically examined its National Socialist past sufficiently or discussed it with their parents. "We have tormented our parents with reproaches, parents, who had been victims, whereas the Germans have not tormented their parents, who were not victims, with reproaches. In my opinion, this is outrageously unjust" (ibid., 238). "Hardly any Germans" says Kugelmann, attended the *Week of the Yiddish Film* in Frankfurt. From the keen interest which many left wing groups otherwise show for other "ethnic minorities", she deduces that there is not only a lack of especial interest in the Jewish milieu, but also that this milieu is unwelcome. She criticises Broder and other Jews who left the Federal Republic for claiming that "it is not possible to get along with the Germans any more" (ibid., 239), whereas she herself assumes that Jews in the Federal Republic are really being stifled by their own inhibitions. "For Jews, the ghetto situation of the Left is dramatically aggravated" (ibid.).

The Prolongation of History:
Germans, Jews, the Palestine Conflict

In August 1982, the daily newspaper *Frankfurter Rundschau* (Frankfurt Review) published a statement from a "group of German Jews belonging to the category of 'intellectual workers' [...] concerning Federal Germany's reaction to the Israeli invasion of Lebanon" (*Frankfurter Rundschau* of August 20, 1982). To a large extent, we are dealing here with the group mentioned above. The central message of the article is the statement that "latent anti-Semitic resentment" (ibid.) is mixed up with justified and necessary criticism of the State of Israel; the reasons for this are to be found not in the Near East conflict, but in the National Socialist persecution of the Jews.

Israeli and Jews are being put on an equal footing with the Nazis. The result is a "gigantic exculpation [...], which hides anti-Semitic resentments under a cloak of universal morality" (ibid.). This is also the approach of the book *Die Verlängerung von Geschichte. Deutsche, Juden und der Palästinakonflikt* (The Prolongation of History. Germans, Jews and the Palestine Conflict) which contains contributions from the very same group and was edited in 1983 by Dietrich Wetzel.[10] This "mixing up" of two elements which has been defined above prolongs the German-European history of the Jews by extending it into the Palestine conflict, where it contributes to shape a hopeless Zionist policy (Wetzel 1983; cf. also the detailed remarks made by Bunzl 1983, Claussen 1983, Diner 1982 and 1983a, Schölch 1983). In post-war Germany, a completely new component of anti-Semitism has appeared in which, as a result of the guilt feelings of the persecutors, the "hate object" which has not been completely annihilated (Wetzel 1983, 8), reappears as an aggressor, thus making it possible to fight it as an "insult to the nationalistic identity" (ibid.). After the oil shock of 1974, the initially philo-Semitic identification with this aggressor (the Israeli troops) was replaced by an increasingly critical and hostile attitude towards this same aggressor, and this makes it possible to frequently voice anti-Semitic remarks.[11] For instance, the democratic public has not, either, really had a critical look at the reproaches brought forward by the former Israeli Prime Minister Begin against the then Federal Chancellor Schmidt; they have not critically considered the reactions to these reproaches, nor in particular, the "problem of historical guilt as part of that national identity which some of the otherwise silent left-wing adherents are just beginning to discover anew for themselves" (ibid., 9).

Misgivings about not being in a position, without supporting the aforementioned tendencies, to criticize Israeli policy because of this "mixing up" of two elements, had been relegated to the background after the Leba-

---

10 | As a reaction to this publication, a number of the periodical *Ästhetic und Kommunikation* (Aesthetics and Communication) appeared in June 1983 under the title of *Deutsche, Linke, Juden* (Germans, Adherents of the Left, Jews) and included contributions from German Jews and non-Jews. In this context, the remarks of Rolf Ebel, Olav Münzberg, Dieter Hoffmann-Axthelm, Eberhard Knödler-Bunte, Hajo Funke (all of them in 1983), which are frequently of a personal nature, as well as the reprint of an article by Dan Diner (1983b) are of particular interest.

11 | Susann Heenen deals with the "radical change of front" of the New Left after the war of June 1967 in her article *Deutsche Linke, linke Juden und der Zionismus* (The German Left, left-wing Jews and Zionism) (1983). "The Palestinians now serve as an object of identification instead of the Israelis formerly loved in the role of victims [...]" (ibid., 109).

non war. However, in addition to actual verbal anti-Semitism, the public in the Federal Republic of Germany exhibited something else still, "namely unanimity in moral condemnation, a so called solidarization with the Palestinians and – above all – an appalling need to misuse the crimes of the Israeli government in order to annul its [own] historical guilt" (ibid.). As a result of his consternation over the massacres in Sabra and Schatila, Micha Brumlik (1983b) expresses doubts about the morality of the Jewish state. It is becoming clear that in this state, which was granted a justification for its existence on the strength of moral arguments, there exists a glaring contradiction between the simultaneous endeavour to achieve sovereignty and the desire to fulfil absolute moral claims.

In a second article, Brumlik (1983a) deals with the aforementioned dispute between Menachem Begin and Helmut Schmidt about the latter's involvement in National Socialism. Brumlik sees the gist of the problem in the inability of the Jews to mourn; this means that they remain bogged down in the past of National Socialism and it "also robs them of a future" (ibid., 95). Thus, the Jews continue to fight with the Germans over the issue of the Palestinians, in order not to be saddled by the survivors' guilt with the responsibility for the repetition of something for which they had never been responsible in the first place. And the children of those who partly bear the guilt for National Socialism try to "escape into the collectivity of the nation" (ibid., 103) in order to find their identity there. "There they will certainly not find an 'ego' that acts in a responsible manner" (ibid.)

Bitburg and beyond

Towards the mid-1980s, the controversy centering about the German "nation" became increasingly important. Whereas the then President of the Federal Republic of Germany, Richard von Weizsäcker, emphasized the guilt of the Germans for the war and for the National Socialist genocide in a speech which attracted great attention and which was held in the German Bundestag (Parliament) on May 8, 1985 on the occasion of the 40th anniversary of the end of the war, the then German Federal Chancellor, Helmut Kohl, repeatedly continued to speak of crimes that had been committed "in the name of Germany" and of the "grace of a late birth", which allowed him to speak in this manner (cf. Haug 1987, 200 et seqq.). In the face of international criticism, the Federal Chancellor managed in view of the increasing economic and political significance of the Federal Republic of Germany to persuade the American President to participate on May 5, 1985 in an act of reconciliation between the former German and US American war enemies (cf. in this connection Levkov 1987). Although there was no handshake between Reagan and Kohl (like the handshake of reconciliation between Kohl and the French President Mitterand in Verdun) – the former US general Mathew B. Ridgeway and the general of the Federal armed forces Johannes Steinhoff did shake hands. However, the place chosen for the reconciliation ceremony, in particular, caused indignation, especially among Jews. This was the soldiers' cemetery of Bitburg, in which Waffen-SS men are, among others, also buried. For the Jews this marked a turning-point of outstanding importance: a turning-point which transformed the National Socialist genocide into the "sacrifice" of a normal war. For both handshakes implied that the peace that had been concluded did not refer to "the war" in its limited sense, but to the whole of National Socialism.

The insistence on this "reconciliation" over the graves of SS men in Bitburg was, in the consciousness of many Germans, to imply that this change of attitude also meant that from now on one must also consider the guilt-fraught German-Jewish relationship as changed, namely as having become "normal". However, what "normality" means for Jews in Germany is precisely not the pleasant feeling of coming to a peaceful rest and of achieving a state of contented serenity, but it means getting used to an undefined disquiet, to fear and exclusion. Thus Detlev Claussen (1986) speaks of the "normality" of *anti-Semitism*: "For the conviction that anti-Semitism is something abnormal is wrong. In modern society, anti-Semitism is on the contrary something normal" (ibid., 232; cf. also Claussen 1987). And David Jonah Goldhagen also points out in the light of a "new way of looking at anti-Semitism" (1996b, 45 et seqq.) that one must assume – in National Socialism – a basically anti-Semitic attitude on the part of the Germans, rather than vice-versa "that on the whole the Germans were not anti-Semites in the nineteenth and twentieth centuries; instead we should have to *show* that they freed themselves from anti-Semitism, if they ever did so. [...] There is practically nothing to show to refute the opinion that the anti-Semitism expressed offensively and publicly could not also be found in people's private opinions" (ibid., 49; transl. by H.H.).

Thus, after "Bitburg", for the sake of achieving supposed impartiality, punishment not only extends to denial of Auschwitz, but also to denial of the suffering inflicted upon those expelled from the former Eastern part of Germany. Or it strikes one that in Fassbinder's play *Der Müll, die Stadt und der Tod* (Garbage, the City and Death) (Fassbinder 1981) only a single person making an appearance remains nameless; he is called "the rich Jew". In connection with the boycott of a performance of this play – in particular, by Jews from Frankfurt who occupied the stage –, the "progressive" culture critic Peter Iden thought it right to speak of the "*sensitivities* of Jewish fellow citizens" and of the fact that "some representatives of *Jewish capital* belonged to a right-wing power cartel, which to a great extent has had its own way in communal politics during the sixties and seventies" (Iden 1985; italics by

K.G.). This choice of words makes clear that Jews are neither accepted as citizens enjoying equal rights, nor is it recognized that in accordance with Marxist theory "capital" is precisely *not* determined by a religious denomination. Iden's sentences look as if they were written in an epoch long past.

One member of the German Parliament, Hermann Fellner, felt emboldened some time after to speak of Jews "who lose no time in turning up when money tinkles in German tills" (*Stuttgarter Zeitung* of January 11, 1986) and one mayor of the Christian Democratic Union, Wilderich Baron Count of Spee was of the opinion that "one would have to kill a few rich Jews" in order "to put the city's budget on a sound basis again" (*Frankfurter Rundschau* of February 7, 1986).

The election of Kurt Waldheim to the office of Austrian Federal President which, in spite of his Nazi past, took place soon afterwards – fifty years after the "Anschluss" – also disturbed Jews in the Federal Republic of Germany. In spite of having been a resistance fighter, Waldheim's adviser Karl Gruber lightly dismissed the criticisms of the candidate for the presidency when he commented in "no uncertain" terms on the report of the Historians' Commission about Waldheim's record as officer of the German Wehrmacht during the Second World War in the following words: "Practically all the commission members were his enemies. The German member is a Socialist, the others are on account of their Jewish origin naturally not friends of his, either, because they are clearly against Waldheim. That is after all the point. He is being attacked because we were not willing, like the Germans, to pay what they had paid. The man Waldheim is only a symbol for the entire complex" (*Frankfurter Rundschau* of February 13, 1988).

The Historians' Dispute

At this time the so-called "Historians' Dispute" had been smouldering in the Federal Republic of Germany for quite a long while; it was triggered off by the article *Die negative Lebendigkeit des Dritten Reiches. Eine Frage aus dem Blickwinkel des Jahres 1980* (The negative vitality of the Third Reich. A problem considered in the year 1980) (*Frankfurter Allgemeine Zeitung* of July 24, 1980); it was the abbreviated version of a lecture given by the historian Ernst Nolte (cf. Diner 1987, Pehle 1990, Augstein et al. 1987, Wehler 1988). Jürgen Habermas (1986) and others criticised the attempt made by historians in the Federal Republic to "get rid of" German history. The historians around Nolte tried to deny the unique character of the National Socialist annihilation of the Jews. Stalin's cruel acts were being misused in order to make the former Soviet leader look like a forerunner of Hitler. The atrocities committed by the Nazis should be interpreted as a comprehensible *reaction* to former events or actions, for instance, say, to the "Asiatic behaviour" of

Stalin or to "something that resembled a declaration of war" (Nolte 1987, 25) against the Germans given by the President of the Jewish Agency Chaim Weizmann in September 1939 "in accordance with which Jews all over the world would fight on England's side in this war" (ibid., 24), a statement which according to Nolte "enables one to justify the momentous thesis that Hitler was entitled to treat the German Jews as prisoners of war [...] and i.e. to intern them" (ibid.).

The former Federal Chancellor Helmut Kohl, occasionally described as having a doctor's degree in History,[12] further distinguished himself by playing down the significance of National Socialism, when he compared the then General Secretary of the Communist Party of the Soviet Union, Mikhail Gorbachev, to the Nazi Minister of Propaganda Joseph Goebbels. However, in public this comparison was regarded as needing to be criticised not because it played down the atrocities of the National Socialists, but because it impaired the relations of the Federal Republic of Germany with the Soviet Union.

Thus many Jews criticised the fact that precisely "this gifted historian and peace-maker of Bitburg" (Grünberg 1993) held an address to Germany's *Jews* on November 9, 1988, in memory of the fiftieth anniversary of the Reich "Crystal Night".

Half a year later, the government spokesman Hans Klein who had the rank of a minister remarked during an interview given to an illustrated periodical: "We accept responsibility for our past. But if the Federal Chancellor today lays a wreath down in Bitburg, there is an outcry as if he had awarded the Order of the Federal Republic of Germany to a concentration camp thug! [...] The Waffen-SS were after all fighting troops, not criminals. They thought that they had to defend their fatherland. Of late, this has not been made clear. And all this has led to our living unreconciled with the dead. A people can tolerate such a state of affairs only with difficulty" (*Frankfurter Rundschau* of May 6, 1989).

It was once again Klein who used an anti-Semitic expression when on the occasion of the Chancellor's planned visit on November 11, 1989 to the former concentration camp of Auschwitz he expressed "understanding for

12 | It has not proved possible to adequately clear up the question whether the designation "historian" can be appropriately used for Helmut Kohl, who was Chancellor for many years. Kohl studied jurisprudence, social and political science as well as history at the universities of Frankfurt/Main and Heidelberg from 1950 to 1956. The thesis which he submitted in order to obtain the degree of doctor of the Philosophical Faculty of the Ruprecht-Karls-University of Heidelberg dealt with a historical subject: "The political development and rebirth of Parties in the Palatinate after 1945" (cf. in this connection also Dreher 1998, 45).

the misgivings of *international Jewry*" (*Frankfurter Allgemeine Zeitung* of November 14, 1989; italics by K.G.).

The 9th of November

In the meantime it is also part of the annals of history that the 9th of November has yet again been endowed with a new significance: following upon 1918, 1923 and 1938, after the Berlin wall fell on November 9, 1989, this date now truly became the "Germans' day" (*Stern*, No. 47 of November 16, 1989). This had been the "night of freedom" (ibid.). In the newspaper *Bild* of November 11, 1989, we read: "Germany embraces itself. Unity and Justice and Liberty. [...] Whatever may now happen – nobody can take this day away from us any more. It was a day for Germany."

And it is only logical that not much later young Germans in Berlin wore T-shirts with the inscription "I was there" (R.C. Schneider 1989). That this was not only a declaration that one had been present at the fall of the Berlin wall, but was also a quotation from the Chairman of the Republican Party, Franz Schönhuber,[13] was probably not the result of a conscious decision. A few citizens also quickly lost no time in giving the "Street of June 17" a new name: now it was to be called the "Street of November 9" (Jacobs 1990).

Reunification

Thus ultimately they were all united in the Germany of the nineties: "Semites" and "anti-Semites", fascists and anti-fascists, perpetrators and victims, Germans in the Federal Republic of Germany and in the German Democratic Republic ... And this much seems to be clear: it was the "reunification", the choice of the "capital" Berlin as the seat of Parliament and of the government which made this possible; the finishing touch was put to the process of normalization: the genocide of the Jews is to be considered as a closed matter to be forgotten; it is to vanish under concrete like the remnants of the Jewish ghetto in Frankfurt/Main (cf. Best 1988). What remains after Auschwitz, is anti-Semitism *because* of Auschwitz. "The Germans", says Henryk M. Broder (Broder 1986, 125), "will never forgive the Jews for Auschwitz."[14]

---

13 | Franz Schönhuber, who joined the Waffen-SS voluntarily, gave his autobiographical book the title *I was there* (Schönhuber 1989).

14 | Gunnar Heinsohn (1988a) ascribes the statement: "The Germans will never forgive us for Auschwitz" to Zvi Rix, who was born in Vienna in 1909 and died in Israel, and Andrei S. Markovits and Simon Reich (1977) quote the following sentence:

Remarks like "This must once come to an end" could no longer be ignored. What was here craving for "Lebensraum" was "nostalgia for normality" (Zollinger 1985, 52) and this meant: 40 years of a "bonus for Jews" were enough. The "honeymoon period" was over. The longed-for "normality" would be finally achieved, after a reconciliation had taken place (cf. Brumlik 1985, 75) and living Jews no longer reminded one of Auschwitz.

The Gulf War

During the "Gulf War" the realization of such ideas came nearer. When a spokesman of the Federal executive of the Green party and leader of a delegation from this party which journeyed to Israel and Jordan in February 1991 expressed the opinion that "The Iraqi attacks with guided missiles are the logical consequence of Israel's policy" (quotation from Christian Ströbele, Süddeutsche Zeitung of February 19, 1991), German conscientious objectors had already been feeling great anguish for a month. Under the title *Talks about beds for wounded GIs, 'Frankfurt on the Gulf'/'Zivis'* [persons doing social and community work instead of military service] *in a moral dilemma* one could read the following remarks in the *Frankfurter Rundschau*: "Conscientious objectors are driven into *severe conflicts of conscience* by the share German hospitals take in caring for Americans wounded in the war. The Zivis are calling for a token strike in all hospitals today. In case of an emergency, their spokesman announced that the Zivis would refuse to work" (*Frankfurter Rundschau* of January 15, 1991; italics from K.G.). One of the founders of the Israeli peace movement, the writer Yoram Kaniuk, expressed quite a different opinion at the same time: "About 100,000 survivors of the Holocaust and their children live here. And they sit here and wait for a guided missile which was technologically improved by Germans [...] and wait for the gas [...]. And gas and Jews do not agree with each other" (*Frankfurter Rundschau* of February 12, 1991).

A Supermarket on Concentration Camp Grounds

On July 19, 1991 the following headline appeared in the *Frankfurter Rundschau*: *Brandenburg's Ministries give Permission for a Supermarket on Concentration Camp Grounds*. One was not astounded any more that business people should begin to erect a supermarket on the grounds of the women's concentration camp Ravensbrück. Just as little was one astounded that politicians on various levels should agree to the building of this supermarket or

"The Germans will never forgive us for Auschwitz. Zvi Rex, Israeli psychoanalyst" (ibid., 325)

that they should withdraw their consent again after protests had been made against this decision. Likewise one was not astounded that a bus entrepreneur should want to use the industrial yard of the former concentration camp or that a tax office should move into the adjacent building of the chief SS administration for concentration camps. It seemed that one had also got used to the street blockades that were erected and to the violence against survivors shown by indignant citizens eager to secure jobs.

In this context, however, a commentary in the *Frankfurter Rundschau*, also dating from July 19, 1991, is interesting; under the title *An Instructive Case* we read: "As seen through the eyes of an outsider, everything might appear to be quite 'normal' [...]. 'After all, this gives new jobs for three hundred people' say the people gathered at the sausage stand. That sentence is a decisive argument. Whoever thinks about the five new Lands [of the former German Democratic Republic], the submissiveness displayed by their governments, the drastic measures which the powerful West German economy adopts without any misgivings, may reflect also upon the plans for the concentration camp of Ravensbrück." Doesn't this mean that one "may" only criticise the building of a supermarket on the grounds of a former concentration camp, if one has beforehand racked one's brains "over the five new Lands, the submissiveness displayed by their governments, the drastic measures adopted without any misgivings by the powerful West German economy"?

Society for the Sponsoring of the Local History of the Administrative District of Verden

The "Registered Society for the Sponsoring of the Local History of the Administrative District of Verden 1933-1945" is responsible for an initiative at the beginning of May 1993 inviting former forced labourers to Verden, in order that they might become acquainted there with "the other Germany". A preparatory course was to help the persons who were to look after the Nazi victims during this visit to cope with the forthcoming meeting.

Various information material was enclosed with the organizer's invitation to this course; in this connection the logo of the promoter attracted immediate attention: two persons in outline who confront each other as in a mirror and touch each other. An interpretation involuntarily came to mind: was one trying to avoid visualizing a meeting with persons with quite a different background of experience than one's own? Instead was one looking for a meeting between equals, a cosy encounter between people, which would if at all possible ignore the rift which National Socialist forced labour represented?

In a covering letter, the wish was expressed "that one might find a so-called 'godparent' for each visitor from Poland and the CIS among the population of Verden. The 'godparent' should already now contact his or her 'godchild' by letter." An information leaflet stated: "The 'godparent' will receive information about the fate and life circumstances of his or her 'adopted partner' from us."

One had the impression that everything was to be precisely planned and that everything should run its course as correctly as possible. The aim was to avoid every conflict before it could even arise. By naming both genders in almost every sentence of the letters and information leaflets, an attempt was made to please everybody. Yet these efforts simultaneously seemed so exaggerated that, as a result of provoking a contrary reaction, one might also reverse the whole: was one possibly unconsciously maintaining the humiliation of the Nazi victims and one's own higher status? Did not the naming of the former forced labourers as "god*children*" (italics from K.G.) and "protégés" serve to fulfil this wish?

The atmosphere which, according to their own description, the organizers aimed at creating suggests that a debate about the latent conflict carried out in the spirit of an authentic encounter was to be avoided rather than carried out, since we read: "Perhaps in this way we can make it possible for them and for us too to successfully cope with the painful past [...]." But is a "successful coping with" history really the aim of a debate about the Nazi past?

International Encounter in Stadtallendorf

The "International Encounter in Stadtallendorf" had taken place already three years before the invitation to former forced labourers to come to Verden was sent off. This event, which as such is to be highly welcomed and which was probably organized against the resistance of conservative politicians, was devoted to the memory of the camp Münchmühle, an external section of the concentration camp of Buchenwald, to which one thousand Hungarian Jewesses who had been selected in Auschwitz were transported, in order to work under inhuman conditions as forced labourers for the Allendorf munition factory of Dynamit-Nobel. The survivors were invited to Stadtallendorf in 1990. The silence about the concentration camp external section that had prevailed for decades was at last to be broken.

In order to give the great event attractive trappings one had presumably had recourse to the services of a graphic designer. He or she designed a logo, which then appeared on every name card, every pamphlet and also on a book documenting the event printed on high-quality paper and clothbound (The Magistrate of the City of Stadtallendorf et al., 1991) which was published afterwards. A quotation set in quotation marks:

3. Jews in Germany Today | 71

"The secret of reconciliation is remembrance" appeared under a coloured rainbow – the Heinrich-Böll-Foundation being one of the promoters of the week's encounter. This quotation (with no indication of its source) had been chosen by the organizers as the motto for the encounter days in Stadtallendorf and in big letters it also decorated the hall in which the encounter took place.

However, there's a not inconsiderable snag to this quotation: because it has been falsified. The original of this much quoted remark made by the Ba'al Schem Tov, the founder of Eastern European Chassidism, reads as follows:

"The exile grows longer and longer because of forgetfulness,
but it is from remembering that redemption comes"
(Sefer Ba'al Schem Tov, II, 190 § 8; quoted from Grözinger, 1992, 32)

Thus "reconciliation" has been substituted for the word "redemption" of the original text. Even though one can pertinently ask whether even an understanding of "redemption" which is based on Jewish tradition should be mentioned in connection with the National Socialist extermination of the Jews, the fact that a term such as "reconciliation" could be introduced in this context calls all the more for an explanation. An inquiry addressed to the then organizers of the Encounter brought no elucidation concerning this significant mistake. The first entry in the minutes already included the aforementioned false wording.

At first glance, one is surprised to find a term which one would rather be inclined to use in a conflict between two individuals. In the context of small or large groups of people, one would at least have to assume that the parties concerned, who are pitting their strength against each other, tend to have equal rights. For instance, two children quarreling over a toy might begin to fight, and afterwards "make it up" (i.e. be "reconciled" with each other). One of them might even forgive the other one for having had recourse to unfair means and vice-versa. They forgive each other and are reconciled. Even if two groups of "fans" start fighting each other during a sports competition, it is conceivable that they might afterwards make it up. The idea of reconciliation might in such cases be appropriate. But in the context of a genocide such a reference is totally inadequate. It involves absolutely ignoring that the National Socialist persecution of the Jews was *not* a dispute between two opponents who tried to assert possibly different or contrary interests with means that are at least capable of being compared with each other. Just as little were two opposing armies in a state of war with each other.[15] And likewise one is not dealing with imaginary controversies, but as far as National Socialism is concerned, one is dealing with a *real* social situation of *violence*, for which patterns of explanation based on concepts which apply specifically to individuals are totally inadequate. When one is dealing with the genocide of a people, the use of the concept of reconciliation stands for reducing a social mass phenomenon to the status of a wrong committed against an individual. Thus this use of the term represents a defence mechanism.

A reference to the *Großer Duden*, a dictionary of the origin of words, provides further clarification. Statements about "reconciliation" can be found under the leading word "expiation": "The group of words [...] is possibly based on the basic meaning 'to make silent, to appease; soothing, comforting'" (Der Große Duden 1963, 695). From the psychoanalytical point of view, one is dealing with a defence mechanism, in which one fends off something in order to relieve superego guilt, possibly also a *feeling* of guilt. If one applies this to persons born after the Nazi period, then one might be dealing with a feeling of guilt unconsciously borrowed (cf. Freud 1923, 50).

What has been repressed and comes back in an involuntary mistake now takes on a more concrete shape. A further look at the "Encounter days" confirms that this is the case.

For the – falsified – talk of reconciliation fell on fertile ground in Stadtallendorf. Among the many speakers there was scarcely no-one who did not mention the motto of the Encounter. Nobody seems to have noticed that the quotation was not correctly reproduced. The then Prime Minister of Hessen, Walter Wallmann, vehemently voiced what he apparently felt very strongly. In his words of greeting, he said, addressing the survivors: "Your coming here shows willingness to effect a reconciliation. [...] 'The secret of reconciliation is to remember'" (Wallmann, n.d., 11). The victims of the Nazi persecution of the Jews were not to be generously wined and dined without having to make a definite contribution themselves. The hospitality of the town of Stadtallendorf should also have a price for the victims. The survivors were to contribute to "making silent, to appeasing", to "soothing, comforting"; they should help bring about the desired relief from guilt. They should be willing to effect a reconcilation.

Not much more than a year then sufficed for the mayor of Stadtallendorf and the Chairman of the society promoting this event to be able to say still more clearly what wishes they associated with the Encounter event. Together with the book documenting the events which has been mentioned above (The Magistrate of the City of Stadtallendorf et al. 1991), a letter of

---

15 | Cf. in this connection the remarks about the "peace reconciliation of Bitburg".

thanks was dispatched in which it was said that the drawing up of the documentation "was something for which we felt both the need and the obligation. Not least because of your commitment was it possible to carry out this *unique event on such a scale* [...]. We hope that you will like the book and that it will help you to think back with pleasure on the event [...] and we hope that you will find enough time to read it at leisure" (letter of December 13, 1991; italics from K.G.).

These sentences are practically self-explanatory. The text's connotations remind one of the controversy of the historians' dispute that centered on the issue of the unique character of the Nazi extermination of the Jews. One feels that there is an unconscious identification with the power and greatness of the Nazis. At the same time, the guilt feeling is warded off, and the political dynamite of the conflict about the experience of Nazi persecution is denied, when the hope is expressed that "you will think back with pleasure" and find "enough time to read at leasure" the book that has been published. The "good" memory of the Encounter days in Stadtallendorf should as it were obliterate the "bad" memory of the days in Stadtallendorf under Nazi Germany. One may, perhaps, object that this is merely an isolated case or – as a Bavarian journalist formulated in terms that made little of the matter – that this was an "admittedly stupid, tactless, well-meant covering letter [...], concluding with – decidedly out of place – wishes for a Merry Christmas" (Chaussy 1992). One might also object that worse things have been known to occur.

However, there is no lack of further examples. And as a matter of fact one can find worse ones. But what seems to be important is that in Stadtallendorf precisely nobody participated who simply denied the reality of Auschwitz, nobody spoke of the "luck of being belatedly born" or believed that they could rid themselves of the burden of German history by concluding peace over SS graves in Bitburg. Here, one is precisely not dealing with people who think that the disappearance of a Jewish ghetto under concrete may bring about peace (cf. Best 1988) nor with people who try to diminish the import of Auschwitz by arguing that in his persecution of the Jews Hitler was merely following in the footsteps of an "Asiatic deed" committed by Stalin ...

On the contrary, here is a position which actually demands – at least on the conscious level – that one should attend to the problem of National Socialist persecution, instead of closing the matter once and for all. It is all the more significant and simultaneously disappointing that one finds that a wish – visible by the slips and mistakes made – breaks through which expresses the original meaning of reconciliation: to appease, to impose silence. Under no circumstances, indeed, can this be regarded as being the same as the remembrance which Judaism demands – as exemplified in the case of Amalek's atrocities for instance. In contrast to this, the demand for reconciliation which is here made, is a violent, destructive act; in a peaceful disguise, it is really an act in which memory is actually *destroyed* (cf. Grünberg 1998a).

What emerges very clearly in this context is that there can be no reconciliation over Auschwitz. The systematic extermination of a people with a prussic acid product used for pest control and carried out on an industrial scale, such an extermination which was prepared by passing legal measures and which was tolerated by the masses, cannot be the subject of a "reconciliation". The intention of a reconciliation is to cloud over the chasm between Germans and Jews which was created by the National Socialist extermination of the Jews and which is indeed difficult to put up with. Reconciliation is intended to appease the Jews and ultimately to stop their mouths.

In order to make a sincere "encounter" possible, however, it would have been necessary to recognize the chasm created by National Socialism as a chasm, which still strongly affects the relations between Germans and Jews even after the involuntary end of the Nazi persecution and which will continue to do so in future. Only the admission that this chasm exists could provide a foundation for an encounter – one which would then, indeed, be a real encounter and would perhaps not be misused. In personal intercourse this attitude should not be branded and misunderstood as "irreconcilable", as if one would thereby imply that one cannot move towards each other or that no attempts to understand each other could be made, or that it is not possible to become friends or to love each other. What is important is to bring light into a very thorny social relationship and to understand collective processes of mass psychology. Not the least important point is the finding of one's bearings on the social and political plane.

Therefore, the slips and mistakes described above are not of importance as individual acts. They are rather of interest, because one is dealing with a form of "contagion". One is dealing with a consensus of opinion, with a collective process in the sense of an ethnic disturbance (cf. Vogt 1995) which can lead to a repetitive compulsion.

It is possible to find a latent threat of this kind, namely that it might not be possible "to exclude comparable catastrophes in the future" if one does not allow the Germans to be a "self-confident nation" in an advertisement placed in the Frankfurter Allgemeine Zeitung by a big new German coalition; this coalition extends from representatives of the peace movement, politicians from nearly all parties, an ex-publisher of the periodical *konkret*, an honorary chairman of the parliamentary group of the Christian Democratic and Christian Social Union party, the former Chief Federal Prosecutor to the chief editor of the extreme right-wing daily *Junge Freiheit*.

In this advertisement, perfidious references were made to the maintaining of silence, to suppression and minimization, but also – precisely by minimizing National Socialism – to the "fresh oppression in the East[ern part of Germany]" and even to the *extermination* (sic!) of the Germans. This big advertisement appeared on April 7, 1995. It bore the title: *May 8, 1945 – Against the Process of Forgetting.*

Complicity and Parallel Perpetrator-Victim Structures

In the "land of the perpetrators" voices were increasingly raised demanding that one should now get rid of the taboos imposed after 1945. The time had at last come "in which it should be possible to express oneself freely". In the "land of the murderers" – a not insignificant detail – most of the Nazi perpetrators remained unpunished. And even after the liberation, Jews were still being abused, despised, persecuted and also killed. The average people in this country avoided the necessity to discuss personal guilt, which should have been the first priority; they denied the reality of the Shoah. Ralph Giordano speaks in this connection of the "second guilt" assumed by the Germans and of the "burden of being a German" (Giordano 1987).

One way of dealing with the suffering of the victims is to present oneself as a victim of "circumstances" and to describe the whole matter as an everyday phenomenon inasmuch as one speaks, say, of the "Holocaust of the trees", of the "nuclear Holocaust" or of the "Holocaust of the unborn" when discussing the legality of abortions. In academic discussion, supposed "similarities" are discovered between the victims and perpetrators so that in this way a confrontation with one's own history is avoided. Jean Améry, on the contrary, demanded that one should not put perpetrators in the same category as victims: "It is out of the question for me to accept a parallelism which permits me to be placed alongside the fellows who castigated me with bullwhips. I do not want to become the accomplice of my torturers; rather do I demand that these should negate themselves and be placed beside me in their negative function. It seems to me that the corpses piled up between them and myself cannot be cleared away in a process of interiorization; on the contrary, this can only be done by transferring the matter to the present, or in sharper words: by working on the unsolved conflict in the field of historical practice" (Améry 1977, 112, transl. by H.H.).

In contrast to this demand, Federal German "practice" is very clearly characterized by placing victims and perpetrators on the same level. In particular, in the course of the "Historians' Dispute" and after reunification, both politicians and academics seemed increasingly to cast off their guilt by minimizing Auschwitz or by branding victims as co-perpetrators. It is no accident that the controversy with Nazi perpetrators has repeatedly promptly degenerated into a perpetrator/victim debate. Agreement is swiftly reached to the effect that the "counterpart" of the perpetrator is the victim, in spite of the fact that a perpetrator/*non*-perpetrator debate would to start with be more appropriate and could even produce far more interesting results[16], e.g. concerning the question what enabled certain people to take up a position in opposition to the majority of their fellows and to the National Socialist persecution of the Jews.

In the Centre for Neurology of the Philipps University of Marburg, during the winter term of 1989/90 the author personally experienced how the controversy about a supposed "complicity" of victims with the perpetrators of National Socialism can be dealt with within the confines of a university seminar. The then director of the Clinic for Psychotherapy, the psychoanalyst Prof. Dr. Manfred Pohlen, announced that he wanted to look into "the constitutive conditions of Nazi Fascism" and that he also wished to explain its inherrent "fascination". However, instead of doing this, he introduced the term "complicity" to the seminar as a central concept. He spoke of "the vertiginous mirror effects" that prevailed between Fascists and anti-Fascists, "Semites"[17] and anti-Semites, perpetrators and victims ... Mention was made of "unconscious complicity" and of "parallel perpetrator-victim structures". Pohlen minimized Auschwitz when he made "the victims of Nazi persecution the accomplices of their persecutors" (Grünberg 1993). Although one can daily find in the practice of psycho-therapists and psychoanalysts that individuals are never identified "only" with victims or "only" with perpetrators, but that a sadist, say, also has masochistic traits or that he or she repels his or her own masochism by means of his or her sadism, yet such insights gained from the treatment of individuals cannot just simply be transferred to groups and masses. In National Socialism, one was dealing with a *real* social relationship involving *violence*. Jews did not allow themselves to be deported in order to be at last able to undergo masochistic submission in this way. In National Socialism there were real perpetrators and there were real victims.

If Pohlen now reduces this difference between "real" and "mental" to the same level, then the result of such a debate cannot be enlightenment, but "a mystification, which precisely allows what is so 'fascinating' about the National Socialist extermination of the Jews to continue" (Grünberg 1993). A "scandal" was the result (Laufner 1990), when a dispute – in which recourse was also taken to legal means – took the pattern that those who dealt critically with National Socialism or with the way National Socialism was being treated at the present time were called persecutors. In Pohlen's opinion, his adversary (Grünberg 1990) engaged in "denunciation"; Pohlen

16 | I owe this insight to a discussion I had with Christoph Scheffer.
17 | No explanation of who the "Semites" were was given.

spoke of "Nazi methods" and accused the author of "calumniation in Gestapo fashion".

The Nazi Past and the
German Psychoanalytical Association[18]

A controversy which was certainly of a comparable nature – not only, with respect to the vocabulary used – took place in court in Frankfurt/Main in 1994/95, after a training analyst and university professor from Frankfurt had called a local psychoanalyst a "Nazi", because he had criticised the way the dead foundation member, training analyst, former Chairman and honorary member of the German Psychoanalytical Association, Professor Dr. Gerhart Scheunert, had behaved as regards his Nazi past. According to information which he himself gave, Scheunert had been an "active party member" until the mid-thirties and later a Medical Officer. Regine Lockot (1994, 227 et al.) states that Scheunert was a block leader, was a member of the medical section of the NSKK (National Socialist Motor Corps), of the medical corps of the army, of the National Socialist Medical Association, and was from 1940-42 an "army medical officer in an advance detachment". Eugen Mahler (1995, 378) writes of his being a member of the SA. The conflict in the German Psychoanalytical Association came to a head when it became public knowledge that a document disclosing Scheunert's party

---

18 | The following chapter should not be understood as implying that it is the privilege of the German Psychoanalytical Association to conduct a questionable debate about the Nazi past of its members. Rather could the *Deutsche Psychoanalytische Gesellschaft* (German Psychoanalytical Society) (DPG) also be the subject of a critical examination of its history (cf. say Brecht et al. 1985, Ermann 1996, Blumenberg 1997). Here we will only refer to the controversy about the publication of Annemarie Dührssen's book *Ein Jahrhundert Psychoanalytische Bewegung in Deutschland* (A century of the psychoanalytic movement in Germany); in his review, Yigal Blumenberg (1995) concluded that the book was "according to all known and usual standards not only not a scientific book, but a document full of resentment. D. uses the language of those who saw the Jews as the undoing of one and all; she hands down the anti-Judaism of centuries and turns a cold shoulder on rational discourse" (ibid., 169; cf. also Hampel 1995, Schultz-Venrath 1995). A further example is the controversy about a letter of invitation to the DPG-conference *Psychoanalyse im Exil* (Psychoanalysis in Exile), which has been criticised by Judith Kraus (1998) in the periodical *Psyche* above all because of its questionable concept of fate and also because of a whole series of slips. Both the Chairman of the German Psychoanalytical Association, Jürgen Körner (1998) and the co-editor of *Psyche* apparently felt obliged to comment on Judith Kraus's position already in the same issue of *Psyche*.

membership was not shown in the exhibition *Hier geht das Leben auf eine sehr merkwürdige Weise weiter ... Zur Geschichte der Psychoanalyse in Deutschland* (Here life goes on in a very peculiar manner ... Psychoanalysis before and after 1933) (Brecht et al. 1985) organized on the occasion of the first International Psychoanalytic Congress held in 1985 in Hamburg, the first one to take place in Germany after National Socialism.[19]

While it is true that the Court of Appeals in Frankfurt/Main meanwhile forbade the university professor emeritus from calling his analyst colleague a "Nazi", in the present context, this judgment and the reasons given for it seem not of such significance as the arguments which were brought forward in the course of the controversy about the Nazi past of one of the "founding fathers" of the German Psychoanalytical Association (DPV). They were published as open letters in the *DPV-Informationen* No. 14 of November 1993 under the heading "Contributions to the debate about our Nazi past". Those who demanded clarification of the role of psychoanalysis under National Socialism and of the attitude later adopted towards this past were described by Jürgen Kenning as a "clique" and as "inquisitors" (Kenning 1993, 4). One was dealing with an "underhanded intrigue" (ibid.), "the prosecutor himself becomes a perpetrator" (ibid., 5). "If we [...] commit a fresh injustice because of an old injustice, then we behave exactly like the Nazis" (ibid.) said Kenning. "Even informer and traitors tell the truth; they do so precisely in order to misuse it" (ibid.) Ulrich Ehebald speaks of a "ruthless interference in the rights of the personality of a person" (Ehebald 1993a, 10) and of a "merciless persecutor mentality" (ibid.) He goes on to say "that certain people [would like] to give expression to their irrational desire for vengeance as if they were vultures" (Ehebald 1993b, 13) and then speaks of "heartless persecutors" (ibid.). According to Jürgen Kenning, one was not dealing with "a crime and therefore not with guilt" (Kenning 1993, 4), if somebody had been a member of the National Socialist party; "Mr. Scheunert had made a mistake" (ibid.). If Scheunert "had left this party" (ibid., 5), it is wrongly claimed, this would have "possibly [...], indeed probably have cost him his life" (ibid.). Kenning's final conclusion which plays down the import of the matter is that "It was Nazi behaviour to reserve rights only for certain people and to exclude others therefrom. The characteristic feature of Nazi ideology is [...] injustice" (ibid., 6).

In the aforementioned remarks, as in others which we have not quoted, it becomes clear that the real state of affairs has been reversed. Critical citi-

19 | This censorship was disclosed to the participants of a conference of the DPV (German Psychoanalytical Association) held in November 1992. But the reference to the fact that a document had been "withheld" in the exhibition in Hamburg was not adequately mentioned in the minutes of the conference.

zens are branded as Nazis and persecutors and the term "Nazi" is brandished as an insult which can be arbitrarily used in the hope of injuring an unwelcome opponent. 50 years after the end of National Socialism tongues seem to wag unrestrainedly, whereas – as far as the truth of National Socialism itself is concerned – a *persistent* silence is observed.

The Pact of Silence

Tilmann Moser (1995; also with almost identical wording in Moser 1996, 124 et. seqq.) argued on another level, whilst structurally using a similar approach to that of Pohlen. Only a few years ago still, says Moser, "it was considered sacrilegious to name the two generations in the same breath, and yet some of their traumatizations are similar. The 'pact of silence' has left vacant spaces in both families, which have been filled with ominous fantasies and mental deformities. Some authors rightly point out that persecutors have experienced nothing remotely like the life under arbitrary humiliation and the threat of death over many years, as well as the loss of all family members which some survivors endured. And yet both sides have frequently gone to extremes by using and also misusing their children in order to cope with the unsayable to which they have been subjected or which they have inflicted. The hope that a process of understanding on both sides might come about during the transition from the second to the third generation arises precisely from this *unbearable kinship*. In this connection it cannot be the goal to level and bring things closer to each other, but rather to reach an understanding that can endure the truth of the other one" (Moser 1995; italics from K.G.).

Moser confuses his readers with his vague wording. By speaking "in the same breath" both of perpetrators and of victims, of "the second generations of both" and then in addition of the "transition from the second to the third generation", he ends up by blurring all distinctions. In particular, the passage in which he speaks of an "unbearable kinship" remains vague. True, one might at first think that Moser refers here to the "second generations of both sides".[20] But a glance at Moser's almost identical, but more detailed description of the same interrelation (Moser 1996, 124-125) throws a clearer light on what is meant. Here, the relevant sentence begins as follows: "Hope springs precisely from this at first almost unbearable kinship of *destructive survival mechanisms* [...]" (ibid., 125; italics by K.G.). The extending to "destructive survival mechanisms" must refer to the generation of the survivors, for the life of their daughters and sons were *not* in danger (which admittedly

20 | But even in that case one might express doubts about the truth of this assertion.

is also true of the perpetrators). Therefore, when he speaks of an "unbearable kinship", Moser does not refer to the descendants of the Nazi perpetrators and survivors, but is thinking of the persecuted Jews and of their persecutors!

The question to be asked then is which "truth" is to be "endured" here? And is not a blatant untruth being produced when Moser construes similarities and a "kinship" between persecuted Jews and Nazi perpetrators? Seen in the light of a "pact of silence" that is supposedly observed by both sides, Moser may be logical in arguing that his moral judgment to the effect that the children were used or even misused applies to "both sides". But this can hardly represent a contribution to "understanding". Moser's line of argument acquires meaning, however, if one imputes a motive to him, which, admittedly, is not openly expressed: is Moser looking for release from guilt in his approach to the Shoah?

As a matter of fact, Moser "betrays" such a motive of gaining release from guilt in the next sentence: "The Holocaust's truth was so dreadful that even Jewish analysts in the USA frequently did not venture to broach its repetition in the life stories told by their patients." If – one might pursue this line of thought – even Jewish analysts in the USA did not venture to come near to what had happened, who would reproach non-Jewish Germans (analysts) – who after all had much more reason to fear "the Holocaust's truth" – for constructing a more bearable "truth"? Moser is trying to get support for "enduring" his approach to National Socialism.

The investigations conducted by Gabriele Rosenthal (1995, 1997)[21] help one to reach a clearer understanding of this way of "coming to terms with the past". On the family level, Rosenthal works out the strategies of reparation to which families resort in order to cope with their Nazi past. "True," in the Federal Republic of Germany "for many years now we increasingly find descriptions of the Nazi crimes in the mass media, but the perpetrators and sympathizers of both genders [...] continue to preserve silence or come forward as guiltless 'contemporary witnesses' with detailed stories of the sufferings they experienced during the war and in the post-war period, without, however, providing documentary evidence of this" (Rosenthal 1995, 30 et seqq.)[22]

---

21 | Rosenthal's study is based upon interviews involving a narrative of one's life history and upon talks conducted with the family members of three generations.

22 | "Nobody will ever be in a position to determine exactly how many people in the National Socialist machinery *were unable to know anything* about the unspeakable atrocities that were perpetrated, and how many knew something, but were able to pretend they knew nothing, and how many again had the possibility of knowing everything, but decided to adopt a cautious stance and to keep eyes and ears (and above

Usually they present themselves "as people not involved in the collective events, and who as a result of the Second World War and its consequences – such as flight from the Soviet army and expulsion – became victims of National Socialism" (ibid., 31) themselves. Their own activities or complicity are "faded out"; the victims, in particular, the Jews, "disappear as a subject" (the Jews disappear from their perception and consciousness, silence is observed about their persecution), the victims are "dehumanized" (their personal and collective identities disappear, as the names of Jews disappear from the history of their life)[23]; responsibility for the genocide is laid at the door of the Jews themselves, or a "perpetrator-victim inversion" takes place. According to Rosenthal, the "pseudo-identification with victims" is also a

all mouths) firmly shut. Be that as it may, since one cannot just assume that the majority of Germans light-heartedly accepted this mass extermination, the circumstance that the truth about the concentration camps was not made widely known must be regarded as involving serious collective guilt on the part of the German people and as clear proof of the cowardice to which Hitler's terror had reduced them: a cowardice that became a habit, and which went so far that it kept men from speaking about it to their wives, and parents from speaking about it to their children – a cowardice, without which the worst excesses would never have been possible and without which Europe and the world today would be different" (Levi 1990, 11 et seqq.; transl. by H.H.). With respect to "knowing" and of the responsibility of perpetrators and observers Raul Hilberg observes: "Moreover, no individual and no official authority alone was responsible for the extermination of the Jews. There was no special budget for the project. The work was spread among the many ramifications of bureaucracy, and everyone could persuade himself that he was only a small cogwheel in an immense machinery. Therefore, civil servants, clerks or uniformed guards afterwards never described themselves as perpetrators. Yet they knew that their participation in the destruction was a voluntary one and that everyone who entered the maelstrom committed indelible acts – and in that respect would, therefore, always remain what he once was, even if he kept resolutely silent about his deeds" (Hilberg 1992, 9; transl. by H.H.).

23 | "Whereas the anti-Jewish actions that had taken place since 1933 are scarcely mentioned, the subject of the National Socialist policy of persecution crops up again with the so-called Reich Crystal Night and is practically condensed to this single event. Even so, in these stories [...] Jews do not usually even appear as persons; rather only the *material damage is described*, the broken glass and the burning synagogues – in accordance with the vocabulary adopted during the Reich night, in which 'crystal' was smashed as a symbol for the prosperity of the rich Jews. Those who were humiliated, beaten and arrested are hardly mentioned just as the perpetrators are not mentioned either" (Rosenthal 1995, 32).

strategy of avoidance which leads to not having to consider what actually happened.

Rosenthal takes individual families as examples in order to demonstrate in detail how Nazi family history goes on in later generations, for instance when the grandson of an interviewed partner, whose grandfather was presumably involved in the building of crematories in concentration camps, feels himself in nightmares to be burning, without seeing the connection with the acts of this grandfather (cf. "Familie Sonntag" – the Sonntag family –, Rosenthal 1995). Rosenthal sums up: "The resistance to uncovering family history does not by any means, however, result in freeing oneself from the family past; rather does it bind the children and grandchildren to the problematic parts of the family's history and thus to a considerable extent blocks the process of detaching oneself from the parents and developing autonomy" (ibid., 47).

Many survivors of the National Socialist extermination of the Jews indeed have hardly spoken of their experiences with persecution. At least, they frequently did not speak of them to their children, or to the "other ones", the "goyim", and least of all to the Germans. But this silence on the part of the survivors must not be misunderstood as *wilful* silence in the sense of lying (cf. Grünberg 1997, 2002). The fact that survivors did not speak of these things should even be regarded as a "mature achievement", brought about for instance to protect their own children. And who would be able to understand at all what Nazi victims really mean, if they do tell their story? Can what is unsayable be said? Can there be real understanding? Moreover, the children of the victims "know" what happened to their parents even *without* verbal communication. One can take it for granted that survivors *cannot* conceal their persecution at all. What is verbally communicated is distinctly overrated in this context. In addition to the verbal aspects, one ought, therefore, to investigate the atmosphere that prevails in the families of survivors, how communication takes place by mimic expression or by gestures, that is to say, by the wordless transmission of the trauma.

The following fact must, however, be noted: a large number of German sympathizers, observers or Nazi perpetrators kept silent about the relevant facts. In contrast to the descendants of survivors, the children of perpetrators or of Nazi sympathizers frequently do *not* know how their parents and grandparents acted under National Socialism; a majority of them do *not* know who their parents really are, who they really love as father, mother, grandparents, as uncle or aunt. By no means do we wish to be understood as saying that this not-knowing has no consequences – on the contrary; but if one bears in mind that the Germans collectively have a tendency to deny the Nazi past, then it becomes obvious that an inner-familial observance of silence about these things will not necessarily "cause a stir" in this country.

Therefore, the confusion which the daughters and sons in average German families experience mostly remains unconscious.

In an endeavour to bring more light into this confusion, Ralf Vogt (1995) refers to Georges Devereux, when he speaks of the "ethnical unconscious" and of "ethnical disturbance" (Vogt 1995, 321) in his *Psychoanalysis of the German Soul [...]* (title on the cover of the periodical *Psyche* 4/1995). Vogt takes the controversy about Rainer Werner Fassbinder's play *Der Müll, die Stadt und der Tod* (The Garbage, the City and Death) as an example showing "that the Germans are today still afflicted to a varying degree with an 'ethnical disturbance', above all as regards the warding off of unconscious guilt feelings and no doubt also of certain kinds of destructive feelings" (ibid., 322).

The Goldhagen Debate

This "ethnical disturbance" would also seem to be involved in a dispute which caused the feelings of many Germans to run high in April 1996 and the following months. "Somebody appears on the scene, puts forward a thesis and proclaims that he has established a new era of research about National Socialist crimes" (Arning and Paasch 1996). In this casual and sweeping manner two journalists introduced a text, in which they contemptuously attacked the research work conducted for years by the US American political scientist Daniel Jonah Goldhagen, when he converted his dissertation into a book bearing the title *Hitler's Willing Executioners*. Scarcely any anti-Semitic cliché is omitted by Matthias Arning and Rolf Paasch (1996) in an article published under the sensational title *The provocative theses of Mister Goldhagen* in the daily *Frankfurter Rundschau*, which is considered as a liberal left-wing newspaper; in this article, they do not examine his theses so much as indulge in a devastating criticism of Goldhagen himself. They speak of a "provocation cunningly designed to produce indignation" and of the accusation against Goldhagen that "with one stroke of the pen he *demolishes* the work carried out during the last five decades by a great many Holocaust researchers" (ibid.; italics from K.G.). A debate was being "staged". And whilst the "[call was being heard] by every publisher" (ibid.), the "publishing house A. Knopf" had secured the publishing rights and "cleverly attracted the public's notice" to Goldhagen's theses. Possibly some readers may have wondered whether the publisher A. Knopf is a rich Jew, for the origin of the protagonists seems to be of great importance in the authors' contribution, in particular since the sub-title refers to "German researchers", whereas only two of the total of nine persons named in the text are Germans at all – in addition to Walter Pehle, a publisher's editor, only the historian Johannes Heil. True, at least one of these "German research workers" is all the more vehemently of the opinion that Goldhagen's theses "are not worth being debated" (ibid.). But perhaps the Australian Konrad Kwiet and the US American Raul Hilberg – incidentally held by Rudolf Augstein (1996) to be an Israeli – were thus "repatriated back into the Reich". The gist of the position adopted by Arning and Paasch seems ultimately to be that US Americans do not apparently ask questions which are of overriding importance to "German researchers". In order to substantiate this insight, we find the following argument: "In this connection, what and how much is really new for historians has hitherto been rarely asked in the US debate, since there this discussion is mostly conducted by Jewish non-historians, that is to say, by journalists and columnists who engage in this discussion on their own" (ibid.; sic!). Once more the Americans are being branded as the spokesmen of Jews[24], and Jews again must be distinguished from the "real", namely the "German" academic authorities.

A great many other publications provided the finishing touches to the cliché of the rich, powerful, clever and vindictive Jew. Rudolf Augstein (1996) brings his article in the periodical *Der Spiegel* under the title *The Sociologist as Executioner*. The "non-historian Goldhagen [...] wants to condemn Holocaust Germans as a whole as the worst kind of anti-Semites there ever were" (ibid.). In the daily newspaper *Die Welt*, Jost Nolte (1996) speaks of a "wrath of Old Testamentary violence"; however, at the end of his article he honestly confesses what he feels to be such a strong threat: "More than half a century after Hitler's death and after the turning-point of 1989/90, which overthrew what had come about as a result of the Second World War, it at last looked as if the history of the Germans had been freed from Sisyphus's fate. Goldhagen has done his best to condemn it to damnation again" (ibid.).

This seems to complete the picture. One can only still ask why so many people are so incensed if Goldhagen's book did "not bring anything that is new", if it is "not worth a debate", if, as Augstein puts it, "the result [...] is a meager one, one might even say, it is practically nil" (Augstein 1996)?

In order to be in a position to answer this question, it is not even necessary to give a detailed review of Goldhagen's theses and critically evaluate them. Just a glance at the *reception* of Goldhagen's book suffices to show how strong are the fear and resistance to admit the supposition that *without* the Germans the Holocaust might possibly not have taken place and that, as Goldhagen (1996a) sets forth, between one hundred thousand and more than half a million Germans *willingly* became "Holocaust executioners". That Goldhagen then still argues that these executioners could not be dis-

24 | This phenomenon was noted repeatedly during the reporting about the second Gulf War.

missed as cruel Nazi monsters, as dreadful and sadistic brutes, who must be seen as forming special sections of society, but rather that they were recruited from the average German population, and that one was, therefore, dealing with "ordinary" Germans, means that he has definitely transgressed a taboo which "ordinary" Germans strive to uphold with all their strength more than 50 years after the end of National Socialism still (cf. in this connection also Arendt 1963, Browning 1992). Goldhagen touched a highly sensitive nerve of the Germans; possibly he struck the centre of the picture Federal Germany has of itself; he struck many Germans individually and also as a collective entity as far as their identity in Germany after the Shoah is concerned.

Collective Guilt

If many Germans were not first and foremost forced to persecute the Jews, but did what they *wanted* to do, – even if this took place only "on the deepest inner level" – then one cannot any more regard a few individual "Nazi brutes" or the leading clique around Adolf Hitler, as having behaved guiltily, but must put a highly disquieting question concerning collective mass guilt. For the survivors of the Shoah and their descendants the question concerning guilt is certainly not a new one. How preoccupation with this problem marked the everyday life of these families in a partly grotesque manner has been described above, for instance when victims of Nazi persecution suffered from a supposed "survivor's guilt" or when their daughters and sons felt "separation guilt" towards their parents. "In the nature of things", the mass guilt incurred by the *Germans* towards Jews is also an essential topic, however. On this point, Jean Améry (1977) makes very forceful remarks: "Collective guilt. This is of course arrant nonsense, inasmuch as it implies that the Germans communally had a joint will, a joint initiative to act and have thus laden themselves with guilt. It is, however, a serviceable hypothesis if one understands thereby nothing else than the objectively manifest *sum* of individual guilty behaviour. Then the guilt incurred in each case by individual Germans – guilt incurred by action, guilt by omission, guilt by speech, guilt by keeping silent – is transformed into the collective guilt of a people. The expression collective guilt must accordingly be demythologized and demystified before it can be used. It then loses its dark, fateful sound and becomes that for which it is alone of any use: a vague statistical statement" (ibid., 117; transl. by H.H.).

If, however, the Germans do not even take note of such a sober analysis of German collective guilt, if they keep silent about it or dismiss it, then the survivors and also their descendants finally find themselves feeling that they have once more been abandoned. And it is again this experience which causes an equally massive disquiet. Thus, a bitter and resigned Améry is obliged to note that once again it is not those who "overpowered" others, but the victims who had to "cope with" the problem; "'cope' in the sense of concentration camp slang; it essentially meant murdering him" (ibid., 129; transl. by H.H.). The victims, he continues, "must and will soon have been coped with. Until this happens, we ask those whose peace and quiet have been disturbed by such reproaches, to show patience" (ibid.). With Améry, such an insight leads to a certain extent to a "reversal" of the collective guilt of the Germans. He turns the guilt against *himself*, when he – logically – "concludes" as follows: "I say, *I* am burdened with the collective guilt: not they. The world, which forgives and forgets, has condemned me, not those others, who murdered or allowed the murdering to be done" (ibid., 120).

Withholding the Truth, Confusion

This "conclusion" to which Jean Améry comes, must also be understood as being a result of the fact that the truth in the Federal Republic of Germany has been withheld by keeping silent about the Nazi past; it is the "conclusion" of a *victim* of Nazi persecution, who himself survived National Socialism, and it is a comprehensible and tragic conclusion. The examples which have been given of the way the Shoah was denied and minimized can be understood as consequences of National Socialism for the non-Jewish German "side", namely as the result of a certain kind of "coping with" the past, as a return of what was collectively repressed. In that sense, the aforementioned equating of the Second Generation of Jewish survivors with the descendants of perpetrators or of Nazi sympathizers, as well as other "slips", would *themselves* be the result of a specific way of dealing with National Socialism; they would in fact be a consequence of the truth about the Shoah having been withheld and silence about it maintained on the part of a great many Germans, regardless of whether these were Nazi perpetrators or "only" Nazi sympathizers. The collective silence observed about these truths by Nazi perpetrators and sympathizers must necessarily leave their descendants in a state of collective confusion.

This confusion is compounded of feelings of *hate* – towards the parents who passed on such a terrible legacy of persecution, murder, deception and lying to their children; of feelings of *angst* - towards parents, whose desire to kill and exterminate was directed not only against the Jews, those who were "inferior" and "of a different kind", but also against their own, weak and naughty children; but presumably also of feelings of *admiration and fascination* – for parents who with respect to their fundamental beliefs would not be persuaded to drop their own convictions and ideas of greatness, who, in their anxious hopes for the "final victory", did not permit themselves to give up hate and destruction, and who even after they had been defeated were still able to lead the world to believe that long before the "end" they had longed for the Allies to come as liberators, who led the world to believe that they themselves had been victims of Nazi dictatorship, and who then after the War brought about the "economic miracle": "Today, Germany listens to us and tomorrow the entire world will do so."

This approach might make it possible to better understand not only the aforementioned examples of denying and minimizing the Shoah, but also e.g. the motives and acts of German terrorists in the Red Army group and the profound hate between the generations. For critical students, the shots that killed Benno Ohnesorg on June 2, 1967, were, in particular, fresh proof of the "older" generation's willingness to murder. The members of the RAF (= Rote Armee Fraktion or Red Army group) felt profound *hate* for their hypocritical Nazi parents and this hate was afterwards to unleash itself in the opposite direction, after they had overcome the *angst* caused by their mighty and dangerous parents. And at the same time they presumably also *admired* these parents. Surely only this *fascination* provides an explanation for the circumstance that these left-wing daughters and sons, who were otherwise so critical of the "old" generation, were able to identify with these very same parents when they proceeded to "select" Jewish passengers after they had hijacked an Air France plane to Entebbe in 1976 (cf. Broder 1986, Der Spiegel 1976).

"Good sons" on the other hand must neither kill their parents, nor must they prove their closeness to them by means of fresh "selections". "Good sons" demonstrate their identification with their parents by trying to take their place *beside* them at the right moment, even if only in an imaginary "dock". In the aforementioned affair about the way the members of the German Psychoanalytical Association dealt with the National Socialist past of their former chairman Gerhart Scheunert, Hans-Volker Werthmann (1997) remarks in the *FPI-Forum* "that the intention was to exclude and denounce Scheunert. If such a man is placed in the dock, then now as before I am of the opinion that he should not be left alone. Unfortunately, nobody is prepared to believe that I have not only put somebody else beside him, but was myself willing to sit there beside him" (ibid., 6).

The children of Nazi perpetrators and Nazi sympathizers, whether they identify with them or as it were counter-identify, remain in a state of partly rigid confusion when confronted with their parents' legacy, with persecution and with the subsequent observance of silence about the past. Only an honest description of the real motives, of the real deeds and of the real participation of the Germans in National Socialism and an honest debate about these questions can bring greater clarity and more awareness into this confusion. This could be a step in the direction of becoming aware of the existence of an "ethnic disturbance", and this might give one reason to see "the world" more optimistically.

3.2 Summary and the Formulation of Hypotheses Concerning the Second Generation's Mental Processing of the National Socialist Persecution of Jews

In the preceding sections we have described what the first generation of survivors from the National Socialist extermination of the Jews was confronted with when it had to "cope with" its experience of persecution; we have also described how, as from about the middle of the 1960s, psychiatrists and psychoanalysts began to face the problems of the Second Generation. We dealt with the "transmission" of the trauma to the next generation and with "aggression and guilt". The question was also raised whether a specific "syndrome" of the Second Generation exists. These questions led us to consider what influence the parents' experience of persecution exerts on the social and pair relationships of their children.

In the course of this stock-taking, phenomena on the various levels – political, cultural, institutional, personal, in the media, in the totality of society – of the world in which Jews live in Germany today were examined, phenomena which are paradigmatic for the occurrence of conflicts in German-Jewish relations in post-Nazi Germany during the last 30 years. The totality of these individual and social patterns of conflict is the background which alone makes it possible to understand the life of Jews in today's Germany and the love relationships of the Second Generation. An isolated study of single persons or families would otherwise inevitably be inadequate. Only if one is able to understand the significance, say, of the political commitment of a Jew in the Federal German left wing, the latter's simultaneous criticism of "community Jewry" and on the other hand the exploitation of the far distant Near East conflict to exonerate the guilt of the Germans, will it be possible to also understand the meaning of certain conflicts which arise between couples. Such conflicts can be caused by a great variety of circumstances: say, by the failure to understand why the Jewish partner in the relationship belongs to the Jewish Community in spite of his or her basically atheistic point of view or of his or her clearly critical attitude concerning the policy of the community; by a failure to understand why one should feel like an outsider in Germany after the "peace proclaimed in Bitburg" or by controversies about the freedom of art in connection with the fact that performances of the Fassbinder play in Frankfurt/Main were prevented. Only if one is able to understand what it means e.g. for a Jew to have an anti-Semitic experience precisely in *that* party which one has joined for general political reasons and convictions, only then can one recognize the impact of such experiences, attitudes or ways of behaviour on Jews in this country. There is a close link between experiences of social persecution or exclusion and social commitment and individual attitudes, the sense of belonging and personal conflicts. The preceding reflections were intended to make one aware of, and lead to a better understanding of this intertwining of social and individual experiences – including those occurring in intimate love relationships.

The question now arises how this approach to National Socialism with its consequences on the social and mental and political levels can be made the subject of empirical observation and critical examination in a "non-clinical" population. While two comprehensive single-case studies above all serve to demonstrate how the parents' persecution has been coped with individually in order to compare these with the different background experienced by the two subjects interviewed, a quantified evaluation of the phenomenon is being performed by contents-analysis and statistical analysis for one of the entire interview material and for the other of various standardized methods used in this study. The specific questions asked lead to the following hypotheses:

- Jews of the Second Generation who live in the Federal Republic of Germany have a particularly strong bond with their parents in the sense of being emotionally "entangled" with them. They feel that it is particularly difficult to distance or separate themselves from their survivor parents, in order to really live a life of their own.
- The Jewish children of survivors are confronted in a special way with their parents' real, essential experiences under National Socialism. They feel a clear awareness of what their parents' essential experiences under National Socialism were.
- Jews of the Second Generation feel exposed to special pressure from their parents to choose partners of the same origin. The parents exercise pressure on them to have Jewish partners and, in particular, they raise objections if they have German partners.
- The experiences which the survivors had under National Socialism specifically cause conflicts in the love relationships of their sons and daughters. We find that conflicts arise in which the different origins of both partners play an essential role.

4. Empirical Analyses

When this study uses the term *empiricism* it is neither implying a merely *quantifying* nor an exclusively *hermeneutic ("qualitative")* mode of procedure. The empirical approach of this study rather follows the trend towards a *multi-methodological procedure* which has been increasingly advocated in the discussion of the last 15 years concerning the methods of data-analysis to be used in the social sciences (cf. among many others, the descriptions in Esser 1987, Engler 1997, Fromm 1990, Früh 1992, Lamnek 1988, Saldern 1995).

The decision to make this choice was determined by the criterion which is mentioned by all authors, that the methods should be *appropriate* to the subjects investigated. On the one hand, it seemed difficult to imagine that one might represent and evaluate the experiences of Nazi persecution and traumatizations of the parents' generation and their possible effects upon the Second Generation in a meaningful empirical manner solely by using standardized techniques of data collection. The subject virtually *demanded* the use of person-centered unstandardized methods of data collection as well as data-analysis that allowed for reconstruction of meaning.

On the other hand, the theoretical discussion of the subject led to *a priori hypotheses* about how Jews who had grown up after the end of National Socialism in the Federal Republic of Germany were to be distinguished from non-Jewish Germans of the same generation regarding the way in which they experienced relations with their parents and partners. Under this perspective, the idiographic comprehension of texts and biographical reconstruction recedes into the background and the supra-individual, group-related comparative aspect comes to the fore. Generalizing statements of the population can be made by means of such quantifying methods that aim to discovering existing differences.

The wish of hypotheses-testing with quantifying methods would not on its own require the use of standardized methods (i.e. questionnaires, psychometric scales). This would also easily be possible by processing "qualitatively" acquired data (cf. in this connection the discussion below). The use of standardized questionnaires in this investigation serves primarily to increase the validity of hypotheses testing by demonstrating that the results are not confounded by the methodological approach.

The multi-methodological approach of the present investigation will be briefly described in the following sections. After describing the design of the study and the sample, the methods used for data collection are introduced. Semi-structured qualitative interviews, which have been supplemented by the use of standardized methods for data-collection (questionnaire scales) are of central importance. Data-analysis has been performed in three steps. To start with, two comprehensive single-case-studies were carried out. This was followed by a text-reducing content-analysis of all forty transcripts through external raters. The results of the external rating were then used in a statistically quantifying manner to examine the hypotheses that had been obtained theoretically and which were listed at the end of the preceding chapter. Finally, the questionnaire data were statistically analysed and correspondences between the two data-sets were demonstrated.

4.1 Method

Research Design and Sampling Frame

An important object of the empirical analyses is to examine the permanent influence of the persecution experience of the family of origin upon the lasting ties to the parents and upon the shaping of the love relationships of Second Generation Jews living in Germany.

In the *quantifying* part of the present study, the aim is to investigate these correlations in a manner as *internally valid* as possible (Cook and Campbell 1979) within the limits of a non- or quasi-experimental design.[1] Figure 1 is a diagrammatic representation of the research design. The parental experience of Nazi persecution is the independent variable which is considered as given in the group investigated – Second Generation Jews who have grown up in Germany – in accordance with the definition of the criteria of selection. Dependent variables are, one the one hand, those indica-

---

[1] An experimental procedure does not of course come into consideration, since in the present case one is not dealing with a "treatment" variable, but with a group variable that already existed before the investigation was made.

tors which refer to the kind of parental bond and knowledge about the essential parental experiences in National Socialism and, on the other hand, those variables which measure the parental influence on the love relationship and its quality among the participants questioned. The dependant variables are operationalized by means of categories of contents analysis and by questionnaire scales.

Figure 1: Diagrammatic representation of the investigation plan

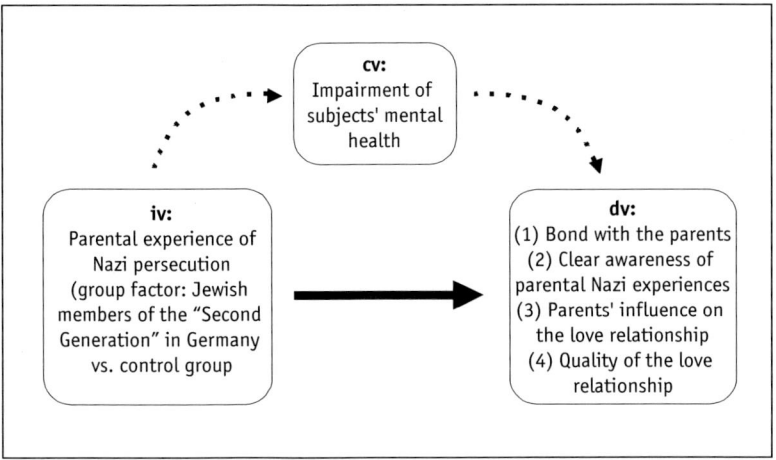

Note: iv = independent variable, dv = dependent variable, cv = control variable

In the chapter about previous research results it has been shown that parental experiences of Nazi persecution can lead to a manifold impairment of mental health in the following generation. Since it is an objective of this investigation to understand the influence of parental Nazi traumatization as a phenomenon that is also prevalent in *clinically inconspicuous* offspring of the Second Generation, it is necessary to control for variables of mental health. Only if one can assure that the two groups investigated do not significantly differ in this respect, – in other words – that the characteristics, "parental Nazi persecution" and "mental health" are not confounded, is it possible to carry through an internally valid examination of the connection between parental experience of persecution and the quality of the love relationship in which we are interested.

In this control group design, the next question which arises is *which* characteristics have to be present in an adequate control group.

The Problem of the "Adequate" Control Group

As far as this is at all possible, the control group should only differ in the respect of interest from the "experimental" or investigated group (cf. Lewin 1986, 53). In an investigation of the consequences of the National Socialist persecution of the Jews for the survivors' offspring in the Federal Republic of Germany, the control group would accordingly have to meet the following criteria: the subjects of the control group must also be Jews who grew up and live in the Federal Republic of Germany; however, their parents should *not* be victims of the National Socialist persecution of the Jews. With such investigation and control groups, one might "test" the "causal connection" between parental persecution and the outcomes for the Second Generation in an internally valid manner.

The problem with this approach is that such a group which differs from the investigated group solely with respect to the Nazi persecution of the parents does not exist in the Federal Republic of Germany. The parents of Jews who have grown up in the Federal Republic are all of them victims of persecution. If one is not dealing with concentration camp survivors or former prisoners in forced labor camps or ghettoes, then the parents concerned survived in an emigration that was forced upon them, that is to say, they were also victims of Nazi persecution. If the parents of the interviewed were Jews who came from countries which were not directly affected by the National Socialist extermination of the Jews, then group differences displayed in the investigation could be traced back to the national origin of these parents. This means that once again the desired connection could not be validly "established". That is to say, it is not possible in the present case to establish a single dichotomous characteristic of differentiation (parental persecution versus non-persecution) which is not also confounded with the influence of other characteristics (e.g. the country of origin).

This is also the case if one endeavours to "vary" not only the fact of persecution as such, but also the *extent* of the persecution. Thus, at the beginning of this investigation the possibility was considered of forming a control group of sons and daughters of emigrees who had returned to Germany. These parents had suffered *less* persecution than concentration camp survivors.

However, in that case, it would only be consistent to also classify the concentration camp survivors in different groups depending on the extent of persecution suffered. Was the survivor "only" imprisoned in a ghetto? Did he or she survive in a labor camp or in an extermination camp with gas chambers? How long was the person incarcerated? How old was that person at the time? How many and which relatives were murdered and in which manner was this done? Was the person subjected to torture or to medical experiments? And might it not be possible that for a certain person the experience of emigration was "worse" than that of being "in the underground" for another? Does it affect a person more or less deeply to have lived with a false identity for years in constant fear of being discovered or betrayed? How must one evaluate the fact that a marriage partner got a divorce in order not to be married to a Jew or Jewess any more? The list of such questions would be endless. The impossibility of a scientific "control" of such interrelated factors in persecution indeed soon becomes apparent. And it is not least of all an *ethical* question whether an investigator takes it upon himself to transform and evaluate in scales such experiences in comparable categories, in order to – seemingly – satisfy the demands for a "proper" empirical design of the investigation.

International comparisons would also be of little help in the present situation – as has already been implied above. True, in this manner one might – say in a comparison with Dutch Jews of the Second Generation – extract the specific German share in the problem; but one would not be able to make any statements about the causal connection between parental persecution and the findings for the Second Generation.

A pragmatic consequence from these considerations resulted ultimately in giving up the claim for this investigation to find causes in a narrow sense for a connection between parental persecution and the findings made for the Second Generation.

Since the fact that they grew up and lived in the Federal Republic of Germany is essentially of central importance for those interviewed, we finally selected a *German* sample, which does *not* exhibit parental persecution experiences. The intention was to a certain extent to deal with "ordinary" Germans, who might be neighbours, acquaintances or friends of the Jewish group investigated, so that one might pursue the question whether processing differences with respect to parental National Socialist experiences could be discovered. However, differences to be found in the study might be based both on parental persecution or the absence of persecution, as well as on the circumstance that one is dealing with Jews in the group investigated and with non-Jews in the comparison group. Both sets of influences are necessarily present in a *confounded* form in the present investigation.

The description of *"causal"* connections – for instance, those existing between the experiences of persecution in a concentration camp on the part of one parent and certain problems in the daughter's relationships – must accordingly finally remain on a level of hypothetical reflection if seen in the light of quantitative-methodological standards of validity. Nevertheless, these considerations – for instance in the studies of individual cases – can acquire a certain value as a plausible explanation for certain phenomena.

Access to the Sample and Matching Procedure

Friends, acquaintances, Jewish communities and institutions were asked to name Jewish interview partners. One requirement was that the interview partners must have been born in the Federal Republic of Germany after 1945 and that at least one parent should be a concentration camp survivor. The mediators were asked to inform the subjects concerned only that this was a psychological investigation in the faculty of psychology of the University of Marburg centering on the problem of the family of origin and their love relationships. In this connection, the experiences of the parents would be significant.[2]

In order to increase the internal validity of the quasi-experimental design, the sample was put together by matching pairs regarding gender, age and professional group, i.e. after a Jewish interview partner was recruited for the investigation, efforts were made to find a non-Jewish German matching person of the same sex, similar age and profession.[3] The characteristics of gender, age and professional group do not stand here "for themselves" (i.e. as indicators of biological or specific professional influences), but must rather be regarded as *carrier variables* for complex gender, cohort and class specific processes of socialization. The objective of the matching is for different experiences of socialization regarding parental experience of persecution and the actual shaping of love relationships, them being the center of interest.

The study group of Jewish offspring of survivors of the National Socialist persecution of the Jews will below be briefly designated as the "Jewish group", and the non-Jewish participants in the investigation usually as the "control group".

To sum up, the design of the study can be characterized as a quasi-experimental matched control group design based on a comparative sample. The circumstance that the Jewish group investigated is not based on a ran-

2 | Seven of a total of 27 interviews made with Jewish subjects could not be included in the analysis because they did not meet the requirements. One person was of non-Jewish origin and in six cases both parents had emigrated from Germany during the National Socialist era. This only became apparent during the interview, however.

3 | Bortz and Döring (1984) speak of "Matching" to describe this procedure of using pairs of persons. By parallelization they describe a weaker kind of control, in which only approximately equal means and variances of the control variables can be established in both samples (ibid., 491). The advantage of matching can be discerned in the fact that not only can the influence of each characteristic be controlled individually, but one can also control possible interaction effects of the matching variables.

dom selection ("representative sample") of all adult Jews of the Second Generation in the Federal Republic of Germany has consequences with respect to generalizations, i.e. the *external validity* of the results and the applicability of procedures that test hypotheses statistically. In the following section they will be briefly discussed methodologically.

The Problem of the Representativeness of the Sample

The concept of "representativity" (of a sample) is not a technical statistical term (cf. Kruskal and Mosteller 1979). Colloquially, it usually refers to the desired feature that the composition of a sample should be such that all significant features of this sample resemble those of the population being investigated, so that the conditions empirically found in the sample – that is to say, e.g. group differences between the Jewish and the non-Jewish participants – can be generalized to the population in question. The term "external validity" is also used synonymously with "generalizability" (Cook and Campbell 1979).

Figure 2: Hierachy of populations and the processes of statistical conclusion and of generalization

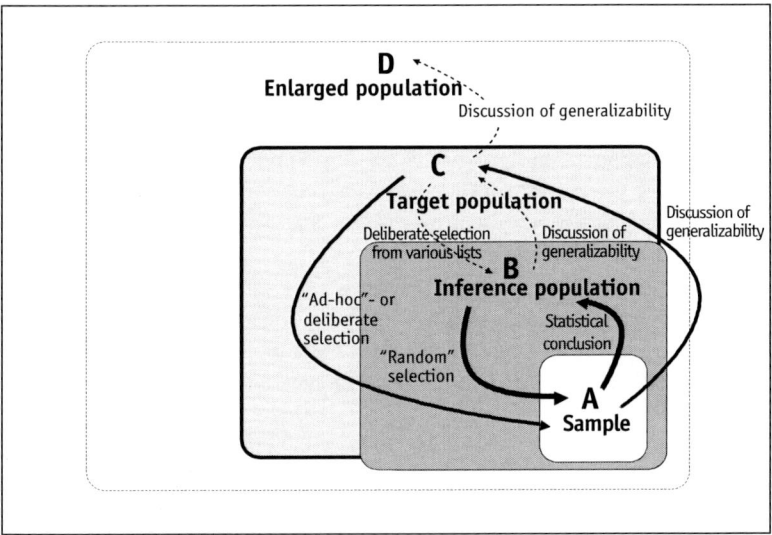

In accordance with Pant 1998.

The process of (justified) *generalization* is often confused with that of *statistical inference-making*, i.e. of the numerical extrapolation of a sample result to the whole population, in our case e.g.: all Second Generation adult Jews in the Federal Republic of Germany (cf. the diagrammatic representation of both processes in fig. 2). The results of statistical inferences are usually reported as significance testings of null hypothesis or the calculation of confidence intervals.

It is an indispensable condition of this extrapolating (statistical inference) that the members of the sample should be selected *at random* from a list of all members of the population (Bortz 1977, Oakes 1986, Schnell, Hill and Esser 1995). In the case of the present study, such a list of all Second Generation (adult) Jews in the Federal Republic is – fortunately, one is tempted to add – not accessible because of the law on the protection of personal data and for other reasons also.[4] This means that a random selection from our population is not de facto possible. Statistical inferences (e.g. significance testing or computation of confidence intervals) cannot, therefore, be unambiguously interpreted, since one does not know with respect to which population one actually makes a statistical inference with these data. In other words: in the present study – as in practically all psychological studies – the use of inferential statistics remains an act of convention, which is not backed up by sampling theory.

Not affected by this is the problem of generalizability respectively of similarity between sample and target population which must also be discussed when one is dealing with a non-random selection. Restrictions in generalizability, result above all in such cases, where certain sections of the target population are systematically not represented in the sample. This is, as a result of the lack of comparative data, only scrutinizable for some few characteristics of the Jews who were born and grew up in Germany after 1945 and will be discussed in the following section which deals with the characteristics of the sample.

Statistically significant results mentioned in this survey can, therefore, merely be regarded as a reference with respect to the form in which results are conventionally reported in the psychological literature. For this reason they should only be regarded as a *heuristic device of discovering* essential interrelations or alternatively as a way of making *tentative hypothesis tests*. An

---

4 | The Central Council of Jews in Germany does have lists of the members of the Jewish communities in Germany. However, these are not available for a probability selection, because of the law on the protection of personal data, since they would involve giving addresses. Moreover, not every Jew is a member of a Jewish community.

alternative form of representing the results via *effect sizes* will be discussed in detail below.

Characteristics of the Sample

This section follows several objectives. Besides the purely *descriptive objective* to characterize the sample, one must, above all, examine whether the paired matching procedure of age, gender and profession has resulted in comparative groups with respect to various other socio-demographic characteristics. All significant group differences (e.g. with respect to the educational status) would have to be regarded as jeopardizing the internal validity of hypothesis-testing at a later point of time. In both cases, i.e. rejection or affirmation of the null-hypotheis, one would have to argue theoretically whether these group differences are responsible for apparent bonds to the parents or for the quality of the love relationship or whether this is due to the independent variable of the parental experience of persecution. Admittedly, however, a statistical *ex post* control of confounding variables identified in this manner does not appear very promising in the light of the small size of the sample.

Special attention will in this connection also be paid to information about the family of origin (e.g. the parents' level of education, the religious education in the family) as well as to the features characterizing the partner situation of those questioned. Finally, this chapter also has the function of showing the sparse sources of *external data* on the target population which can be meaningfully compared with the composition of the Jewish study group.

The sample comprises ten female and ten male Jews, who were born or grew up in Germany after 1945 now living in the Federal Republic of Germany. The mediators in the finding of interview partners were asked to only name persons at least one of whose parents was a concentration camp survivor. Since it proved impossible to always adhere to this criterion of the surviving of a concentration camp, the interview partners should be refered to as children of survivors of the National Socialist persecution of Jews in Germany or in the territories occupied by the Germans. The control group consists in accordance with the remarks set forth above of 20 matched non-Jewish Germans.

As can be seen in figure 3, the two samples are perfectly matched with respect to gender; there are also no significant pair differences regarding the two other control variables (age and profession). The maximum age difference between the pairs is four years and lies in the average of $\bar{x}_{|diff|} = 1.5$ years (SD = 1.1). Thus, there is no significant age-difference between the groups (Jewish group: $\bar{x} = 32.35$ years; SD = 6.4 years; control group: $\bar{x} = 32.25$ years; SD = 7.0 years). As far as profession is concerned, it is striking that lower income groups are under-represented and that there are no unemployed at all, whereas as a result of their greater accessibility students ($n = 12$) and psychologists ($n = 3$) were noticeably overrepresented among those questioned.

Figure 3: Result of the matching procedure for gender, age, and profession

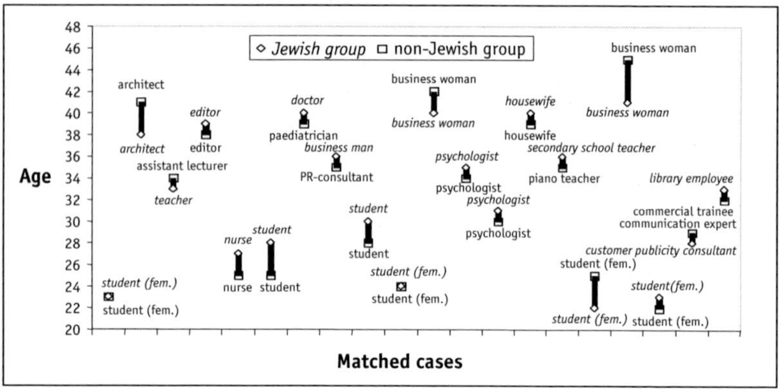

```
                    ◊ Jewish group   □ non-Jewish group
```

Age axis (20–48) with data points:
- architect, editor, architect, assistant lecturer, teacher (Jewish group)
- doctor, paediatrician, business man, PR-consultant, student, nurse, student, student (fem.), nurse student, student, student (fem.), student (fem.)
- business woman, business woman, housewife, housewife, psychologist, psychologist, psychologist, piano teacher, secondary school teacher
- business woman, business woman, library employee, commercial trainee, communication expert, customer publicity consultant, student (fem.), student (fem.), student (fem.), student (fem.)

Matched cases

Religious Membership

Half the members of the control group belong to the Protestant church; about a third are non-denominational and the rest are Catholics (cf. fig. 4). A glance at the religious affiliations in the parents' generation (cf. fig. 5) shows that with the exception of one mother, all the parents in the Jewish group also adhered to the Jewish faith or had at least – as was the case with two mothers – converted to it. From the point of view of achieving as great a homogeneity in both groups as possible, it is above all significant that both the parents of the control group and those of the Jewish group belonged predominantly (16 of 20 pairs of parents) to the same denomination (coefficient of contingency $C = .66$; $p < .01$). In the control group, the denominational ties of those participating are predominantly the same as those of their mothers. In 16 of 20 who were questioned, they tally with respect to the generations ($C = .72$; $p < .001$). Only four subjects left the church in which their mothers were and do not today belong to any denomination (cf. fig. 4 and fig. 5 in chap. 6).

The Jewish participants showed a tendency to answer the question regarding a religious upbringing in the family more frequently in the affirmative ($n = 15/20$) than those of the control group ($n = 10/20$), although it is not possible to speak of a substantial difference when one compares them in pairs (p<.56). The same applies to the question regarding religious education outside the family (cf. fig. 6 and fig. 7).

Altogether the group that was investigated and the control group do not differ significantly with respect to the formal characteristics of religious ties and religious tradition – apart from the adherence to different religions.

Nationality

Whereas all those questioned in the control group were German nationals, we find two subjects among the Jewish participants with double nationality (German-Israeli), as well as an US national and a stateless subject (cf. fig. 8). The proportion of non-German fathers and mothers among the parents' generation of the Jewish group was less than a fifth, whereas the parents of the members of the control group were all Germans (cf. fig. 9).

Educational Status

Thanks to the pairwise matching for professional affiliation, hardly any difference can be found between the two groups even on the highest educational levels. In each case, three quarters of the subjects interviewed had passed the "Abitur" (school-leaving examinations entitling one to study at a university) and they thus characterize the sample as clearly weighted towards the academic (cf. fig. 10). This does not apply to the parents' generation in similar fashion. The majority of the fathers of the Jewish subjects questioned, in particular, had not completed their school or university education, or they had had an education that had ended before the "Mittlere Reife" (conclusion of intermediate secondary school education) (cf. fig. 11) and on the average their status was, therefore, much below the educational status of the fathers of the control group.

Moreover, a glance at the parents' education shows that the "education capital" in the Jewish group clearly lay on the mothers' side. In eight families they had a higher education than their husbands; the opposite applied to only four cases. In contrast to this, in the non-Jewish parents' generation we find that a majority of the fathers had "a better education" (10 as against 2) than their wives (cf. fig. 12).

Slight group differences were also found with respect to the *inter-generational educational mobility*. If one compares the education of male participants with that of their fathers and that of the women questioned with that of their mothers, one finds that no-one "underachieved" in the Jewish group, while there are three "underachievers" in the control group (cf. fig. 13).

Regarding the internal validity of the study, the "educational dominance" of the mothers and subjects who "underachieved" are, consequently, characteristics which distinguish the Jewish group from the control group. Theoretically, one will, therefore, have to consider the factor of the parents' ambitions for the education of their children as one that ought to be added to the experience of persecution when one considers the quality of the parental bonds. In addition, the question whether both results are of significance in the light of generalizability (external validity) must remain unanswered; this question asks whether the superior education of mothers in comparison to that of the fathers and whether a strong educational advancement motive can be considered as "representative" for all the Second Generation Jews in Germany.

Age of the Parents when the Children Were Born and the Parents' Death

The age of the parents at the time when those questioned were born has been considered a factor that had a possible influence on the parental bonds (cf. fig. 14). In the group means neither the fathers nor the mothers differ essentially. The range varied in the case of the fathers of the Jewish group from 26 to 52 years ($\bar{x} = 36.6$; $SD = 7.4$), whereas it varied between 18 and 53 years ($\bar{x} = 34.3$; $SD = 9.6$) for the fathers of the members of the control group. When the participants were born, the mothers' age ranged from 23 to 45 years (Jewish group $\bar{x} = 30.4$; $SD = 5.1$) and from 19 to 43 years (control group $\bar{x} = 30.5$; $SD = 7.3$).

As a further potential confounder it was examined whether the death of fathers or mothers occurred with the same frequency and at which point of time this happened in the life of the subject interviewed. In both groups, 10 fathers and two mothers were dead when the interviews were conducted. Whilst those interviewed were on average 21 years old ($SD = 9.9$ years) when their fathers died, this loss happened in general somewhat earlier in the control group, i.e. at the age of $17^1/_2$ years ($SD = 10.0$ years). However, the point of time in both groups was spread over a considerable range, i.e. in one case, the father died when the person interviewed was one year old, in the other case this only happened when the person was 36 years old. As far as the causes of death are concerned, there were no significant differences between the groups (cf. fig. 15). In both cases, cardiovascular diseases dominated, followed by cancer.

From the perspective of internal validity, it is again essential that these familial characteristics are very similarly distributed in both groups and cannot, therefore, exert any influence on the links which interest us here between parental experience of persecution on the one hand and specific bonds to the parents and the quality of the love relationship on the other.

Size of the Household of the Families of Origin

The size of the family of origin of the subjects interviewed can be regarded as a further potential confounder. The closeness of the parental bonds of those questioned might perhaps be affected by the number of siblings or of other persons living in the household. Therefore, it would be desirable that similar conditions should also prevail in both groups. With respect to the number of siblings, the conditions are practically identical (cf. fig. 16). No significant differences can be discerned, either, as far as the presence of further persons in the household is concerned. Whereas the nucleus family of the Jewish subjects interviewed was enlarged in four cases by relatives and others living in their home, additional others – usually a grandmother – also lived in the parents' household of seven non-Jewish participants.

Current Love Relationship

The majority of those questioned was unmarried in both groups (cf. fig. 17). Nevertheless, 15 of 20 Jewish participants and 18 of 20 non-Jewish interviewees stated that they were living in a permanent intimate partnership. A discernible difference between the groups can be seen when asked whether participants were living in a joint household with the steady partner. Only 8 of the 15 Jewish couples lived together, whereas as many as 13 of 17 couples of the control group did so (cf. fig. 18).

In this connection, reference to another characteristic that is confounded with respect to both groups may on the one hand prove helpful: the size of the city of residence. Whereas the Jewish partners of those interviewed nearly all came from large cities (16 from 20), in which single households constitute the majority, the control group participants were mostly recruited in small and medium-sized towns (cf. fig. 19).

On the other hand, the small number of Jews sharing an apartment with their partners might also be seen as a factor of their own origin, here expressed in greater distance towards the non-Jewish partners, to whom one is not "allowed" to come too close or does not wish to do so. This interpretation is supported by the fact that only three of the ten Jews who had a non-Jewish partner lived with them in one household, whereas *all* five Jews who had Jewish partners shared a household with them.

Regarding the internal validity of the group comparison, one must note that Jewish and non-Jewish participants lived in different city milieus. This apparently had no effect upon the fulfilment of the wish to have children, since a similar number of children was born in both groups. In both cases, however, the participants who had no children made up the majority of both groups at the time of investigation (cf. fig. 20). A detailed analysis is of interest here. Whereas only three of ten Jews with non-Jewish partners had children, four of five Jews with Jewish partners did so.

Considering the nationality and religion of the partners of the interviewees, one is, moreover, struck by the following. Whereas the non-Jewish subjects had without a single exception also a relationship with non-Jewish Germans, a clearly different situation can be seen in the Jewish group (cf. fig. 21). Here, only 8 of the 15 partners were non-Jewish and German. With respect to the hypotheses formulated it seems necessary to pay attention to the fact that not only the group factor, i.e. the parental experience of persecution, but also the cultural-religious concordance in present love relationships may vary systematically, thus possibly influencing the bonds and quality of the partnership. On the other hand, one might adopt another perspective to the effect that one is confronted here with a dependent variable namely "choice of partner". If one adopts this outlook, Second Generation Jews sought Jewish or at least non-German partners in order to avoid a confrontation with the German perpetrator problem in their own love relationships.

Comparison of the Jewish Group with External Data Sources

Jews born in Germany after 1945, who grew up here and whose parents were survivors of National Socialist persecution were defined as the target population for which we have endeavoured to make generalizations in this study. If one consults the *Statistical Yearbook of the Federal Statistical Office* (1991) as well as statistics from the Central Welfare Organization of Jews in Germany as external sources of data in order to describe this population, the possibilities of making comparisons remain slim. With the help of these data sources, one can merely approximately examine whether gender, age group and denomination of the (marriage) partners clearly deviate from the parameters statistically available.

In accordance with the information of the census of 1987 (Federal Statistical Office 1991), the proportion of gender in "members of the Jewish denomination" is slanted slightly in favour of men (53%) and thus scarcely deviates from the sample value of 50 per cent ($p<.49$).[5] The same applies to the two age groups in question (22-30 years old and 31-40 years old), for whom reference data for the year 1989 are available from the statistics of members of the Jewish communities (Central Welfare Organization of Jews in Germany 1998). As in the Jewish sample (60%), 61.7% belong, accord-

---

5 | As a statistical test an exact binomial test with a one-sided formulation of the significance level has been carried out.

ing to the statistics of the Jewish communities to the category of those over 30 years old ($p < .53$).

From the Statistical Yearbook (1991) we can see that of the Jews who got married in Germany in 1989 ($N = 253$) a quarter married a man or woman who was also Jewish. The proportion of subjects questioned in the sample of those who had a steady Jewish partner amounted to a third and is thus not significantly above these population data ($p<.32$).

In conclusion, it can be noted that the sample data of the 20 Jewish subjects questioned scarcely deviate with respect to the corresponding population parameters. It has already been mentioned that there is a high probability that this does not apply to the characteristic of educational level. On the whole, this comparison of data with population figures certainly does not claim to "prove" the generalizability of the results described below. All that could be determined is that the comparison of a few, basic socio-demographic characteristics does not already speak *against* such a generalizability.

Conclusion of the Description of the Sample

On the whole, the detailed comparison of the Jewish and non-Jewish groups that were interviewed shows that the method of pairwise matching has resulted in very homogeneous comparison groups with respect to many more characteristics than the mere matching variables of age, gender and profession. This is essential for a quasi-experimental study with a small sample size, because it strengthens confidence in the *internal validity* with respect to the correlations. Exceptions only had to be registered regarding the following characteristics:

- In contrast to the control group, there are no cases in the study group showing an educational decline compared to their parents; this is partly due to the fact that the level of education of the Jewish fathers was lower in comparison with that of the other group.
- In the parents' generation of the Jewish participants, the mothers had a clearly better education than their husbands, whereas the opposite is the case as far as the non-Jewish parents are concerned.
- For this study Jewish subjects were recruited more frequently in larger cities and they lived more seldomly with their partners in a common household than the participants of the control group.
- It is necessary to take all three differences into consideration as alternative or additional explanatory factors when the interpretation of the results is reviewed.
- Indications for the external validity, i.e. being able to generalize the sample results as valid for the population of the Second Generation in

Germany remained fragmentary. Although this does not in itself restrict a generalizability of the quantitative statements of this investigation, it does at all events give them a more speculative character.

Investigation Methods

Semi-structured Qualitative Interviews

Semi-structured qualitative interviews constitute a central component of the investigation. "The main task of the qualitative interviews lies in the representation of the individual case in the light of the problem to be investigated; at the same time, comparable material is to be gathered from the multiplicity of subjects interviewed" (König 1952, 143). To distinguish them from pre-structured questionnaires, König (ibid., 145) describes such interviews as "qualitative", "intensive" and "detailed". The terms "depth interview" or "intensive interview" are frequently used synonymously (Friedrichs 1973, 224).

The use of an interview guideline made it possible on the one hand to adopt comparable interview behaviour, whilst on the other hand this could also be flexibilized. Each individual interview could allow supplementary questions and questions designed to probe the problem (cf. König 1952, 143).

The interview method has been strongly influenced by the "narrative interview" evolved by Fritz Schütze (Schütze 1977), even though my own interviews have been conducted much more on the basis of a dialogue than as actual narrative interviews. What has been attempted, however, is to let the interviewees tell their stories from time to time in their own way. The narrative interview is suitable if one is to achieve "the reconstruction of cognitively complex and/or potentially revealing circumstances which might be risky for the informer if they become known" (ibid., 143). Over long stretches of the narrative interview the researcher holds back, thus giving the interviewee the opportunity to speak in accordance with his or her own assessments of what is relevant and enabling him or her to shape the topic as he or she thinks fit. In doing so, one can assume that the person gets really "involved" in the stories he or she is telling. He or she will, therefore, frequently express himself or herself in a highly detailed and exact manner which he or she had by no means originally intended. "The pattern of presenting circumstances causes the informer to feel compelled to supply details and give his or her tale a definite form" (ibid., 52) as well as to condense it.

The questions or remarks made by the interviewer are intended to induce the interviewee to communicate important and difficult circumstan-

4. Empirical Analyses | 107

ces, including very personal and intimate experiences. In order to create a good atmosphere for the conversations, use was consequently made of relevant parameters of humanistic psychology, in particular those of Rogers' approach to client-centered conversational psychotherapy. The idea is to create an atmosphere of acceptance and encouragement. Pavel (1975, 26 et seqq.) refers to a style of communication on the part of conversation psychotherapists intended to allow the client "to reflect about his person and engage in deep self-exploration and reflection about his behaviour and about how he experiences things". Tausch and Tausch (1960, 31 et seqq.) talk of a sympathetic non-evaluating understanding as an encouraging attitude and activity on the part of helpers. The idea is to get close to the "reference background" of the interviewee; it is an attempt to get nearer to the "client's inner terms of reference" (Rogers 1951, 44 et seqq.; transl. by H.H.).

The conduct of the interview was, moreover, guided by psychodynamic insights. The interviewer's questions or remarks were intended to bring about free associations on the part of the interviewee. This also applies to additions to statements inserted at the end of the interview. These additions may be understood as a projective technique.

The remarks made by Mitscherlich and Rosenkötter (1975), when they emphasize the "instrument of empathetic understanding" (ibid., 1161) of psychoanalysis were also relevant in ascertaining data. Beier et al. (1980, 81) refer to the "receptive understanding attitude" of the interviewer who "largely follows the associative flow of description of the subject with inquiries and interventions" (ibid.). According to Mitscherlich and Rosenkötter (1975, 1151) understanding is based on "sensing the similarity in other people of processes one has already experienced oneself". In this connection, the circumstance that both the interviewer and those interviewed in the study group are Jews is important. The similarity of origin certainly also helped to establish a contact with those interviewed (cf. König 1952, 146 et seqq.). To a certain extent this also applied to the control group, if, say, one lived in the same place or if e.g. both had had a university education. Here one must keep in mind that the subjects of the control group did not necessarily see the interviewer as a Jew, but rather as a German graduate student and qualified psychologist, who wanted to conduct an interview with them because of a scientific research project. One can, therefore, assume that the Jewish origin of the interviewer did not have a negative influence on the non-Jewish interview partners' willingness to tell their story.

In drawing up the guiding principles of the interview as such certain questions were taken over from Robert Prince's thesis (1975, 320 et seqq.) and from the author's own diploma thesis (Grünberg 1983). Before the questions were put, brief explanations concerning the investigation and a review of the course the interview would take were given.

Part A of the interview deals with the family of origin and the parents' experiences during the thirties and forties; part B concerns the love relationships of the subjects interviewed.

In Part A of the interview the following topics are dealt with:

- the parents and one's relationship with them;
- childhood and youth in the parents' home;
- changes in comparison with the past;
- parental experiences during the thirties and forties which had the most permanent influence on them;
- the effects of these experiences.

The contents of part B of the interview are:

- a description of the relationship with the first boy-/girlfriend (the partner, the relationship, the partner's family, one's own family, separation);
- a description of subsequent relationships (see above);
- persons who are at present important for the partner of the interviewee;
- the most important love relationship (the partner, the relationship, children, parents, the partner's parents, relations, sexuality);
- supplementary information (problems, wishes);
- fears and hopes for the future;
- influence of the parents' experiences during the thirties and forties upon the love relationships;
- how one feels at the end of the interview.

On the whole, the attempt was made to avoid questions which can be answered only with "yes" or "no". Thus, the question was not put: "Were there typical problems between your parents and yourself?", but: "which typical problems were there between your parents and yourself?".

Questions concerning the complex of problems dealing with sexuality were put at the end of the interview on purpose, since an atmosphere of confidence must prevail when one discusses intimate questions and this atmosphere does not exist from the beginning. Before entering this field, it was explicitly stated that the interviewee did not *have to* answer these questions.

At the end of some interview units time was allowed for giving supplementary details concerning the subject dealt with in that unit. At the end of part A, direct questions were put concerning the influence of the parental experiences during the thirties and forties upon the family and one's own life. At the end of part B, a direct inquiry was made whether the interviewee could discern any consequences the parental experiences during the thirties and forties had had on his or her love relationships, and if so of what nature these consequences were. At this stage, the point at issue was to a certain extent to directly test the basic hypotheses of the investigation.

At each stage of the interview, there was an opportunity to offer comments, express ideas or feelings. At the end of the interview, the interviewer inquired how the interviewee felt at that moment and what the interview had been like for him or her.

For the concept of the investigation, it is of central importance that no one in the two groups should be brought into a defensive position already as a result of using certain terms (e.g. Nazi persecution, collaborator, annihilation of the Jews etc.). Thus, when the questions about the parents' National Socialist experiences were put, the interviewer was careful never to use the term "National Socialism" or, say, "persecution of the Jews", *of his own accord*. Instead, he inquired about the important experiences of the parents "during the thirties and forties". After that, those subjects were always dealt with which had before been indicated by the interviewees as being important. The structure of this complex of questions is identical in all interviews; the contents vary in each case.

Preparing the Interviews

The investigator called the potential interviewees up. He communicated the above remarks about the investigation to them. It was pointed out that for methodological reasons no information about hypotheses or about the background of the thesis project could be made before the investigation had been carried out. After the interview, there would be an opportunity for a detailed discussion. The interviews would be recorded on tape. The promise was given to the interview partners that one would endeavour to secure their anonymity.

After they had promised to take part in the investigation, three questionnaires were sent to the interview partners before the date fixed for the interview (data about their own person and family, FPI-R and PFB, which are described in detail below). These were to be filled out before the interviews took place. Six subjects did not fill out the PFB questionnaire, because they did not have a partner relationship at the time; one woman applied the PFB items to a relationship that had recently come to an end.

Conducting the Interviews

The interviews were usually conducted in the interviewee's apartment or at least in their city of residence. As a rule the talks lasted for about 5 hours

($3^1/_2$ to 9 hours). Some of the interviews were also carried out on two consecutive days.

At the end of Part A and Part B of the interview, a further, self-constructed questionnaire was in each case submitted (scale of bonds with the parents and scale of couple autonomy).

Questionnaire Investigation

The use of standardized methods of investigation should fulfil three functions within the framework of this study. First, data concerning the subject and family of origin were collected in an economical manner, thus relieving the interview of the need to ascertain them. The evaluation of these data has already been described in the section about the characteristics of the sample.

Secondly, it was necessary to psycho-diagnostically guarantee that the claim to make statements for *non-clinical* populations was met. Therefore, the factor "mental health" which was seen as a control variable in the design was operationalized by means of the Freiburg Personality Inventory (FPI) in its revised version (FPI-R) (Fahrenberg, Hampel and Selg 1970a, 1970b).

Thirdly, the use of questionnaires to be filled out by the interviewees themselves made it possible to attain independence from any expectations harboured by the interviewer or by the rater of the interview, an independence which should at least not reduce one's confidence in the objectivity of the testing of the hypotheses. (All objections which have been adduced against overly interpreting the procedure of hypothesis testing remain unaffected by this argument). In order to operationalize the dependent variable complex, Hahlweg's (1979, 1996) Partnership Questionnaire (PFB) was used; the self-constructed rating scales "scale of *bonds to parents*" (R I) and the "scale of *couple autonomy*" (R II) were used to determine bonds to the family of origin and the influence it exerted.

On the whole the complementary use of qualitative and quantitative strategies for determining facts was to contribute to the *reciprocal validation* (triangulation of methods) of results obtained by standardized and non-standardized methods (for a discussion of triangulation concepts, cf. Denzin 1970, Flick 1991, Lamnek 1988, Schründer-Lenzen 1997).

The scales FPI-R, PFB, Scale of Parental Bond (R I) and Scale of Couple Autonomy (R II) will be briefly characterized below and an account given of the *internal consistencies* (reliabilities) of the scales used in the sample involved.

4. EMPIRICAL ANALYSES | 111

The Freiburg Personality Inventory (FPI-R)

Westhoff (1993) describes the Freiburg Personality Inventory as "the most popular personality inventory in Germany" (ibid. 314) and speaks of its "good qualities as a descriptive inventory in clinical practice and research" (ibid. 315). The FPI is a method based on an analysis of factors and items which is designed to determine multi-dimensional personality structures, which has been standardized with a representative population sample of $N = 2035$ subjects (Fahrenberg, Hampel and Selg 1985). Its usefulness above all in non-clinical samples has been proven in several hundred individual studies (for an overall view cf. Fahrenberg et al.'s manual of 1970b, as well as Schmidt and König 1986), and it is, therefore, not necessary to give a detailed report here.

The FPI-R is a fully standardized method with a total of 138 items, in which a person provides a self-assessment. The subjects are asked to answer statements about certain patterns of behaviour, attitudes and habits with "applicable" or "not applicable". Twelve items are in each case classified in 10 standard scales which bear the designations *satisfaction with life, social orientation, efficiency orientation, inhibitions, excitability, aggressiveness, behaviour under stress, physical complaints, health worries* and *openness*. In addition, there are two secondary scales (*extroversion* and *emotional responses*), for which 14 items are in each case provided.

Internal consistencies of the FPI-R sub-scales in the sample

The internal consistency (Cronbach's α) varies not inconsiderably from sub-scale to sub-scale ($a_{max} = .80$, $a_{min} = .52$) (cf. table 1 in chap. 7). In view of the smallness of the sample, however, only the values for the sub-scales *inhibitions, aggressiveness* and *openness* ($\alpha < .60$) must be regarded as not very satisfactory, in particular since the reliability values indicated by the test authors can on the whole only be regarded as fairly satisfactory (cf. also table 1). If only on account of the relatively low reliabilities and the high proportion of measurement errors connected therewith, scarcely any significant differences can, therefore, be expected to exist between the Jewish group and the control group for the three scales mentioned. Both, indeed, also exhibit partly clearly different consistency values for each sub-scale. What especially strikes one is that the scale for inhibitions did not "function" at all in the control group as intended by the test authors ($\alpha < .19$)[6] and it is, therefore, not possible to interpret group comparisons as regards this characteristic.

---

6 | After a thorough examination, it was possible to exclude the possibility of errors in the encoding of variables.

On the whole, however, the FPI-R has been shown to be a satisfactorily reliable instrument in the present sample as regards the investigation of possible group differences in the control variable "mental health".

Partnership Questionnaires (PFB)

The partnership questionnaire (PFB) (Hahlweg 1979, 1996) is an instrument for the analysis of partner behaviour in love relationships existing at the time which was evolved within the framework of behaviour therapies for married couples. It records the quality of the partnership and the degree of satisfaction with it. The PFB consists of 30 items[7], which are classified under the three sub-scales *quarrel behaviour* (example item: "He/she is sarcastic when he/she criticises me"), *tenderness* (example item: "Before we fall asleep we snuggle together in bed") and *shared experience/communication* (example item: "He/she asks me in the evening how I have spent the day"). All questions must be answered on the four-point Likert scales (never/very seldom – seldom – often – very often) and refer to a "recent period of time". In addition to the sub-scale values, one can also form a total score in accordance with the formula (*30-quarrel*) + *tenderness* + *shared experience/ communication* which covers the range of values of 0 to 90 points.

A high value on the scale *quarrel behaviour* indicates that during a conflict the partner shows ways of behaviour with which a successful solution of the problem cannot be achieved. In the *tenderness* scale, a high value means that the partner seeks direct bodily contact and also expresses positive feelings verbally. In the scale *shared experience/communication*, a high value indicates that many activities are pursued and discussed jointly; there is a strong attachment (Hahlweg 1996). The PFB includes as its 31st item the so-called *Terman assessment of happiness* (Terman 1938) which makes it possible to assess the actual state of the partnership on a six-point Likert scale ranging from "very happy" to "very unhappy".

As a standard sample, the author indicates $N = 534$ subjects with an existing intimate love relationship; a little more than half were subjects in Catholic marriage counselling centres ($N = 299$); the rest consisted of subjects who had no partnership problems ($N = 235$), and were found over contact networks (Hahlweg 1996). According to the author, the PFB can be regarded as having construct validity; in addition, it exhibits successful external validations in the light of observed behaviour.

---

7 | An earlier form evolved for the PFB (Hahlweg 1979) had 45 items, of which 15 were eliminated because they did not exhibit any significant changes after a marriage therapy intervention had been made (Hahlweg 1996).

Internal consistencies of the PFB scales in the sample
In contrast to the FPI-R sub-scales, the sub-scales of the partnership questionnaire throughout exhibit satisfactory to very good internal consistencies (cf. table 2), which lie between $a = .79$ and $a = .88$ for the total sample. The entire PFB scale is also very reliable in the two sub-groups ($a = .92$ for the Jewish group and $a = .83$ for the control group), so that from the aspect of test theory nothing can be adduced against a discovery of group effects in the quality of the love relationship, if they exist at all.

Scale Ratings for Ascertaining the Bonds to the Parents (R I) and the Autonomy of Couples (R II)

Two rating scale questionnaires designed to ascertain the *bonds to the family of origin* and the *love relationship* were designed for the investigation. The scales were primarily intended to be used to also secure a quantitative record of the questions discussed in the interview and to render possible a mutual validation.

The male and female subjects in each case received specific gender versions (m/f) of the questionnaires. All items had a 6-point response format ("does not apply at all" to "is very applicable"). The *Parental Bond Scale* consists of 15 items, which are designed to ascertain the bonds with the parents, the parents' relationship to each other and to other persons, as well as the consequences of the National Socialist experiences of the parents (item example: "How easily my parents give me feelings of guilt").

The *Autonomy of Couple Scale* consists of 11 items, which aim at measuring the bonds to one's own family as regards the choice of partner and the upholding of traditions, as well as distance towards the partner's family (item example: "How much I like being with my partner's family"). A single twelfth item serves to evaluate one's satisfaction with life.

Those questioned were able to give separate answers for father and mother for some of the items. In these cases, the average of the values from both answers for each item was taken in order to evaluate the result.

Internal consistencies of the Scales for Bonds to the Parents and Autonomy of the Couples
In the total sample, both scales can be regarded as fairly reliable (parental bond scale: $a = .72$, couple autonomy scale: $a = .68$). A look at the values in the sub-groups, however, clearly shows that the two constructs measure a very different homogeneity in the Jewish and in the control group (cf. table 3). Since quite a number of items both in the parental bond scale and in the pair autonomy scale correlates negatively with the (corrected) total score of the scale, it cannot obviously be expedient to use these two collections of

items as constructs that are to be understood as being one-dimensional. Instead, factor analyses were separately conducted for both scales, in order to determine the dimensionality of the item sets more precisely.

Factor analyses for the Bonds to the Parents Scale and Couple Autonomy Scale

An analysis of the principal components with subsequent varimax-rotation was in each case conducted for both sets of items, in order to produce a simple loading pattern of the items on the factors which is as easy to interpret as possible (Bortz 1977). In order to determine the number of factors to be extracted, the plot of the Eigenvalues was inspected.[8] As can be seen in figure 22, two factors for the 15 items of the parental bond scale emerged.

Not all 15 items could be unambiguously used for the interpretation of the factors (cf. table 4). In accordance with this selection of items, the first factor which accounts for 21.8 per cent of the variance after the rotation can be described as *"bonds with the parents originating from the family history"*, whereas the second can be regarded as a *"general bond with the parents"* (18.8% of the of the variance explained).

The Eigenvalue plot in the factor analysis of the 11 items of the scale couple autonomy would actually seem to suggest a 3-factor solution (cf. fig. 23). Nevertheless, only two factors have been extracted, since the "leap" clearly occurs after the first two factors considered "worthy of interpretation" as a result of this dominance.

As regards this scale also, the loading pattern (table 5) shows that not all items ought to be used for the interpretation. The first factor with 25.3 per cent variance explained after the rotation is described as *"Positive relationship to the partner's family"*; the second (variance explained 25.0%) is described as *"Significance of the family background in the love relationship"*.

In the results of the testing of the hypotheses regarding bonds to the parents and couple autonomy described below, the two scales are not used as independent variables beside the individual items any more, but this is the case rather with the factor values of the interviewees with respect to the four factors "bonds to the parents resulting from the family's history", "general bonds to the parents", "positive relationship to the partner's family" and "significance of the family background in the love relationship".

---

8 | It is recommended that one extracts those factors which lie before the break from which the Eigenvalue curve takes an asymptotical course to the X-axis (Bortz 1977).

Evaluation Methods

Analysis of Individual Cases

Two of the twenty interviews conducted with Jews have been selected for a qualitative analysis of individual cases. Whereas when dealing with the purely quantitative methods and the evaluations with external ratings of a qualitative analysis of contents the point is to use objective methods or to bring about a control of the evaluation by having recourse to external judges who are independent of the investigator, the analyses of individual cases are subject to one's own criteria of evaluation. The object of the studies of individual cases is to show how the subjects interviewed coped with the history of persecution and the later behaviour of their parents. In particular, the point at issue is the formative influence of the parents' persecution on the modes of relationship adopted by those interviewed. The case studies are based especially on subjective assessments on the part of the investigator. His counter-transference reactions must be especially taken into consideration when an analysis is made of the "scenic" aspect of the interviews. The interpretations to be submitted should exhibit an inner conclusiveness. The subjective understanding displayed by the investigator should be plausible. Nevertheless, the interpretations made in each case should be documented by passages from the text of the interview transcriptions. The criterion for the selection of such statements made by those interviewed should be exclusively based on the contents. This has been done regardless of whether it involved the possible repetitions of remarks.

Because of the necessity to preserve the anonymity of the interview partners it is not possible to publish the entire transcriptions. Nevertheless, in order to afford as deep an insight into the two individual cases and in the conduct of the interviews as possible longer passages from the interview also in each case partly follow upon the investigator's interpretations. On the one hand, the remarks made by those interviewed shall – as has been set forth above – serve to document the interpretations; on the other hand, the readers can in this manner also form their own idea of the interviews (at least of parts thereof).

Analysis of the Contents of the Interviews

Lisch (1978) deals with basic demands which are to be satisfied by the category systems dealing with the analysis of contents. "The basic object of every model for the analysis of contents is to reproduce the reality, such as the investigation has made available in a text, as adequately as possible by the question put in each case, and to analyse this reality by reducing the information basically available to what is relevant to the intention of the question. In view of the incredible complexity of oral remarks, this presupposes that categories are formed" (ibid., 69). According to Lisch (ibid., 70 et seqq.) category patterns should fulfil the following conditions:

- the category patterns must be comprehensive;
- the categories should be unambiguous;
- the categories should be independent of each other;
- the categories should refer to the same dimension of meaning (cf. also Holsti, quoted by Ritsert 1972, 51 et seqq.).

Herrmann and Stäcker (1969, 409 et seqq.) distinguish "empirical systems" and "a-priori systems" as classification systems for the analysis of texts in the light of how they obtain their data. Groeben (1987) describes this distinction in deriving the categories as an inductive versus a deductive way of proceeding: "The inductive method of forming a category can be suggested by the semantics of the text [...]; the deductive method deduces categories in as stringent a manner as possible from theoretic models, hypotheses, the formulation of the questions" (ibid., 5).

For the qualitative evaluation of all the interviews of the present study, a method was adopted which combines a *deductive* method of analysing the contents with the *inductive* method of the "summarizing analysis of contents" (Mayring 1988). Three independent external raters were given central questions for the fields to be studied. With the aid of these central questions, relevant passages were selected from the interview transcriptions – without the hypothesis being known –, and were then paraphrased and reduced. These categories which were obtained inductively were allocated to the categories derived from the theory (categories arrived at deductively).

Deductive Analysis

Based on the insights of the relevant literature, categories were established in a deductive analysis for the field of "relationship with the parents"; these deal with the sections "bond of the Second Generation with the parents" and "National Socialist experience of the parents". In the field of "love relationships", categories were established which deal with the sections "pressure on the part of the parents on the selection of partners" and "conflicts in love relationships". All categories have been clearly assigned to one of a total of 18 superordinate categories. The tabular listing of the fields, sections, superordinate categories and categories are listed in table 6 and 7.

Inductive Analysis

To start with, the external raters each read an identical transcript from the group that was investigated and from the control group (the external raters are not acquainted with the group divisions). In accordance with the *central questions for codification* which are given they should mark all the passages of the interview relevant for the four central questions with different colours. The results are then discussed together. The object of this discussion is to agree upon a joint selection of the passages.

Thereupon the concept of the "summarized analysis of contents" (Mayring 1988, 1991) is explained to the external raters, in accordance with which the selected passages from the interviews are at first *paraphrased* in prepared tables. After this a *generalization* of the statements is effected. Finally, a *reduction* of the generalizations is carried through, which are characterized as numbered *categories*. The paraphrases, generalizations and reductions which have been set up by the external raters independently of each other are then discussed by them. The object is to agree upon *common* categories.

The same procedure is adopted with a further interview transcript. After that, *different* transcripts are submitted, upon which the external raters work independently of each other. At a later point of time, the external raters again receive an identical, then again different interviews for evaluation. One proceeds in this manner until all the interviews have been dealt with. That is to say, several identical interviews are dealt with separately, but jointly discussed in order to reach an agreement. Most interviews are only dealt with by one external rater.

At the end, the total result of the external rating is summarized by the group. *All the categories that have been extracted* are separately listed in a table under central questions. When doing so, one attempts to allocate each category to an superordinate category (e.g. *entangled* or *non-entangled affection* or *rejection*, *open* or *concealed pressure* etc.). The frequency with which these phenomena occur in each category in the individual interviews is then listed in the columns of the table. (For purposes of control, the number of the interview paraphrase is also indicated.)

The category collections are then compared with the deductive categories derived from the theory (cf. Groeben 1987, Groeben and Rustemeyer 1995). This comparison is effected by allocating the inductive categories to those gained deductively.

Quantitative-statistical Analysis

In order to make the rating results accessible for a quantifying analysis, the frequency of all 86 categories listed in the last section were registered for each subject. These data were electronically stored for later evaluation.

The use of consecutive quantifying methods following qualitative evaluation steps of data reduction is a disputed issue in the discussion of the methods of procedures analysing the contents of an investigation, and it is frequently also treated as a dichotomous conflict of a qualitative versus a quantitative analysis of contents (cf. Giegler 1992, Groeben and Rustemeyer 1995, Mathes 1992, Mohler 1992, Schmidt 1997, Saldern 1995).

Whilst some authors (e.g. Schmidt 1997, 560) would like to see the statistical treatment of rating results limited to the function of an overall view of the material, which might then, when selecting cases, prove to be useful for the analysis of an individual case, Groeben and Rustemeyer (1995) see the analysis of content precisely as the "connecting link between the hermeneutical and empirical structure of science" (ibid., 547; cf. in this connection also Leuzinger-Bohleber 1995, Leuzinger-Bohleber et al. 1992). They argue emphatically in favour of making "the (quantitative) evaluation models hitherto developed and introduced fully available" (Groeben and Rustemeyer 1995, 549).

This is by no means a new controversy; it was already dealt with as a detail aspect in the so-called *methods dispute* conducted within German postwar sociology in the sixties and seventies of the past century. In his criticism of quantitative methods, Adorno (according to Ritsert 1972, 28 et seqq.) at the time indicated four points which the qualitative analysis of contents should have in contrast to the quantitative one:

1. it should classify individual elements of the text in their meaningful context with regard to the entire text (*context*). "Taking the theoretical knowledge of a syndrome as a point of departure, a quantitatively incidental or even irrelevant characteristic may acquire an outstanding significance for the context" (Adorno according to Ritsert 1972, 29);
2. it should comprehend the latent structures of meaning (*latency*) of a text (thus differing from the idea that analyses of contents can only refer to the *manifest* contents). Lorenzer also emphasizes that the "'latent meaning' beneath the language structure which is important in practical life" (Lorenzer 1981, 171; cf. also Fischer 1982, 182 et seqq.; Kriz 1978, 44 et seqq.) must be worked out; in this connection, one must, however, bear in mind that the meaning of the latency term varies in accordance with the theoretical position adopted;

3. it should take the *singularity* of individual objective circumstances into consideration, i.e. the importance of statements should not depend on how frequently they are made;
4. one should also take omissions, i.e. statements that are *not* made, into account when making the analysis (*presence*). According to Ritsert, however, the endeavour to adopt a "strict non-frequency approach" (Ritsert 1972, 27 et seqq.) leads to a dead end. "Why should an analysis of contents which is inspired by the criticism of ideology do without quantifications if these are found to be useful (say, when summarizing material)?" (ibid., 28). Kriz (1978, 49) summarizes the controversy about "quantity versus quality" as follows: "The alternative of a 'qualitative versus a quantitative analysis of contents' can thus largely be seen as an illusory problem and a dispute concerning this issue is irrelevant."

Ultimately, as regards the possibility of interpreting the contents of a quantifying analysis within the framework of analyses of contents, *what* remains centrally important is to clear up the question what is actually being measured by the rating of the data which have been obtained. For instance, if the allocating of a passage in the text to a certain category (e.g. "Suffering from relationships with partners who are not of the same origin, without this circumstance being named") has been effected by a rater, it is certainly questionable whether the variable resulting therefrom can still be regarded as a characteristic of the subject questioned or rather as what is the result of complex interrelations between the subject, the interview situation, the text, the rating rules and its understanding by the rater.

As regards the *scaling level* of the category variables, one must ask whether these shall only be understood as dichotomous characteristics (the category "occurred" versus "did not occur"), or whether the repeated allocation of various passages of the text to one and the same category also means a "linear more" of the characteristic involved and whether the contents of this "more" are possibly to be interpreted as a greater intensity, a more frequent occurrence and a greater subjective importance of the characteristic.

In the relevant texts and manuals on qualitative methodology one finds throughout only surprisingly vague remarks concerning this *measurement and validity problem*, if indeed it is not ignored altogether.

Therefore, when testing hypotheses, specific operational definitions of variables have been made in the present study which take these problems into consideration. As has already been set forth, the problem of the validity of the quantifying category variables has been made accessible to empirical evaluation by the parallel use of fully standardized questionnaire scales. The following section casts a light on the fundamental procedures and problems of statistical analysis, which in principle concern both types of variables – questionnaire data and category data.

Statistical Analysis of the Questionnaire Data

Like the data of the rating of the analysis of the contents, all the questionnaire data were electronically stored and analysed with the statistical program SPSS (SPSS for Windows 1998).

It has been explained why in the case of the present non-random samples tests of statistical hypotheses can only serve to draw cautious and temporary conclusions concerning the actual magnitude of a group difference between Second Generation Jews in Germany and their non-Jewish co-citizens. Incidentally, statements about the statistical significance of this study rather have the function not to "disappoint" expectation concerning conventional models of reporting results.

This basic opinion should not, however, free one from the obligation of using a test method which is appropriate for the evaluation problem involved in each case.

The circumstance that the findings in this study were made with matched samples of pairs, therefore, exclusively requires test procedures for *paired samples*, such as e.g. one-way or multivarate t-tests for dependent samples, the Wilcoxon-test or McNemars χ-test (Bortz 1977).

As far as the present size of the sample of $N = 20$ pairs is concerned, one must, however, – quite apart from the fact which test methods were used in detail – expect fundamental problems with respect to the *test power* which will be briefly discussed below.

Considerations to Power and Effect Size

The probability of being able to show that an effect (i.e. a mean difference or correlation of a certain magnitude) is significant in the sample and to then consequently decide to reject the null hypothesis (Buchner et al. 1996, Cohen 1988) is designated as the power of the test. Besides fixing an accepted error probability α, one requires a value indicating how large the effect in the population is or could be, the so-called *effect size*, in order to indicate the power of the test in a concrete case. In doing so, one can be guided e.g. by the results of earlier investigations of the same or at least of a comparable hypothesis. If such possibilities of comparison are not available, one can make reference to the conventions established by Cohen (1977, 1988, 1992) which serve as a guide line up to the present day (Buchner, Erdfelder and Faul 1996). Cohen has defined effect size indexes for all commonly used

4. EMPIRICAL ANALYSES | 121

test methods, and he has for each of them indicated limit values gained from experience regarding the point from which an effect in the behavioural sciences should be regarded as "small", "medium" or "large".[9] If one applies these conventions to the concrete situation in this study, then the problems concerning the power can also be expressed in numbers. For instance, if one wishes to make a simple comparison of the mean values between the Jewish group and the control group (e.g. in one of the FPI-R sub-scales), then one would by means of a t-test for dependent samples in general discover an actually existing "medium" effect when (two-sided) testing conventionally with an error probability of $a = 5\%$ only with a probability of 19%.[10] As for the remaining probability of 81% (the so-called b-risk), the t-test would supply a non-significant result. The probability of discovery would look even more dismal (7%) if a "small" effect were involved. Only in the case of a "large" effect would the strength of the test exceed the guessing probability of 50%. Only in that case, would the use of a t-test with $N = 20$ couples provide somewhat more information than if one were to toss a coin, if one wants to decide whether a mean difference in the random sample actually exists.

Since the 1990s there has been a growing demand to abandon the logic of null hypothesis testing for psychology as a way out of this unsatisfactory situation (and for some other reasons also). Instead attention should, it is argued, be directed rather towards reporting the effect sizes themselves and, if possible, the qualification of the contents should be directed to what is practically or clinically significant or not so very significant (cf. especially Cohen 1994, Meehl 1990, Schmidt 1992).

In the part in which the results of this study are set forth, I have, as a consequence of this discussion, abstained from making *decisions* about accepting or rejecting null hypotheses or from making significance statements. It is, therefore, logical that no *a priori* error probabilities (e.g. $a = 5\%$) have been fixed as limit values for decisions, either. Besides the conventional representation of the p-level[11], the effect sizes are reported for all impor-

---

9 | Thus, a medium effect (for two independent groups) would concretely mean a group difference of $\bar{x}_{diff} = 7.5$ IQ-points (Cohen 1992) in the intelligence tests commonly used which are standardized for a mean variation of 15 IQ-points.

10 | The program GPOWER of Erdfelder, Faul and Buchner (1996) was used to calculate the power of the tests.

11 | The statistical program SPSS provides alternative methods for a number of test types (e.g. Wilcoxon-test or McNemar's χ-test) as to how the level of significance (p-level) should be calculated (Bühl and Zöfel 1998). The method usually found in psychology for asymptotic testing is thereby linked to pre-conditions concerning the size of the random sample, the distribution of the values and the minimum fre-

tant group comparisons and described as "small", "medium" and "large" in accordance with Cohen's (1988) suggestions.

The demand for a "strict" *theory testing* by the testing of hypotheses has, therefore, not been applied in this study not only because of the lack of a random sampling procedure, but also on account of the reasons which derive from an unsatisfactory power of the test which is inevitably the case in small-scale investigations.

4.2 Results

Analysis of Individual Cases[12]

Extracts from two individual interviews are described and analysed below. The extracts serve as examples which show how the history of the parents' persecution and their later behaviour were experienced by the partners of the interview and how this shaped the pattern of their relationships. Even if one is not dealing here with psychoanalytical interviews, the point at issue in the interpretations is in particular to work out the latent ideas held by the partners of the interview. Counter transference reactions were at work both in shaping the conduct of the interview and in analysing the material. Special attention was accordingly paid to the "scenic" aspect of the relationship between interview partners as defined by Argelander (1967), beginning with the unusual "recruiting" of the interview partner. In this connection, it is also of especial importance that the interviewer himself belongs to the Second Generation.

The selection of the two interviews for an analysis of individual cases

quencies to be expected in crosstables, which have partly not been observed in this investigation. Therefore, wherever possible, recourse has been had to the more appropriate procedures in accordance with the *exact method* or the *Monte-Carlo method* (Bortz 1977, Büssing and Jansen 1988).

[12] The two analyses of individual cases of the interviews with Rachel G. (interview No. 27) and with Samuel N. (interview No. 3) have been published as brief case vignettes (Grünberg 1991) and both of them again in a detailed version (Grünberg 1995, 1998b). The documentary quotations from the transcripts are in each case indicated in parentheses. The first number refers to the interview, the second indicates the page; e.g. the indication "(3;4-5)" means that the quotation indicated in interview No. 3 (Samuel N.) can be found on pages four to five. Passages printed in italics indicate a special emphasis expressed by the interviewed person. Remarks printed in italics in parentheses describe certain conspicuous features noted during the talk, e.g. laughter, crying or a clearing of the throat.

was made in accordance with the following criteria: one of the interviews was to be conducted with a woman, the other with a man. In one case, both parents were to be survivors of the Shoah, whereas in the other case this should apply only to the father or the mother. One individual study was to refer to a survivor who had spoken a lot about his or her experience of persecution; in the other interview reference was to be made to a survivor who was inclined to speak very little about it.

For a better understanding, the study of both cases is preceded by indicating the biographical data of those interviewed. The sections have headings which indicate which subject is treated.

Rachel G.

Synopsis of Rachel G.'s Biographical Data

Rachel G. is in her early forties and is a freelance photographer. She is single, lives on her own in a big German city and has no children. When the interview was conducted, she had a German friend called Rudolf. Rachel's parents came from Czechoslovakia. They survived in ghettoes and in several concentration camps.

In addition, her father was also interned in a Stalinist camp. Most of her relatives were murdered by the Germans. Both parents died at a comparatively young age and within brief intervals of each other. Rachel has a brother who is also unmarried and has no children. The interview with Rachel lasted for a total of about seven and a half hours.

Interaction with the Interviewer before and after the Conversation with Rachel G.[13]

A confusion on Rachel's part, which – as will become clearly apparent later – also involved the *contents* of the interview, could already be discerned before and after the conversation. On the one hand, the issue was whether Rachel could trust me. On the other hand, the issue arose of whether there were possibly problems involving her family, and in particular her parents. When Rachel's coping with parental persecution was revealed – say, the idealisation of her parents, which served to maintain close bonds with them –, Rachel was very soon in danger of losing her balance. For the revelation of the idealisation of her parents also revealed the existence of aggressive-

---

13 | The *interaction with the interviewer before and after the conversation* is given "in the first person", since the interviewer's own counter-transference reaction is a constitutive component of the analysis of the individual cases.

ness that had been denied. In the course of the interaction, this confusion became apparent as follows: It had already not been easy to gain Rachel's consent for the interview. She did not have much time: at the time her situation at work was that radical changes were being made. However, because of the mediator, a common acquaintance, she gave her consent after a long telephone conversation to have the interview despite the lack of time.

However, when I appeared in her apartment on the date which had been arranged months before, Rachel tried to back out. She had not filled out the questionnaire which had been sent to her, and she said that she did not have a real "love relationship", either. Therefore, she was probably not "interesting" for my research project. Nonetheless, after half an hour's discussion, she agreed to co-operate and have the interview after all. We agreed to use the intimate personal "Du" form.[14]

The first part of the interview lasted two and a half hours, the second one just under three hours. I spent a total of seven and a half hours with her.

A few days later, Rachel sent me the questionnaire which she had filled out by mail. A card reading as follows was enclosed:

Dear Kurt,
I enclose the forms which I have filled out. – Perhaps you will be interested to hear this – the interview has helped me in spite of a sleepless night! I became aware of several things.
Many regards,
Rachel.
N.B. It would interest me to know what you made of the interview.

In subsequent telephone calls, we discussed the question whether Rachel would allow me to evaluate her interview more thoroughly so that I might make use of it for lectures and publications. She agreed to this. She did request, however, that she might look at the work beforehand, in order to be able to make alterations "to protect her person" if need be.

After the first text for a lecture had been drafted, Rachel was nonetheless beset by doubts as to whether she should keep her promise. A longer conversation and the alteration of a few passages in the text of the lecture made it possible for her to give her consent again.

Long after the interview had taken place, during the Gulf War, Rachel

---

14 | The form of address was agreed upon with every interview partner before starting the interview. In each case, the interviewer accepted the form of address which the interview partner wished to adopt.

phoned me up in a very nervous state. She was very upset and needed professional help. Rachel asked me to help her in her search for a psychotherapist or psychoanalyst.

The Interview with Rachel G.
The Good Parents

When Rachel was asked to characterize her parents, it became obvious how much she idealized them. She described her parents as very human, affectionate and good persons. They had never done anybody any harm; they had not so much as *wished* anybody any harm. She mentioned the names of friends who could confirm this. As a matter of fact, her parents had been "too good (*laughs*) and as a result also too foolish (*laughs*)", for they had permitted others to exploit them. In the process of identifying with her parents, she thinks the latter also applies to herself. Altogether "she had very much in common with her parents". Whilst she considered her father to be the weaker one, she ascribed more strength and ability to assert herself to her mother. In a later part of the interview, Rachel mentioned business failures as a weak point of her father's character; he had let relatives cheat him (27;6-7).

The idealization of her parents is accompanied by splitting processes. The "bad people" are confronted with "only good" ones. On the one hand, we find above all Rachel's persecuted parents, the Jews, and on the other hand we find what is evil, in particular the Nazis. On a conscious level, the interviewee denies this splitting, however, which ultimately opposes the Jews to the Germans. Her parents had taught her that not all Germans had been perpetrators. The splitting process has principally the function of closely binding the daughter to her parents. Aggression is projected outwards, for "the parents who are solely good" must not be subjected to any criticism (cf. below). The family's equilibrium rests upon this denial of aggression towards the parents. How dangerous it is to disturb the family's equilibrium will be seen in the conflicts which arose during adolescence (cf. below).

R.G.: Yes, it is of course very difficult that – my father was a – altogether both were very good people, as far as their character is concerned, that is to say, they were emotionally very human, very good, very loving; that is to say, not bad persons. Never expressed any bad wishes of any kind towards anyone in any way or --- Yes, it is really very difficult, to describe it in this way. My father, when I now look at the relationship of my parents, if you mean that, I don't know ...

K.G.: Well, we could perhaps speak about this right now. But to start with, if you now look at them each one on their own and so say "My father was like this and this; my mother was a person, who ..."

R.G.: Let us say, my mother was the stronger one, my father the weaker one, if I look at this today in this way ... (K.G.: hm, hm) ... well not, during my childhood, but today as an adult. Let's say, that he was perhaps really weaker; she was stronger. But I can really only express this by saying that both were really *incredibly* human, they were good, they were warm-hearted; that is to say, one can say that this really applies to them both in the same way. It works ... (K.G.: hm, hm) ... really in the same manner. I can not now put it in this way or that way. I can only say that I can see today that my mother was a stronger woman, and my father was weaker.

K.G.: In what manner do you think, say, that she was stronger and he weaker?

R.G.: In the way it is today also; as regards life in general, I think. As regards one's ability to assert oneself, I would say. (K.G.: hm, hm) yes, assertiveness, I would say. (K.G.: hm, hm) That in any case the strength was to be found more there and the weakness there and actually I find it difficult to say now, what I have just told you, that about so many positive things; perhaps you would say that that is not possible. But you know, eh, I well remember friends of mine who really liked coming to us at home. But they came more for my parents than for me ... (K.G.: hm, hm) [...] because they like that is to say they liked my parents and always said: "what wonderful parents you have", because they were, you know, so warm-hearted, so good. That is to say, they would both of them – it does not now matter which of them had given their last shirt to a stranger, who came to us – a bed, a meal and well, really everything, yes? (K.G.: hm, hm) They were just, I think, too good (*laughs*) and even perhaps too stupid (*laughs*) or whatever. I don't know. You know, *today* I compare this with my own experience in some way, so that I say – and by this I also describe myself because I have taken over much from my parents, yes – if one is actually too good, then one is exploited by the world and it soon turns into a kind of stupidity. (K.G.: hm, hm) Because one can then assert oneself less on account of one's good-naturedness, on account of one's – well, that is how I would see it. (27;2.3)

At a very early stage of the interview already, Rachel mentions – without being expressly asked (!) – the National Socialist persecution of her parents. The parents had not been able to work any more "as a result of the war"; they had suffered much. It is of interest to note that she uses the expression "war" when she is referring to the National Socialist persecution of the Jews. This must be regarded as indicating adjustment to the non-Jewish German environment. For in the aforementioned context, the word "war" does not cause any offence in contrast with the controversial theme of the National

Socialist persecution of the Jews. As Rachel sets forth in a later part of the interview (27;35), her parents had brought her up so that she would not call attention to herself. The adjustment to German society is also to be noticed in her way of expressing herself.

K.G.: Hm, hm. What was your parents' profession?

R.G.: Both were pensioners, well as a result of the war. They were very young, but, well also unable to work: they were incapacitated from work to the extent of 80 per cent. Well, as a result of the war, both of them had gone through terrible things; they were very ill physically and in any case they were always at home for 24 hours really. (27.3)

The Father

The father's persecution for a large part remains vague. He seems to have been both a victim of National Socialist persecution and interned in a Stalinist camp (27;28-30).

It is obvious that Rachel has not had the courage to put more detailed questions to her father, which would have put her in a position to appreciate and understand his persecution more precisely. Possibly she imagined that she might receive information that would have damaged her idea of her father. In this connection, also, the splitting processes which have been mentioned above, are important. The point at issue is not to jeopardize the relationship to a father who is "solely good". The father appears as a man who permits himself to be cheated rather than do something wrong himself. At the same time, he tends to recede into the background compared to the mother. She has influenced the family atmosphere more strongly, she was the more dominating one.

The Mother

Rachel's mother was one of the few survivors of the extermination camp Majdanek. In contrast to her husband, she felt compelled to talk about her persecution again and again. The interviewee intimates that her mother tells guests the story of her persecution more or less as an entrance ticket to her apartment. Presumably this was meant to make it clear to the guest that one could only build up a relationship on the foundation of knowledge of the mother's traumatic National Socialist experiences.

How Rachel Experiences the Story of her Parents' Persecution

If Rachel was repeatedly a witness of these descriptions of her mother's persecution, this must doubtlessly also have caused aggression. One can surmise that guests must have experienced a similar reaction. Rachel does not, however, mention such reactions. Such a denial of aggression might be comprehensible against the background of the splitting processes, which only allowed her mother to appear as solely "a good victim". Such a mother must not be called into question.[15]

R.G.: Well, I must tell you that the topic "Third Reich" was *always* present for my mother. So, regardless of who came to us, she *immediately* told her whole story to everybody. (27;23)

Already when she began to describe her experiences with her mother's persecution, Rachel also spoke of her *own* fears which had been passed on to her by her mother. The interviewee sees her phobic fear of going into the woods as resulting from her mother's persecution. Rachel described how her mother's survival had depended on coincidences and the help given by other people. She admittedly also stressed her mother's strong points, which helped her to survive, but on the whole she conveyed the impression that her parents' experience of persecution and their survival also had somehow been determined by fate.[16] She spoke of intuitions, visions and the hopes resulting therefrom, as if certain events and ways of behaving had been predetermined. Possibly one is dealing here with an attempt to endure terrible events which had irreversibly taken place, in order in some way to make them "more bearable", and to do so by removing them from one's own sphere of influence. Rachel wants to banish something from her consciousness which causes her great pain and many conflicts.

R.G.: Yes, ph (*moans a little*). My mother's experiences were also so, as I have said, eh, eh, first a – it's all a bit far away – well at first the ghetto; and then she was in two or three concentration camps, before she got to Majdanek. Terezin, oh, what was the name of the other one, I can't remember just now. And then she came to Majdanek. Had to work in the woods there, well, to fell trees. Since then, I must say, ever since I heard this when I was a child, I have at the most been three times in a wood in my whole life for over 40 years. I panic at the thought of a wood or forest. That has come from hearing the story. And, well, she naturally gave many more details than my

---

15 | How this interrelation works in adolescence will be described below.

16 | Later Rachel will place her own experiences also in a similar context involving fate, namely, when she speaks of the loss of her unborn child.

father. She naturally told – one of the stories was that when she came to Majdanek, or perhaps to another concentration camp [...] that there were these notorious roll calls, like right-left-right-left; and she stood in this way in the queue and then she said: prompted by a sort of intuition she suddenly moved to the other queue – that this most probably saved her life. Then there were situations that she was I don't know how many times in the gas chamber, and they called out "Everybody out again. We need these people for work." Then there was a situation, I don't know why, but she was somewhere in solitary confinement and she told us of a vision which she had, because my grandfather had died shortly before the war, that is my mother's father. And, since, yes, she is a very religious woman, well, – he supposedly said to her: "You will survive." – so that was what she hoped. Then in Majdanek she had, well, typhoid fever and typhus, as I have said before. That she was so lucky as to have a Jewish doctor there, in – the what's it, in that sickness camp. When a, what do you call it, a kind of delegation came to see at what stage the patients were; whether they were fit to work or were to die, that is to say to take a decision about life or death.[17] And this doctor – it's all fate or whatever you want to call it – had pumped her full of morphine and he had said to the commander : "No, this woman can go back to work again tomorrow." Although she was lying there with I don't know how high a temperature, with typhus; and he had really pumped her so full that she got up the next day, in order to, well. Those are the stories in which she was practically always brought back to life. Then her leg, I don't know why, the one leg was broken three times, it was not put into a splint properly, well, the lower leg. Then she had an experience, when they all stood in the open space in Majdanek for some roll call or other and the commander [...] called my mother out from all the rest. And, yes, she only said how he stood there with his two big German shepherd dogs and she stood there and he said: "Hey, you, come over here." And she thought, now your life is once more at an end. And he asked her "How long are you already here?" And she said, I don't know how long, one year, a couple of months "God knows what." And he answered: "Considering that you still look quite good" and sent her back to her place. But this psychic terror, that she survived then – So, my mother was now a woman, as I have told you at the beginning already, not only that she was a good-looking woman. She also looked very Aryan. She was blonde and had blue eyes. And was a very clean person. She also told us that she washed her hair every day; and she also washed the only blouse which she had every day. That is to say, she always attached much value to this. That was her instinct for

---

17 | This statement refers to the fact that in a concentration camp "life" could only be understood as being identical with "work". This problem was very impressively dealt with in May 1990 at an International symposium held by the Evangelische Akademie (Protestant Academy) Arnoldshain together with the Jewish Museum Frankfurt. The symposium had the same title as the exhibition in the Jewish Museum: *Our only way is work ... the Ghetto in Lódz 1940-1944*.

self-preservation, I suppose, you know. And yes, well, those are the kind of stories which she told us. (27;33-34)

Rachel was about five or six years old, when she first heard of her mother's persecution. We will clearly see below how the fact that she was exposed at a very early date already to continually repeated descriptions of persecution whilst at the same time living in Germany oppressed her and gave rise to internal conflicts. Rachel suffers from this contradiction. Her parents' statements about pogroms that took place in Poland after the war supposedly to show that hatred of Jews was not confined only to Germany, or such things as the mention of denunciations presumably on the part of Jews exercising the same function, cannot solve her problem.

The Family Atmosphere

One must assume that Rachel's parents had to deny their hatred and aggressive impulses in order to keep on living in Germany. Moreover, one might ask whether they were obliged to do so in order to be able to go on living *at all* after the National Socialist extermination of the Jews.

In addition, it becomes apparent how Rachel experienced the circumstances of her own life as a contrast to those of non-Jewish Germans of her own age. Whilst she saw herself confronted with her parents' persecution and its consequences – she heard "horror stories" of Nazi persecution; she has no relatives[18] – other children have grandparents, who give them presents and they listen to ordinary fairy tales.[19] In this connection, Rachel's aggression about this difference between Jews and non-Jewish Germans can after all be felt, in contrast to the tendency to deny these; this becomes especially clear when she explains how "ridiculous", say, the "compensation" given to her parents had been in view of what had been inflicted upon them. She underlines this statement when she says that one had had only to *look* at her parents in order to notice the injury that they had suffered as a result of National Socialist persecution (cf. 27;36).

R.G.: [...] It was like in a fairy tale. You know, other children are told the fairy tale of "Snow White and the Seven Dwarfs", and I am told a horror fairy tale. Incomprehension, eh, couldn't, somehow, eh, believe it, well, because the word "Germans" has

18 | Rachel says during the interview: "And I didn't know what Grandma means, what Grandpa means, yes?" (27;36). This shows that something more than a feeling of being a stranger is involved.

19 | Proof of this is given not only in the following extract from the text, but also further below still (27;36).

fallen, "Germany"; and then of course I also then said: "yes, why do we live here?" Yes, but now it is not that this was the object of my education, not from the point of view of my mother, either: *the Germans*. You know, she also told me about the tattooing, how the others. Everything that you also know. I mean, she told me these stories; what they did with the teeth, with the hair, how their hair was shaved and so forth, you know. And, eh, she never told this, you know. We live in Germany and this hatred of the Germans, who are there *now*. It was only so, it was then; then the stories also came, that my father perhaps, to say this again, then also told perhaps a little bit more clearly still, what happened in the pogroms *after the war*, in Poland. That there the Poles were not *better* than the Germans; true, there were no concentration camps and nothing, but that their hatred of the Jews was just as strong, yes? And of course also what happened inside the camp with one's own people, one's own Jews, you understand with the overseers; and, eh, this denunciation, what happened in that way. Of course my mother also told me these things. (27;34-35)

Like her parents, Rachel tries to fend off conflicts by denying their existence. By using this strategy in coping with conflicts, she tries on the one hand to protect herself from being overwhelmed by the stories of persecution,[20] for the persecution of the Nazis is also reflected for years in Rachel's nightmares. From a certain point of time, she was not able to listen to her mother's descriptions any more.[21] But on the other hand, the problem is to find a way not to disturb the harmony within the family, which her parents have more or less made into a law. For in that case Rachel would have touched on precisely those conflicts the denial of which only made it possible for her parents to live in Germany at all. Moreover, one possible consequence resulting from the problems of life in Germany might have involved a separation from her family. – As an adolescent, Rachel wanted to emigrate; her parents did not allow her to do so, however.

The family's efforts to achieve harmony is nonetheless of importance not only within the family, but also in connection with their co-existence with the non-Jewish German environment. When Rachel says, for instance, that her parents had brought her up not to attract notice, then this may be founded on fear of renewed persecution from a hostile environment. Not to hate the Germans, not to provoke the Germans, was intended to preserve

---

20 | Even during the interview itself, one can sense Rachel's efforts to protect herself from a loss of distance whilst she describes her parents' persecution. She often refers to events "with which one is acquainted", she speaks of stories, which her mother reported. She finds the necessary distance in a way by staying on the surface of things.

21 | Here there is a suggestion of forbidden aggressive impulses directed against her mother.

the family from attacks on the part of Germans. This also made the rather withdrawn life of Rachel's parents comprehensible, if one does not choose to see it solely as an injury *directly* caused by the persecution.

R.G.: Well, she, I must tell you, she always repeatedly spoke of it and she spoke and spoke and spoke: that is to say until, most probably I had so much of it, until at some point of time I could not hear it any more, and the answers that I got – to my questions: why do we live here, why don't we go away? You know, when I was 16 years old, I wanted to go to Israel, yes, my parents didn't let me, yes? And, yes, it's clear, they didn't want that and eh, and oh, what I wanted to say before, and this bringing up my mother gave me: it was not full of hate against – because we live here now. Always be reserved, only so that it should not happen again and so on and so on. And at some point of time everything came – as I have already told you, into my bottom drawer; because, when I also think of it today, if I only think of it and the older I got I started to reflect this, I could not actually have lived here.

K.G.: What do you mean when you say: "that went into my bottom drawer?"

R.G.: Into my system of repression. (K.G.: hm, hm) For, eh, at a later point of time also, as soon as I only thought about it, and if I looked at my parents, yes? I couldn't understand why we live here. And I did not *want* to understand, see? I had always – I was born here, you know, and I grew up here and like all the others also, that is to say my generation and so on. And always whenever I began to think about it and looked at my parents to see how they were feeling, in point of health and financially and at what they had received as compensation, that that was really so ridiculous, you know, in view of what they had gone through. And actually also during my childhood, when I think that *I* – all the others who were at school spoke of their grandma, she had given them this and the grandpa had given them that; and then a fairy tale.

I did not know what a grandma is, what does a grandpa mean, yes? That is to say, these were things that were totally *strange* for me, yes? And, and I see that, I saw the whole thing. I could only live by repressing these thoughts. And above all, you mustn't forget one thing, that I had dreams *every* night, that is to say, I really had these nightmares; I really heard soldiers running around; always, you know, soldiers and war and so on. And this went on for years. And then also my mother's fears. Which she had of course naturally passed on to me. Not to go out in the twilight, yes? That is to say, all these things. Above all fear; I was – o.k., this possibly also resulted from the way I was brought up, that I was brought up more as a girl than as a boy or a normal child, say, with climbing or such things, yes? That fears, fears, fears, yes! That I was afraid of thunder, that I was afraid of being alone in a room, yes? That I was afraid, eh, of going into a forest; that I looked inside the wardrobe to see if somebody was not hiding there or under the bed, do you know. I mean, I dragged these fears along with me for years. (K.G.: hm, hm) And in order to be able to live in Germany at all; and I had no hate, because hate was not instilled into me, yes? I would most probably have felt better if they had brought me up to feel deep hate. I could have had my own experiences in life *myself*. And as a result of the fact that I had no hate, who was I to *hate*? Do you understand, I could not hate the schoolchildren with whom I went to school or their parents and so on. Therefore the only point was to be able to live here without thinking about this. It was already bad enough to see them, how *they* felt; I could only put it in the bottom drawer. (27;35-36)

Whereas Rachel was, on the one hand, given to understand that she should not feel any hatred towards Germans, she was on the other hand aware of the fact that her parents cut themselves almost completely off from their non-Jewish environment. Besides a few relatives, who had also survived the Shoah, and other Jews, closer contacts only existed with people who had supported Jews during the National Socialist era (who were "O.K.") or with people who could not be identified as Nazis because of their age. Rachel herself also had few contacts with non-Jewish Germans – at least during her childhood and youth. Rachel finds the reasons for this mainly in her non-Jewish environment. She was not invited to other people's homes and she remembers hearing anti-Semitic remarks from other children. Above all, however, the mistrust of Germans is no doubt based on the history of the National Socialist extermination of the Jews, even if Rachel's parents had tried to bring up their daughter precisely *not* to hate the Germans as such. One can see from the circumstance that Rachel has absorbed this mistrust so profoundly how strongly she suffers from the contradiction of living precisely in Germany after the Shoah. In addition, one has to bear in mind that Jews who live in Germany after the Shoah are under pressure to justify their remaining in Germany to Jews who live in other countries. If one hated Germans, how could one then live in Germany? Thus, Rachel's parents have presumably tried to bring up their daughter to have an attitude which did not correspond with their own deeply-seated feelings and convictions. It is clear that Rachel feels something which – on the conscious level – she should not feel.

R.G.: Yes, yes, so my parents had contacts with *non*-Jews, actually *only* neighbours, with whom they had a very warm-hearted and close relationship, it was really almost intimate; who were also younger. That is to say, they could not actually have done anything like what happened during Nazi times because they themselves had been children at the time. But apart from that I, eh, can hardly actually remember anything *non*-Jewish.

K.G.: And that was the case with you children, also?

R.G.: Eh, – yes and so it was also like this in my childhood at first, I can also remember, this came up just now also, I could remember that other children had called me names. Yes, but what this was, I cannot say any more, either. But it had some connection or other with Jewishness. Well, and that was, say, at the beginning of the fifties. I also know that to come to me at home – I was never invited, that is to say, during my childhood to anything non-Jewish. Although, eh, right at the beginning, when I was still very young, three years or so, maybe four years old, when my father still had the shop, there was such an older German woman. She was then really inordinately old. She was something like our Grandma, but she was *not* Jewish, and at that time she partly did some housework for us. And, but she was somehow O.K., yes? Then I can remember that my parents also knew a non-Jewish woman, who had *hidden* a Jew. Well, they were really only people who were really not, one cannot say, philo-Semites, they were just *human beings*, you know? Who had really done something good for Jews; or well, eh, really Jews and later, O.K., one was just automatically together with Jewish children through the religious education and the youth centre. And then for some time I was together with three other Jewish girls in one class. And that of course led automatically to friendships, only much later did it come about that sometimes a non-Jewish girl from my class came *home* to me, yes? But she was *the only* one then. Because *I* was invited nowhere, so she was the only one with whom we had such a contact. That all happened much later. (27;25)

Rachel states that there was great harmony in her family. In particular, her parents' relationship to each other was incredibly harmonious. Many people had envied her parents. Nonetheless, one can see how her family here is strongly idealized and that this is intended to cover up another aspect of the family's relationships, that aspect which involves aggression and destructive wishes. Yet, precisely those aggressive and sadistic impulses establish a connection to the Nazi persecution of her parents.[22]

The impression that her parents are idealized by Rachel is confirmed by reference to a person outside the family, the family doctor, who to some extent "confirms" how happy her parents had always been with each other. It is exceedingly important for Rachel to see her parents in such a positive light and to keep them in this light in her memory. The experience of family tensions seems now as in the past, i.e. also during the interview, to constitute a threat.

R.G.: [...] So we lived in harmony, my parents were very much in harmony; their relationship was a very harmonious one; their relationship to us was harmonious. (27;26)

22 | This will have to be worked out later as a determining element in Rachel's present couple relationship.

R.G.: [...] My parents' relationship, actually a film. If I told you this, you would say to me: "That's Hollywood". Because something like this, I have never experienced it with anybody else, and all my friends and everybody who actually knew me really envied me this very very much. Even our family doctor said something very wonderful to me to console me after the death of my parents. He said this to me then: "You know, you had parents who were very happy with each other and you were a happy family. And that will be of help to you later; not now, but later – as a memory". Possibly this says a good deal. (K.G.: hm, hm) My parents had a marriage, which really. If you buy yourself a cheap novel at a kiosk today, and you read that, and you then say: "A wonderful fantasy; but that's not real." That was my parents' marriage. There was much, much love. That is to say, each one only lived for the other one, but jointly they lived for their children. They could, they could *always* busy themselves together. There was actually only a dispute or there was actually never a loud word spoken. There was a lot of harmony, very much love, which my parents felt for each other. They quarrelled if my father said that he thought that my mother was a fanatic for cleanliness; you know, that she should not wear herself out and become ill, on account of the fringes of the carpet being absolutely straight, or when she took the vacuum cleaner and my father said: "But it's already clean. What for, yes?" (K.G.: hm, hm) "Why do you wear yourself out?", yes. Those were, as I tell you, issues for discussions and quarrels, yes. (K.G.: hm, hm) It was really, oh, only love, only worry. (27;9-10)

Adolescence and Attempts to Separate from the Nuclear Family

In the course of the interview, it became increasingly clear how much Rachel is still suffering from the stifling atmosphere in her family. Contradictions torment her, as has been shown, say, by the remarks above about the problems caused by the fact that the family lived precisely in Germany (27;35-36). True, Rachel attempted to uphold the idea that extraordinary harmony had prevailed. However, she also senses that nothing should be allowed to shatter this harmony. Open controversies within the family were taboo. The mother used the power with which her suffering has endowed her in order to bind her daughter to the home.

When a question was put about the typical problems that existed between her and her parents, she at first categorically denied their existence.

R.G.: Really there were none. Ty-, what does typical problems mean? I mean, there are no, one can say in principle there are *no* problems. Problems, ph., perhaps I might mention as an example of a problem what occurred when I wanted to go out when I was 16 or 17 years old, yes? As it is also today, to come home at a definite time; and so if I mostly came home a bit later, but then I knew, one day I did find this out, that my mother always had *special* heart attacks (*laughs*), if I came home late. So I knew – I was almost always sure that if I went away and so came home later that usually the *emergency doctor* was there. (K.G.: hm, hm) Or that, how old was I then, 17 years old or something like that, or maybe 18 years old, and I wanted to go to Munich with two girl friends, or some such place; that my mother also fell ill again solely so that I could not go. You know, some kind of psychological pressure. At some point, I found out, eh, that this was the case, because she simply – those were her fears, that something might happen to me. But on the other hand, again such an extreme, yes, come, these are, *were* extremes, and I am like that *also*. In some way, my parents were really *selfless*. Selfless, that was, eh, when at some point I wanted to go to Switzerland with friends, that eh – and then my mother was *really* ill. She fell, had a concussion, and for instance she asked the doctor not to tell me the truth, *in order* that my holidays should not be spoilt. Or I was, what do I know, in Spain and eh I still wanted to stay a few days in Paris on my way back – no, I was older then, over 20 years old – and then I called from Paris : "Is everything O.K.?" "Yes, everything's O.K." Yes, I arrived in B; and well, daddy had had a heart attack. But well, that is again the *other side*. They didn't want to *spoil* my wonderful time. (K.G.: hm, hm) So it always depended *what* it was. On the one hand, this oppression with, eh., suddenly an emergency doctor and always falling ill, if I were. But, whether these can now be regarded as problems, I ... (27;19-20)

The above passage reveals (after an initial denial) the other side of the coin of harmony, and simultaneously the strength of the parents-daughter bond. Where not very serious events are involved, such as when Rachel goes out in the evening, her mother reacts with heart attacks, whereas Rachel is "spared" the knowledge of a really serious illness of the father, in order not to spoil her holiday. The result is that Rachel feels great insecurity, and she cannot acquire any clear standards as to how she is to react appropriately to family events. This confusion of standards practically represents a reversal of relationships which can be lived in a normal way. The result of this insecurity is an even stronger bond with her parents, for Rachel can never know how alarming crises really are. Here guilt, – an essential factor in the parents-daughter relationship – appears in a very striking way. Every move away from her parents involves the danger of being guilty of leaving them alone possibly at an important point of time in their life, whereby, however, no clear criteria exist as to which situations can be regarded as "important". Ironically, these statements are confirmed precisely by the fact that in the interview Rachel emphasizes the fact that she "was spared" from hearing the news about her father's heart attack as positive evidence for the *selfless* behaviour of her parents. Occasionally Rachel cannot recognise her own confusion for what it is.

The pronounced symbiosis in her parents' marriage plays a very important part in Rachel's development. Her father died a few months after his wife. Both died at an early age, but were very much aged by the experience of persecution.

R.G.: Both of them wanted to die before the other one. My father did die nine months later from a diseased heart, doubly diseased heart, once *really* from a diseased heart and then out of love for my mother. During those nine months he did not really live any more. He was 59 years old, if one thinks of that, and he said "I only wait for my wife to take me to her. Life has no meaning for me." (K.G.: hm, hm) "Even my children will go away, but I am alone." I mean, perhaps that says everything, eh ... (K.G.: hm, hm) Perhaps, eh, I don't know, either, it was really a very, very happy marriage. (27.10.)

Rachel's Love Relationships

Her bond with the parents is also apparent in Rachel's love relationships. She recognises that it is hopeless to find a man who can devote himself to his wife as her father did. He would have to be a Jew of the Second Generation with the same background experiences as she had. Rachel has adopted a radically different way: she lives as an unmarried woman who does not have a child with a man who – as she later learns – maintains innumerable sadomasochistic contacts to women who are in his thrall. From time to time she can assume a position of power in this relationship. Beside his mother, she is the only woman whom her partner respects.

Rachel can only find a place for the aggressions and destructive wishes which were denied in her family in a sadomasochistic relationship. Only a "sadist" can bear Rachel's destructive wishes, without being destroyed himself. But at the same time there exists here – and this is the focus of the problems of the interrelation of the investigation – a bond with her mother's concentration camp experiences. For it is not, say, the existence of a sadomasochistic relationship on the part of the interview partner which is necessarily questionable as such, but on the contrary the fact that the topic of Nazi persecution extends into the next generation. One is inclined to remember, say, her mother's description of her encounter with the commander of the concentration camp which has been quoted earlier on. In the secondary description given by the interview partner, this encounter acquires a certain erotic connotation. When Rachel meets a woman who is in thrall to her partner, she is fascinated and simultaneously humiliated. After she has been confronted with the sadomasochistic orientation of her partner, she has a breakdown, but sexual intercourse also takes place. In this way, the intertwining of her parents' persecution by the Nazis with the personal relations of the interview partner becomes apparent.

R.G.: (*clicks her tongue*) Yes, he showed it to me. I did not want to believe it, and he said to me, because again these were the kind of women, who I actually found nice and likeable – actually I still find them nice and likeable. But when they are then involved with him (*laughs*), then I do *not* find them nice and likeable any more – and he said to me: "You know, the women do what I want. Yes, and at times that *also* gives me pleasure. And during the time when this gives me pleasure, you must just leave me in peace. For I must then go through with it." And that, it is of course also a very serious problem for me today, I can tell you. To manage it, because I have not the disposition for this. I am not masochistically inclined. I tend rather to be sadistic. So I would be inclined to be a dominant woman rather than to be masochistic. And anyway, I did not want to believe him. We sat in a café and then came one of these women, whom I *also* know. From whom I knew that he had an affair with her, but how, what and when. And then he says to me: "I will prove it to you. She does what I want." And well, then I said – and I saw this woman differently, I as a woman – said: "I don't believe it." "O.K., we'll do it." And then she came, sat down at our table and he said to her: "What are you doing now?" "Yes, I wanted to have a coffee." And then he says, he says to her: "Well, go home. I'll call you up right away." And well, then she got up and went. I must say here, well, everybody knows that we have a kind of relationship. But nobody, nor this woman either, knows *what* kind of relationship it is. Because they see us when we are awfully nice with each other, or they see us when we bicker in a dreadful manner (*laughs*) and when we quarrel. (K.G.: hm, hm) That is to say also in public. That is to say, nobody knows; and if somebody mentions me to him, then he doesn't give an answer. That is to say, he does not speak about me. And well, we then got up and went out of the café; and well; he rang her up, he would call with me. No, he would call on her now. She should undress, and *I* would come with him. Yes, I wanted to see her naked. Anyway, he said something of that kind to her. And well, I was quite convinced, I must say, when we already stood before the door to her apartment, that she would *not* be naked when she opened the door. Well, and he still says to me: "Well, if you say, she can now serve us tea; we'll sit there together and she'll serve us tea naked." Or if you say, well, if you want to hit her or that I should hit her or whatever, then, well, that will happen, if you. And I said: "I don't believe you." I am, do you know, I had never been confronted with something like that, yes? And we ring the bell, and I thought I couldn't believe my eyes, because I had thought of what I would do *myself*, and of how *I* would have reacted. I would have stood dressed behind the door and would have said: "Yes, do you want to drink tea. Come in". Well, you know; but I must also try to understand the psyche of these women somehow or other, shall we say. Because I think they need that, like somebody else needs something else. I mean, I would not describe that as perverted, because it is not a perversion. But, well, to make it short, this woman opens the door, naked with garters and, well with a garter belt and black stockings. Well, I must tell you I (*very emphatic*) could not believe my eyes, he was right.

4. Empirical Analyses | 139

K.G.: How did you react to it?

R.G.: Well, he found it quite wonderful, that I, because he knew me, as I normally am, all that I have already done, and how I reacted. Then we went, you know, to her in her room. She sat down on the bed. There was a chair there and there I also, there, well I also sat down there, lit a cigarette and well, he also sat down; and somehow or other, I could not bear it. You know, I felt ashamed for this woman somehow, because I am not like that. I, and this is perhaps not *normal* either, I don't know, at all events, I felt so – how can she allow herself to be humiliated in such a way as a woman. Well, I felt it to be a humiliation, what is not a humiliation for her, if one understands it, her situation, yes? But in that moment the fact was after all that I was seeing it from my vantage point, you know from my own situation and I found that so bad that I said: "My God, how can a woman allow herself to be so humiliated." Do you know, to allow herself to be so degraded. You know that she does what he tells her, yes? And that another woman *accompanies* him, you know that? And then I lit myself a cigarette, and then she asked me whether she despise her. And then I said: "No, I don't do that." Whether I would now despised her. And then I said: "No, I don't do that. She had done it for me, too, because I had behaved in such a funny way." That's obvious, I had or I do behave in a funny way to all women, who have a connection with him, yes? And she wanted so much, because she also liked to be my guest; she wanted so much to be, well, acquainted with me, I think, not friendship, that's perhaps exaggerated, but my obliging her. And I had the cigarette, not five minutes had passed, and then I only said: "I must go now. I must go to work and if you want to stay" – to him – "you can stay". "No. There's no question of that. I'll drive you", although we were there with two cars, yes? And so, we were outside and he only said how wonderfully I had behaved, that I had now neither laughed, nor screamed, nor had I had some kind of hysterical outburst, but that I had not, well, either hurt her feelings by my behaviour, either, for that's how she is and, well, that's her way, and that is not a humiliation. I must say that it also did not, well, excite me sexually either, yes? Really not, although we then went to my place and we *did* sleep with each other. But that was *him* rather than I. Actually it rather turned me off, I would say, more than it turned me on. And, but before, I, we went, as I said, to my place and I said: "Do you know, I have a feeling that I must phone up this woman again and that I must tell her again that I do not despise her, because I am awfully *sorry* for her." Well (*clicks her tongue*), because it still, you know, was caused by *me*, yes? And then I said to her, well, I wanted to tell her again she should not think about it any more. I did not despise her. And, well, she asked me then whether he was with me. Of course I said: "No", because I did not want to hurt her by saying this still. And, as I have said, and, then we also went to – bed, but, I don't know, you know? And well, I then had a kind of breakdown for myself in the evening and cried terribly, because I could not cope with this for myself. It all made me feel sick again that I had said: "Okay, on the one hand I find it terrific of him that he confessed it so openly to me, because few men do that. That means something that a man admits his – true *(clicks her tongue)* how does one say, well, *inclinations*, and stands by it, to his partner or even non-partner, as one wishes to describe us. That this involves a great deal of trust, a lot, actually a very great trust, to disclose this in such a way, because a great many do it *in secret*. Well, because they are ashamed of this facing the partner, they are embarrassed or something like that, yes?" I mean, on the one hand, I thought a lot of him for that. You know, that, that he revealed himself in such a way to me. Because it really takes a lot, I think, an awful lot to do so. On the other hand, I somehow could not cope with it at the time, because I had to cry awfully. I did, well, I did not understand this woman, you know, or the situation, because I had never tackled the fact that women feel *pleasure* in such things, yes? Well, that there is a kind of feeling of pleasure, which I do *not* feel, yes? And that in my eyes they are really humiliated or degraded in this way, which possibly is not at all the case for them, but. And that this goes as far as a kind of bondage to do what such a person tells them to do, yes? That someone comes and says. But perhaps this is because, I don't know, that I also, that I always had my career or so, you know this professional thinking and cannot therefore understand these things, yes? I don't know, well, whether it has something to do with it. (27;71-73)

The Wish for Children

A later section of the interview deals with the question of the wish to have children.

Rachel, dejected, admits that she had a miscarriage only a few weeks before the interview was held.[23] The extent to which the parental experience of persecution exerts an influence in this respect also can be seen from the following extracts from the text. Rachel declares that she would bring up a child from her partner on her own or leave Germany. During the course of the interview she increasingly explains the reasons for this. She would like to spare the child the difficult experiences which she herself had in Germany, she would like to "make something good". She reflects upon the possibility of emigration also for herself, for the overcoming of her own "history". Here, the extent to which the Nazi persecution of her parents influenced Rachel's love relationships becomes quite clear.

Rachel points out emphatically that Rudolf is not Jewish. Although she emphasizes that her partner is not "the typical German" and that his family had also been opposed to National Socialism, yet she cannot prevent herself from seeing him as a German. She could not have done her parents the injury of "having a child from a German". Thus, against the background of

---

23 | Possibly the miscarriage which was only mentioned at a late date of the interview represents one reason for Rachel's original reluctance to participate in the interview.

the miscarriage, the climax of this passage is the remark that she would no doubt have had to have the child "done away with", if her parents had still been alive. Here, too, we find the existence of a putative guilt entanglement on the part of the Second Generation. Rachel would assume guilt if she did not follow the law laid down by her parents in her choice of a partner.

The statement "what does not want to live, does not live" wakes associations with the National Socialist policy of exterminating "life that does not deserve being lived". And this again means that in confronting a love relationship with Rudolf as a non-Jewish German on the one hand and her parents as Jewish survivors on the other hand, associations become virulent, which represent a close bond with National Socialism.

The differentiation drawn by Rachel between her parents as regards their reaction to the relationship with Rudolf would seem to imply that the surviving of a National Socialist extermination camp resulted in greater harm having been done to the mother in comparison with the (admittedly less clear) persecution of her father. However, one must bear in mind that in the line of argument pursued by the interview partner this differentiation can in the last resort be regarded as irrelevant because the father does not appear as an independent, autonomous person. This has been documented above when we mentioned e.g. the symbiotic relationship of the parents. Thus ultimately it is unimportant for Rachel whether her father was perhaps really more tolerant than her mother. The bond with both parents remains the decisive factor, i.e. in particular, the bond with the Nazi persecution of her parents.

K.G.: hm, hm. Do you want to have children?

R.G.: Yes, half a year ago, I did want to have children. And I must tell you that I had a miscarriage four weeks ago. (K.G.: hm, hm) – But I wanted to have the child, I must say this here, if it had been possible, which realistically was *not* the case; I mean, it would have been my *first* child and I am older than forty, which is very difficult. That it should be kept and the job, which I have; I must carry my equipment. And then such a pregnancy cannot take place anyway; I'm not a calm housewife who can lie down at home, yes? So I would never have been able to keep it, because I am not twenty, either. But I had actually said to myself, had it been possible then I would have had the child, because it would have been from a man, whom I – loved, or who was *special* in my life. But I have always made it understood that if I were pregnant, I would bring up the child on *my own*, that is to say, as a single mother.

K.G.: Why was this so important for you?

R.G.: Yes, I can't tell you that, either, well somehow again in being independent.

Well, again, not that, perhaps we go back again. That is to say, in this connection, maybe I am a case for a therapist, eh. Not this family business again! Well, you know, as a *complete* family. (K.G.: hm, hm) Once again, I was against that actually. A *child* yes, *alone*, but not, eh, as a complete family.

K.G.: Was that your first pregnancy?

R.G.: hm, hm

KG.: hm, hm – How then did you experience your, the miscarriage? How, yes, what was it like for you?

R.G.: (*clicks with her tongue*) Yes, it was actually, eh, somewhat painful for me, I must say. – And I also still dreamed afterwards. I mean, from the psychological point of view, I'm still dragging it with me, I must tell you, today after four weeks, because I a) at the moment I cannot imagine anything at all. Actually I am pleased that we had such a row. That we do *not* have any contact, because at the moment I just cannot imagine having sexual contact with him in any fashion; but not only with him, in *general* at present with a man. I assume that it has something to do with it. Well, that I do not have any sexual desires, either. I'm not, shall we say, so oversexed now, either. But in particular, that in any case I have a kind of phase at present in which all that does not interest me so much. Assume that it has something to do, eh, possibly with the whole hormone system or something of that kind. I mean, the pregnancy was right at the beginning. It was in the sixth week. (*clicks her tongue*) And well, – from the rational point of view, I said to myself: "It was not to be. What does not want to live, does not live. And how can you have a child if you have such a job just now. It is not, well, possible." I mean, I would then have organized my life differently. That's what I say, if I then. (*Draws a deep breath*) I did not then definitely know it at the time, either, yes? But had I known that I am now in the third or fourth month, then I would have changed my life entirely. That is to say, I should have taken a normal job, in order to, well, get a certain security.

K.G.: What did you not definitely know at that point of time?

R.G.: About the pregnancy. There were only symptoms. (K.G.: hm, hm) Well, it was still too early. I had gone to the doctor, but then the t-, that thingamajig was still too early in order to find out during the examination. But all the symptoms were there, and – that I am pregnant; and well that it was a miscarriage is also a fact.

K.G.: hm, hm And how did Rudolf react to the pregnancy or to the symptoms of the pregnancy and the miscarriage?

4. EMPIRICAL ANALYSES | 143

R.G.: Well, yes, to the symptoms of the pregnancy, I did not tell him anything, because shortly after I had gone to O. And I had that in O. And from there I called him up, because at the moment I had had the feeling: With whom am I to talk about it? I, he is the only one to whom I could say how bad I feel psychologically. And yes, well, what can he say at all. On the telephone his reaction was: "Oh, my God", yes? Well, I mean, it came so from the heart, from; I mean, well, how can he help or what can he say in such a moment, yes? It is clear that there is nothing, eh (*clicks with her tongue*) there, yes? And – well, yes –. It has to be digested. (K.G.: hm, hm) Although I think, as I have said, then it was not to be! And now I have also got away from it, what am I to say? Well, I should *not* like to try this once more, to become pregnant.

K.G.: What would then have been changed through your, for your relationship if you would have been having a child now?

R.G.: Yes, eh, it would also have been a process of separating from him because I would, eh, to start with have lived a different life, as I have said. I would have had to look for a normal job, in order to, well, eh, have a regular income, in order to first live through the pregnancy. When the child would have been there, for a certain time still also, in order, shall we say, to live a *normal* life to a certain extent and not a life such as I am living *now*, you know with much insecurity. And I also think that, that I would have definitely insisted upon having the child *alone*. Well, I don't know, maybe I would have given up everything also and would have left Germany. I have also thought of that.

K.G.: Why? What would that have had, why, what has that to do with Germany?

R.G.: Yes, because I would perhaps have wanted to make something good for the child that was *not* done for me, *not* to grow up here, *not* to be born here. It was, let us say, one of my trains of thought in which I imagined or, I mean, I do not *know* whether I would actually have done it. But I imagined it, I played with the idea of it. If I, that is to say, before the miscarriage happened, if I am pregnant, if it should definitely all turn out that way; perhaps you will sell everything here and go to Israel or somewhere else and have the child there and will live *there* under different circumstances. (K.G.: hm, hm) Perhaps that was really for me such a – *that* would have helped me to overcome my own history, if I had done that. That is to say the conclusion of a process. Assume that it would have been that and.

K.G.: Now this question does not arise?

R.G.: No, it doesn't arise and eh, (*exhales loudly*) I do not *want* it any more, either. Well, at present, as my mental situation is, I have somehow done with it and the affair is closed. I've said: "The work which I do now, I can do, but *no* pregnancy can continue", yes? I mean, the older you are, the more difficult it is in any case, to become pregnant. So, nothing is so easy, and eh – until I again find that there is a pregnancy, I will again have so very many commissions for photographs, and will have dragged so many things along, that it is again kaput. So, – what for? (K.G.: hm, hm) And very probably, I must tell you, it is not my job to do so in my life, either. That's where I am today, yes? Perhaps I was already there ten years ago or even earlier. That I was unaware of it then, and today I am aware of it. That the job in my life, that is to say, no children, no family, but actually in the first place my profession. And that this is what most probably satisfies me and fulfils me and. And if one recognizes that this is so it is most probably *good*, if one can accept it. That years ago I was unaware of this, and that I am actually today, let's say, more aware of this.

K.G.: And if you imagine, you would now have children, what would be particularly important for you as regards these children?

R.G.: (*clicks her tongue*) If I *had* children it would *indeed* be important for me somehow or other. I think I would be a very crazy kind of mother. Do you understand, well, that I would somehow be perhaps a *super* mother, although I am against this and say: "No, I would not do what *my* mother did." You know, well, this *Jewish* mother. That most probably I would be even worse as a mother and; and that I might perhaps have felt so, well if I had children here, I don't know. I don't know.

K.G.: "Here", what does that refer to?

R.G.: Yes, to Germany. I don't know. Perhaps also after my present experiences, if I were to look back upon them then. I don't know, you know, most of my girl friends have put their children in boarding schools abroad, yes, and they want them to study abroad. You know, they have the financial means. If I didn't have these financial means, I do not know whether I would have been so happy to have children here.

K.G.: Would you think that there would be agreement on these things between Rudolf and yourself?

R.G.: About what, agreement about *what*?

K.G.: Well also precisely, would these things have been important for him too, as regards the children? That they should not actually live or grow up here?

R.G.: Rudolf is not Jewish!

K.G.: Yes.

R.G.: Well, but I must say in this connection that he – and I found that very positive or very good of him, that his family has nothing to do with the past. Otherwise all that would not actually have been possible. That he is not the typical German, either, yes?

K.G.: What do you mean by that?

R.G.: Not in his *ways*, not the typical German. But that when people meet him they do not even think he is, except as regards the way he speaks, that they think he is a Jew rather than *I* or so on. You know, from his ways, yes? And eh, – well, I don't know, eh. Since I could never *marry* him, either, and never be married, but that really it would have to be *solely my* decision, in case of a child, there would be *no* alternative but what I had de-, decided.

K.G.: And if you now had children, what contact would these children have with their grandparents? If, your parents do not live any more, then to *his* parents.

R.G. Yes, only one, that is to say, only his mother is there. And his mother is, in any case; his family was also more or less a socialist-communist family, that is to say, which had not been in favour of the Third Reich, eh, but had been rather against it, yes? And well, as a result, one can say, he also had a different upbringing than most Germans of his age.

K.G.: Has his father been dead a long time already?

R.G.: No, they are divorced.

K.G.: Oh, I thought he was no longer alive.

R.G:. No, no.

K.G.: Both of them are alive.

R.G.: Both are alive, but he was a small child when his parents got divorced.

K.G.: And what is the attitude of his parents to your relationship?

R.G.: Well, his, I do not know his father, and in any case he does not have any contact with his father, either. Most probably that is also one of his problems, I think. Well, (*exhales loudly*) his mother likes me a lot. She would of course be very happy if she knew that he and I, had, let us say, a normal (*laughs*) relationship, such as parents wish.

K.G.: Would that, hm – that's a difficult question to put – but, if you were to imagine your parents were still alive. What do you think, what would their attitude to your relationship be?

R.G.: – Well, ph, yes, I don't know, eh, first, if they were alive, if the relationship had existed, I would probably have kept it *secret* from my parents. If they had got wind of it, well, I must say my father was more tolerant than my mother in that respect. That is to say, I could always speak with my father about certain things, which I could not do with my mother. Well in quite a peculiar, pe-cu-liar way . My mother would have shown absolutely no understanding for this. I am absolutely sure of this. I should have –, let us say it this way, either they would not have known about it or I would have broken this affair off or whatever. Or had it in such a way, that they would *not* have been confronted with it, my parents. Well, because, I could not have done that to my mother, to them.

K.G.: What could you not have done to them?

R.G.: I don't know, eh, if I now, eh, had had a child from a German or with a German. My life would have taken a different turn. Well, I could not have confronted them with that. Well, if I had had the child today and they would have been alive. Well, then I would, if I had not lost it, I would have had to have it done *away* with or I don't know what. Because somehow I could not have done that to them, I must say. Whether these are once again feelings of *guilt* or what, do you know, this bond that we have with our parents as the Second Generation, I don't know. Eh, if my father were living on his own; yes I would very probably have had understanding from *him*, I must say, and tolerance, somehow. That is to say, with him it would have been possible. (K.G.: hm, hm) Not with my mother. And with the combination of both, since she had a very very strong influence on him, in any case not, so there we are. I should very probably not have been able to do that to them somehow, either, I must say – in all probability. Or I would have had to go away from B. in order to live a life somewhere else, of which they would know nothing, let us say. (27;80-85)

Towards the end of the interview, we also speak about Rachel's brother who does not have any children, either. Resignedly, she sums up:

R.G.: And so I assume that our family dies out with us. – Yes, I don't know how I am to see this differently. That we have actually got so far. That is to say, or whether we have unconsciously or consciously got so far that actually our name will finally die out. – Perhaps one can also think about whether it does not also all hang together. (27;97)

Rachel G. can bind herself to a man, from whom separation is also repeatedly experienced. The relationship is a stable one and at the same time it is questioned. This insecurity goes along with a "life on packed suitcases". She does not find it possible to settle permanently in one place. This is also significantly affected by an encounter with a Nazi perpetrator. In the foyer of a theatre in Munich, she overhears a German who boasts of having murdered only *one* Jew. She is unable to defend herself against this man. Later she speaks of *"her* murderer", who killed her illusion, the illusion of being able to defend herself before it is too late.

R.G.: [...] After all, I had said to my parents: "How was it that you could not then defend yourselves? Why did you not defend yourselves? Why did you go along like so many sheep?" Yes, and suddenly *myself,* nineteen hundred, you know, [...] eighty, I am a sheep! (27;43)

The above case description has shown two things in particular: on the one hand, it becomes clear that one can see that there is an extraordinarily close bond between Rachel and her parents against the background of Nazi persecution; on the other hand, it shows that the present love relationship of Rachel is also affected by her origin.

It has become possible to see in what a problematic manner the separation-individuation of the interview partner has been shaped. Aggressive impulses are accompanied by strong feelings of guilt. The denial of aggression is an essential defense mechanism in the family context. Endeavours to achieve harmony with the parents (inwardly and outwardly) serve to strengthen the bond between the generations. In her present love relationship, Rachel finds a possibility of introducing aggression into her life, but in her attitude towards National Socialist persecution, she remains a captive, a circumstance which is of especial relevance in particular against the background of her life which she leads precisely in Germany.

Concluding Interpretation of the Interview with Rachel G.

The "scenic course" of the talk with Rachel G. is characterized by her uncertainty as to whether she should grant the interview at all. She hesitates, wants security, expresses a vague fear and demands that she should inspect the publication "to protect her person", as if she were exposed to danger as a result of the interview. The long interval of time which elapsed after the interview until she requested therapeutic help shows most impressively how closely outside events affect her. A remotely threatening political reality (the First Gulf War) directly affects her private sphere. A political crisis becomes a private one. Much more than can be conveyed by a great many verbal descriptions, this shows how very much a social "buffer" is missing in Rachel's life, a "peer group" – not a nuclear family, but not the big alien world, either – which helps to shield one against real angst. Ernst Hartmann's concept of "thin boundaries" (1991) describes such a state of mind. What does the interview reveal with regard to the genesis of this angst readiness?

The interview begins with the idealization of Rachel's parents, which is a "making good" process. One is practically dealing with a process of identifying the parents with being good. The idealization has something affirmative; it looks like an agreement between Rachel and her parents, which gives one the impression as if it had to be just so and on no account otherwise. The family balance which is produced in this way by including the children in their traumatic experiences serves to render these more bearable for the parents. The price paid for this is the denial of aggression, of the need for vengeance, of depression, and finally of being annihilated. The "making good" does not then involve the family sphere only, but also the non-Jewish German environment. For that reason, Rachel does not speak any more of Nazi persecution, but describes the genocide in less vigorous terms such as "war" and "Third Reich". Presumably when her father speaks of National Socialist persecution and the Stalinist camp in the same breath this also serves to exonerate the Germans and to eliminate aggression.

Even if one later interprets her own symptoms (nightmares and phobias, diffuse fears, etc.) as the expression of a hate that has been inadequately lived and dealt with, Rachel holds on to this family agreement: "On no account inquire what the father's experiences were"; the mother's reports are to a certain extent played down as gossip stories. This shielding oneself from a hostile environment makes it possible to create a "family ghetto" in an environment that is only latently understood as hostile. As a child, Rachel seems to have only rarely heard anti-Semitic remarks.

On the conscious level, too, Rachel gradually discovers that the relations between the parents and the children are too harmonious to be true ("like a Hollywood film"). During adolescence she begins to suffer from being confined and cautiously wants to separate herself. Here the great need for endogamous solidarity now becomes clear: attempts to effect a separation are foiled by her mother's heart attacks. Now the father absolutely wants to die before the mother (and vice-versa), no doubt also because the children who are freeing themselves do not guarantee solidarity any more. Thus the cautious attempts to effect a separation and achieve distance reveal to what a large extent the family was a kind of comforting community. The role of the daughter is that of a self object which served to supplement and preserve the symbiotic feeling of self. Without this comfort and her faithful presence, the traumatized parents could not cope with their trauma any more. Since there is not enough strength for aggression, for vengeance any more, depression is what remains.

What remains open is to what extent this self object significance of Rachel was not inscribed from the very beginning in the modes of object selection. It is a fact that Rachel does not seem able to have a stable love relationship. This would seem to indicate that her faculty to establish a bond was irritated and obstructed at an early date and that this impediment also survives the end of the original family, even her parents' death. Rachel's descriptions and her behaviour towards the interviewer suggest that her ability to engage in a permanent exogamous love relationship has to a certain extent been used up during her childhood and youth, that it has stayed stuck for ever in the original family. For her, a complete family is a group that is fenced off from the outside world, which is organized around comfort and the denial of aggression and the fending off of depression. More clearly even than in her choice of a partner inclined to engage in sadistic practices this can be seen in the problem posed by the wish for children. She does not want a child, and certainly not from a German – at least as long as her parents are alive. The child is, shall we say, a much more precise indication of what a true relationship is. Possibly Rachel is protecting the child from what she has lived through herself. Therefore, in this quandary, she takes flight to a strenuous profession which is not compatible with having a child.

Whilst the parents in spite of their traumatic experiences managed to create a loving relationship which prevented aggression internally and externally (comfort, the partner as a self object, the fending off of depression, and so forth), precisely this is not possible for the daughter any more. The interview provides little information as to why no Jew came into consideration as a partner. But a possible explanation can be derived from the scenic relationship with the interviewer (K.G. speaks with R.G.): for here one can discern that in that case the victim situation of the parents is difficult to accept as an element making for a relationship, for it takes one's freedom away, it places the couple around the trauma and the family with a child around the topic of denial and avoidance of aggression. A relationship with a Jewish partner which is shaped rather by exogamous rules would include the risk that the latter might become a critic, as has also been intimated in the relationship with the interviewer, a critic who understands the denial of what is aggressive and of the wishes for vengeance as being a betrayal of Judaism.[24]

Even if Rachel cannot love a German man and can on no account have children with him, because ultimately he is a representative of those who persecuted her parents, the fact that she has a German friend means that in

---

24 | Horkheimer and Adorno were for instance also exposed to such accusations of betrayal when they returned to Germany.

this loose arrangement with the sadistic qualities he displays he does allow her precisely the amount of freedom she needs and which she can experience in a love relationship. Rachel cannot have a family with a Jew because this fixates the relationship too much on mourning, trauma and incest. But she cannot live in a different, rather "exogamous" relationship resembling a marriage, because this would make her guilty and would possibly mock her parents a second time or represent an arrangement which had always frightened her parents.

As a result, Rachel manages to have a compromise relationship with a partner who is not a "real" German. But her childlessness allows her to say the truth nevertheless, namely that he is a German after all. And so the overall conclusion is that the disturbed love relationships refer back to a history that has not been "worked out": true, Rachel is denied a permanent relationship with a partner with whom she could fulfil her wish for a child. What she can find, however, is a possibility of living her "unfulfilled" abhorrence of Germans in the form of a latent (sexually sadomasochistically tied) hate; but this can indeed only be done fluctuatingly and it is very remote from that intimacy which her parents had established.

Samuel N.

Synopsis of Samuel N.'s Biographical Data

Samuel N. is 40 years old and has no brothers or sisters. After having passed the "Mittlere Reife" (first public examination in secondary schools, usually at the age of 16 years), he went through training at a broadcasting corporation, where he works today as a radio editor. Soon after the birth of his daughter, he married a non-Jewish German woman, who – in contrast to his own mother – did not convert to Judaism. The marriage is a difficult one. He has had many extra-marital relationships.

Samuel's father who came from a Polish family of tailors was the survivor of several concentration camps, and witnessed the murder of several siblings. Besides himself, only a sister and a female cousin survived Nazi persecution. Samuel's mother is German. Her family owned a haulage firm, which supplied concentration camps with raw materials, among them the camp in which Samuel's father was a prisoner.

Later, in connection with their marriage, Samuel's mother converted to Judaism. The marriage, however, was very fragile. Thus, his parents lived separately for a long time. His father lived with his family permanently for a period of only two years. He only rarely spoke of his persecution experiences. He died at home in Samuel's arms, at the age of only 40 years.

The interview with Samuel N. lasted for a total of about seven hours.

Interaction with the Interviewer before and after the Interview with Samuel N.[25]

The interview with Samuel N. was arranged for me by a Jewish organization. Only after several obstacles (e.g. data protection) had been overcome, was I allowed to call him on the telephone. In the course of this call, Mr. N. called my attention to the fact that I was to bring my identity card to the interview. He would make a note of the registration number.

Another female partner for an interview from the same town, whose name had been given to me, had taken back her promise to participate in an interview at short notice and Samuel N. knew about this. Apparently doubts had arisen as to the seriousness of my investigation. The immediate cause of this refusal were doubts about sexuality in the Hahlweg "Partnership Questionnaire" for which I had supposedly not prepared the interview partner.

Samuel N. at first kept his promise. In view of the very long journey to his town, I had decided to arrive there on the preceding evening already. Mr. N. must have tried to call me before his departure in order to also cancel the appointment. However, as he could not reach me, he turned up at the agreed place of the appointment. When we were sitting in the car, he told me that he did not wish to participate in the interview after all. I tried at great length to persuade him to change his viewpoint. My attempts to persuade him seemed to have some success. His attitude changed a little. Now the main obstacle was the lack of the key for the building in which the interview was supposed to have been conducted originally. Unfortunately, it was not possible to procure the key at short notice.

Mr. N. then suggested having the interview in a restaurant; on no account could it take place at his home. Here, again, I was unable to give my agreement to this arrangement. One had to find a place, I argued, in which one could speak without being disturbed. It occurred to Mr. N. to use the place where he worked. I followed him there in my car. Whilst doing so, I had the feeling of being an agent who meets a client, who is at first hostile, in a secret place, in order to then follow him to a further secret place, where the conspiratorial meeting which is planned can really take place. I wondered whether there might really be something in the interview with Samuel N., which had to be concealed, a family secret. Something prohibited seemed to be involved or else it was important not to expose this forbidden something to the light of day.

---

25 | The *Interaction with the Interviewer before and after the Interview* is being reproduced "in the first person", since one's own counter-transference reaction is an integral component of the analyses of an individual case.

At the beginning of the interview, I principally felt how much I depended on the decision of the potential interview partner. I was very much aware of the enormous difficulties I had encountered in finding "experimentees" for my investigation.[26] So I had to repress my annoyance that after complicated negotiations and after having driven a long roundabout way my interview partner told me that he had now changed his mind about the whole thing. Yet at the same time, an intimacy arose between us in this tense atmosphere. Mr. N. trustingly offered to use the familiar "Du" (you) form in speaking with me and ultimately we spent more than seven hours together. Perhaps the important thing for him had been to test whether I was trustworthy. I also wondered whether Samuel's ambivalence in establishing a relationship mirrored a family pattern in which on the one hand a desire to establish contact and closeness and on the other hand the desire to disparage and distrust play a big part.

After the interview, there was an exchange of letters between Samuel N. and myself. He wrote:

> With regard to my marriage I reproach myself for being inconsistent. And this releases enormous feelings of guilt[27] in me. Thus, until now I have had 13 extra-marital relationships (always highly emotional and therefore self-destructive) with other women. Sometimes even two at once. I always had to lie to everybody which involved me in moral conflicts. On the other hand, I did not manage to break up my marriage, either, and to separate from my wife. Whilst I go for closeness to other women for self-confirmation (they were not always beautiful or great in bed, but always interesting and warm-hearted; frequently they also had to cope with problems themselves), I was not able to give up the cosiness and security of my marriage. Somehow I even love my wife and until now I have confessed every infidelity to her sooner or later. She forgave me and remained faithful to me.

Afterwards, he thanked me for the interview.

> You not only listened to me, you have also understood me. Although I was somewhat tired afterwards, but I was also relieved to a great extent.

In my reply to him, I also opened up myself to him by referring to my own problems. This was an attempt to qualify my position as the interviewer to a

---

26 | It took over a year to find the forty interview partners.

27 | Samuel's guilt feelings remind one of the alleged "survivor's guilt" experienced by survivors (thus also by Samuel's father), which recur in the Second Generation as diffuse, often unconscious guilt feelings (cf., say Grubrich-Simitis 1979, Niederland 1980, M.V. Bergmann 1982).

certain extent. And it also satisfied the feeling I had that I wished to return the confidence which had been extended to me by something that corresponded to it.[28]

In a further letter Samuel gave me permission to use his interview for publication. That was "a matter of course". He compares his life with that of the Jews who had been persecuted by the Nazis:

I am in good health, have a roof over my head, I have work and enough to eat and to drink. For our co-religionists these facts would have amounted to paradise during the Nazi regime. I, for my part, am dissatisfied with my fate, with the fact that I haven't enough money to be able to separate from my wife (my daughter is not a very small child any more and I am extremely proud of her), and that there is no other woman who is happy with me and gives me fulfilment.

In a third letter, Samuel talks of a problem central to his identity:

Actually I still don't know who I really am and where I stand. To say it without judging and in an objective way: for the Germans I am a Jew and for the Israelis I am a German. For they cannot imagine how a Jew can live in Germany.

This confusion of Samuel's will have to be made clear in the following description of the interview. Nevertheless, one must rather question whether his confusion can really be reduced to the difference in the attitude of Germans as against those of Israelis.

The Interview with Samuel N.
How Samuel Experiences the Story of the Persecution of his Father's Family

Samuel's father's big Jewish Orthodox family – they were tailors – came from Poland. Nearly all his relatives were murdered under the National Socialist regime. Besides Samuel's father, only an aunt and a female cousin of his father survived the National Socialist annihilation of the Jews. The father's sister

S.N.: [...] only survived by pure coincidence [...]; she had, she was on the way to

---

28 | This touches upon a fundamental problem. My contacts with the interview partners had therapeutic connotations, but were not therapies. They were not supposed to be, either. Thus, I also told them things about myself after the interviews. Ultimately, however, one cannot do away with the one-sidedness that has arisen. Therefore, the interviewer retains guilt feelings about having "used" the interview partners for his own investigation.

Auschwitz and was able to flee, she was given shel-shelter by peasants. Hm. My father in any case w, was really also only an accidental survivor, he eh, shortly before the Americans liberated that camp, they, they had, SS people had beaten him up badly so that he became unconscious and they actually thought he was already dead. But the Americans were then able to patch him up again in hospital. (3;7)

Samuel's father was the survivor of several concentration camps. Like many survivors he hardly spoke about the experiences of his persecution.[29] Nonetheless Samuel knows some details about the National Socialist persecution of his family, and these play a large part in his life. In the following account given by Samuel, we clearly see how he attempts to make it more bearable for him to cope with the reality of the Nazis' sadism in the concentration camps as well as with the unavoidable arbitrariness of survival, whilst others were brutally murdered; he does this by drafting a "hero's story" so to speak, which allows the victims of the persecution of Jews a possibility to become active in spite of the unavoidable annihilation. Samuel's remarks can be interpreted as a defence mechanism against the reality of the annihilation of the Jews, without denying the existence of the Shoah.

S.N.: [...] Well I heard about this, eh, in great detail, how how my, eh uncles and aunts were killed, hm, for instance, they stuck a water hose 'n,' 'n, 'n, in the mouth of a boy and opened the faucet until, until he was, well, dead, and they shot an an older brother and by chance the younger one saw this. Apparently they were both of them in the same camp, and he threw himself upon his brother: so, if you kill *me*, well, if you kill my *brother*, then you must *also* kill me. And of course, they were willing enough to do him this favour, weren't they? And m' my father's model was undoubtedly his oldest brother, also a very strong man, actually they were rather hefty, which I have been able to notice, so, he was also able to survive in the camp until until the end and a S', SS man said to him: "You needn't think that you will survive this here, eh, you haven't a chance, I will kill you, yes?" Then he said: "Listen, then allow me at least that I can at least properly shave once more and that I can still have a bath, then you can kill me." And they really allowed this and when he came, freshly washed and shaved, they killed him. (K.G.: hm, hm) And I find this unspeakable, a thing like that, no? (K.G.: hm, yeah) To bring, that eh. I don't know whether I, whether I, whether I have that inner *greatness* or could ever have it, I do *wish* I had it, but, hm, hm. (3;18)

Samuel says that his father's oldest brother had been his model. His father had always carried a photograph of him with him and it also hung on the

---

29 | In contrast to his father, Samuel's mother constantly spoke about how hard her experiences in the "thirties and forties" had been (3;44-45; cf. also Grünberg 1997).

wall in their apartment.[30] And this uncle is equally important for Samuel himself, for instance when he asks himself whether he would ever be able to behave as he had.

However, it may not only have been his uncle's courage which made him a model. At the same time his father's brother did something in the scarcely imaginable reality of a concentration camp which to a certain extent can be understood as an instance of self-determination. In Samuel's description he also determined the point of time of his death, however absurd this may sound. And moreover before he was murdered he shaved himself. This act would appear to have a profound significance. For according to Samuel, his father's family was very religious. But in accordance with Jewish orthodox tradition, the shaving off of the beard represents a degradation. Under National Socialism the Nazis frequently had fun shaving the beards of orthodox Jews or cutting off their sideburns. But Samuel's uncle deprived the Nazis of such a triumph inasmuch as he himself became active[31] He was persecuted and murdered as a Jew, but at the same time he preserved the "dignity" to decide himself which part of his Jewish identity he wished to retain. And it is precisely this that may have been essential for the fact that he was regarded as a model, both by father and son.

How Samuel Sees his Mother's Experiences under the Nazis

It is much more difficult to evaluate the experiences of Samuel's mother and of her family under the Nazis. The reason for this is that the involvement of this part of the family in National Socialism is difficult to make out. It is possible to consider Samuel's mother as a Nazi sympathizer who did what she was expected to do. She can also be regarded as a *co-agent* whose family as well as she herself ultimately profited from the exploitation of concentration camp inmates. However, she can also be regarded as a brave woman who took the risk of helping a concentration camp prisoner.

Samuel's mother comes from a German-Catholic family, described by Samuel as conservative. Her parents owned a haulage firm, in which she worked as a truck driver. She supplied raw materials to the concentration camp in which Samuel's father was a prisoner. Because she secretly gave food to her later husband he spontaneously married her after the war. "You helped me then; today I help you", said Samuel's father when he led her to the registry office. Samuel's mother converted to Judaism.

30 | The behaviour of Samuel's mother with regard to the uncle's photograph will be explained in a later passage.

31 | The fact that he washed himself must also be understood as an act of self-determination under the conditions prevailing in a concentration camp.

Samuel's Parents, their Wedding and their Marriage

According to Samuel, for his mother to marry a former Jewish concentration camp inmate in the uniform of the American army in post-war Germany must have been a useful step to take. Her story could stand "being subjected to the public gaze"[32] and possibly she took the decision to convert to Judaism for that reason. This, again, had the important consequence that Samuel was accordingly a Jew.

When Samuel was asked to describe his parents, it became clear that they had been separated for a long time. His father only lived permanently with his family for a period of two years. Actually, he had not really known his father. At all events, he had never been given affectionate attention from which he might have profited in his later life.

S.N.: Well, yes, I don't kn, know what kind of a person my father was. Hm, the reason for this is that I saw him too little. Really only for two years over a longer period of time. (K.G.: hm, hm) I was then about 12-14 years old. So he died when I was 14, and when I was 12 he came back to our joint home. During those two years, I got to know him as a truly helpful, merry person who liked to drink, hm (*small pause*), but also as a weak person. He was selfish, unjust, hm, with respect to, of his intelligence he was rather a simple man – he did not really give me anything.

K.G.: What do you mean: he did not give me anything?

S.N.: Hm, yes, well, I would, say, describe that as being a help for one's life. (K.G.: Hm, hm) In every respect. I was just there. He did not bother about me or do anything with me or so on. (3;5)

To start with, Samuel ignores the question about what kind of person his mother was. Later he says the following about her:

S.N.: (*exhales loudly*) My mother (*small pause*). A negative person. Well, a person with an extremely negative attitude to life. Always sensing filth everywhere and behind everything, fearing lies and deception, hm, suspecting treason, having a foreboding of evil. Well, here's an example: I, I say "I'm going to Yugoslavia for my holidays." "Be careful, the roads are so congested, and there are sharks there", and so on. She doesn't say "Okay, go with God, in the name of God, relax and come back well." You would never hear anything of that kind from my mother. Eh – I don't know whether

---

32 | It is conceivable that this story had the function of a so-called "Persil certificate" (proof of denazification) for Samuel's mother.

she was always like that. I knew her, ah, as rather gay in the past. She took part in those drinking sessions[33] in her parents' home, which I can still remember. (3;10)

Thus Samuel also experienced his mother as someone who was not there for him and looked after him, but rather as someone who was unaware of his needs. On the one hand, she is described as mistrustful; on the other hand, at least in earlier days she was open – like his father – to the convivial sides of life. As a boy, Samuel witnessed an instance of libertine sexual behaviour on the part of his parents.

His mother must have been very dissatisfied with her husband, for instance when items of furniture were seized by bailiffs. Moreover, she felt that he oppressed her. In the course of the interview, it became increasingly clear that Samuel himself regards himself as a victim of his parents.

S.N.: [...] In love with life, eh. Mind you, hm, she [his mother] felt oppressed and treated like a child by my father; undoubtedly she was also often disappointed, when, for instance the bailiff came to seize the furniture because once again something had not been paid. But even so, such impressions, like when I once lay in bed in the evening and people came from the, former colleagues from the trucking times and, eh, what they then did I can only guess (*laughs*). Eh – or I do know, once two had a fight over my mother at home, in the apartment. (3;10)

So as to be understood, Samuel wished at first to describe his complicated family history in a connected manner. In the end, he wanted to explain how it was possible for him to arrive at the clearly negative attitude towards his parents which has been described above. He wished to make one understand the background against which it was possible for him to regard himself as a victim of his parents, the fact that he sees himself as a victim.

In the following description given by Samuel, it is possible to recognize which moments of his life determined his development. Possibly one can discern a first indication of Samuel's own problems with alcohol in this passage and in the aforementioned brief pause after the remark about his father's fondness for drinking. Samuel sees both his parents equally as victims. The persecution of his father in the concentration camp and the "odyssey" of his mother during the "chaos of war" are placed beside each other as having almost the same import. This way of seeing things on the part of Samuel is probably principally due to the fact that his mother was one of the few Germans who risked helping persecuted Jews. In addition,

---

33 | Possibly one can discern a first indication of Samuel's own problems with alcohol in this passage and in the aforementioned brief pause after the remark about his father's fondness for drink.

she helped precisely those Jews who were the weakest ones. In contrast to this, the work in her parents' haulage business is described as a necessity. Samuel expresses this by saying that his mother was *forced* to qualify for the permit to drive trucks, because the drivers had been conscripted. Nonetheless, her older sister did not try to acquire this permit.

The parents' marriage to a certain extent marks a kind of compensation; at first, one helps the other one and then the position is reversed. In this context, it seems almost a matter of course that Samuel's mother should have converted to Judaism. She was to be a member of the Jewish people. This represents an unconscious attempt to negate the Nazi regime as regards the actual perpetrator-victim relationship, and to practically negate the persecution which had occurred. It will be seen during the further course of the interview that such a compensatory act can hardly be maintained. Above all, however, it will be necessary to work out the significance which his parents' attitude towards the National Socialist persecution of the Jews finally had for Samuel.

In the following passage, it becomes clear how very important one character trait of his father's, namely an inclination to seek sexual adventures regardless of social conventions, was for Samuel. This is emphasized also by Samuel's first laugh during the interview, when he referred to this. Samuel can find pleasure in these actions of his father. Here he finds a possible way to identify with him.

S.N.: Hm, my father comes from a family of tailors from T., a very religious family, hm, there were eight brothers and sisters and more relatives. My father had *also* learnt to be a tailor in the family business, and was then drafted into the Polish cavalry. Hm, I have heard, but only recently *(laughs)* that there, he was I think a corporal, he fell out of favour because he, well because he was found in the bed of the captain's wife, who had seduced him. Then he was disgraced and demoted. And, eh, then the Nazis already came and put him into the concentration camp. That's where he got to know my mother. Jump[34] – my mother comes from a rather conservative family, she was a Catholic. The parents were Catholics, my mother also and she has a sister. Well her parents had a haulage business [...], truck trailers, two of them. Hm, when my mother was born in 1926, my father was born in 1915, when *(clears his throat)* the drivers were drafted, my mother at the age of 18 had to get a driving permit II with a special permission, and she then drove trucks; my grandfather had been a sergeant during the First World War and he was drafted again during the Second World War;

34 | This "Jump" of Samuel's could be a hidden indication of the fact that he senses that there is a problem here, which appears to him to be insoluble, namely the lack of clarity as to how his mother's family must be actually judged with respect to their involvement in National Socialism.

that was the grandfather on my mother's side, and he then came to Poland and then he seems to have decided that he would rather have the status of a person who could not be spared from work, and, well then went on running his business again. And my mother once, well, she had to sign a declaration that under penalty of death she would never tell anybody anything about what she saw when she visited these camps, because she had to deliver raw material there and collect finished products. Well, she did see that people there, the inmates, were in a very poor state, and she then smuggled, well, food under the seat in the truck-trailer; she then selected the weakest, that is to say, the inmates most in need of the job of unloading the goods and she then slipped them the food. And one of those was my father. (K.G.: hm) Well, then that connection was broken off, my father came then to Mauthausen, and my mother had another odyssey; where they then got exactly during the chaos of war and how or what, wa, wa, I don't know any more. (3;6)

The stuttering at the end of the preceding passage reveals Samuel's own confusion.[35] This confusion may also be connected with the "Jump" in his story which has been mentioned above. Above all, this may refer to the vagueness as regards the involvement of his mother's family in the Nazi regime.

Samuel describes below how his parents met again after the end of the National Socialist regime and married without further ado. Samuel's father then did not leave Germany for his wife's sake – a further link in the chain of his parents' act of mutual "compensation".

S.N.: Well. And it was in 1945 or 46 at some, at some street corner or other in F. My, mother had agreed to meet her parents, that is to say, if it should be any where, we will all meet again in F. My grandparents on my mother's side, they came via Czechoslovakia, what do I know, everything was broken up. And she stood there in F., in F., well with two suitcases and was looking for the home of a distant relative. Well, and then an American jeep stopped near her and a man in an American uniform got out, that is my father, who says: "Well, what do you say, we know each other." Yes. Then my mother had to have papers in order, in order to be able to stay in F., that is to say, a permit of residence and one only got this if one had a work permit and you only got the work permit, if you had a – well, it was that kind of game. (K.G.: hm, hm) Father says: "You helped me then, I help you today." Well, he got her into the jeep and the two of them drove to the town hall and they went to a door and it said "Registry office". And then my mother said: "No, we seem to be in the wrong place here", and my father retorted "No, now the first thing to do is to get married." And so they got mar-

35 | The word for "confusion" in the German text is "verwirrt" and the word for "chaos of the war" is "Kriegswirren"; "wie oder was, wa wa weiß ich nich mehr" (how or what, wa, wa, I don't know any more).

ried. Only with fingers raised and the only personal document a driving license. (K.G.: hm, hm) My father was to be brought to Norway. They took him there because he could not return to his old home place any more, and actually he did not want to stay in Germany any more, either, and so he wanted to go to Norway and he had already taken all the necessary steps. And now he stayed there after all, for my mother's sake. (3;7)

Samuel describes his parents' sad experiences in similar fashion in another passage of the interview. The sufferings of one partner are meant to a certain extent to cancel the sufferings of the other one. The significance of this does not, nonetheless, reside in that there should be *no* suffering any more in the end. The point is rather that the *gulf* between his parents was to be eliminated. This gulf is the difference existing between Jews and non-Jewish Germans as a result of the National Socialist annihilation of the Jews, a gulf which went on existing.

When Samuel was asked about the relationship his parents had with each other, he answered:

S.N.: Yes, well – the right expression for this is chaotic. That is to say, actually, their relationship in my opinion went on as it had *begun*, in extreme circumstances, under extreme preconditions. Eh, – in point of fact they had had no real youth; life had been unkind to them, to both of them, in one way to one of them, in another way to the other one; they now tried to make up for it. (3;17)

Both suffered in their *own* way. The consequence for *both* of them was to want to make up for what they had missed.

Then Samuel described the business life of his parents. They bought a great many businesses and enterprises; but in doing so they experienced many failures. They, too, built up a haulage business, which once again they lost later. Thereupon, his mother worked as a long-distance driver for another haulage firm, whilst his father was employed there as an "odd job man" (3;8). As far as his father was concerned, infractions of the law seem to have been frequent: he "did not take [...] the law very seriously" (3;8). Samuel mentions "shady deals" (ibid.), and later in the interview also brawls. As a result of such a physical dispute, his father was charged with having caused a "bodily injury leading to death" (3;42). Samuel learnt of this when he secretly rummaged through his parents' files containing records of court proceedings. Samuel's secret discoveries and actions[36] also remind

---

36 | On several occasions Samuel described how he made interesting discoveries during such secret prying (cf. 3;21 [postal savings book] and 3;88 [the daughter's letter to Samuel's secret girl friend Elisabeth]).

one of the interviewer's feelings during the interaction with him, when he felt that the interview with Samuel N. was a not quite legal, conspiratorial meeting, in which it was important to keep family secrets (cf. the section *Interaction with the Interviewer before and after the Conversation*).

Childhood

Apart from the explanations given for the parents' behaviour, the suffering which Samuel felt as a result of his parents' neglect now becomes quite clear. Already as a small child, he was looked after by frequently changing persons. After a nanny had left, he was sent to his grandparents; then an aunt took him into her home and finally neighbours or acquaintances looked after the boy. When his mother at last took him back again at the point of time when he started going to school, she took on a full-time job. His father only returned to his family two years before he died, when Samuel was twelve years old. Towards the end of the interview, Samuel repeatedly refers to the difficult circumstances under which his parents suffered. When he declares that what was no doubt important for his parents was to make up for something which had been denied to them in the past, he is trying to calm down and curb his anger and disappointment. This too must be regarded as an attempt on the part of Samuel to deny the fact that his parents had frequently neglected him (cf. the remarks about the parents "mutual making up for the past" made above). The problematic behaviour of the parents is placed in a meaningful context in order to thus make his own suffering under them more acceptable.

At the same time, there are indications that the father attempted to overcome his persecution experiences in a specific manner. Besides the attempt to deny what happened during National Socialism[37] which has already been described, one interpretation of the "making up for the past" mentioned by Samuel on several occasions may be seen to reside in the fact that, as a result of the abolition of all laws governing human intercourse by the Nazis, one should not after such experiences show any particular willingness to *oneself* accept certain social conventions now. This "making up for the past" may then mean not showing any special consideration for the needs or wishes of others, who after all had not helped one in the past either. Finally, one may even consider whether Samuel's father might possibly have been unable to accept his own son as such, because in a certain way he belonged to "the others". This way of seeing things would make Sa-

---

37 | Cf. the "compensation" effected by the parents' marriage which has been described above or the father's remarks about relations with former Nazis quoted below.

muel's neglect by his father understandable to a certain extent. Yet at the same time one can sense a tormenting conflict of identity on the part of Samuel here. To which side does he really belong? To that of the victims or to that of the perpetrators? To the children of those who were exploited in the concentration camps or to the children of those who ultimately profited from precisely this exploitation? To the Jews or to the Germans?[38]

S.N.: No. I had sev, *also*, well to put it precisely, I had, the persons who looked after me were constantly changing. (K.G.: hm, hm) To start with, when my parents were still in F., I had a nanny, and when they could not afford her any more, my grandparents looked after me. Then my grandparents went, these are always my mother's parents, because those of my father were after all dead. (K.G.: hm, hm) But then my grandparents *also* went to West Germany, and my aunt, my mother's sister looked after me. And she also more or less went her own way and then they had to have recourse to the neighbours or other acquaintances or such. (K.G.: hm, hm) I was very often alone at home. Well, actually had little contact with with with other boys or girls of my own age. Well. My mother, when she did come, to start with worked on a full-time job as saleswoman at K. in F., she was then also, she went out of the house in the morning and she only came back very late in the evening. And yet this is also a woman, whom life has bypassed, hasn't it ... (K.G.: hm, hm) ... who did not have much enjoyment during her youth and she then made up for it, no?

K.G.: Yes.

S.N.: She still spent the evenings with colleagues and so on. (3;8-9)

Samuel felt lonely. When he had contact with other children, it hurt him to compare himself with them. The others were much better off. He, on the other hand, was hungry and thirsty. The description of a friend of his father's whom Samuel in the interview at first describes as an SS man, is particularly striking. Later he puts this right, the man had been a parachutist, who, in contrast to his own parents, cared very much for his children. Samuel feels envy and also admires this parachutist.

S.N.: [...] of whom we all knew that he was, well, an SS man, but in some way or other he really knew how to enjoy life. So he always somehow or other, well, yes, there are fellows who, as one says so well can still win something from the dirt under their fingernails. (3;11) [...] Now whether he was an SS man, I don't know, well, he had had training for single combat, he was, no, sorry, he had been a parachutist. (K.G.: hm, hm) Wrong. Somebody else had been an SS man. I'll return to this later. He was a

---

38 | This conflict will be dealt with in more detail later.

parachutist during the Second World War, well quite a hearty fellow. Actually I admired him, what he, because he was actually still worse off than we, but what he did for his children, how he, they actually wanted for nothing and and and I lacked everything, in point of fact, didn't I?

K.G.: Oh yes, hm.

S.N. I really, the Red Cross then gave me things, because we had no money, I had nothing, nothing to drink, I then had the cheapest jam there was, a spoon in wat, a spoon of jam in a glass of water, I drank water from the tap, that's what I drank in the summer, yes. (K.G.: hm, hm) Often I was also hungry. (3;12-13)

Relationship with Samuel's Mother

When he describes his relationship with his mother, Samuel explains how he suffered from the prohibitions she imposed. He hesitates before saying that he did not and does not like his mother. She forbade him to have contacts with other children. These contacts were regarded as dangerous for him. This seems all the more remarkable if one bears in mind his mother's "way of life" (c.f. the "drinking sessions" mentioned above etc., 3;10). A mother who allows her son to witness contacts of an undoubtedly licentious nature with men from her circle of acquaintances (cf. colleagues who fight for her favour, 3;10) at the same time forbids him to have contacts with other children because Samuel would not learn "anything good" from them.

S.N.: To my mother (*small pause*), well (*longer pause*) (*exhales loudly*) difficult, very difficult. Actually I didn't *like* her. For I didn't understand why the children in my class went away on holiday, during their holidays, why they, why their parents had cars, why they made excursions, why they went on school outings, and I was not allowed to take part in them. So, I was not allowed to take part in school outings, I was, yes, occasionally I was allowed to take part in an excursion, but, well, I never went away, if, well, well, well, during my childhood. And I actually remember that, yes, as I have said, often alone, my mother forbade me to have co, contact with other children using the motto: they will only harm you, you will learn nothing good from them. (3.21)

Then Samuel speaks of an experience with his mother which severely shook his trust in her. Without telling him, she took Samuel's savings. Although she promised to do so, she did not even repay him.

S.N.: Well, actually at that time I was keen to buy something for myself and I opened a postal savings account into which I, well, I religiously paid in every penny and deutschmark that I got or earned somehow, well, I saved everything. At any rate, I had saved about 250 deutschmarks and that was actually, I was really proud of this, well, I thought it is quite wonderful. And one day I had again managed to save a small amount and I wanted to pay it into this postal savings book, and I didn't *find* it in the, in the usual place where I always kept it. Thereupon, once, when I was alone I began to look for it and I found it hidden in a handbag of my mother's in her clothes cupboard and it only still had one mark to my credit on it without her having told me that she needed the money or that she had taken it or so on. (K.G.: hm, hm) Thereupon I challenged her and she answered: "Yes, I needed it now urgently, father is in hospital and I haven't any money any more and some time or other you'll get it back". I did *not* get it back. (K.G.: hm, hm) But some of the things I wanted to buy, I could then not buy any more, nothing whatever.

K.G.: Hm, that was a big disappointment for you.

S.N.: Very big. Then I lost, I then lost any trust which I, before, I don't know if I had any, but, but what one might call respect, was all gone. And then I must say that I was *often* beaten by my mother. (K.G.: hm) Well, as I have said, less by my father, but, well yes, he hardly had the opportunity to do so, but very often my mother did. I still know it today.

K.G.: *How* did she beat you?

S.N.: With a coathanger. With a wooden coathanger.

K.G.: Also very hard?

S.N.: Yes. (3;21-22)

Not least as a result of these disappointments, Samuel speaks in a very critical and distant manner of his mother. Whilst filling out the scale dealing with the ties with his parents at the end of the first part of the interview, he remarked:

S.N.: [...] I shall never be willing at any point of time to take my mother into my household; however I would see to it that she is looked after in a suitable old age or nursing home and if need be, I will always bear the cost. (3;48)

Relationship with Samuel's Father

Samuel probably experienced separations during his childhood as traumas. He described such an experience with his father, who came home for the Christmas holidays.

S.N.: Well, he then, he, I was very happy that he had come and it was also very nice and we ate and drank and that sort of thing. And then he had to go away again, or he wanted to go, or whatever, and I didn't want to let him go. (K.G.: hm, hm) So I then, yes, I then locked the apartment door, hid the key, yes. And then they talked and talked to me and so on, that he needed the key and I then also found it or handed it over and then he went away, and I was then very sad. (3;16)

Ultimately, Samuel's relationship with his father is a very ambivalent one. On the one hand, he wanted to be near him, yet most of the time his remarks are decidedly critical. He had been frequently beaten by his parents (cf. above, 3;22).

He had been unable to understand why his father punished him. His father had only given him support once – for a youthful escapade.

S.N.: Actually, I had, well, never felt much for my father, he also beat me, as I think, without having any reason for doing so.

K.G.: Often?

S.N.: Nope, not often, I cannot say often. But when he did so, I didn't know why. Well, I only know that he helped me once, I had as a young boy done something foolish with a neighbour's boy on the street, we'd shot staples on cars driving by, well, you know, that kind of thing, but we did not use any stones, but only small cardboard balls or suchlike. (K.G.: hm, hm) One driver then stopped and chased us, and the other boy could run quicker than I, and he then took me home with him, and my father, he scolded me, but actually he was on my side and said to the man, he should not make such a fuss or something of that sort. That was already a positive experience for me, yes, ... (3;15)

A bit later, Samuel then explains:

S.N.: Essentially my relationship with my father is really marked by his death. (K.G.: hm) And those two experiences of which I have told you, the positive one, when he stood up for me, and the negative one when he went away, although I would rather have had him near me. And then, well, what actually put a great strain on me, the vi, the constant visits to the hospital. He was, yes, he was there for two two years, but you must, you must understand that he would in any case, hm, hm, the man would in any case have spent more than half a year in these hospitals. And I always had to come along ... (K.G.: hm, hm) and I didn't really want to. But one, I, had to come along, yes? (K.G.: hm, hm) And then I saw him lying there, only a shadow of his former self. (3;20)

Samuel describes his father's dying in a very vivid manner. He was the one who called the doctor and his mother for help. In that situation, Samuel was close to his father, but at the same time he must have felt his father's death as if he were being abandoned. However, he was abandoned by a father who had never really been there for him. One feels his mourning and fear, but above all his anger and disappointment.

According to Samuel, his father died as a result of inefficient medical treatment. The final reason for his death was a heart attack. That he died so young, at the age of 49, may also have something to do with his persecution.[39] At that time, Samuel had "prayed to God for my father to live". (3;16)

S.N.: In this connection, I must mention that I can still *very* well remember it, because he, well, he died, if if you can say so, in my arms. I was alone at home then, my mother was at a friend's, well, a a woman from this couple, they had, w w what do I know, they wanted to do their hair or God knows what. My father felt sick, I had just come home from school, the meal was, it was to be warmed and, well, he then felt sick and he lay down, and because I know how, well, well, what one then has to do, because he had already been often ill at home and so on, I rubbed eau de cologne on his forehead, fanned him with fresh air and phoned the doctor and he said, "yes, I'll come, I'll come, but I can't just now. You'll still have to wait a bit" and so on. Then he turned blue and he was gasping for breath and foam came out of his mouth and, well, I actually, *then*, at that moment I was really afraid. (3;15)

S.N.: [...] Well, yes, and then I also phoned my mother since my father was in his death throes, she also wanted to come. Yes, and I do not know any more who came first, whether it was the doctor or my mother, I believe my mother came first. And I still know this much, I went away then, out of the apartment, ran into the street and prayed to God for my father to live. (K.G.: hm, hm) Well – because I didn't know how I could help him in any other way any more, yes? (K.G.: hm, hm). And it wasn't any use then, though, he died on the way to hospital. – Yes, and then the affair was also settled for me.

K.G.: Hm. So, at that point of time you were very close to him.

39 | Cf. in this connection Baeyer, Häfner and Kisker 1964, Medical Commission of the Fédération Internationale Résistants (FIR) 1973, Stoffels 1991.

S.N.: Yes.

K.G.: That is to say, perhaps much closer than before.

S.N.: That's right. (K.G.: hm) – But, as I have said, soon afterwards it had already passed again, yes, then he went, he was gone, well he was dead then, and I can remember, two days later or so I already listened to the Beatles on the wireless again, and I was quite relaxed, that's what I think at all events. (3;16)

In the last part of the sentence one senses that Samuel to a certain extent himself discovers how he may be unconsciously guided by other feelings than those he experiences consciously. Later we will work out that Samuel experiences important repetitions which are intimately connected with the ambivalent relationship with his father.

This shall for instance be documented by sayings of his father's which Samuel quotes and which have remained fixed in his memory. Samuel quotes such aphorisms of his father's four times during the interview (3. and 4. are almost identical, but they appear in different contexts):

1. "You helped me then, I help you today." (3;7)
2. "Don't *you* condemn any German about whom you do not know for sure that he did you harm." (3;17)
3. "You cannot have all the women of this *world*, but you must *try* to do so." (3;26)
4. "You cannot have all the women of this world, but you must at least try to do so." (3;92)

The first saying has already been interpreted above as an attempt to deny the different perspectives of their life which Jews and non-Jewish Germans entertained after National Socialism. The second aphorism can also be understood in this light.[40] The context here is how Samuel's father helped a

---

40 | An alternative interpretation of this saying can be seen in the circumstance that Samuel's father here adopts a moral stance or alludes to an utopia which can contribute to bridging the rift between Jews and Germans: individuals are to be judged in accordance with their personal actions, not just on the strength of their belonging to a group. Nonetheless, this interpretation does not seem so plausible to the author as the one mentioned in the text above. A judgment about what a person has done ought not – if the moral attitude should really be a constant one – be limited to actions which only applied to the person who is doing the judging. But this is precisely what is being said by Samuel's father here and is even emphasized by the repetition of the word "you".

former SS man by giving him food. Samuel is unable to understand how his father could do this. This SS man

S.N.: who was very likeable in my eyes, as I had got to know him, he gave him, although he knew exactly that he *had been* an SS man, he gave him, when this Winkelmann was a student, food or so, when they still owned the shop. Somehow, I never understood this. (K.G.: hm) One day, I then broached the question to him, and he said: "Arno Winkelmann never did *me* any harm, me personally. And he's a decent fellow, so, why should I not help him?" And he said: "don't *you* condemn any German about whom you do not know for sure that he has harmed you, you." (K.G.: hm, hm) So that was also another lesson for me take on my way.

K.G.: What did you feel, then, when your father said this to you?

S.N.: Yes, I found this tremendously inconsistent, no? (K.G.: hm, hm) I could not make any sense of it. Well, well, on the one hand they didn't leave me in doubt as to what the Germans had done to the Jews. Well, I heard all that very exactly, how how my, well, my uncles and aunts were killed. (3;17-18)

So Samuel learns how his father succeeds in building up a positive relationship to a former SS man, by means of a strategy in which he ignored his Nazi past. Samuel himself also feels a certain sympathy for this man. Yet at the same time he senses the contradiction which this involves.

The third and fourth sayings will be interpreted in the following chapter *Adolescence.*

Adolescence

Upon being asked when he first heard of his father's persecution, Samuel remembers incidents when he was beaten up by schoolchildren.

S.N.: Yes, when when I began to be able to understand things. As soon as I was, well, able to under understand the situation they told me.

K.G.: Hm, can you somehow remember, *when* that was, *what* it was like, how you *felt* at the time?

S.N.: (*small pause*) (*exhales loudly*). Not in detail. Hm, I only know one thing still. At, at school, when I first started going to it, they had religious instruction, Christian religious instruction, I could not take part in it.

K.G.: Who said that, that you could not take part in it?

S.N.: My mother ... (K.G.: hm, hm) ... she forbade it, she gave me a letter for the headmaster, and says: My son is not to attend Christian religious instruction, because he is a Jew. (K.G.: hm, hm) And I hm did not then *do* so and I, naturally, since religious instruction was usually, well, during school hours, that is to say, immediately afterwards there were still other lessons, and I had *free* time. And now I hung around either on the school playground or I was in the school's garden, or whatever. And that aroused or incited envy on the part of my schoolmates, schoolmates. "Why is he free and we have to swot up religion here?" (K.G.: hm, hm) That created tension. My schoolmates beat me up and so on, I then felt bullied by them and so on, and I approached my mother on the subject and said "What is the point actually?" And thereupon she tells me, she tells me why and how and so on. Hm.

K.G.: What did she tell you then?

S.N.: Yes, that's just it, you are *different* from the others. (K.G.: hm, hm) You are Jewish and you believe this and that. And not what the others believe, and so on. [...] For the first time, I felt, it was then that I felt the *consequences* of being a Jew. Possibly I had been told that already *before*. (3;37-38)

That is to say, ultimately, the fact that Samuel was Jewish implied suffering and exclusion for him. He did not grow up in a Jewish environment, in which Jewish traditions would have been transmitted to him.

With regard to Samuel's first sexual experiences, these seem to have been influenced by his father's sayings, which have been quoted above. First, he had not known how to deal with the statement that one cannot have all the women of this world, but that one should at least try to do so (3;25). This saying comes to his mind when he speaks of the "upbringing" which his father gave him, i.e. here he speaks about something that he has heard from his father. That he also "learned" it can be seen from his first sexual experiences, which he had with the daughter of an acquaintance of his father's. This acquaintance was a Jew who had also married a non-Jewish German woman. This marriage had (also) broken up quite early. And this man had not been able to look after his daughter properly, either. Therefore, Samuel's parents had for a while taken this daughter into their home.[41]

Samuel was fascinated by this girl. He describes her as a "little tigress" and a "Lolita type" (3;52), who already dressed modishly and went to discos.

S.N.: She was, she was once, she was once at our place, and caused a lot of unrest

---

41 | This is interesting in view of the fact that the means for their *own* son were so limited.

because she did not fit in with the ideas my parents actually had about her. And I found her *good* for precisely that reason.

K.G.: And what was it, what did it mean that she did not fit in with the ideals ...

S.N.: She did not accept anything that one told her. (K.G: hm, hm) She always went her *own* way. And for that reason I *admired* her. (3;53)[42]

What Samuel therefore admired was the independence of this girl who did not observe the prevailing conventions (the rules laid down by adults). That is to say Samuel was able to find approval for his own sexual acts in his father's saying which has been quoted above.

This saying of his father's occurs to Samuel a second time towards the end of the interview when he is asked about recurring sexual fantasies.

S.N.: (*small pause*) Hm, these sexual fantasies remind me very much of my father's saying: "You cannot have all the women of this world, but you must at least try to do so." Try, because because because in reality I cannot do so, so I at least try to do so in my fantasy. So I imagine when I spea', I see a woman or a girl somewhere in the street what it would be like to sleep with her. (K.G.: hm, hm) Or what I like about her or not, sometimes I like her legs, sometimes I like her breasts, sometimes her hair, sometimes her face, I like something or other or I absolutely don't like anything. But, all right, that eh, and then I think: Ooh, hmhm, hmhm, hmhm and so on.

K.G.: hm, hm What sexual difficulties do you have?

S.N.: Actually, none at all. – Really not. (K.G.: hm) I cannot act as I *want* to. I'd much rather fuck around, but marriage forbids this, that is to say, it does *not* forbid it, but it makes it very difficult for me, I'd then have to lie again or so, nope. (K.G.: hm, hm) The possibilities would be there.

K.G.: And you avoid that at present; at present there is no further relationship beside your, your marriage.

S.N.: I wouldn't say that, no, no, no, no.

K.G.: Well, I mean a *sexual* relationship?

S.N.: A sexual relationship just now, no, the oth, the last one came to an end only a

---

42 | Samuel and Martha were still in contact with each other later. However, both of them seem to have given up making attempts to meet again.

few weeks ago, with a woman from whom I had, to be honest, hoped to have more, which did not then come about in this way and since I know what the consequences are if one prolongs something like that artificially, I decided to leave it as it is. (3;92)

Samuel then talks of a somewhat older woman with whom he has very intensive conversations, and about a politician with whom he had "a tremendously intensive sexual experience" during a trip to Israel. (3;92-93)

What Samuel associates in this connection are therefore extra-marital sexual adventures or relationships.

The meaning shared by the four aforementioned sayings resides in the fact that Samuel's contradictory nearness to his father is revealed by them. They deal with precisely those activities in which Samuel does so to speak the same things as his father did. Samuel also married a non-Jewish German woman and he also had close contact with the parents-in-law[43] – this is where the relationship with non-Jewish Germans dealt with in the first two sayings comes into play -; and Samuel repeats his father's behaviour by acting upon the advice given in the other two sayings to actually have extramarital experiences.

Samuel's Love Relationships

The love relationship described by Samuel as his *most important* one is precisely an *extra*-marital relationship with a woman (Elisabeth), whose acquaintance he made in a night bar. It turns out that she is the mother of his daughter's best friend.[44] As a result of this relationship a son was born, whom Samuel never got to know. He was released for adoption without him being informed of this.

But before we go into this relationship in greater detail, Samuel's marriage shall be described. For the discussion concerning his marriage gives us important insights into Samuel's problems with his identity.

At the age of 17, Sam met his wife Anne at a party; today she works as an administrative clerk, Anne was the only one who was not dancing. So the boys had a bet about who would manage to ask her to dance. It was precisely this bet which Samuel won. Laughingly he says that in the meantime he regrets having won this bet (3;57). The devaluation of a woman which consists in having approached her as a result of a wager is expressed by Samuel

---

43 | Samuel's relationship with his parents-in-law will, however, later lead to a serious rupture.

44 | The incestuous character of this relationship is emphasized by his close bond with his daughter. She is also the one who later found out what her father was doing and wished to interfere.

making the ironic remark which brings him to laugh that he meanwhile regrets having won the bet. Samuel describes Anne as a

S.N.: [...] rather unprepossessing girl, hm, averagely intelligent, but honest, faithful, extremely reliable, thinking and acting straightforwardly. – But again intolerant, eh – very moody at that time (*small pause*), humourless, or at least with very *little* humour, no fanta', hardly any fantasy, no charm. (3;57)

Whilst Samuel was at first happy to have at last found somebody, who took an interest in him at all,[45] his feelings for Anne became more and more negative during the many years of their relationship. To start with, however, Samuel found that this relationship gave him an opportunity to rebel against his mother.

S.N.: Ah, I don't know, I simply, eh, acted according to the, eh, in the knowledge that my mother had repressed me long enough and and and and eh kept me away from life. And I now wanted to catch up with this now out of spite and opposition. (3;68)

At the same time, Samuel again sees the chance to "catch up" with something (cf. the "making up" for something on the part of his parents that has been described above). Samuel wants to have an experience of life, which he has been denied in the past. On the one hand, one can here again recognize a repetition of the way his parents acted – both his parents and Samuel make up for something. On the other hand, at the same time Samuel sees a possibility of achieving a separation from his mother. So

S.N.: [...] I seized the very first opportunity to move out, namely to move to my girl friend's. And since then I have been away, I have been away from home. (3;30)

At first, Samuel was very happy about how warmly he was welcomed by Anne's parents. They then lived as an engaged couple with Anne's parents. And later they built a two family house, in which they still live today, with Anne's parents.

Yet Samuel had already separated from Anne and "was together with another girl" (3;46), when he learnt that she was pregnant. It was his mother who then, as against her initial rejection of Anne, urged him to marry

---

45 | The description of Samuel's relationship with his wife reminds one of the way the interviewer took up contact with him, which has been described above. In both cases, we have on the one hand a devaluation of the other person and on the other hand the fact that Samuel is glad if someone takes an interest in him.

her. At the time, his professional career had been very important for him. And

S.N.: [...] precisely in, in in that phase my mother said to me: "You have made this girl pregnant, now you must also marry her. I do not want that anybody should say anything bad about a Jew." (K.G.: hm, hm) "You have the responsibility and I do not want that the child should grow up, I don't know, with people who beat it, who beat each other up, or where it will not be treated well or so on." So well, and then I got married, ... (K.G.: hm, hm) ... at the registrar's. This marriage still exists today, the daughter is meanwhile 18 years old and already out of the house, but perhaps we shall return to this point later. (K.G.: hm, hm) And even today I do not take back this this this reproach from my mother. I hold it very strongly against her that she forced me into this marriage. The *question*, the other question why I *allowed* myself to be forced into it, that is 'nother question. (K.G.: hm, hm) I can only answer this by saying that I was in spite of all still comparatively unable to stand on my own feet then, that my career had priority for me and I said to myself, that is to say, a good friend even advised me "Do not get married!". But I said to myself, at the moment your career is the most important thing for you, the rest will get settled somehow. In addition, it would not be the *first* marriage to be divorced. (3;47)

That is to say the possibility of a separation had already been considered when Samuel decided to get married. It is interesting that Samuel's mother should have spoken of the Jewishness of her son, when she formulated the "moral question" of the decision about what was to happen with his relationship with Anne, to which she had objected before, when she got pregnant. Thus the question of what was to happen with Samuel's Jewish identity, when he decided to get married, becomes significant.

In the passage quoted above, Samuel states that the marriage took place at the registrar's. It is only at a later point in the interview that Samuel is more explicit: in contrast to Samuel's mother, Anne was not willing to convert to Judaism. This means that Samuel had asked her to do so. Moreover, in the same breath he mentions that Anne was absolutely against his contacts with the Jewish community and that this is an important reason for the distance between them. Samuel's evident emotional involvement in this connection becomes clear when he suddenly says he has lost the thread of his thought. That underlines how important this state of affairs is for him. A further meaning implicit in the same figure of speech possibly resides in the fact that in this way Samuel has also lost the thread which bound him to the Jewish community.

S.N.: *Only* at the regis ..., yes, well, my, my Anne had been a Protestant (*exhales loudly*) eh, she was not prepared to convert, she was actually *against* my, my contacts with the

Jewish community, wanted me, that has certainly also contributed a lot to my having detached myself inwardly from her, she did not *want* it.

K.G.: What didn't she want?

S.N.: My contacts with the Jewish community, she wanted me to keep away from it. Then, the Jewish community in F., yes? (K.G.: hm, hm) And, eh, now I have lost the thread.

The further course taken by this part of the conversation is extremely informative. When Samuel is asked whether it had been considered that *he* should give up *his* faith, his emotional excitement becomes even more apparent. It seems almost to annoy him that one should put such a question to him at all. Samuel explains the impossibility of taking such a step by referring to the suffering which he had experienced as a result of his Jewishness. At the same time he chuckles. He wishes to adhere to his faith.[46]

Samuel as Father

Then Samuel begins to speak also of his daughter Andrea, and this is scarcely accidental since the issue is the problem of the continued existence of Judaism after National Socialism. However, it would seem that when Samuel expresses the opinion that the question of his daughter's religious denomination is not so important he is inclined to rationalize. She was not christened so that she might later herself decide whether she wished to adopt a faith, and in that case which one of the two it was to be.[47] In accordance with the Jewish law, she could only have become Jewish if she had converted, since her mother is not Jewish. The decision later taken by Andrea to become a Protestant also appears to be of considerable significance. Samuel vehemently denies that this has resulted in creating a distance between him and his daughter. He idealizes the circumstances when he remarks what a fantastic relationship he has with his daughter. At the same time, one cannot help noticing that no sooner has Samuel made a statement, than he frequently qualifies it. Andrea does not drink or smoke – but

---

46 | Here a reference to his father's oldest brother is again important. As has been shown above, he was not only a model for Samuel's father, but also for Samuel himself. Even when he was about to be murdered, he refused to renounce his Jewish identity.

47 | Andrea's second and third Christian names ought, in contrast to her first one, be probably regarded as rather "Jewish names". So in choosing her names part of a possible Jewish identity had to a certain extent been established.

then she does occasionally smoke. She is a "normal girl" without any problems of any kind – but then he mentions her dyslexia. After Samuel has stressed how "very satisfactory" everything is, he immediately admits that it has not been easy for his daughter and that for some time she also lived in a foster family. The last circumstance to a certain extent shows how crucial experiences are repeated in the following generation. Samuel himself had also been looked after by one person after another when his parents had been unable to care for him.

That is to say, in the context that has been described here one can clearly discern a tendency on the part of Samuel to deny unwelcome realities. One fundamental question which may not be put is the one concerning the continued existence of Judaism in his family.

K.G.: – I only asked you about your marriage with Anne and, because you said, you only got married at the registrar's.

S.N.: Yes, well yes. Yes, well, so she was a Protestant, and for that reason no religious wedding took place, she was not prepared to convert, either. Which I had not *demanded* that she do, either. The daughter ...

K.G.: Did you wish this?

S.N.: What?

K.G.: That she should do so? That she should convert to Judaism?

S.N.: Yes, I'd have thought it *good*, I'd have thought it *good*, but if one does not *want* to do so, one should not be forced to do so.

K.G.: And did *you* consider doing so, changing your faith?

S.N.: Never, nope. (K.G.: hm, hm) In that connection, I already had to take too much upon myself on that account. I can't shake that off by changing my *religion (laughs a little)*. That can't be done. I also want to *stick* to it. (K.G.: hm, hm) Eh, and so, we just got married at the regis, registrar's, our daughter was *not* baptized. We both said, she should once decide herself at a later point of time whether she wished to be a member of a religion or not. (K.G.: hm, hm) And my wife at some later point of time formally left the church, when she found that the the the religious taxes were too high. (K.G.: hm, hm) In that respect she is rather calculating.

K.G.: And your daughter?

S.N.: I made it possible for my daughter to to take part in Christian instruction at school, did *not* forbid it. (K.G.: hm, hm) For there are not any Jews at all where we are, altogether there are only very few Jews in the community. And to that extent I am not not eh sure about the rites and and the customs, so that I might have been able to teach her anything about them. And I would not, would not have known, either, how I could have *convinced* her. So it came about that she had contact with her Christian friends, who took her along to events of some kind and, eh, she also enjoyed going with them to church and so she said, well, she did want to become a Protestant after all. Two months before being confirmed, she was baptized and then she was confirmed. In the meantime, eh, eh, she is also rather slack as regards the church, she only goes there for Christmas sometimes. But that's not *my* concern.

K.G.: You say: "that's not *my* concern". Here, well, I sense a very big distance to her.

S.N.: Yes, yes, yes – nope, to to her *faith*. (K.G.: hm, hm) Eh, and, and, for God's sake, not towards my daughter! She is the only human being, whom I perhaps *really* love. (K.G.: hm, hm) Well, we have a *very, very* close relationship to each other.

K.G.: Can you say something about this?

S.N.: Yes, the this relationship with my daughter is, it is on a reciprocal base. We both love each other very much, we have also said this to each other quite openly and have also written this to each other, and we get on *so* well that we do not *have* to talk about many things at all. We just look at each other and we know what's what and so on. I was also tolerant when she had friends and so on. I was not *at all* jealous then and she is a girl who actually gives me only pleasure, who grows up to be like *this* or has grown up to be like this, well, yes God – so it's been really *better* for her than it was for me, yes? Not because I made it *possible* for her, but – perhaps I also made it partly *possible* for her, because eh she she gives me *only* pleasure. She doesn't smoke, she doesn't drink, she has, well yes, in the meantime she does occasionally smoke, but she's an *absolutely normal* girl! Without any diff, difficulties of any kind whatever. She *did have* difficulties with reading or spelling once for a short while, but that has gone, and that we also, eh, at a point of time when she hm – hm, yes when we were busy *building*, and we were unable to look after her properly. (K.G.: hm, hm) So, there. Nope, but then – and for that reason I do not talk about her so very much, because, that's super, no? [...] She does have problems with the *boys*, because they, eh, all of them like her and she can't offend any of them and she also has several relationships *at the same time*, yes, well, she is very chaotic, but ...

(*Both clear their throat*)

4. EMPIRICAL ANALYSES | 177

K.G.: Hm, hm, but that is something that you, eh, also like, let's say, that is quite good.

S.N.: Hm, hm?

K.G.: That is also something that pleases you ...

S.N.: That pleases *me*?

K.G.: That pleases you, that she is so ...

S.N.: Yes, yes ...

K.G.: that so many boys or men are there, who ...

S.N.: Yes, because we speak openly about it

K.G.: ... are attracted to your daughter.

S.N.: Yes, yes. We speak openly about it, I know them *all*, they also come, they also come home to us and eh, to us, I have also undertaken things with *those* people.

K.G:. hm, hm Yes, would you at the moment like to still add something about this, about your marriage, about your relationship with Anne, about your relationship with your daughter, which is important, what you think, is something missing, an important aspect that we haven't touched upon?

S.N.: Yes, actually, only one: I do not wish to say anything more about my daughter, that is really absolutely satisfactory and it has not been *easy* for the girl, either, because I was often also – *also* frequently absent, but it has turned out well *after all*, yes? We even were, partly we even had to put her in families, in *foster families*, when I was in B. I worked full-time and my wife also, Andrea was there. And then we found a very *good* family who did it. But also only for half a year and since that time, she actually, since her fifth, fifth year she has been always with us. (3;69-72)

Contrary to Samuel's description of things, one can assume that his daughter is also confused about her own identity. In the present context, however, the important point at issue is Samuel, who compares his own life with that of his daughter. For instance, he mentions immediately that in contrast to him, his daughter was allowed to take part in religious instruction. For it was here that we find the cause for the first conflict he experienced in connection with his Jewish faith (cf. above).

Samuel implies how much he missed having grown up in surroundings which would have passed on the Jewish tradition to him when he speaks of the difficulties he felt about what he was to teach his daughter, or could teach her, if she had been open for Judaism. Here one actually feels despair. Samuel sees himself as a Jew, when his environment makes him so. On the other hand, this suffering may have a libidinous component whenever Samuel establishes a connection with the sufferings of his forefathers (cf. his uncle as a model). The reactions of other people are always of essential importance for Samuel.

Samuel's "Crucial Experience" – German or Jew?

Upon being questioned about his contacts with Anne's parents Samuel makes very important statements. He himself speaks of a "crucial experience".

S.N.: The contacts with Anne's parents are eh eh subject to great changes. When I became *acquainted* with them, I admired them, precisely because they gave their daughter everything they had. Although eh, they were refugees who had come over from the German Democratic Republic after August 13, 1961, that is to say, on the last day, the day the wall was built; and they were not financially well off, *either*, but they did everything they could for her. And eh, when I got friendly with her, with Anne, they immediately accepted *me* and integrated me in the family. In their outings, whatever they undertook, and so on. And I also lived in their home after I, eh, had left my parents' home, that is to say I lived with my then fiancée Anne in her parents' house, that is to say in her parents' apartment. Actually I felt very good there and eh, although I knew, well yes, whether her father had been a Nazi, I am not sure about this – no, no, he wasn't a Nazi, he was a soldier. But there was always, *afterwards* it did disturb me, always the those so-called *good Germans*, who who just stubbornly did what they were told. If they had said: "shoot this person", then he would have done it. That is to say, had one said this or the other to the mother, then she would *also* have done it, quite uncritically. (K.G.: hm, hm) And as against this, their flight from from the German Democratic Republic was actually only because because the father of my father-in-law was in very bad shape and they had had high hopes that they would be better off over here or something of that kind; so I don't know, they already *also* had good jobs again and were in better positions. Only much later did I notice that they were very, eh, well very *ordinary* people, who could give me absolutely nothing, and eh, a a a crucial experience was when I was once at home and an acquaintance visited them, that is to say my parents-in-law – oh! You can't be aware of this at all. Eh, when I was then in M., in 1975, my wife and I had decided to do something on our own, to build a house, which we could not, however, have managed to do with our own financial means. And since at that time I still got on very well with my parents-in-law and I

4. EMPIRICAL ANALYSES | 179

also thought to myself: Well, you would rather have *them* in the house than your mother, we said: So, let's put things together and let's build a *two*-family house. On balance, it comes to the same thing, but we save money because they contribute. And so that's how it went, too, we have, I built a house, and they moved into it then. However, there were two absolutely separate apartments ... (K.G.: hm, hm) ... and actually it went off quite well up to a point of time which is also already some years ago, when it was exactly, I do not know; yes, so I was at home during the dinner break, I was lying on my bed in the bedroom and I was having a nap when I heard how my parents-in-law spoke about me with an acquaintance of theirs from B., and then made nasty remarks about my mother and so on. And eh I *didn't* like *that* at all, yes?

K.G.: Do you know what they said, can you still remember this?

S.N.: Yes, they had had said: "yes, she doesn't love him really, it's only a kind of stupid infatuation" and and so and eh "he is not a *real* Jew, either, he is only a *half* Jew" and this and that, yes. And then I was also irritated by them having an acquaintance with whom they are still very familiar today, from S., and this is *certain*, he *was* a Nazi and he is still one *today* and he even *admits* it. And eh, he doesn't want to admit what has been done to the Jews.

K.G.: hm, hm Could we still go back briefly to the situation, when you were in the bedroom ...

S.N.: Yes.

K.G.: ... you heard ...

S.N.: Yes.

K.G.: ... how they talked about you and your mother ...

S.N.: hm, hm

K.G.: ... spoke about them. You said they had said, hm, you were only, not a *real* Jew ...

S.N.: hm, hm

K.G.: ... but only a "*half* Jew".

S.N.: Yes.

K.G.: What would that mean, say, what did that count with them and what does it mean for *you*?

S.N.: I saw it, I saw it in such a way that that they looked upon it as a blemish, that I am a *Jew*.

K.G.: hm, hm That's just it, that is say almost: well yes, he isn't like that, he's not quite *so* bad, he's in point of fact not *wholly* a Jew, but only *half* one.

S.N.: Correct. (3;64-65)

Samuel could also have refused to give his consent, for the interviewer assumes that he had only partly understood the import of this "crucial experience" during the interview. Presumably the point at issue for the parents-in-law was *not* to find Samuel more acceptable as a "half" Jew. The great hurt felt by Samuel may rather reside in the fact that he had been seen by others *not* as a "whole", that is to say a "real" Jew. When his mother's love for him is questioned at the same time – by others –, then this scene touches upon a central identity conflict on his part. We are dealing with the question which has already been discussed above about who Samuel really is, to which "side" he actually belongs. Does he belong to the side of the perpetrators or of the victims? Is he a German or a Jew? In this "crucial scene", Samuel becomes aware of the fact that he is regarded by his parents-in-law, whom he had held in esteem before, as someone who is *between* these groups. On the one hand, they see him as a Jew, but then again he is a German, one who is considered as not "really" belonging to the one group, nor "really" to the other one.

Samuel's confusion is also expressed by the fact that on one occasion he sees his father-in-law as a Nazi, but then again as a soldier, at all events as a "good German" who obeys commands.[48] Afterwards, the Nazi is at least an acquaintance of his parents-in-law. Moreover, it is striking that Samuel suddenly uses the more distant form "Sie" in addressing the interviewer. In the light of the above interpretation of his identity conflict it would have been

48 | The strict distinction between "Nazi" on the one hand and "soldier" on the other must already be questioned. Soldiers could also have been Nazis and perpetrators. The alternative distinction between Nazi/soldier must already be seen as an expression of confusion on the part of Samuel and as an attempt to describe his father-in-law's service in the *Wehrmacht* as unproblematic, in order to avoid examining his actual behaviour. This can undoubtedly be regarded as a typical way of "coming to terms with the past" adopted by a great many non-Jewish Germans (cf. in this connection, e.g. Goldhagen 1996b, Heer 1997, Hilberg 1992, Rosenthal 1997).

logical to feel that the interviewer in this scene belongs to the *one* group. The slip made in using the form "Sie" seems to express the distance which apparently seems appropriate.

Samuel had been "very shocked"[49] about this conversation which he overheard (3;66). "And from that point of time, the contact was, I *radically* limited contacts with the parents-in-law to what was absolutely necessary" (ibid.). Anna "took note of his experience without commenting on it" (ibid.); yet he had hoped to have her support in this.

S.N.: Yes, I had I had I had hoped that she eh *(exhales loudly)* hm, that she would stand by *me*, that she would say: "They can't do something of this kind, and they must be out of their mind" or something like that.

K.G.: And she didn't do this?

S.N.: Don't know any more. Well, she did, I can still remember that she tried to, eh, hm, play it down: "You can't have heard it properly" or "They certainly did not mean it like that" or so. (K.G.: hm, hm) Said: "Nope, that is how they had meant it!" "Hm, well yes." "Eh, yes, man, neither do I know, what, what." In the meantime, she has *also* become more critical towards her parents, which she wasn't before. (3;66)

A bit later Samuel says the following about his parents-in-law:

S.N.: [...] From that point of time, they might as well have been *dead* as far as I was concerned. (3;67)

And all the more towards the end of the interview, when is he asked to complete sentences started by the interviewer, Samuel spontaneously speaks very critically about Anne's parents.

K.G.: hm, hm I have problems with the fact that Anne's father ...

S.N.: ... – well, fought for the Germans.

K.G.: I have problems with the fact that Anne's mother ...

S.N.: ... was always a good German. (3;94-95)

K.G.: I wish that Anne's father ...

---

49 | Cf. In this connection the secret rummaging of files, the reading of a letter written by his daughter and other secret activities indulged in by Samuel.

S.N.: ... may kick the bucket soon.

K.G.: I wish that Anne's mother ...

S.N.: ... may also soon kick the bucket. (3;95)

In this situation, Samuel therefore sees his parents-in-law as Germans connected with National Socialism and wishes them to die.

Extra-Marital Relationship

Finally, the aforementioned relationship with Elisabeth should still be dealt with in detail. As has already been mentioned, this extra-marital relationship is considered by Samuel to be his most important one. This is a relationship that lasted for several years and only came to an end a short time before the interview was conducted. The pain about the failure of this relationship can still be clearly felt during the interview. Samuel had considered divorcing his wife, but Elisabeth did not seem willing to also separate from her husband. Although she had become pregnant by Samuel, she had – without Samuel's knowledge – immediately released their joint son for adoption as soon as he was born, instead of complying with his wish to try a new beginning with him. She had stayed with her family.

Samuel describes Elisabeth as tall, and he loves tall women. She was

S.N.: [...] well, yes, eh she is *not* attractive, but she looks *good*, you know, she is a certain *type*. (K.G.: hm, hm) She looks good. She represents something, so she is not mousily unprepossessing, but she has *tremendously* wonderful brown trusting eyes and a warm-hearted way of the kind I need so much, if I am to be attracted by a woman who must be *warm-hearted*, craving for love, but also able to give love, to give feeling, to show feeling. (K.G.: hm, hm) Moreover, she is what I would describe as a housewife and a *whore*. An, an exemplary mother, who keeps her household ship-shape and who is moreover also still exceptionally attractive sexually. A woman who makes men turn round. (3;78)

In answer to the question what kind of a person Elisabeth is, Samuel replies:

S.N.: Yes, a person who is sociable, just as I am. In the same way, somebody who likes giving parties and likes to be invited, something that Anne does not like *at all*. Anne is very introverted, finds it difficult to make friends, seen in that light we are really not at all *suited* to each other. What is probable, now I do not know why, but Elisabeth is now, eh – somebody in whom I would find the fewest minus points, if I were now, eh, to draw up a list, that may now really sound banal, or, I don't care, I must describe it like that: positive qualities – negative qualities, yes? And then, in the sum total that, for me, the positive would *predominate* in my eyes, yes?

K.G.: hm, hm

S.N.: A caring mother who looks after her children, eh, also with – I know her husband, he is *really* a washout. And she exactly, and that was really what united us so, slipped into marriage just as I did.

K.G.: hm, hm Yes, there is actually, eh, if I see this rightly, there is a similarity between Anne and Elisabeth's husband.

S.N.: Correct. 100 per cent! Both of them absolutely alike, cast in one mould. (K.G.: hm, hm) Only with the one difference that Anne afterwards made real progress so as to please me again and get me back, and her husband did nothing of the sort. (3;78-79)

Samuel thus draws a parallel between his wife and Elisabeth's husband on the one hand and between Elisabeth and himself on the other. Samuel believes that Elisabeth's mother treated her daughter just as his mother had treated him (3;91). So the ideal constellation might have looked like this: Anne with Elisabeth's husband and Samuel and Elisabeth. That possibly incestuous wishes towards his daughter might have found their way in the attraction he felt towards Elisabeth has already been mentioned above. What Samuel wanted to see in Elisabeth is at all events the picture of a woman to whom he can really surrender, who is attractive, but who also looks lovingly after him. Time and time again he contrasts Elisabeth with his wife:

S.N.: I feel very close to her [Elisabeth] in the field of sexuality – and in the field which which which which, yes, I would say, the field of warmth, feeling, a lot gets across. Well, when I was at her place for instance, when her husband wasn't there, she put candles on the table and this and that, everything of that kind, and we prepared a meal together and did it lovingly and danced and so forth, yes?

K.G.: hm, hm

S.N.: I miss something of that kind, yes? Anne, she puts – in the morning she still serves me the coffee cup of the evening before, without in the meantime having washed it up or so, yes? (3;83)

Samuel is desperately looking for a woman who can give him what he missed in his childhood and what his wife now also seems to deny him now: warmth, care, reliability and the acceptance of his Jewish identity. And Samuel is obliged, in the end, to also give up his hopes in the relationship to Elisabeth. This failure is in the end evident in the difference of opinion about Elisabeth's pregnancy and perhaps about an abortion which she possibly had. More and more Samuel feels that he has been cheated; he increasingly loses the trust he felt for her:

S.N.: [...] This trust is comple', hm, then ultimately, it definitely, hm, vanished when she gave the boy away. (3;79)

In a fantasy Samuel states that an abortion did not take place and plays with the idea of taking his son home by finding out where he lives and kidnapping him. On the other hand, he feels how senseless such an action would be, for he could not even be sure that he would be doing something good for the boy if he fetched him.

S.N.: So I would have at first a) to find out where he is b) crop up there at dead of night and c) kidnap him. And this would mean that I would have committed an offence; but I could always get on a roof of a high building with my son and say: if you take him away from me, then I will jump down with him. Nope, then I would *not* do the boy any favour at all, for possibly he *also* likes his foster parents. (3;87)

Once again one can feel Samuel's despair. His hope of living another life is frustrated by reality. When he admits the impossibility of his relationship with Elisabeth in the final part of the interview, he simultaneously confesses something.[50] He mentions a therapy which he had undergone one and a half years ago (3;81). Samuel had had treatment as an in-patient because of a problem with alcohol. That is to say, it was a cure for alcoholism. These had been "the hardest six weeks of his life", but they had also helped him. At the time he had been "absolutely at the end of his tether with his nerves".

In reply to the question what changes the treatment had had, Samuel answers that he had been able to think more clearly and that he had become more self-critical.

S.N.: And ultimately and in the end I am, I am, I, hm, don't drink so much any more, yes? (K.G.: hm, hm) Drink sometimes, as I have said, here[51] now, for instance, or at some celebration, a bit, and was then all, yes?

50 | One is possibly dealing here with the last of the "family secrets", which the interviewer sensed in the course of his first contact with Samuel.
51 | Here Samuel hints that apparently he is still addicted to alcohol.

4. EMPIRICAL ANALYSES | 185

K.G.: hm, hm It stabilized you?

S.N.: Yes. However, how long it will last, I don't know. I still manage, still manage, yes? (3;82)

It becomes clear once more that Samuel is afraid. He would like to change his life and in this connection repeatedly thinks of divorcing. But he also is aware of his limitations. He is

S.N.: [...] a person who can just not be on his own. It's not that I might be afraid of being alone, but I just *cannot* be alone, I'm afraid of this, very much afraid. It is possibly the only thing of which I am afraid at all. (3;73)

Repetitions and Identity Confusion

Instead of being able to engage in separations and make changes, we find repetitions in Samuel's life which can only be understood against the background of his family history. It may be assumed that his father's experiences of persecution led to the loss of his basic trust in other people. Close relationships become a threat if there is no security any more. Other persons can turn out to be persecutors. And they can just as suddenly vanish as reliable partners in a relationship. Such a massive disruption of basic trust can also have far-reaching consequences for the following generation.

In this connection, the history of Samuel's mother is, however, of equal central importance. For the special quality of Samuel's family background resides in the fact that his father to a certain extent married a woman from "the other side". The position of Samuel's mother is ultimately not clear. On the one hand, she is a brave woman who at the risk of her life helped inmates of a concentration camp.

She is a woman who converted to Judaism and at the end also got her mother a place in a Jewish old people's home. At the same time, however, she is also the member of a family which profited from the National Socialist system of the exploitation of concentration camp inmates. For Samuel's grandfather, the carrier firm which was possibly vital for the war effort was also an argument not to be conscripted. Therefore, Samuel's mother was at least indirectly involved in persecution. It is not possible to say to what extent this involvement was a guilty one. At all events, Samuel's mother was a witness. She cannot any more be someone who "knew nothing" of the crimes committed on the Jews.

These experiences of his parents had, to start with, the consequence for Samuel that they grossly neglected the needs of their son. Samuel experienced this as the victim of his parents. From his vantage point he is the one who was more or less at their mercy. With regard to his father, the possibility was broached that he may possibly not really have accepted his own son as a Jew and as his son. Here, the father appears as an aggressor[52] who looks down upon the other person and dominates him. The frequent absence of his father could in this context also mean that he tried to preserve his son from his own even worse impulses. And once again one would have to ask what his mother's position is. Already in the first part of the interview, it is clear how very troubled Samuel is about this point. When Samuel spoke about his father's oldest brother, he mentioned the photo of this uncle which the father constantly had with him and which also hung on the wall in the living-room. After the death of Samuel's father, his mother took the picture down. She felt "pursued" by the "piercing eyes" of this uncle.

S.N.: My mother took it down some day because she could not bear the look of it, she said. She said the man had such, had such piercing eyes, and she felt pursued by these eyes. Then she put the picture away.

K.G.: Did that happen *after* your father had died?

S.N.: Yes.

K.G.: Hm.

S.N.: He wouldn't have allowed her to put the picture away. But I believe we have already got away from the subject we were discussing. Eh.

K.G.: We were talking about your parents' relationship.

S.N.: Yes, my parents' relationship. (*Hiccups*) (3;19)

Samuel gets a hiccup when he speaks of his mother's reaction to this photograph of his uncle, who – as has already been set forth – had a great importance both for his father and for himself. The mother feels that the glance of the persecuted man "pursues" her. Possibly Samuel felt that his mother was a "perpetrator" in this case, as she had been when she took his

---

52 | One should, however, be careful before one applies the defence mechanism of "identifying with the aggressor", because if one ascribes "perpetrator" qualities to the persecuted Jew this can serve the purpose of relieving guilt (cf. in this connection for instance Krell 1984).

savings book without telling him. We may suspect that there is a link with National Socialism on the unconscious level involved here so that the term "perpetrator" is associated with "Nazi perpetrator".

This means that Samuel is in the position of a person who is confused because he cannot find any clarity in the past of his father and of his own self. What identity has he got? Is he a Jew or a German? His experience of the continuity of the past gives him a broken identity. Like his father, he marries a non-Jewish German woman. Like his father, he is on a desperate search for a place where he can settle. Like his father, Samuel also engages in a great many extra-marital relationships in the course of his search.

This continuity of his past can also be recognized in the way certain words occur repeatedly. During the interview Samuel uses the adjective "chaotic" five times to describe relationships (3;17, 46, 61, 72 and 88). One is when he is characterizing the relationships of three generations; then he applies it to his parents' mutual relationship, and to his relationship to Elisabeth and his daughter's relationships. The conflicts of the love relationships involved in each case exhibit a structural similarity. That is to say, the "chaos" is transmitted from generation to generation. In many passages of the interview one can sense how much the entire family attempted to deal with the "chaos" by denying reality – when, say, the victim-perpetrator relationship of National Socialism is denied, in order to as it were undo what happened.

Ultimately, Samuel feels that he is left alone with his conflicts. His parents had not cared enough for him. They had

S.N.: [...] pursued their own interests [...] and I [...] yes, they just brought me into the world. "Now you happen to be there and just see to it that, now swim, now get on!" (3;29)

Finally, Samuel can only draw hope from the prediction of a fortune-teller, who told him that he would get divorced in two years' time and find a woman with whom he would be happy. And his wife would also find another man (3;73-74).

S.N.: [...] She [the fortune-teller] says, she says, I, she quite clearly sees two marriages for me. Even says that to start with, eh, I would live with a woman, but that then, when I am older, between 48 and 49 years old I would get married a second time and this marriage would then be a happy one and it would be absolutely wonderful and that so the second half of my life would be much better, and, moreover, there would even be financial independence. I would be successful in my profession, later then. Eh, n' n' normally I am a very critical person, but I believe this already to this extent, first, because I should like to believe it and *(laughs)* and *(laughs)* second, because she told me some things from my past life quite clearly, things which she could not know, yes? I do not wish to go into this now, it would go too far. (3;93)

Concluding Interpretation of the Interview with Samuel N.

Samuel's history is the history of a member of the Second Generation, which, however, is characterized by various special features. It is above all determined by the circumstance that his father was a survivor of the Shoah and his mother a German who to a certain extent was even involved in persecution. In the First Generation, that is to say, with respect to Samuel's parents, this made it more or less impossible for a core family to be created which is organized to provide mutual consolation and to a large extent to shield itself against the outside world, a circumstance that was considered as a justification for its existence in the case of Rachel G. Rather the story of the persecution was revived and experienced again within the family. The numerous attempts to bring about a compensation and to neutralize what had happened which have been described above were unable to expunge the irreconcilable reality. On the contrary, the gulf between the victims and the perpetrators of National Socialism was only inadequately "covered up" when Samuel's parents got married and his mother took the step of converting to Judaism. Thus, the marriage of Samuel's parents can be considered as an attempt to break with a taboo that finally failed. The marital relationship was doomed to fail, regardless of the individual personal experiences and actions of those concerned. Especially in Germany such a form of "reconciliation" turned out to be impossible and could not work.

Samuel's history, however, is not only the history of a late traumatic development which has been transmitted to the Second Generation by the parents and continues to be effective there. It must, in addition, be seen as a second primary trauma experienced by Samuel. The parents do not appear solely as victims who carry their memories with them and impair their child's life as a result of earlier wounds (depression, physical illnesses, suppressed impulses for revenge) and need their child as an auxiliary ego. The parents' conflicts permeated the family's reality so violently that they did not allow a secure environment to come into being. On the contrary, their son was exposed to a great many dangers. Some things Samuel reported about his father's behaviour (the manslaughter story, his early separation from his wife) at all events indicate possible murder fantasies on the part of his father, even towards his own son. Did he leave the family for that reason and did not care for it at all for many years? His dreadful (early) death in the arms of the helpless boy may have been experienced as a direct repeat of the extermination action that only now came to an end. His mother did not only not protect her son from such fantasies and experiences, but also had an active part in giving him a trauma. When he was a small child, she sent him to relatives, she cheated him financially and confronted him with sexual experiences which overtaxed him.

Seen from that angle, it is at first surprising that Samuel is able to have love relationships, to marry and have a child. With all due caution as regards a diagnosis of his mental conflicts, it cannot be denied that the traumatic consequences seem first to become evident rather in the disturbed development of his personality and of his ego structures and not so much in a fundamental disturbance of his ability to form relationships, as was the case, for instance, in Rachel G. With regard to Samuel, we are faced with an identity problem, with the question as to who he really is; only in the second place does this then lead to problems with his relationships, as seen in his conduct towards his daughter, in his alcoholism and in the way he behaves towards the interviewer.

Samuel seems to try to evade this extremely disquieting identity confusion by idealizing his father, by identifying with his Jewishness and by taking over his life maxims. The ambivalences which are part of this process are painfully covered up, possibly also by a polarizing devaluation of his mother. This appears as an attempt to save himself, which, however, also fails because he never found *lasting* access to a Jewish group, a community and so on. For a certain time, rescue seems to come about with the help of his non-Jewish German wife Anne, who won him in a similarly stranger-kind manner as his mother won his father. Samuel was accepted by Anne and accepted as a Jew. And just as his father helped his mother after the war by marrying her, so Samuel does not let his later wife down, when she becomes pregnant.

Yet ultimately this marriage cannot prevent the breach which has only been patched up – which makes him repeat his parents' attempted taboo violation – from continuing to live in Samuel's fantasies nevertheless. For Samuel's broken identity represents an internal mental conflict, which he carries around like an explosive inside him. Irreconcilable paternal and maternal components cannot be "reconciled". For some time Samuel feels relieved by raising his identity problem upon an inter-personal level by his marriage. He is "wholly" Jewish provided that Anne is "wholly" German. In this fashion she saves him from being involved in an unfinished intra-psychic battle between irreconcilable paternal and maternal components. The intra-psychic tension can now run free in an inter-personal field. Samuel is very grateful to her for this proffered solution, which endows him with a Jewish identity.

However, when this proffered rescue turns out to be a fiction as a result of a "crucial experience", when he has to recognize that he is not seen by the others as a "real" Jew, but only as a "half Jew", Samuel forfeits the recognition of having a clearly defined identity. He becomes somebody who will possibly arouse less compassion or fewer feelings of guilt. The marital relationship breaks down – at least internally. From this point onwards, it seems only possible to engage solely in detached love relationships, such as his father had. Samuel looks for and find a new love relationship (with Elisabeth), which, however, is organized in such a way that it must fail again. The extent to which he feels that his marital relationship is now alien to him is revealed by the fact that he does not want to go to his apartment with the interviewer. He does not want to have to describe his past history in the presence of his wife and of his parents-in-law.

To notice how Samuel has repeated the important events of his family history in his own marriage, right down to the repetition of his own "expulsion", when he farms out his little daughter, is a striking experience. In his fantasies about fetching a fictional son back, he reveals what ties it is at all possible for him to still form: a relationship with a child that has been abandoned by its mother, a pattern of relationship which is very close to the death scene of his father.

When the progress of the interview takes on the character of a conspiracy or of a secret agents' meeting this is not the expression of paranoid tendencies on the part of Samuel. It is more probable that it assumes this form because the theme of the investigation, the person of the interviewer, and Samuel's preoccupation with his longing for a good relationship with his father, for a Jewish identity which he has not yet given up, can find an expression in this manner.

Analyses of Contents

Inductive Formation of Categories (Bond with the Parents)

The categories for the section *Relationship with the Parents*, which the external raters have worked out in their "analysis from below to above" as a result of their qualitative analysis of the entire interview transcriptions[52] are listed below. Essentially the external raters were able to apply the superordinate categories used. In one instance (superordinate category 1.5), the name of the superordinate category remained open, as the raters were unable to decide whether to assign the findings to the category *"caring"* or *"rejection"*. In accordance with the investigated problem, the subsumed categories "disappointment", "neglect", "hurt feelings", and "ambivalent attitude" are, however, to be understood as an *"entanglement"* and their contents regarded

---

52 | There was a total of approximately 4000 pages of interview text to be considered. Each transcription of an interview comprised about 100 pages.

like the categories which have been collected under the superordinate categories 1.1 and 1.3.

In another case (superordinate category 2.5) no designation has been chosen, either. The one category (private experiences with family, profession etc.) which appears here is later counted in the statistic evaluation like the superordinate category 2.2 (confrontation with the covering up of essential National Socialist experiences), since the circumstances of the National Socialist society which are socially relevant are not specifically named. The result of the inductive finding of the categories and classification appears in table 8.

Table 8: *Results of the inductive finding and allocation of categories by external raters for the field "relationship with parents"*

Section	Superordinate Category	Category
1. Bond with Parents	1.1 "entangled" devotion	1. Contacts out of a feeling of duty 2. Avoidance of direct disputes 3. Identification with parents (one parent) 4. Feeling of being enfolded by parents (one parent) 5. Feeling of dependence (financial, emotional) 6. Disunity between the parents
	1.2 "unentangled" devotion	1. Satisfaction with education, positive memory 2. Caring for parents (one parent) 3. Good relationship with parents (one parent) 4. Sympathy and esteem for parents (one parent)
	1.3 "entangled" rejection	1. Debate about education methods 2. Feeling of excessive demands by parents (one parent)
	1.4 "unentangled" rejection	1. Rejection of the parents' personality 2. Distant relationship with the parents (one parent) 3. Rejection of parental wishes (separation)
	1.5 [no designation]	1. Feeling of disappointment 2. Feeling of neglect 4. Hurt feelings 5. Ambivalent attitude
2. Nazi experiences of parents	2.1 Confrontation with	1. Helping Jews 2. Relating of parents' sufferings under National Socialist crimes

	important experiences under Nazism	3. Reports about the war experiences as soldier, post-war period in captivity
	2.2 Confrontation with covering up of important experiences under Nazism	[no assignment made]
	2.3 Silence with clear knowledge about important experiences under Nazism	1. Hesitant and incomplete reports about experiences of persecution
	2.4 Silence with covering up of important experiences under Nazism	1. Incomplete reports about experiences during the Nazi era 2. Parents refuse to talk about experiences under Nazism (taboo)
	2.5 [no designation]	1. Private experiences with family, profession etc.

Inductive Formation of Categories (Love Relationships)

The categories of the section *Love Relationships*, which the external raters have worked out as a result of their qualitative analysis of the contents of all forty interview transcriptions are listed in table 9. In all cases the given superordinate categories have been used.

Table 9: Results of the inductive finding and allocation of categories by external raters in the section of "love relationships"

Section	Superordinate Category	Category
3. Pressure by parents concerning choice of partner	3.1 open pressure exercised regarding origin (religion, national identi-	1. Demand made by parents: Jewish partner 2. Rejection of the partner because of a non-Jewish origin 3. Parents' expectations after marriage with a partner with the same religion

4. EMPIRICAL ANALYSES | 193

	ty) of a partner	
	3.2 open pressure, which has no connection with the origin of a partner	1. Parents' demands on the qualities of the partner 2. Marriage as a result of parental pressure (because of a pregnancy etc.) 3. Interference by the parents in the partnership (criticism, compulsion) 4. Rejection on account of character, because of jealousy etc. 5. Quarrels between the parents and the partner
	3.3 concealed pressure because of a partner's origin (religion, national identity)	1. (decided) approval of the partner because of the same religion 2. Tacit rejection because of German origin 3. Acceptance combined with wish for conversion
	3.4 concealed pressure irrelevant of partner's origin	1. Parents' wishes for a marriage and financial security ("being in good hands") 2. Unspoken reservations because of the partner's social status etc.
	3.5 no pressure	1. Acceptance of partner 2. Lack of interest 3. No interference
4. Conflicts in love relationship	4.1 open confrontation with the issues of origin/ National Socialism	1. Problems on account of different religion as regards joint life perspective/conversion 2. Non-acceptance of the partner's parents on account of their Nazi past or of their religion 3. Difficulties with the upbringing of children on account of different religion 4. Political/religious differences of opinion
	4.2 open confrontation with other issues than origin/ National Socialism	1. Accusations and aggression because of partner's character 2. Quarrels on account of differences of opinion (e.g. upbringing of children, money problems, interests, opinions) 3. Separation because of a new partner 4. Separation because of differing plans for the future/drifting apart 5. Jealousy as conflict issue 6. Criticism of partner's family and friends

		7. Separation for a fresh orientation
8. Feelings of restriction
9. Struggles for power/rivalry
	4.3 concealed confrontation with the issues of origin/ National Socialism	1. Difficulties with partner's behaviour patterns which are attributed to past history (e.g. shouting, socialization)
2. Inner reservations bec. of partner's relig.
3. Feeling of being left along with the upbringing of the children because of the non-Jewish partner
4. The partner does not assume responsibility for Jewish traditions and customs
	4.4 confrontation with other issues than origin/ National Socialism	1. Dissatisfaction with partner's personality
2. Dissatisfaction with sexuality
3. Different expectations concerning the intimacy of the relationship
4. Disappointment about the partner's lack of openness
5. Discrepancy as regards cultural/intellectual/professional level
6. Indirect attempts at separation (journeys, moving affairs)/(thinking about separation)
7. Dissatisfaction because of partner's lack of solidarity
8. Guilt feelings (because of adultery, affairs)
9. Mistrust/breach of confidence
10. Feeling of being misunderstood in the partnership
11. Lack of intensive feelings
12. Unspoken jealousy of other (sexual) relations of the partner (also of child)
13. Inner feelings of distance
14. Fear of intimacy, of being pinned down
15. Symbiotic relationship (lack of freedom)
16. Strong adjustment to the partner's person and interests
17. Disappointment about having no children
18. Difficult external circumstances – secrecy
19. Lack of time for each other because of children
	4.5 no conflict	1. Esteem for the partner
2. Finding understanding for (joint) problems
3. Shared interests (profession, hobby, family)
4. Good contacts with partner's parents
5. No problems or quarrels, contentment
6. Sexual satisfaction
7. Feeling of security, agreement on educational aims

4. Empirical Analyses | 195

Defining Leading Categories for Statistical Evaluation

The inductive formation of categories for the subjects of "bond with the parents" and "love relationships" produced categories, which – as has been shown in the preceding section – could be subsumed under superordinate categories in each case.

Leading Categories are defined below (i.e. one for each section), which should be used to form the leading variables for a further statistical examination of the hypotheses. Such superordinate categories will in each case be collected under these leading categories, in which the Jewish group should have more entries than the control group in accordance with the theoretical considerations.

Entangled bonds with the parents
Here all the categories that belong to Section 1 (bonds with the parents) are collected which fall under the superordinate categories 1.1 *"entangled" devotion*, 1.3 *"entangled" rejection* and 1.5 *(no designation)*. The distinction between devotion or rejection is of no significance for the actual evaluation. The sole point at issue is whether to allocate categories that can be regarded as an "entangled bond with the parents" or not.

Clear knowledge about the parents' essential experiences
under National Socialism
Here all the categories that fall under Section 2 (parents' experiences under Nazism) are collected which have been found in the superordinate categories 2.1 *confrontation with important experiences under Nazism* and 2.3 *Silence combined with clear knowledge of important experiences under Nazism*. The distinction about whether the parents were silent about their important experiences under National Socialism or not is not relevant in the present context. The point here is whether – in spite of whether the parents kept silent or spoke about these experiences – it was clear to their daughters or sons, that is to say, the subjects being interviewed, what their parents' important experiences under Nazism were.

Parental pressure due to the partner's origins
Here all the categories that fall under Section 3 (pressure exercised by parents concerning choice of partner) are assembled which have been found under the superordinate categories 3.1 *open pressure regarding origin (religion, national identity) of a partner* and 3.3. *concealed pressure because of a partner's origin (religion, national identity)*. The distinction as to whether the parents exercise *open* or *concealed* pressure is irrelevant in the present context. The

sole point at issue is the question whether parental pressure was experienced in connection with the religious or national identity of the partner or not.

Conflicts with the partner caused by issues of origin/National Socialism
Here all the categories that fall under Section 4 (Conflicts in love relationship) are assembled which have been found under the superordinate categories 4.1 *open confrontation with the issues of origin/National Socialism* and 4.3 *concealed confrontation with the issues of origin/National Socialism*. The distinction about whether those interviewed confronted their partners in an *open* or *concealed* manner with their origin or with issues of National Socialism is irrelevant here. But admittedly the point at issue here is whether these problems represent contents to be found in the conflicts in their relationship or not.

Statistical Analysis and the Examination of the Hypotheses

At first a description is given as to how far the two groups differ regarding the *absolute frequency* with which the categories occur in the total interview and with respect to each leading question, that is to say, whether one has to take a different base of comprehensive data as the point of departure. In this respect, one will also have to consider the possibly systematically different *duration of the interviews*. Depending on possible group differences, the final definition of variables for the subsequent testing of hypotheses will be made.

A second step will describe to what extent the *relative distribution of the total number of rated responses among the four leading questions* (ties with the parents, National Socialist experiences of the parents, pressure exercised by the parents on the choice of partner, conflicts in love relationships), is the same in both groups. As a result, one can assess whether these four subject areas which were determined by the interview guidelines have been taken into consideration in a similar manner or whether central issues, which are typical of the group involved, have emerged.

Finally, a third step is to "examine" whether the Jewish group really shows more rated responses in the *leading categories* defined in the last section, which deal with the consequences of the parental experiences of persecution in accordance with theoretical considerations (*entangled* bond with parents, *clarity* concerning the parents' important experiences under National Socialism, parental pressure *due to the partner's origins* and conflicts *caused by the topics origin/National Socialism* in love relationships) than the comparable non-Jewish group.

Most of the interviews in the Jewish group required rather more time

4. Empirical Analyses | 197

(cf. fig. 24). In thirteen cases the talks with Jewish subjects required more time than the corresponding pairs; only in four cases was this reversed. From the time aspect, this at least explains why the Jewish participants were able to "produce" more text and that, solely for this reason, there would be more categories in their evaluation.

This extra number of categories can indeed be observed as being not only spread over the entire length of the interview, but also in every individual section (cf. table 10). Altogether 176 ratings less (i.e. on the average just nine per interview) were needed for the interviews of the control group than for the Jewish group.

The *percentage distribution* of all category assignments among the four subject sections which were found by external raters is practically identical in both groups (cf. fig. 25). The conceptual focal point of the interviews was consequently equal in both groups as regards the subject *bonds with the parents* (Jewish group: 40%; control group: 38%) and the section *conflicts in love relationship* (33% and 36% respectively). What is, above all, important, is that the subject *parents' experiences under Nazism* was apparently given the same intensive treatment in both groups (18% and 16% respectively). That is to say, whereas the length of the interviews and the quantity of category assignments resulting therefrom were systematically different, the *thematic interview structure* can be regarded as very homogeneous across groups.

As a consequence of the different number of category assignments under categories which are characteristic for the groups, the four variables (leading categories) for the statistical testing of the hypotheses must be defined for each subject as *proportionate values of the classifications regarding the leading categories involved in the total number of statements of the corresponding section*. Otherwise, if only the absolute number of assignments are used, the Jewish group would achieve higher average values solely as a result of the longer interviews, which involved more material. Regarding contents, this would reflect the percentage of categories e.g. in the leading category *Entangled bond with parents*, which deal with such entanglements, regarding the total number of those categories which focus on what was said about the *Bond with the parents*.

The relation between the Jewish group and the control group in the leading category variables which have been thus defined, can already be graphically derived from figure 26 to Figure 29. Whereas about half the category assignments of the section *Bond with the parents* for the Jewish participants concern "entangled bonds", these amounted to only 29 per cent in the control group (fig. 26). This difference is mainly produced by the difference in the superordinate categories "Entangled devotion" and "No designation", which – as has been set forth above – can be regarded as indicative for entanglement (table 11 provides an overview of the definition of the variables, which have been taken in this manner from the category entries).

Figure 26: Average percentage of the superordinate categories of the section "bond with the parents" in both groups

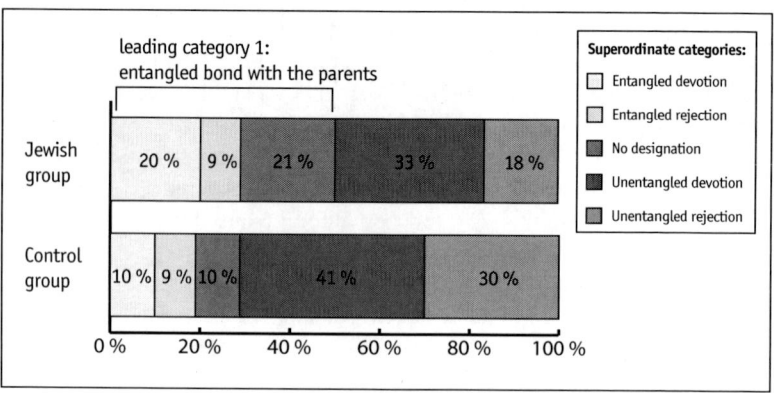

The group-difference is even more distinct in the range of categories dealing with the *Parents' important experiences under Nazism* (fig. 27). On average nine out of ten statements of the Jewish group concerning this subject clearly illuminate the parents' experiences under National Socialism, compared to on average 17 per cent in the control group.

Figure 27: Average percentage of the superordinate categories of the section "parents' important experiences under Nazism" in both groups

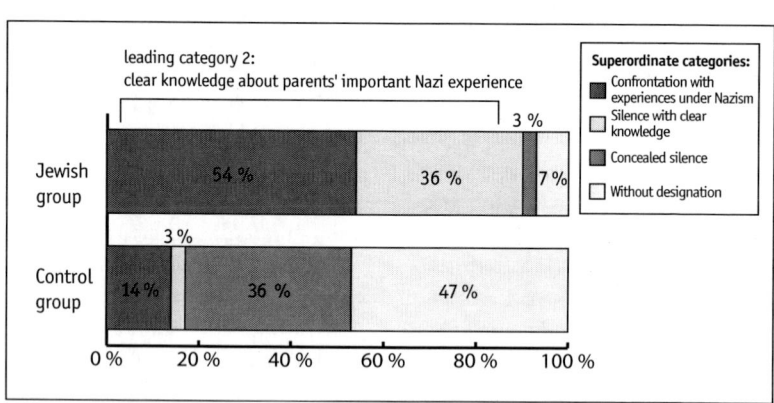

A completely different content can also be determined in the third thematic section dealing with the *Parents' pressure on the choice of a partner* (fig. 28). Whereas interviewees with a Jewish origin give statements amounting to 48 per cent assignable to categories revealing a feeling of – open (36%) or concealed (12%) – parental pressure exercised because of a partner's origin, these practically do not appear in the control group (1% of the statements). All the rated statements in this group dealt with contents in which the parental pressure experienced could not be ascribed to the partner's religious denomination or national origin.

Figure 28: Average percentage of the superordinate categories of the section "pressure exercised by parents on the choice of partner" in both groups

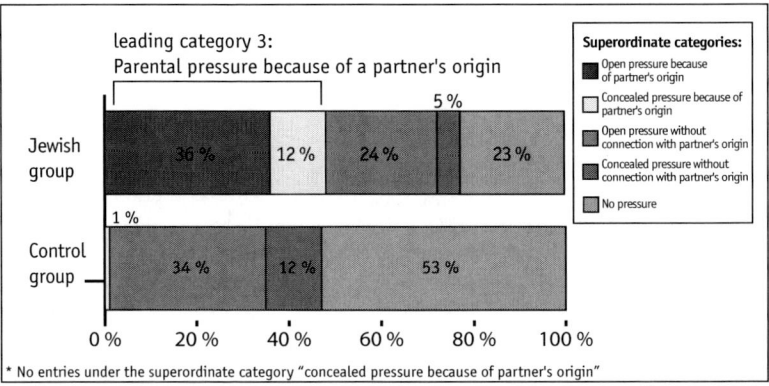

The results of the fourth thematic section, *Conflicts in love relationships*, are structurally similar (fig. 29). Admittedly, in the opinion of the external raters only every tenth rating in the Jewish group dealt with conflicts in love relationships existing or arising as a result of the origin of one of the partners or of the topic of National Socialism. However, in the case of the non-Jewish interviewees *not a single* statement was made regarding this leading category, i.e. all the rated text passages in this field contain statements about conflicts which in the opinion of the raters had nothing to do with National Socialism. That is to say, this topic does not occur at all in this context in the control group.

Finally the differences between the groups with respect to the statements thus rated regarding the leading categories were calculated and the hypothesis formally tested. As expected (cf. graphic representation), the multivariate analysis showed a distinct difference between the groups regarding the four leading categories of interest here, $F(4, 16) = 20.07$, $p < .001$ (table 12 illustrates the univariate effects for the four leading catego-

Figure 29: Average percentage of the superordinate categories of the section "conflicts in love relationships" in both groups

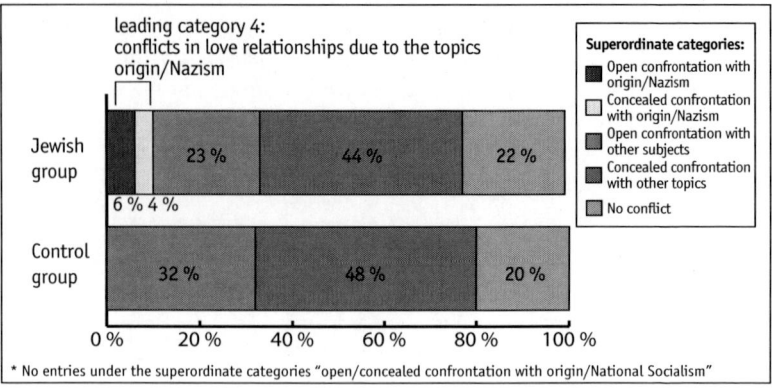

ries, which can all be regarded as significant in accordance to the conventional logic of significance testing).

In the chapter "Reflections on the Strength of the Test and on the Representation of Effect Sizes" we have, however, set forth that the logic of null hypothesis-testing are of doubtful value in the social sciences for various reasons. Therefore, the empirical difference between the groups should also always be classified by means of *effect sizes*, in addition to the results of significance tests. A group-mean-comparison with dependent samples asks for the effect size d_z (Buchner et al. 1996).[53] As a help in interpreting the results, reference is made in the tables below to the conventions introduced by Cohen (1988), in accordance with which a certain effect size (difference of the mean value) can be classified as being *small* ($0.10 \leq d_z < 0.25$), *medium* ($0.25 \leq d_z < 0.40$) or *large* ($d_z \geq 0.40$).

According to this classification, all four mean-differences can be regarded as large. Consequently, the hypotheses can be regarded as having been "accepted" in accordance with which members of the Second Generation of Jews in Germany tend to have *entangled bonds* with their parents and simultaneously to have greater *clarity about their important experiences under*

---

53 | The effect size d_z is defined as the mean value of the differences between the couples, divided by the mean variation of this difference value $\mu_{x\text{-}y}/\sigma_{x\text{-}y}$. The population parameters $\mu_{x\text{-}y}$ and $\sigma_{x\text{-}y}$ are estimated by the random sample values $\bar{x}_{x\text{-}y}$ and $SD_{x\text{-}y}$.

National Socialism than comparable non-Jewish Germans. The same is true for the hypothesis stating that, Jews in post-war Germany experience stronger *parental pressure to choose partners of the same origin* and more frequently attribute *conflicts in love relationships* to the topics *origin and National Socialism*.

Questionnaire Results

The presentation of the results of the data obtained from the questionnaires will be performed in three stages. At first, an examination is made as to whether the Jewish group and the control group exhibit striking differences in the readings of the FPI-R ascertained in the control variable "mental health" (cf. fig. 1). In a second step the principal hypotheses are examined, i.e. the group differences for the "bond with the parents" and "couple autonomy" are examined – on the level of the individual item and respectively for the factor values obtained by the factor-analysis – as well as the group difference in the quality of the love relationship (PFB-values). Finally, the congruence between the results obtained from the questionnaires and those obtained from the formation of the categories regarding contents-analysis (triangulation) is shown.

Comparison of the Groups in the Freiburg Personality Inventory (FPI-R)
The sub-scales transformed by standard nine serve as the basis for the comparison of the participants (cf. fig. 30). A first glance at the mean-profile of both groups suggests the hoped for conclusion that both groups can on average be found in the range without pathological findings (Fahrenberg et al. 1970b, 53), i.e. within the range of the mean 54 per cent of the standard-validation-sample. In accordance with this, both groups would have to be classified as non clinical. However, this examination of the means covers up the fact that a total of 49 readings with extreme values (i.e. Stanine values of 1, 2, 8 or 9) were recorded for 19 interviewees of the Jewish group (out of 240). This was also the case in the control group for 19 interviewees for a total of 37 readings. In other words: The individual results are beyond the normal range to a considerable extent in both groups. But in none of the twelve subscales does the proportion of interviewees with extreme values deviate significantly from those in the control group.

Statistically significant differences between the Jewish and the control group cannot be found in the multivariate mean comparison of the raw scores, either: $F(12, 8) = 1.02$, $p < .51$. All the same, the univariate comparisons between groups (two-sided testing) do suggest that there are interesting differences[54] in the sub-scales "Satisfaction with one's life": $F(1) = 4.06$, $p < .06$, "Excitability": $F(1) = 7.58$, $p < .02$, "Physical ailments": $F(1) = 2.72$, $p < .12$ and in the sub-scale "Emotionality": $F(1) = 2.96$, $p < .11$. This is of significance inasmuch as these four scales are precisely those in which, according to FPI validity studies (Fahrenberg et al. 1970b, 62), subjects of the standard-validation-sample who are *psychotherapeutically* experienced show significantly increased means.

It was set forth that, besides the fundamental reservations about significance testings in such a small sample as is involved here (which has already been mentioned), one may in addition have a problem with the test power and thus come to mistaken judgments concerning the effects. Differences between the groups which are quite considerable will then possibly be regarded as "not significant". With regard to the FPI-scales a slightly modified evaluation results when one uses effect sizes. The mean raw score differences in the scales satisfaction with one's life and excitability must be classified as *large*, those in the scales achievement orientation, behaviour under stress, physical complaints and emotionality as medium and those in the scale health problems as at least still a *small* effect (cf. table 13).

As a result of the examination of the FPI-R scales, one can conclude that constant, marked differences with respect to personality diagnostics do not appear in the sample. Although single pronounced characteristics outside the "non-clinical range" certainly occur, one can on no account speak of a clinically conspicuous sample. In accordance with the test results, one cannot, however, overlook that there is a slight tendency in the Jewish group towards greater physical excitability, a tendency towards psychosomatic disorders and towards a reduced satisfaction with one's life. But, with respect to the question of a clinical versus a non-clinical sample, one should also keep in mind that the samples were – in contrast to the numerous previous studies – neither accessed via clinical institutions nor via non-hospitalized psychotherapy patients and that the statements of this study can legitimately refer to a non-clinical population if only for that reason.

Altogether, one need not fear any threats to internal validity regarding further testing of the hypotheses through the effect of mental health characteristics, as assessed here.

---

54 | For the interpretation of statements concerning significance in this study, reference is again made to pages 103 et seqq. and 156 et seqq.

Hypothesis Testing for Scale "Bonds with the Parents"

The multivariate comparison of the means of all 15 items of the newly designed scale Bonds with the parents shows a clear difference between the Jewish and the control group, which meets conventional significance standards despite the small size of the sample: $F(15, 5) = 5.37$, $p < .04$. When one looks at the individual items (cf. table 14) it becomes clear that markedly stronger bonds with the parents exist in the Jewish group. Very large effects ($d_z > 0.45$) occur, as was to be expected, for the questions concerning the decisive influence of the parents' experiences during the "thirties/forties"; here, the majority of Jewish interviewees has chosen the extreme response category. Further clear differences can be seen in the statements which dealt with the mutual dependence directly felt between parents and interviewees. The Jewish participants of both sexes think it is much more difficult to detach themselves from their parents; they accordingly see themselves as being more dependent, and believe that without them their parents would find it difficult to manage and that they are not well able to find friends on their own. In this respect, the discrepancy or congruence which is to be found between the felt (item 12) and the desired independence (item 13) from the parents is revealing. Since both groups hardly differ in their wish for autonomy, the lesser autonomy that is felt by the Jewish group must simultaneously be interpreted as a felt autonomy deficit, whereas in this respect wish and reality seem to be in harmony for the non-Jewish participants.

With respect to active behaviour, the Jewish group estimates that they are more frequently in contact with their parents than their non-Jewish participants and the bonds resulting from feelings of guilt and worry are in their subjective evaluation here much stronger.

In the chapter on "Scale Ratings for Ascertaining the Bonds to the Parents (R I) and the Autonomy of Couples (R II)" it was explained that the 15 items do not entail a one-dimensional construct "Bonds with the parents". The factor analysis produced two factors which were described as "Bonds with the parents originating from the family history" and as "General bond with the parents", as the case may be.

When taking the factor values into consideration, which can be interpreted as characteristic values of the subjects interviewed for these two "bond" factors[55], we find both multivariate: $F(2, 18) = 39.2$, $p < .001$ as well

---

55 | Factor values are z-standardized variables with a mean value of $\bar{x} = 0$ and a standard deviation of $SD = 1$ in the total sample. In the case of two equally big groups – that is to say in the present instance for the comparison between the Jewish and

as univariate very clear differences. According to Cohen (1988), both the group difference with respect to the bond with the parents originating from the family history as well as that with respect to the general bond with the parents show effect size indices of $d_z = 1.45$ and $d_z = 0.83$ which can be regarded as very large effects (cf. table 15).

Thus the Jewish participants feel more strongly bound to their parents both in general and also specifically as a result of the family tradition than the comparable subjects from the non-Jewish group who were matched with respect to age, gender and profession.

Hypothesis Testing of the Scale "Autonomy of Couples"

The eleven items of the scale Autonomy of Couples are intended to cover the influence of the family of origin and of family tradition on the organization of the present love relationship of those interviewed. The multivariate comparison of mean values in this respect shows – as was already the case for the scale Bonds with the Parents – clearly different circumstances in both groups: $F(11, 9) = 8.42, p < .003$.

The univariate comparisons of the individual items (cf. table 16) plainly show that the Jewish participants of both genders experience the direct and indirect influence of tradition and parental generation on their partner relations much graver than their non-Jewish comparative pairings. Very large effects can be found for four items. The strongest individual effect ($d_z = 1.67$) of all 26 items on the two self-designed scales for bonds with the parents and autonomy of the couples can be found for the question concerning Parental pressure on the choice of partner, which the Jews have on the average experienced as considerably heavier. In addition, it is apparently much more important for the Jewish participants to continue family traditions in the upbringing of children ($d_z = 1.4$), whereby the Partner's religion logically plays a prominent part ($d_z = 1.29$). Corresponding with the item "parental pressure" it can finally be seen that the Jewish participants attach much more value to the Acceptance of the partner by one's own family ($d_z = 0.59$).

Thus, whereas considerable differences exist with respect to the normative pressure to conform and to observe tradition, this hardly seems to have an effect on the daily interactions and contacts with the family of origin. In all the items which deal with the evaluation of such daily contacts, one can discern only very small effects or none at all.

This result is also confirmed when one looks at the group differences

non-Jewish group – the mean values of the groups in the factor values with different signs are, therefore, numerically equally big.

for the factor values, which resulted from the 2-factor solution of the factor analysis of all eleven items which was carried out beforehand (table 17). Whilst the relationship to the partner's family on the level of everyday life is seen as equally good or bad in the Jewish group as in the control group, a very strong effect in the expected direction emerges for the factor "Significance of the family background in the love relationship". The multivariate difference between the groups which can be ascertained: $F(2, 18) = 29.7$, $p < .001$, must consequently be ascribed solely to this second factor.

Hypothesis Testing of the Experienced Quality of the Present Partnership

The general quality of the love relationship has been determined by means of the questionnaire of the PFB (Hahlweg 1996, 19). There, the subscales as well as the entire scale showed satisfactory to good reliabilities. In accordance with our hypotheses, it was expected that the general quality of the present love relationships of the Jewish participants of both genders would suffer as a result of the experiences of persecution under the Nazi regime of the parental generation.

This hypothesis, however, is not confirmed in the present sample (cf. table 18). The multivariate test with the three subscales quarreling behaviour, tenderness and common interests/communication: $F(3, 12) = 0.53$, $p < .67$, suggests the "conclusion" that Jews of the Second Generation in the Federal Republic of Germany by no means experience their love relationships as basically more problematic than their non-Jewish German fellows.

On the contrary: In the total value of the PFB we find a medium effect ($d_z = 0.26$) in the sample in the direction that the Jewish interviewees on average experience their life with the steady partner or husband/wife even somewhat more positively than the interviewees of the control group. This slight "lead" is consistently found, at least in the comparison of the mean values, in all three subscales (cf. table 18).

Compared with the mean values of the non-therapeutic standard sample of the PFB (Hahlweg 1996, 19) both the Jewish and the non-Jewish participants in this investigation experience their love relationships as somewhat less positive (cf. fig. 31). These differences are almost solely due to the higher values of both groups in the subscale "quarreling behaviour" (standard sample: $\bar{x} = 5.4$; $SD = 4.6$; Jewish group: $\bar{x} = 8.1$; $SD = 6.4$; control group: $\bar{x} = 10.1$; $SD = 5.8$).

An ad-hoc hypothesis to explain the absence of a group difference might suggest that in the Jewish group only those interviewees whose partner was not Jewish and of German nationality experienced the quality of their love relationship as worse. As far as the questioned Jewish participants who on the contrary have a non-German or a partner who is also Jewish are concerned, the conflict potential of the "victim-perpetrator opposition" of the parental generation is not at present felt in the present love relationship, or if it is felt, in a much attenuated manner.

But this hypothesis cannot be confirmed by the data available, either. True, the Jewish subgroups thus defined differ in the total value of the PFB and in all the subscales in the expected direction (cf. table 19). Questioned Jews who had non-Jewish German partners experienced their love relationship as somewhat more problematic in all three partial aspects (quarreling behaviour, tenderness, common interests/communication). However, all these effects can merely be classified as "small" according to Cohen (1988) and – what is more important, the Jewish subgroup with non-Jewish German life partners does not show an experience of their partnership, either in the total value or in any of the three subscales, that might be regarded as more negative than that of the control group.

Finally the result that the PFB total scores across pairings are clearly correlated with $r = 0.55$ ($p <.05$) is worth mentioning. As far as the contents are concerned, this means that with the matching characteristics of sex, age and profession, important influence sizes affecting the quality of partnership experiences were already kept constant and that, seen statistically besides this, the issue of the parents' experiences of persecution under the Nazi regime cannot become effective as an explanatory factor for a different experience of satisfaction with the partnership. In other words, the quality of partnership experiences, as assessed with the partnership questionnaire, is related more to the specific background of the subjects questioned with respect to gender, age and social level than to the parental persecution under the Nazi regime and its possible consequences as regards socialization and psycho-dynamics upon the following generations.

Congruence of the Results of the Questionnaire Data and of Content Analysis ("Triangulation of Methods")

The structure of the parental and partnership relationships of the participants of this investigation was operationalized in the present study both by means of questionnaire data and by an analytic summary of the contents of certain passages of the interviews by external raters. The information obtained for each of these two methods (questionnaire and analysis of contents) has been "condensed" in such a manner that in each case four variables finally emerged for the testing of the hypotheses (cf. table 20).

Table 20: Variables for determining the structure of parental and love relationships by questionnaire data and data gained from content analysis

	Method of obtaining data	
	Questionnaire (factor values)	content analysis (variables)
VARIABLES	Bonds with parents due to family history ⟷	entangled bonds with the parents
	general bonds with the parents	Clear knowledge about the parents' experience under Nazi regime
	positive relationship to family of partner	parental pressure due to origin of partner
	Significance of family background in love relationship ⟷	conflicts in love relationships due to topics origin/ National Socialism

Note: Double arrows characterize variables which should cover the same or similar characteristics.

As far as the questionnaire data are concerned, these were the 2x2 factor values which resulted from the two factor analyses of scale items concerning bonds with the parents and the love relationship (cf. "Scale Ratings for Ascertaining the Bonds to the Parents (R I) and the Autonomy of Couples (R II)".

For the data obtained through content-analysis, variables were defined by building leading categories, which determined the percentage of certain allocations in each category for each subject with respect to the total of allocations within a certain thematic topic (cf. table 11).

Hence the question with respect to the triangulation of methods is whether those among the eight variables which according to the idea of the author operationalize the same or at least similar characteristics by different methodological approaches, also do so empirically i.e. whether substantial positive correlations can be found among them. Accordingly high correlations were expected between the questionnaire variable "Bonds to the parents originating from family history" and the leading category "Entangled bonds with the parents" regarding the domain bonds with the parents, and with respect to the domain love relationships high correlation were expected between the questionnaire variable "Significance of the family background in the love relationship" and the leading categories "Parental pressure due to the partner's origin" as well as "Conflicts in the love relationships caused by the topics origin/National Socialism" (cf. table 20).

Looking at the corresponding correlations of the total group, a first glance confirms the assumptions that have been made. "Bonds with the parents due to family history" correlates with $r = .36$ with the leading category "Entangled bonds with the parents", and the "Significance in the love relationship of the family background" correlates even more clearly ($r = .59$ and $r = .52$ as the case may be) with the corresponding leading categories for the topic conflicts in love relationships (cf. table 21).

However, these are not the only clear coherencies in the total group of 40 subjects questioned which can be empirically noted (cf. table 21). Another five of the remaining 13 coefficients between variables to be found in the questionnaire data and those resulting from content-analysis with correlations of $r > .35$ also exhibit substantial correlations even though these cannot be conclusively explained in content. Only the questionnaire variables "General bonds with the parents" and "Positive relations with the partner's family" exhibit lower ($r < .35$) correlation coefficients throughout.[56]

Such a correlation pattern in which all variables related to the experiencing of conflicts in both the love and the parental relationships correlate, irrespective of the method used, rather suggests that these correlations are mainly due to the circumstance that – as was already shown in the tests of the hypotheses – all Jewish participants exhibit high values in these variables and all non-Jewish participants low values. The correlations would accordingly have to be regarded as statistical artefacts produced by the heterogeneous composition of the total group and not due to the fact that the characteristics measured here are identical in contents. In other words: If the questionnaire variable "Bonds with the parents due to family history" would indeed measure something that is similar to the variable "Entangled bonds with the parents" obtained through content-analysis, then it should do so consistently in each subgroup of this investigation.

That this is not the case is confirmed by the results of the analyses conducted separately for the Jewish group and the control group. Quite different correlation patterns which can barely be interpreted result for both groups and, moreover, all the correlations turn out to be markedly lower (cf.

---

56 | Thus, a factor analysis of all eight variables shows a clear 2-factor structure. Only the two questionnaire variables "General bonds with the parents" and "Positive relationship with the partner's family" substantially load on the one factor, whereas all other variables load on the other factor. This result at least clearly shows that there is no pure "methods factor", that, therefore, variables resulting from analysis of contents and from the questionnaire do not consistently load on different factors. Possibly, the one factor can be interpreted as a "conflict" factor, whereas the factor formed by the two other aforementioned variables tends to reflect "daily life and normality" in experiencing the parental and couple relationships.

tables 22 and 23). Moreover, all the subjects questioned in the control group have the value "0" in the leading category "Conflicts in love relationships caused by the topics origin/National Socialism" as well as in 19 of 20 cases regarding the variable "Parental pressure due to the partner's origin". Therefore, it is pointless to indicate correlations for these characteristics which in this sub-group represent constants rather than variables.

The correlation pattern between the leading category variables of the content-analysis and of the scales of the partnership questionnaire (PFB) of both groups seems somewhat more consistent. This pattern suggests that "Entangled bonds with the parents" in both groups are accompanied by reduced "tenderness" and "common interests" as well as by an overall more negative experience of the quality of the partnership (cf. table 24). Moreover, all three PFB scales mentioned correlated negatively in the Jewish group with the data from the category "Parental pressure due to the partner's origin".

This result that entangled bonds with the parents and pressure exercised by the parents on the present love relationship which is explained here by the family history are accompanied by a rather negative experience of the partnership, can certainly be interpreted as a proof of the validity of the the categories built.

The following conclusion can be drawn as a result of the "triangulation of methods". Both methods of to data acquisition – content-analysis and questionnaires – are appropriate measures to clearly show differences between the Jewish and the non-Jewish participants with respect to the experiences of both parental and love relationships of those questioned. Nevertheless, both methods do not measure the same phenomena, even though very similar names were in part given to the variables. Without further investigations with other samples, it is not possible to determine which of the two methods of data acquisition is more suitable to show the structure of the relationships which have been experienced with parents and the partner in a "better" way, i.e. which has more validity. What must once more be emphasized here is that both methods, even if they are perfectly valid, certainly do not show the "objective" quality of relationships of couples or to parents, but at best they represent the quality that has been perceived and experienced by those questioned.

These reflections, however, already lead us directly to a discussion of the contents of the empirical analysis.

5. Discussion, Perspectives

After the empirical analyses have been completed, one has to ask not only how far the hypotheses listed at the end of the third chapter must now be regarded as confirmed or as rejected, which correlations between certain phenomena can be viewed as substantiated on the basis of the results now available and which reasons might be regarded to explain the absence or the corroboration of certain phenomena, but in addition one has to face here the critical question whether it has really been possible to illuminate in essential respects the investigated subject of love relationships of the Second Generation in the Federal Republic of Germany. In addition, one must subject the methodological approach of the study to a critical judgement. In what way have the different methods of investigation contributed to the results? Has it been possible to successfully "combine" the analyses of contents, in which external raters collaborated, with the questionnaire investigations in a meaningful manner? How can the results of the "triangulation of methods" be assessed in terms of the construct validity of this study? And last, but not least, an important question is how the results from the two analyses of individual cases are to be evaluated in this context.

The analysis of contents by external raters which have been made within the framework of the present investigation confirm that the descendants of Jewish survivors of the National Socialist persecution of the Jews are more strongly bound, in the sense of being emotionally entangled, to their parents than is the case with the paired paralleled control group of non-Jewish Germans. This result of the empirical analyses is seen as indicating a disturbance in the separation-individuation process of the Second Generation. Already in their childhood or adolescence sons or daughters of survivors frequently do not dare to distance themselves from their family, to express aggressive impulses or to turn away from parents whom they experience as helpless and dependent on their children. With regard to the closeness to parents, who look for an "replacement" for their former family that was murdered under the National Socialist regime, one must find and maintain an extremely delicate family balance. Wishes for a separation frequently provoke reactions of violent anxiety and severe guilt feelings in the children. Even when they are adults, the descendants also find it difficult to detach themselves from their parents, in order to live their own lives.

These findings do not, however, mean that the participants of the control group are not also "entangled" with their parents and unconsciously bound to them in another sense which has not been investigated here. A conceivable "entanglement" of this kind would for instance exist if the son of a National Socialist doctor would also become a doctor, in order to take over his father's "practice", without recognizing the nature of the inheritance which is actually being assumed. Indications which prompt such reflections arise from the second important result of this investigation: The Jewish group of the investigation showed much more "clarity" and knowledge concerning the actual, fundamental experiences of their parents in the society they were living in during the National Socialist era, whereas the non-Jewish German control group saw itself confronted rather with experiences of their parents in private life which were not connected with National Socialism. Whether these parents maintained silence concerning the truth about their active or passive participation in National Socialism, whether they lied, denied it or tried to be honest, cannot be said. Within the framework of this investigation, such results may at best be inferred from the analysis of individual cases taken from the control group. However, in view of the great amount of work this would have involved, it was not possible to carry out such an operation. In addition, one must ask whether even interviews conducted for this purpose with non-Jewish German parents would have been likely to throw light on such well-kept family secrets as their real attitude and their actual behaviour under National Socialism. Here, it becomes clear that investigations conducted concerning the consequences of Nazi persecution for the next generation fundamentally follow other "rules" than would be the case when one does research on the handing down of National Socialist experiences in non-Jewish German families.

In their love relationships – such was the result of the testing of the third hypothesis – the Jewish group that was investigated experienced stronger parental pressure to choose partners of their own origin. Whether, however, the fourth hypothesis to the effect that specific conflicts caused by origin or by how the issue of National Socialism had been coped with arise in the love relationships of the sons and daughters of survivors as a result of parental experiences during National Socialism, the question whether this hypothesis can also be regarded as having been confirmed cannot be so clearly answered. For, according to the judgments made by external raters, only ten per cent of the categorised statements concerning conflicts in the relationships of the Jewish group can be ascribed to the topic origin/National Socialism. On the one hand, this may be regarded as a small percentage. On the other hand, it can be seen from the comparison between the groups, that practically no statements of this kind whatever were made in the control group. It is thus inferred that there are specific conflicts in the Second Generation in their relationships which are connected with the topics origin/National Socialism. But it remains an open question what conceptual significance and what status these conflicts have for the attitude to love relationships that has been investigated. This would have to be worked out in further investigations.

The results of the questionnaire investigations also largely confirmed the hypotheses. To start with, the application of the Freiburg Personality Inventory assured that one could assume that the precondition of a non-clinical investigation sample was fulfilled. The scale Bonds with the parents that was specially constructed for the investigation revealed a clear difference between the groups investigated here: The Jewish group has markedly stronger bonds with parents. A similar picture also emerged from the group-related testing of the factor values of the two factors extracted by factor-analysis Bonds with the parents caused by family history and General bonds with the parents. The application of the self-constructed scale Couple autonomy also produced quite clear results. The Jewish group experiences the direct and indirect influence of tradition and of the parent generation on their love relationships in a much more massive way than the control group. Nonetheless, the calculation of the factor values for the two factors extracted by means of a factor-analysis Positive relationship to partner's family and Significance of the family background in the love relationship showed that the difference between the groups cannot be ascribed to a more critical relationship of the Jewish subjects questioned to their partners' families, but is due solely to the second factor.

The evaluation of the partnership questionnaire PFB did not confirm the hypotheses. Contrary to our expectations, a lower quality in the partnership was not measured in the Jewish group; the group that was investigated even tended to express slightly more satisfaction than the control group. A more exact analysis of the PFB data rather showed that the social-demographic parallelizing variables sex, age and profession must be taken into account to explain differences in the quality of partnership experienced.

Examining the congruence of the results from the questionnaire data and from the rating of the content-analysis ("triangulation of methods") also casts doubts on some of the investigation results that at first seemed to be so clear. Actually, in view of the availability of meaningful results from different methods one would have expected that those variables would strongly correlate, which purport to measure something that is similar. However, it was not possible to confirm this in this manner. Rather did a correlation pattern emerge in which – independently of the investigation method used – all the variables which are related with the experiencing of conflicts in both the couple and the parent generation strongly correlate. Only the correlations of the PFB scales with the leading categories of the content-analysis produced a result which accorded with what was expected, namely that in both groups that were investigated, "Entangled bonds with the parents" were accompanied by less "tenderness" and "common interests" as well as with a negative experience of the quality of the relationship. This, again, can be regarded as a positive sign of the construct validity of the variables measured here.

Apart from this, a consistent pattern, however, emerged, showing that whilst all methods were able to very clearly differentiate between the research and the control group, indeed different contents were measured with the opertionalized variables that were named quantitatively or qualitatively the same or similarly. Therefore, the categories derived from content-analysis and from the questionnaire scales do not measure the same things.

In spite of these results, the multi-method approach of this investigation need not be fundamentally questioned. Both the content-analysis by external raters and the questionnaires are undoubtedly suitable in order to show differences between Jews of the Second Generation and a non-Jewish German control group with respect to the experience of parental and love relationships of those questioned. However, since both methods do not measure the same thing, further research with other samples would be required in order to clarify which approach can be considered to be "more suited" for which measuring dimension. Moreover, the present investigation made an attempt not to get stuck in certain investigative approaches in order to obtain the desired results with these methods. The attempt was rather made to close in on the subject that was being investigated by means of strongly divergent approaches. "Pure" qualitative methods were combined both with standardized methods of obtaining data and with scales for ascertaining bonds with the parents and couple autonomy that were constructed specially for this investigation. The linking of the deductive with the inductive analysis of the contents in which the external raters collaborated serves to further statistically process information from the comprehensive analysis of contents obtained and condensed in accordance with qualitative rules.

Nevertheless, fundamentally critical remarks are called for. These become necessary above all when the results from the "freely" evaluated analysis of individual cases are related with the "more objective" methods (analysis of contents with the collaboration of external raters and questionnaire methods). Here, we discover the weak points of *both* approaches, which are difficult to "even out" by the other method involved in each case. Whilst in the group-related investigations differences with reference to manifest, more consciously experienced characteristics are examined, in the individual cases one can also ascertain the latent dimension, the unconscious dynamics. The difficulty in answering the question as to how valid the method of ascertaining facts in each individual case can be considered, will now be discussed by referring to one concrete example.

When Rachel G. evaluates the relationship to her non-Jewish German partner Rudolf in the scale of couple autonomy, she ticks the extreme value *"not at all"* for the third item (*how much does my partner's origin trouble me*). She does the same thing for the sixth item (*how reserved am I towards my partner's relatives*). She would also *"very willingly"* leave her child in the care of her partner's parents (item 8). On the other hand, it is *"very important"* for her that her partner should be accepted by her own family (item 4). And she comments the seventh item (*how important is it for me to continue my family traditions in a child's upbringing*) where she has put a tick beside *"very important"* with the sentence: "would be fully brought up as Jews". In view of one's knowledge of the interview conducted with Rachel G., it should not be particularly difficult to discern that the first aforementioned questions were answered as part of her defence mechanisms, in accordance with which she also emphasized that Rudolf was "not a typical German", but that rather his family had been in opposition to the Nazis. As a result, she was able to encounter his family in a very open way. During the further course of the interview, it became clear, however – as has been set forth in the analysis of her individual case – that she did not find it possible to realize her wish for a child in her relationship with Rudolf. In this context, she suddenly stresses that Rudolf is *not* a Jew and that she would have "had" the child "done away" if her parents were still alive. It is quite inconceivable to "have a child from a German". This concrete example clearly shows how important it would be to interpret the subject's "answering behaviour" with reference to the specific history of the individual concerned. This would be possible and enlightening in an individual case. When one makes a comparison between groups, such references can only be taken into consideration if the defence mechanisms would also be operationalized, in order to then measure them as an influencing factor in the total group. If Rachel turned out not to be an isolated case, one would have to question some of the evaluations made with reference to the groups.

To a certain extent this critical view also applies to the question how expedient it was to use the Freiburg Personality Inventory (FPI-R) as a standardized questionnaire method and the Hahlweg Partnership Questionnaire (PFB). The partnership questionnaire in particular refers to the *con-*

sciously perceived behaviour of those questioned, to the quality of partnership that has been *experienced*. The method is mainly used in couple therapies using the behaviour therapy approach. Thus one could in a concrete instance – as has been set forth for Rachel G. by means of the couple autonomy scale – contrast the answer consciously given in the PFB with the love relationship dealt with in the interview. And here too, one would be able to produce comparable results. But here it again becomes clear that this would go beyond the bounds of such an investigation.

Psychoanalytically-oriented questionnaire methods and projective tests for personality diagnoses or for the investigation of love relationships are available: Beckmann and Richter's Giessen Test (GT), the Rorschach Test, the Thematic Apperception Test (TAT) in accordance with Murray, the Rosenzweig Picture Frustration Test or the Object Relations Technique according to Phillipson, and numerous other procedures. However, ultimately, the selection of the standardized methods for the present investigation also had a connection with the behavioural orientation of the Department of Psychology of the University of Marburg. Similar considerations apply to the conduct of the interview itself. Without a sound psychoanalytic training – this refers to the training stage of the interviewer at the point of time when the study was made – it was hardly possible to conduct psychoanalytic interviews in the narrow sense of the word. For these reasons, today other possibilities would exist of raising the topics of the unconscious predetermination of bonds with the parents and of conflicts in love relationships already during the interview itself and it would be possible to analyse how one should deal with interpretations in the context of transference and countertransference. Yet, although one must admit the limits of the present investigation both with regard to the methods of ascertaining facts which were selected and with regard to the conduct of the interviews, it nonetheless proved possible – in particular, as far as the analysis of the individual cases was involved – to work out a number of remarkable results and structures by means of this study.

When one looked at the existing bonds with the parents, the knowledge about the parents' experiences during National Socialism, the pressure exercised by the parents with regard to the choice of a partner and at the existence of specific conflicts in their love relationships, the present study enabled one in a multi-methodological approach to show how different the realities of the Second Generation appear in comparison with those of a non-Jewish parallel group. Admittedly, only the exact analysis of individual cases provides insight into the manner in which the parental trauma is passed on in each case. Here, important differences emerged depending on which partner the parents had in each case.

In spite of the small size of the sample, the empirical findings noted in the description of the sample, can show what are at least indications of the special difficulties experienced by Jews of the Second Generation in their love relationships with non-Jews, and in this connection, in particular, with German partners. It is to be regretted that corresponding data were not available for the total group of the Second Generation living in Germany. For, upon looking at the nationality and religious denomination of the partners of the Jewish interviewees of this study, it strikes one that – in spite of living in this country – only eight of the 15 partners are not Jewish and German. And moreover, it strikes one that again only eight of the 15 Jewish couples live with their partners (compared to 13 of 17 couples in the control group). An even more differentiated picture results upon noting that of the ten Jews, who have a non-Jewish partner, only three live with them, whereas all five Jews, who have Jewish partners, share their home with these partners. In addition, it was found that only three out of ten Jews with non-Jewish partners have children, whilst this is the case in four out of five Jews with Jewish partners.

Roughly all this is evidence of something that was to be worked out in the analyses of individual cases as the personal pattern of coping with the parents' experiences of persecution and with one's own life in Germany after National Socialism. Unfortunately, it was not possible in the framework of this investigation to effect further individual analyses besides those that have been made. But already the interviews with Rachel G. and Samuel N. made it possible to work out the methods of coping with the parents' persecution which emerged in the talks conducted to such an extent that one was able to recognize specific mechanisms of handing down the trauma.

The analysis of the interview with Rachel G. deals with survivor couples in the parents' generation of those questioned who were only able to secure their life *after* the Shoah as long as they had a partner who had essentially been exposed to the same trauma of persecution. The children were necessary in order to open up the hope of a future perspective – in spite of the genocide – for the few "who were left" and in order to support them in bearing their difficult fate and not leave them alone. A marriage that was internally symbiotic and simultaneously established a blockade against the outside world resulted in the handing down of a trauma, which might be conceptualized as a return of a *supposed* survivor guilt of the parents in the form of guilt regarding separation on the part of their daughters and sons. Every attempt by the children to distance or separate themselves then jeopardizes an extremely delicate family balance. Children are needed here as self objects in order to symbiotically supplement and preserve the self. Such families to a certain extent appear as "consoling communities", who can only maintain their function as long as nobody "drops out". Such a "dropping out" can occur by turning away to take up an exogamous love relationship or also it may take the form of the death of one parent, which can threaten or actually bring about the destruction of the entire family unit. In these families, the parents must be idealized, since only then can the "price" be justified which the descendants "pay" if they give up separation from them and the process of individuation or if they collaborate in denying their aggressive, depressive and destructive components, because the survivor parents, who have already lived through so much that was terrible, have in reality to be spared. To break away from such a closely-knit "community sharing the same fate" must provoke massive practically intolerable guilt feelings.

Additional tension arises in connection with the life of these families precisely in Germany, where now as in the past silence is usually maintained about the active and passive participation of the Germans in National Socialist crimes and where they are even denied. Only in very rare instances were the Nazi perpetrators in this country condemned and punished. That such a manner of dealing with National Socialism is hardly likely to cope with the anti-Semitism that prevails is hardly to be wondered at. For survivors, who even after the end of the Nazi regime had to reckon with being exposed both to anti-Semitic attitudes and corresponding actions, this certainly had dramatic consequences: they live with the fear of meeting their persecutors again, they live with the fear of renewed persecution.[1] If one has at the same time to justify the fact that one continues to live in the "country of the murderers" towards other Jews (whether these live abroad or are critics at home) or also in the light of one's own doubts and self-reproaches, then the result is not only to deny inwardly directed aggression, but in addition one has to deny outwardly-directed revenge impulses and aggression. On the other hand, however, the picture of the Germans as persecutors and enemies of the Jews has, again, to be upheld, because this is the only way to prevent the family "consoling community" from breaking up, the sons or daughters from being orientated outwards and in this way supposedly "betraying" their parents. Rachel G. is then confronted with the dilemma either of seeking a quasi incestuous, endogamous love relationship with a Jew, which would continue the defence of her family, or of

---

1 | Ignatz Bubis seemed to feel something of this kind of anxiety when he noticed, after Martin Walser's speech on the occasion of being awarded the Peace Price of the German Book Trade, that besides himself and his wife there was nobody in the audience who, like them, did *not* join in the applause, but respectfully rose from their seats. Here – and in many other points of the "Walser-Bubis debate" – did Bubis feel that he was standing alone against many others, against many, who did *not* recognize him as being one of them – alone against "the Germans"? (Cf. also "Critical" Jews and "Community Jewishness").

"clearing out" by means of an exogamous relationship, which would mean that ultimately she would "abandon" her own parents. She finds a compromise in being able to live out her "unfulfilled" abhorrence and her "unfulfilled" hate of the Germans with a sexually sadomasochistically fixated partner; but no permanent relationship, in which her wish to have children can be satisfied and an intimacy found such as she knew from her parents, can come about in this manner.

The analysis of the interview with Samuel N. brings us to members of the First Generation, who did not marry survivors, but men or women from the "other", non-Jewish German persecutor or sympathizer side. The children of such families can find themselves faced with a tremendous identity problem, for they do not know to which side they now belong, to that of the perpetrators or to that of the victims. Here, also, an attempt to find a solution can consist in identifying with the survivor parent, in order to thus avoid imminent confusion. This concrete case shows, however, that identification would have to be made with a love object, that one would have to fantasize and organize in opposition against too much that is real, so that finally an idealization cannot come about or fails. The ideal and the real father are too far from each other. Samuel's father turns out to be too torn as a result of persecution trauma and of his subsequent way of coping with this (e.g. in his marriage, in his social environment and not least in his relationship with his son) to be a father whom one can in fact idealize and internalize in the aforementioned sense. He remains too much a victim and too untrammelled in his aggressiveness for Samuel to be able to make him into an ideal father. The world from which he came was almost entirely destroyed by the Germans. Evidently nothing remained from the Jewish Orthodox life of his family, which he might have passed on to his son. What he did pass on to Samuel, on the contrary, is brokenness, restlessness, violence and destruction.

Samuel's situation comes to a climax when he finds that his mother cannot keep him. She entrusts him to the care of relatives, of foster families, she steals from him and expects him to be confronted with sexual experiences which he is not able to integrate. She appears to him as associated with the picture of a "perpetrator", when, after his father's death, she takes down his uncle's photograph, from whose glance she feels persecuted. Since the uncle was a model both for his father and for himself, he must regard this action as a betrayal with which – seen in this light – she reveals her true character. What remains is the picture of a wrecked family, which does not permit Samuel to find an identity of his own.

What conclusions can be drawn from these results? On the one hand, it seems worthwhile to continue work on the interviews that have already been made. As has already been intimated above, it would be interesting to also deal with the talks with the non-Jewish control group in order to make analyses of individual cases, to investigate here too above all the unconscious passing on of historical experiences. Would one find indications, say, in actions that are Freudian slips, which allow one to draw conclusions concerning the active or passive participation of the parents in National Socialism? Would one find indications that a confusion on the part of the non-Jewish interviewees would have to be ascribed to possible experiences or actions on the part of the parents?

It would, moreover, be important to study further interviews with Jewish interview partners as individual cases. In this way, it might be possible to examine the process through which this trauma has been transmitted to the Second Generation, as was expolored in the analyses of Rachel G. and Samuel N. Would one obtain further findings which one could integrate in the process of transmission which has been described? Or might one find other mechanisms by means of which the parental experiences of persecution are passed on to the Second Generation by conscious and unconscious psychic communication? To this end, it would also be expedient to work on detailed reports about psychoanalyses conducted with the descendants of survivors, in order to gain further insights into the unconscious dynamics of the transmission of the trauma. In this connection, one must also think of the Third Generation. What do the descendants of survivors pass on to *their* children, in particular, when they live in Germany? How does the Third Generation experience the way their parents cope with their grandparents' persecution? How does the Third Generation experience their life in the "country of the perpetrators"?

It is an open question whether such kind of investigations should be made in the form of group or individual studies and whether the interviewees themselves should be questioned or also their parents, unmarried and married partners and children. Every investigation design has its strong and weak points. But all investigations in the Federal Republic of Germany concerning the consequences of the National Socialist extermination of the Jews point to the question of the transmission of Nazi behaviour, the transmission of Nazi attitudes, the transmission of anti-Semitism. In Germany, the most important task would be to trace the way in which active persecution and, respectively, collaboration are passed on. For, from the viewpoint of the survivors and their descendants, it is essential to understand the non-Jewish German environment, in order to be able to bring about necessary changes.

German-Jewish relationships will remain strained. The rift between the families of the victims and the families of the perpetrators and sympathizers cannot and should not be "filled up". But in this relationship that is burdened by genocide and extermination, an authentic encounter can only take place if *both* sides were to understand something concerning the way in which the relationship has been determined, from where one really comes. In order to prevent future persecution, attention must be directed to the non-Jewish side of the transmission of National Socialism. One would have to be aware of what the reality is. It would be important to pay more attention to mass phenomena, to the "ethnic unconscious", to collective Freudian slips, which are communicated as consensual attitudes by "contagion". Future studies should, therefore, deal especially with three topics and with each of their interactions, namely with the *traumas* themselves, with the way the status of the perpetrators and victims is dealt with in collective and individual *memory* and with the dissemination and communication of actions, fantasies and attitudes within the *generations* involved.

6. Figures[1]

Figure 4: Religious membership in the control group (N=20)

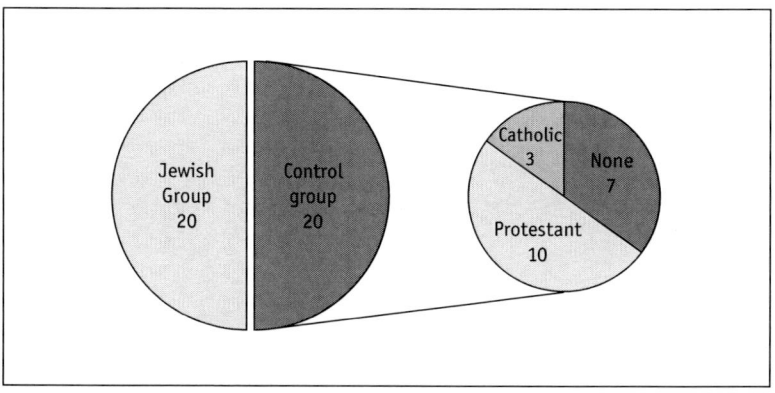

---

1 | You will find the figures 1 to 3 and figures 26 to 29 in chapter 4 »Empirical Analyses«.

Figure 5: Religious membership of the subjects' parents

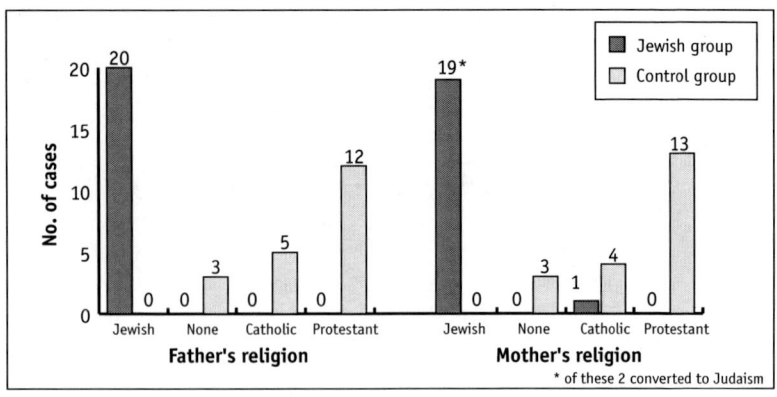

Figure 6: Religious upbringing in the family (N=40)

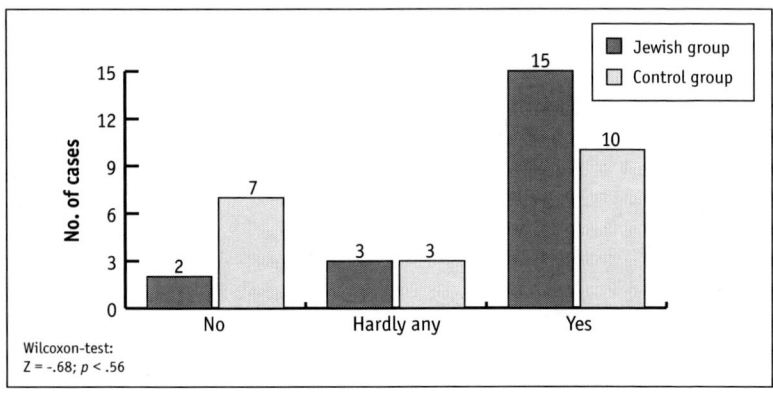

Figure 7: Religious education outside the family

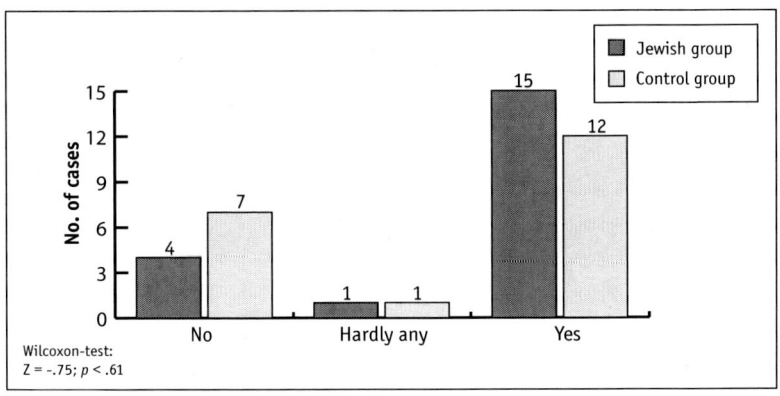

Figure 8: Nationality of the subjects

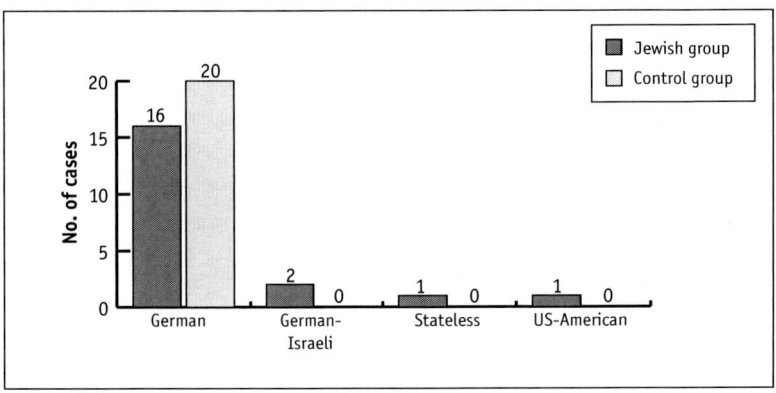

Figure 9: Nationality of the parents' generation

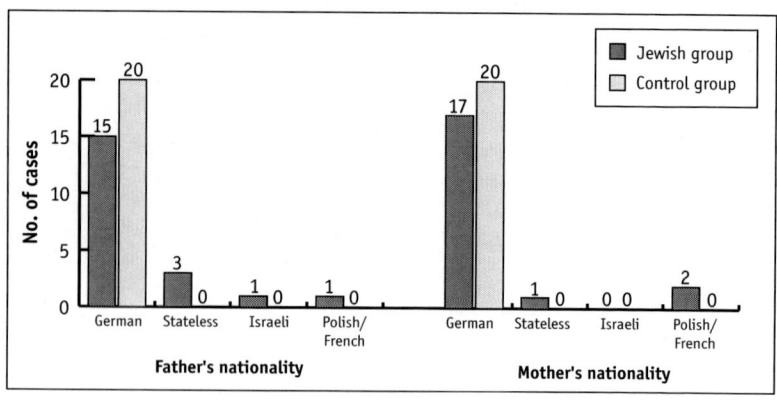

Figure 10: Completed school education of the subjects

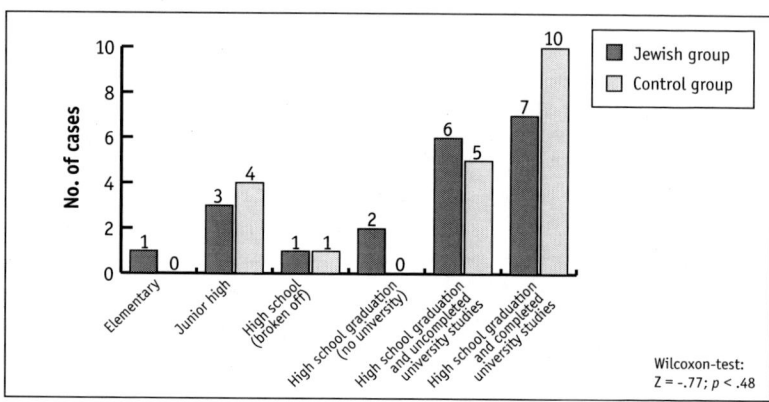

Figure 11: Education in the parents' generation

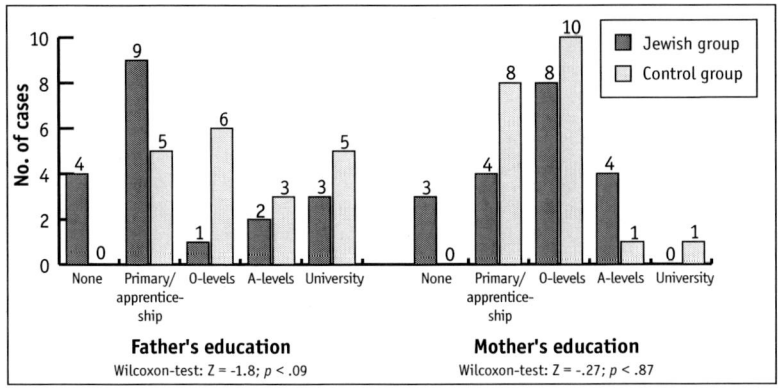

Figure 12: Comparison of the education of subjects' mothers and fathers

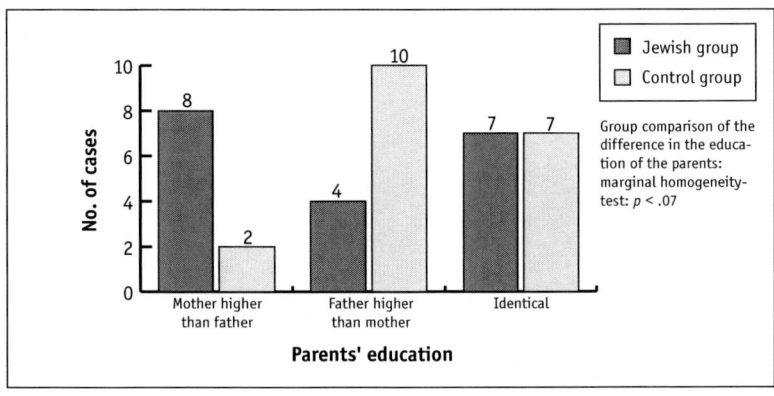

Figure 13: Intergenerational educational mobility

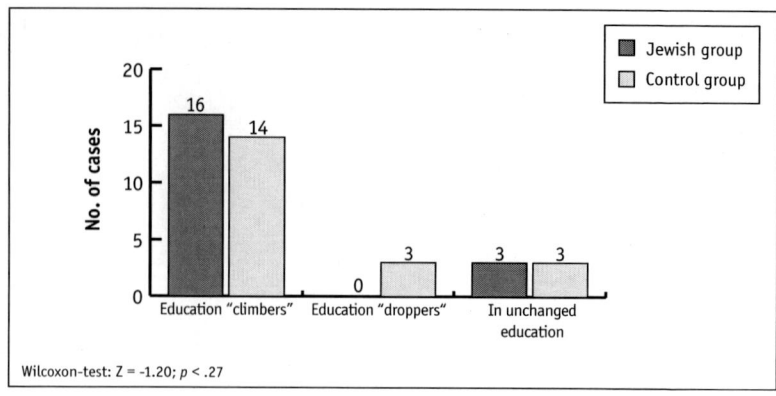

Figure 14: Average age of parents when the subject was born and standard deviation

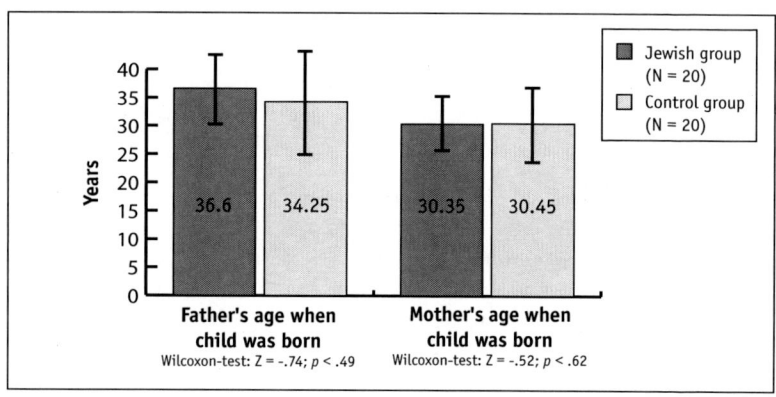

Figure 15: Causes of the parental deaths

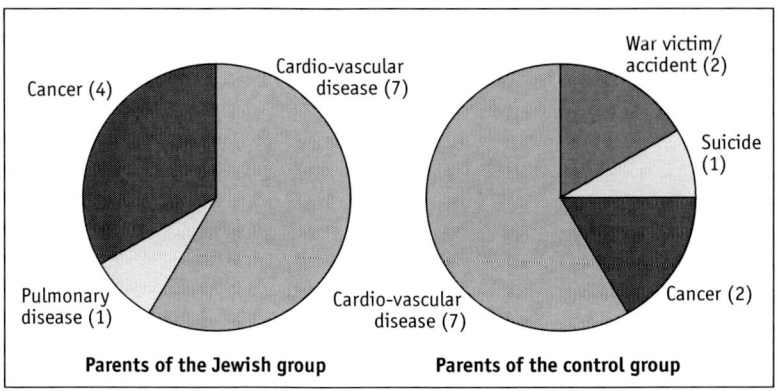

Figure 16: Number of siblings

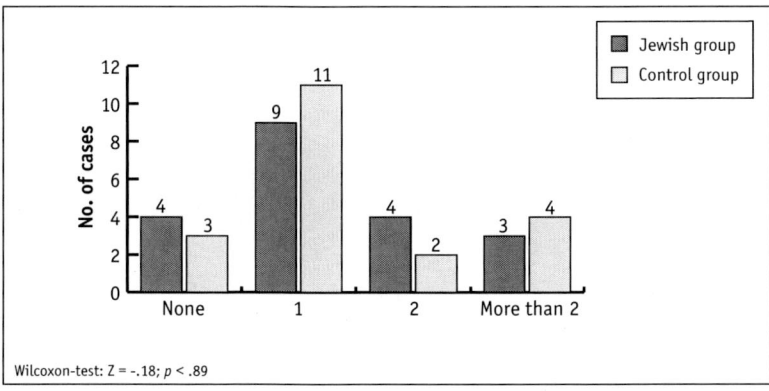

Figure 17: Marital status

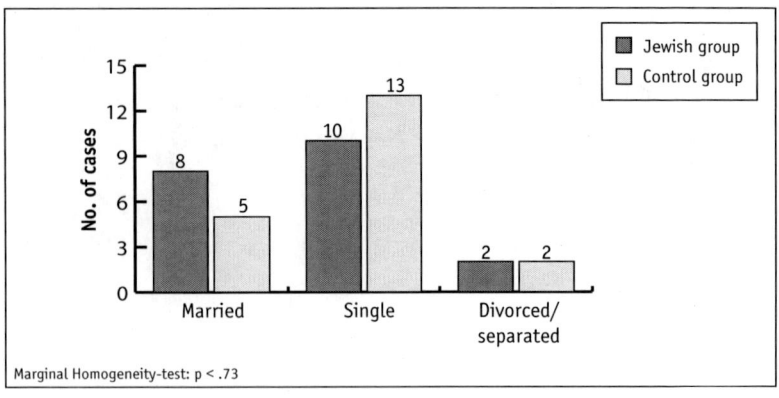

Figure 18: Information about the existence of a separate or joint household with the steady partner

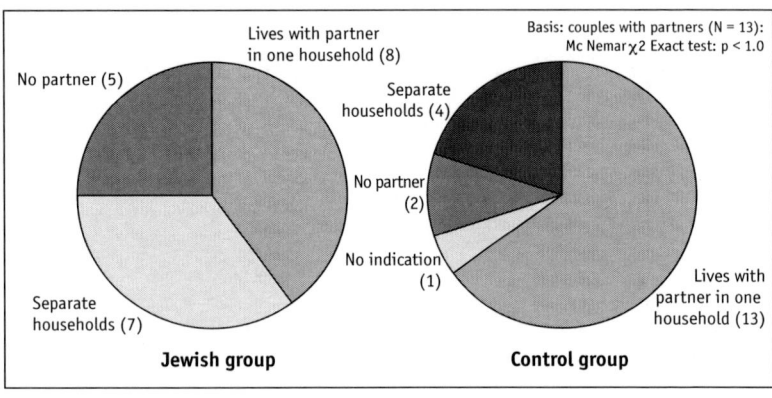

Figure 19: Size of the city of residence

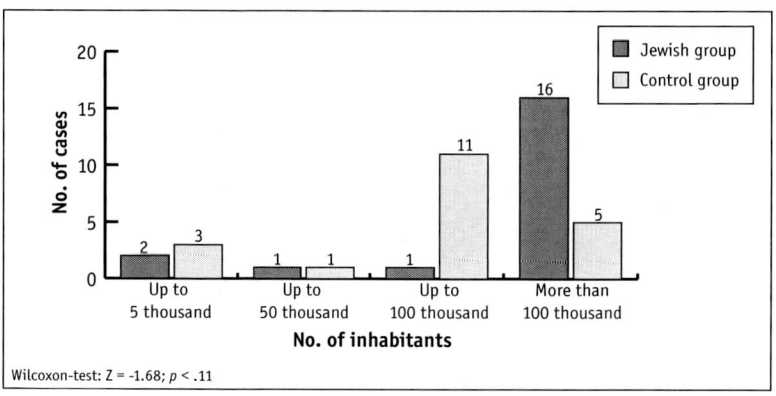

Wilcoxon-test: Z = -1.68; p < .11

Figure 20: Number of children

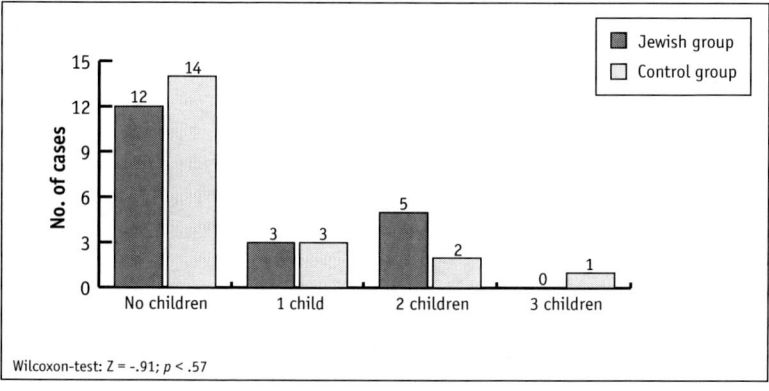

Wilcoxon-test: Z = -.91; p < .57

232 | LOVE AFTER AUSCHWITZ

Figure 21: Religious denomination and nationality of the steady partner

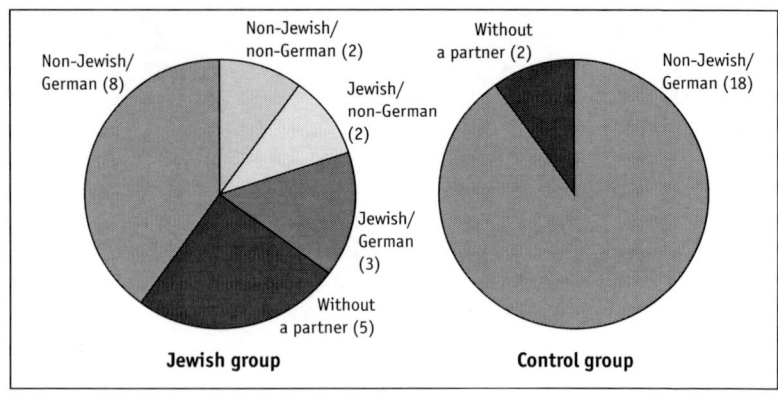

Figure 22: Eigenvalue curve (Scree plot) for the factor analysis of the items of the scale "parental bond"

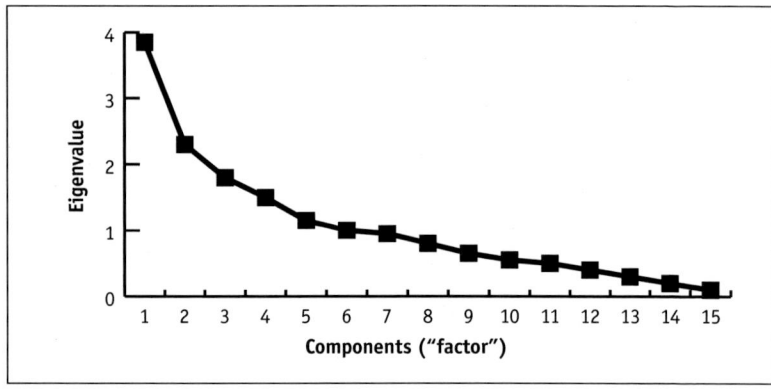

Figure 23: Eigenvalue curve (Scree Plot) for the factor analysis of the items of the scale "couple autonomy"

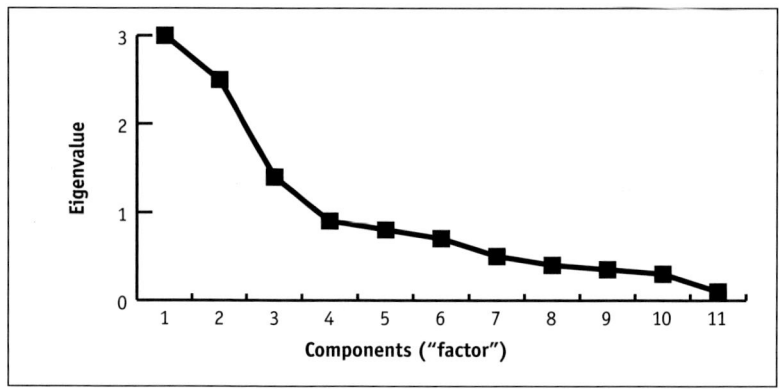

Figure 24: Duration of the interviews

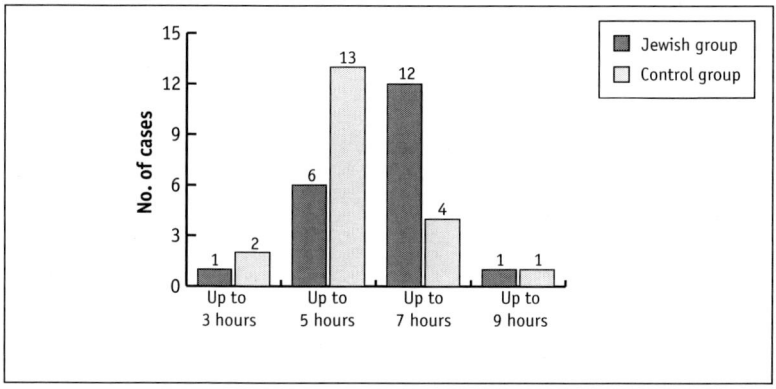

Figure 25: Percentage distribution of all assignments among the sections in both groups

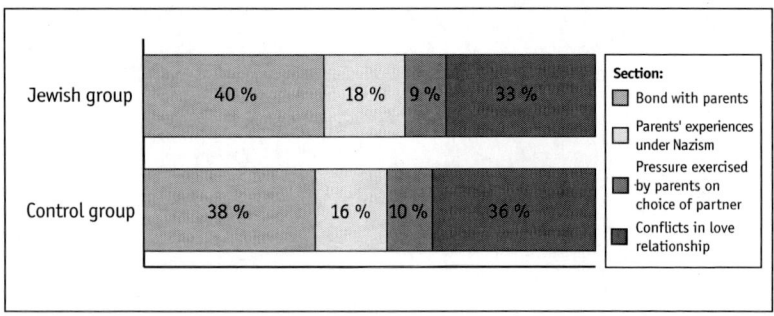

6. Figures | 235

Figure 30: Mean profile of the Jewish group (N=20) and of the control group (N=20) in the subsidiary scales of the FPI-R (Stanine values)

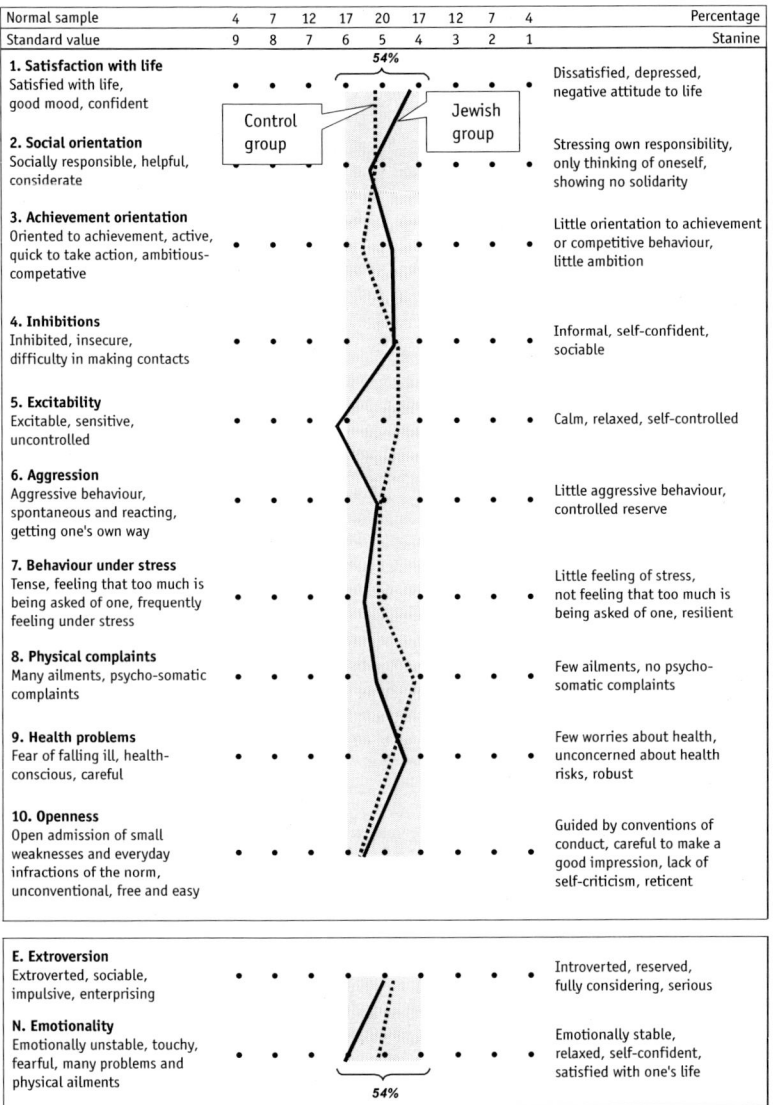

Figure 31: Mean values and standard deviations in the partnership questionnaire (PFB) in both groups and in the calibration sample (Hahlweg 1996)

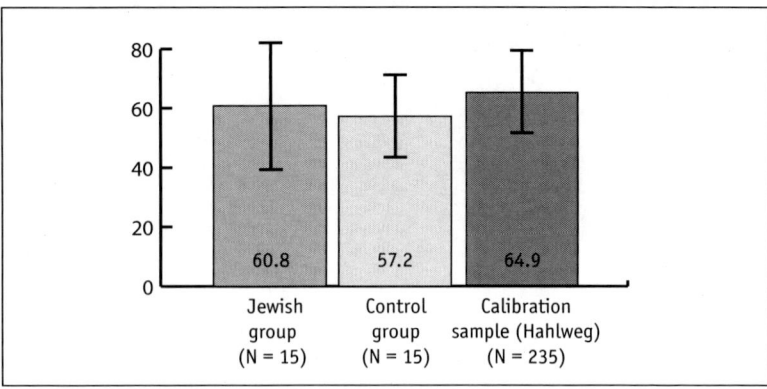

7. Tables[1]

Table 1: Internal consistencies (Cronbach's α) of the FPI-R sub-scales in the total sample and the two groups investigated as well as a comparison with the values of the standard sample

Scale	Total group (N = 40)	Jewish group (N = 20)	Control group (N = 20)	Test authors*
Life satisfaction[a]	.75	.74	.69	.78
Social orientation[b]	.68	.74	.60	.71
Efficiency orientation	.73	.80	.56	.77
Inhibitions	.52	.67	.19	.77
Excitability	.80	.82	.71	.75
Aggressiveness	.59	.59	.61	.74
Stress tolerance	.71	.77	.62	.84
Physical complaints	.73	.76	.66	.79
Health worries	.73	.76	.74	.79
Openness	.73	.70	.74	.79
Extroversion	.71	.63	.57	.74
Emotionality	.74	.82	.54	.80

Note: * Fahrenberg, Hampel & Selg 1985
[a] N = 3 values missing, [b] N = 1 value missing

1 | You will find table 8 and 9 in chapter 4 »Empirical Analyses«.

Table 2: Internal consistencies (Cronbach's α) of the sub-scales and the total scale of the partnership questionnaire (PFB) in the total sample and the two groups investigated as well as a comparison with the values of the standard sample

Scale	Total group (N = 31)	Jewish group (N = 13)	Control group (N = 18)	Test author*
Quarrel behaviour	.87	.87	.87	.93
Tenderness	.86	.93	.69	.91
Shared experiences/ communication	.79	.86	.68	.88
Total scale	.88	.92	.83	.95

Note: * Hahlweg 1996

[a] N = 6 subjects did not fill out the PFB because they did not have a partner relationship at the time; N = 3 subjects questioned did not reply to single items and have consequently not been included in the calculation of reliabilities.

Table 3: Internal consistencies (Cronbach's α) of the Parental Bond and Couple Autonomy Scale in the total sample and the two groups investigated

Scale	Total group (N = 40)	Jewish group (N = 20)	Control group (N = 20)
Bonds to the Parents (15 items)	.72	.60	.46
Couple Autonomy (11 items)	.68	.39	.80

Table 4: Factor loadings of the 15 items of the scale Parental Bond (N=40) Representation of the varimax-rotated 2-factor solution

Scale Parental Bond Item	Factor 1 Bonds with the parents originating from the family history	Factor 2 General bond with the parents
Parents' ability to acquire friends	-.56	.03
How well the parents match each other	-.58	.07
Similarity in the parents' attitude to life	-.55	.37
Frequency of contacts to parents	.00	.65
Parents cause guilt feelings	.46	.19
Devotion for parents	-.05	.63
Importance of the parents' welfare	-.21	.74
How well parents manage without me	-.61	-.34
How frequently one worries about one's parents	.28	.69
Difficulty to detach oneself from one's parents	.31	.65
I dare to be aggressive towards my parents	.15	-.08
How independent I am from my parents	-.60	-.40
How independent I should be from my parents	-.16	.02
Parents' experiences during the thirties/forties have shaped family life	.79	.13
How much has my own life been shaped by parents' experience during the thirties/forties	.70	.25
Variance explained Σ = 40.6 %	21.8 %	18.8 %

Note: Item loadings that have been used to interpret the factors have been printed in bold.

Table 5: Factor loading of the 11 items of the scale Couple Autonomy (N = 40). Representation of the varimax-rotated 2-factor solution

Scale Couple Autonomy Item	Factor 1 Positiv relationship to the partner's family	Factor 2 Significance of the family background in the love relationship
Importance of the partner's religion	-.07	**.72**
Parents' pressure on the choice of partner	-.03	**.82**
Burden caused by the partner's origin	-.15	**.55**
Importance of the partner being accepted by my family	.59	.60
How much I like being with partner's family	**.86**	.00
Being reserved towards partner's relations	**-.53**	-.23
Importance of own family traditions in the bringing up of children	.25	**.76**
How willingly are children left with the partner's parents	**.75**	-.07
Stabilization of the love relationship by the partner's family	**.62**	.10
Stabilization of the love relationship by one's own family	.43	.30
Satisfaction with the love relationship	.44	-.39
Variance explained Σ = 50.3 %	25.3 %	25.0 %

Note: The item loadings used to interpret the factors have been printed in bold.

Table 6: Sections, superordinate categories and categories of the deductive analysis of the field »relationship with the parents«

Section	Superordinate category	Category
1. Ties to the parents	1.1 »entangled« devotion	1. Devotion resulting from parents' pressure 2. Devotion resulting from guilt feelings 3. Devotion in order not to leave parents alone 4. Devotion so that the parents do not feel alone 5. Devotion resulting from fear of being rejected by the parents 6. Devotion shown by assuming responsibility for the parents 7. Devotion shown to avoid a rejection from the parents from being understood as aggression 8. Devotion shown to meet the parents' expectations 9. Devotion shown because one has not emancipated oneself from the parents in material respects 10. Devotion shown to spare the parents the experience of separation
	1.2 »non entangled« solicitude	1. Devotion shown because one likes one's parents 2. Devotion because one gets along well with one's parents 3. Devotion because one wishes the parents to have a share in one's life 4. Devotion because the parents enrich one's own social life 5. Devotion because the parents help to look after one's children
	1.3 »entangled« rejection	1. Turning away from the parents in order not to be exposed to the parents' difficult life 2. Turning away from the parents in order to hurt them (revenge) 3. Turning away in order to free one self from the parents 4. Turning away accompanied by guilt feelings 5. Turning away in order to get away from one parent whose position during the National Socialist era is not accepted

	1.4 »non entangled« rejection	1.	Turning away because one's own life is of central importance
		2.	Turning away out of lack of interest
		3.	Turning away to establish a distance to the parents' life (e.g. criticism of their views on life)
2. National Socialist experience of the parents	2.1 Confrontation with essential National Socialist experiences	1.	Confrontation with parents' private experience without reference to the social milieu of National Socialism
		2.	Confrontation with parents' professional experience without reference to the social milieu of National Socialism
		3.	Confrontation with the »good old times« as an idealization of the circumstances then prevailing
		4.	Confrontation with parental war or expulsion experience without reference to the causal connections and to the guilt question
		5.	Confrontation with parental war imprisonment without reference to causal connections and to the guilt question
		6.	Confrontation with parental experience during the first years of the Nazi regime, as if no possibilities whatever had existed from the very beginning of exerting influence or of fleeing
	2.2 Confrontation with the covering up of essential National Socialist experience	1.	Confrontation with parents' private experience without reference to the social milieu of National Socialism
		2.	Confrontation with parents' professional experience without reference to the social milieu of National Socialism
		3.	Confrontation with the »good old times« as an idealization of conditions then prevailing
		4.	Confrontation with parents' experience of war or expulsion without reference to the causal connections and guilt question
		5.	Confrontation with parents' war imprisonment without reference to the causal connections and guilt question
		6.	Confrontation with parents' experience during the first years of the National Socialist regime, as if there had been no possibilities from the very beginning of influencing things or of fleeing

7. TABLES | 243

2.3 Silence allied with clarity about essential experiences during the Nazi era	1.	»Mute« confrontation with parents' persecution by the Nazis (which left their mark on atmosphere, without the experiences being talked about)
	2.	»Mute« confrontation with physical illnesses or psychiatric symptoms resulting from the parents' experiences under the Nazis, without these experiences being treated as a subject to be talked about
	3.	»Mute« confrontation with parental helplessness, social isolation, mistrust of their environment (excepting persons with a similar background of experience) as a result of experiences made under the Nazis, without these experiences being treated as a subject to be talked about
	4.	»Mute« confrontation with parents' war or expulsion experiences, including reference to the causal connections and to the guilt question (e.g. books, films)
	5.	»Mute« confrontation with parents' war imprisonment, including reference to the causal connections and the guilt question
2.4 Silence with covering up of important experiences under Nazism	1.	Silence about the parents' experiences under the Nazis, because »nothing out of the ordinary« had happened during the Nazi era
	2.	Silence about parents' experiences under the Nazis, because one had not »known anything about« National Socialist atrocities
	3.	Silence about the parents' experiences under the Nazis, because they had not been involved in National Socialist atrocities
	4.	Being silent about possibilities of fleeing during the first years of the Nazi regime (in order e.g. to evade the question why one had not left Germany)
	5.	Parents' silence about their experience under the Nazis in order to avoid being reminded of an alleged survivors' guilt
	6.	Hints of parents' war or expulsion experiences, without reference to the causal connections or to the guilt question
	7.	Hints of parental war imprisonment without reference to the causal connections or to the guilt question

Table 7: Sections, superordinate categories and categories of the deductive analysis of the field of »love relationships«

Section	Superordinate category	Category
3. Pressure by the parents exercised on choice of the partner	3.1 Open pressure with respect to origin (denomination, national identity) of a partner	1. Argument that one can only really trust persons of same origin 2. Argument that one bears a responsibility towards »History« and the future of one's own people even in one's love relationships 3. Threat that a partner who is not accepted will revive former experiences of suffering 4. Warning that an inter-denominational relationship can never turn out well 5. Immediate raising of objections to a partner of different origin if parents so much as suspect that a love relationship is beginning 6. The immediate voicing of reflections regarding marriage if a partner has the same origin 7. Demand that the partner should be of the same origin
	3.2 Open pressure that is not connected with the origin of a partner	1. Demand that the partner should share one's own ideas concerning profession, status and income etc. 2. Demand that the partner should »be able to behave well« and be »decent« 3. Demand that the partner should not fundamentally contradict one's own political opinions 4. Demand that both partners should agree upon one denomination in the event of a marriage, without strong pressure being exercised to the effect that one must absolutely insist upon one's own denomination being chosen
	3.3 concealed pressure concerning origin (denomination national identity) of a partner	1. Hint that a mistrust exists of persons who are not of the same origin 2. Hint that one has a responsibility towards »History« and for the future of one's own people, without explicitly saying so 3. Hint of renewed suffering on the part of the parents without explicitly referring to the reasons

			4. Furthering of relationships with partners of the same origin without mentioning these reasons
			5. Suffering as a result of relationships with partners who are not of the same origin, without mentioning the reasons
	3.4 concealed pressure which has no connection with the origin of a partner	1.	Support provided by the parents' behaviour for relationships with partners who correspond to the parents' ideas, without mention being made of the reasons (profession, status, income, political stance, denomination, »decency« etc.)
		2.	the sanctioning of relationships with partners who do not correspond to the parents' ideas, without expressly mentioning the reasons (profession, status, income, political stance, denomination, »decency« etc.)
	3.5 no pressure	1.	no parental pressure
4. Conflicts in love relationships	4.1 open confrontation about origin/National Socialism	1.	National Socialism, National Socialist persecution as a subject of conflict
		2.	the state of Israel, the Jews as a subject of conflict
		3.	frequent discussion of the possibility of emigration
		4.	drawing of distinctions between the partners (victim vs. perpetrator), disparagement of the partner
		5.	confronting the partners with the National Socialist history of his/her family (he/she should break with his/her family, what does his/her family have to conceal?)
		6.	the reduction of contacts with the families, that are seen as connected with National Socialism to what is absolutely necessary
		7.	the partner, whose family is seen as connected with National Socialism is repeatedly »subjected to a test« (Can one trust the partner? can he/she provide adequate protection? would he/she stand by the partner in the event of renewed danger?)
		8.	the partner, whose family is seen as connected with National Socialism must »prove« himself/herself in special ways in order to guarantee the continuation of the relationship (he/she should also deal

		comprehensively with the problem of National Socialism; he/she should seize the initiative in approaching survivors of National Socialist persecution, he/she should distance himself/herself from the perpetrator and collaborator sides; conversion etc.)
		9. Children must absolutely be brought up in the family tradition
	4.2 confrontation with other issues than those of origin/ National Socialism	1. Issues of the social (professional) position of the partner as a conflict problem
		2. Interests, leisure pursuits as a conflict problem
		3. Political ideas (environment) as a conflict problem
		4. Plans for, and attitudes concerning one's future life as a conflict problem
		5. Sexuality as a conflict problem
		6. Financial ideas as a conflict problem
	4.3 concealed confrontation with the issues of origin/National Socialism	1. Avoiding conflict by restricting oneself to partners of the same origin
		2. Avoiding conflict by restricting oneself to non-German partners
		3. not entering into any permanent or »normal« relationships (marriage, children, love relationship)
		4. looking for partners who come from persecuted groups
		5. after a partner has e.g. adequately distanced himself/herself from his/her family e.g. by converting, in order to ensure the continuation of the relationship, avoiding open confrontation with his/her origin
		6. seeking intensive familiarity with the families of perpetrators to demonstrate that one has freed oneself from the persecution complex
		7. A descendant of National Socialist perpetrators »demonstratively« enters into a relationship with a Jewess or a Jew
	4.4 concealed confrontation with issues other than those concerning origin/National Socialism	1. Issues of the partner's social (professional) position are not openly discussed
		2. Differences of opinion about interests, leisure pursuits are not openly discussed
		3. Political views (environment) are not openly discussed

		4. Plans and attitudes concerning future life are not openly discussed 5. sexual conflicts are not openly discussed 6. financial problems are not openly discussed 7. restricting oneself to partners with certain qualities, interests etc., accord with one's own ideas in order to void controversies about these subjects
4.5 no conflict		1. no conflict

Table 10: Total number of assignments under categories
per section and group investigated

	Jewish group			Control group		
Section	Σ	Min	Max	Σ	Min	Max
Bond with parents	378	10	37	294	7	21
Parents' Nazi experiences	167	4	17	123	1	15
Pressure exercised by parents on choice of partner	89	2	9	77	1	7
Conflicts in love relationship	311	4	31	275	2	21
All categories	945	26	77	769	25	52

Note: Min and Max = minimum and maximal assignments under categories per text

Table 11: *Definition of the variables for examining the hypotheses of the category assignments obtained from the analysis of the categories*

Variable (leading category)		Operational definition
1. entangled bond with the parents	= $\dfrac{\Sigma}{\Sigma}$	Category assignments under the sections »entangled devotion«, »entangled rejection«, »no relationship« (1.5) Category assignments under category »bond with parents«
2. clear knowledge about	= $\dfrac{\Sigma}{\Sigma}$	Category assignments under the sections »Confrontation with important experiences under Nazism«, »Silence with clear knowledge about important experiences under Nazism« Category assignments under the category Parents' experiences
3. parental pressure because of partner's origin	= $\dfrac{\Sigma}{\Sigma}$	Category assignments under the sections »open pressure concerning a partner's origin«, »concealed pressure concerning a partner's origin« Category assignments under the section »parental pressure on choice of partner«
4. Conflicts in love relationships caused by the issues of origin National Socialism	= $\dfrac{\Sigma}{\Sigma}$	Category assignments under the superordinate categories »open confrontation« with the issues of origin/National Socialism Category assignments under the section »Conflicts in love relationships«

Table 12: Average proportion of variables per section

Variable	JG	CG	SD_{diff}	$p <$ [a]	effect size d_z	conventional classification of the effect size[b]
entangled bond with the parents	49 %	30 %	0.24	.002	0.83	large
Clear knowledge about important experiences under National Socialism with the parents	91 %	17 %	0.43	.001	1.70	large
parental pressure because of the partner's origin	48 %	1 %	0.29	.001	1.61	large
Conflicts in love relationships caused by the topics of origin/National Socialism	10 %	0 %	0.10	.001	1.00	large

Note: JG = Jewish Group, CG = Control Group, SD_{diff} = standard deviation of the difference values of couples, [a] t-test for dependent samples, [b] Classification in accordance with Cohen (1988)

Table 13: Means and effect sizes in the subscales of the FPI-R
(N = 20 Jewish/non-Jewish pairings)

FPI-R scale [a]	JG $\bar{x}$	CG $\bar{x}$	SD_{diff}	$p <$ [b]	d_z	Conventional Effect size classification of the effect size
Satisfaction with life	5.35	7.15	3.99	.06	0.45	large
Social orientation	6.90	6.75	2.91	.82	0.05	no effect
Achievement orientation	6.55	7.95	3.97	.13	0.35	medium
Inhibitions	4.45	4.30	3.53	.85	0.04	no effect
Excitability	7.45	5.00	3.98	.01	0.62	large
Aggression	4.45	4.30	3.70	.86	0.04	no effect
Behaviour under stress	7.10	6.00	3.73	.20	0.30	medium
Physical complaints	3.50	2.30	3.25	.12	0.37	medium
Health problems	4.25	5.10	3.98	.35	0.21	small
Openness	7.55	7.55	2.94	1.0	0.00	no effect
Extroversion	7.50	7.30	4.30	.84	0.05	no effect
Emotionality	8.05	6.10	5.07	.10	0.38	no effect

Note: JG = Jewish group, CG = control group, SD_{diff} = standard deviation of the difference values of pairings, »[a] raw scores«, [b] t-test for dependent samples, [c] classification according to Cohen (1988)

Table 14: Means and effect sizes for the items of the questionnaire bonds with the parents (N = 20 Jewish/non Jewish pairings)

Item	JG $\bar{x}$	CG $\bar{x}$	SD_{diff}	$p <^a$	Effect size d_z	Conventional classification of Item of the effect size[b]
how are parents able to make friends	2.75	3.80	1.91	.02	0.55	large
how well do the parents match each other	3.65	4.25	2.19	.23	0.27	medium
Similarity of parents' attitude to life	3.40	3.85	1.88	.30	0.24	small
Frequency of contacts with parents	4.85	4.00	1.27	.01	0.67	large
Parents induce of guilt feelings	3.85	3.00	1.69	.04	0.50	large
Being considerate to the parents	4.08	3.80	1.98	.54	0.14	small
Importance of the parents' well-being	5.20	5.30	0.97	.65	0.10	small
how well do parents manage without me	3.25	4.65	1.79	.01	0.78	large
how frequent are worries about parents	4.25	3.05	1.85	.01	0.65	large
Difficulty of detaching oneself from parents	4.80	2.80	2.05	.001	0.97	large
I dare to be aggressive towards parents	3.80	3.60	2.02	.66	0.10	small
how independent I am from the parents	3.65	5.05	1.79	.01	0.78	large
how independent I should be from the parents	4.70	5.00	1.53	.39	0.20	small

how strongly parental experiences during the thirties/forties have marked family life	5.30	3.45	1.84	.001	1.00	large
how strongly one's own life has been marked by parental experiences during the thirties/forties	5.15	2.75	1.79	.001	1.34	large

Note: JG = Jewish group, CG = control group, SD_{diff} = standard deviation of the difference values of pairings, Scale from 1 =»not at all« to 6 =»very much«, [a] t-test for dependent samples, [b] classification according to Cohen (1988)

Table 15: Means and effect sizes for the factor values of the 2-factor solution, which result from the analysis of the factors of the scale »bonds with the parents« (N = 20 Jewish/non Jewish pairings)

Factor	JG $\bar{x}$	CG $\bar{x}$	SD_{diff}	$p <$ [a]	Effect size d_z	Conventional classification of effect size[b]
Bonds with parents originating from family history	0.65	-0.65	.90	.001	1.45	large
General bond with parents	0.35	-0.35	.85	.003	0.83	large

Note: JG = Jewish group, CG = control group, SD_{diff} = standard deviation of the difference values of the pairings, factor values are z-standardized, [a]t-test for dependent samples, [b]classification according to Cohen (1988).

Table 16: Means and effect sizes for the items of the questionnaire autonomy of couple (N = 20 Jewish/non-Jewish pairings)

Item	JG $\bar{x}$	CG $\bar{x}$	SD_{diff}	$p <$ [a]	Effect size d_z	Conventional classification of effect size [b]
how important is the partner's religion	4.60	1.75	2.21	.001	1.29	large
parental pressure on choice of partner	4.20	1.40	1.67	.001	1.67	large
partner's origin is a burden	2.45	2.05	2.39	.46	0.17	small
important that the partner be accepted by one's own family	4.80	3.60	2.04	.02	0.59	large
enjoys being with the partner's family	3.15	3.35	2.61	.74	0.08	no effect
reserved towards the partner's relatives	3.00	2.80	2.26	.70	0.09	no effect
important to continue family tradition in upbringing of children	5.05	2.35	1.92	.001	1.40	large
how willingly one leaves children in the care of partner's parents	3.25	3.40	2.87	.82	0.05	no effect
love relationship is stabilized by partner's family	1.70	2.05	1.50	.31	0.23	small
love relationship is stabilized by own family	2.60	2.25	2.52	.54	0.14	small
satisfaction with the love relationship	3.95	4.65	2.58	.24	0.27	medium

Note: JG = Jewish group, CG = Control group, SD_{diff} = standard deviation of the difference values of the pairings, scale 1 = »not at all« to 6 = »very much«, [a] t-test for dependent samples, [b] classification according to Cohen (1988).

Table 17: Means and effect sizes for the factor values of the 2-factor solution resulting from the factor analysis of the scale »pair autonomy« (N = 20 Jewish/non-Jewish pairings)

PFB-scale	JG $\bar{x}$	CG $\bar{x}$	SD_{diff}	$p <$[a]	Effect size d_z	Conventional classification of effect size[b]
Positive relations to partner's family	-0.05	0.05	1.64	.80	0.06	no effect
Importance of family background in the love relationship	0.73	-0.73	.84	.001	1.74	large

Note: JG = Jewish group, CG = control group, SD_{diff} = standard deviation of the difference values of the pairings, factor values are z-standardized, [a]t-test for dependent samples, [b]classification according to Cohen (1988).

Table 18: Means and effect sizes in the subscales of the partnership questionnaire PFB (N = 15 Jewish/non-Jewish pairings)

PFB-scale	JG $\bar{x}$	CG $\bar{x}$	SD_{diff}	$p <$[a]	Effect size d_z	Conventional classification of effect size[b]
Quarreling behaviour	8.1	10.1	6.5	.24	0.32	medium
Tenderness	19.3	18.7	7.4	.76	0.08	no effect
Common interests/ communication	19.6	18.7	6.0	.56	0.16	small
Total value	60.8	57.2	13.6	.33	0.26	medium

Note: JG = Jewish group, CG = control group, SD_{diff} = standard deviation of the difference values of pairings. As far as five pairings are concerned, at least one of the two matching partners did not fill out a PFB questionnaire. [a]t-test for dependent samples, [b]classification according to Cohen (1988).

Table 19: Means and effect sizes in the subscales of the partnership questionnaire PFB for two Jewish subgroups with or without a non-Jewish German life partner ($N_1 = N_2 = 7$)

PFB-scale	JG with non-Jewish German partners $\bar{x}$	JG with non-German or Jewish partners $\bar{x}$	$p <$[a]	d_z	Conventional Effect size classification of effect size[b]
Quarreling behaviour	8.7	6.9	.62	0.27	small
Tenderness	18.1	20.6	.60	0.30	small
Common interests/ communication	18.7	20.4	.65	0.26	small
Total value	58.1	64.1	.53	0.35	small

Note: JG = Jewish group, [a]t-test for independent samples, [b]classification according to Cohen (1988).

Table 21: Correlations of the variables from the questionnaires and from content analysis dealing with the parental and love relationship in the total sample (N = 40)

Questionnaire variables	Leading category variables of content analyses			
	entangled bonds with the parents	clear knowledge about parents' experiences under Nazi regime	parental pressure due to partner's origin	conflicts in love relationships caused by topics origin/National Socialism
Bonds with parents due to family history	**.36***	**.58*****	**.38***	**.45****
General bonds with parents	-.06	.30	.32*	.20
Positive relationship to partner's family	-.17	-.03	.03	-.16
Significance of family background in the love relationship	**.37***	**.60*****	**.59*****	**.52****

Note: Interrelations between variables of both methods of ascertaining data which correspond with respect to contents are shown in bold; *p <.05, **p <.01, ***p <.001

Table 22: Correlations of variables in the parental and love relationships obtained for the Jewish sample from the questionnaires and from the analysis of contents (N = 20)

Questionnaire variables	Leading category variables of content analysis			
	entangled bonds with the parents	clear knowledge about parents' experiences under Nazi regime	parental pressure due to partner's origin	conflicts in love relationships caused by topics origin/National Socialism
bonds with parents due to family history	-.07	-.33	-.30	*.13*
general bonds with parents	-.21	.34	.10	-.02
positive relationship with partner's family	-.22	.13	.18	-.18
Significance of family background in love relationship	.09	.20	.15	.24

Note: Correlations between variables in both methods of determining facts which correspond to each other with respect to contents have been printed in bold.

Table 23: Correlations of variables in the parental and love relationships obtained in the non-Jewish sample from the questionnaires and analysis of contents (N = 20)

Questionnaire variables	Leading category variables of content analysis			
	entangled bonds with the parents	clear knowledge about parents' experiences under Nazi regime	parental pressure due to partner's origin	conflicts in love relationships caused by topics origin/National Socialism
bonds with parents due to family history	**.34**	.32	_a	-
general bonds with parents	-.35	-.16	-	-
positive relationship with partner's family	-.09	-.04	-	-
Significance of the family background in love relationship	.00	-.11	-	-

Note: Correlations between variables of both methods of ascertaining facts which correspond to each other are shown in bold.

[a] Calculation not possible or meaningful as all those questioned, or all those but one in one case, exhibit the value »0« in the variables »parental pressure due to partner's origin« or »conflicts in love relationships caused by the topics Origin/National Socialism«.

Table 24: Correlations of variables from content analysis with the relationship with parents and couples and with the sub-scales of the partnership questionnaire (PFB) in the Jewish (N=16) and in the control group (N=18)

Questionnaire variables	Leading category variables of content analysis				
		entangled bonds with the parents	clear knowledge about parents' experiences under Nazi regime	parental pressure due to partner's origin	conflicts in love relationships caused by topics origin/National Socialism
quarreling behaviour	JG	.20	-.16	.01	.07
	CG	-.02	-.29	-a	-
tenderness	JG	-.34	-.17	-.32	.12
	CG	-.44	-.23	-	-
common interests/ communication	JG	-.47	-.14	-.38	.16
	CG	-.12	-.10	-	-
total value	JG	-.42	-.07	-.30	.09
	CG	-.22	.04	-	-

Note: JG = Jewish group, CG = control group.
[a] Calculation not possible or not meaningful, since all or all but one of those questioned show the value 0 for the variables »parental pressure due to partner's origin« and »conflicts in love relationships due to the topics origin/National Socialism« as the case may be.

8. Bibliography

Améry, J. (1977), *Jenseits von Schuld und Sühne*. Bewältigungsversuche eines Überwältigten. Stuttgart: Klett, 1980

Appelbaum, P.S., L.A. Uyehara & M.R. Elin (eds.) (1997), *Trauma and memory*. Clinical and legal controversies. New York/Oxford: Oxford University Press

Arendt, H. (1963), *Eichmann in Jerusalem*. A report on the banality. New York: Viking Press

Argelander, H. (1967), *The initial interview in psychotherapy*. New York: Human Sciences Press, 1976

Arning, M. & R. Paasch (1996), Die provokanten Thesen des Mister Goldhagen. Der US-Soziologe stößt mit seinem Buch »Hitlers bereitwillige Helfer« bei deutschen Forschern auf viel Kritik. *Frankfurter Rundschau* of April 12th 1996

Augstein, R. (1996), Der Soziologe als Scharfrichter. Rudolf Augstein über Daniel Jonah Goldhagens »Hitler's willing executioners«. *Der Spiegel* 16 of April 15th 1996, 29-32

Augstein, R. et al. (1987), *»Historikerstreit«*. Die Dokumentation der Kontroverse um die Einzigartigkeit der nationalsozialistischen Judenvernichtung. München/Zürich: Piper

Bachar, E., M. Cale, J. Eisenberg & H. Dasberg (1994), Aggression expression in grandchildren of Holocaust survivors – a comparative study. *The Israel Journal of Psychiatry and Related Sciences* 31, 41-47

Baeyer, W.R. v., H. Häfner & K.P. Kisker (1964), *Psychiatrie der Verfolgten*. Psychopathologische und gutachtliche Erfahrungen an Opfern der nationalsozialistischen Verfolgung und vergleichbarer Extrembelastungen. Berlin/Göttingen/Heidelberg: Springer

Barocas, H.A. & C.B. Barocas (1979), Wounds of the fathers. The next generation of Holocaust victims. *The International Review of Psychoanalysis* 6, 331-340

Barocas, H.A. & C.B. Barocas (1980), Separation individuation conflicts in children of Holocaust survivors. *Journal of Contemporary Psychotherapy* 11, 6-14

Bar-On, D. (1989), *The legacy of silence*. Encounters with children of the Third Reich. Cambridge: Harvard University Press

Bar-On, D. (1995), *Fear and hope*. Three generations of the Holocaust. Cambridge/London: Harvard University Press

Becker, D. (1997), Prüfstempel PTSD – Einwände gegen das herrschende »Trauma«-Konzept. In: Medico international (ed.), *Schnelle Eingreiftruppe »Seele«*. Frankfurt a.M.: Verlag medico international, 25-47

Becker, J. (1969), *Jacob the liar*. New York: Plume, 1997

Becker, J. (1986), *Bronstein's children*. Chicago: Chicago University Press, 1999

Beier, C., K. Horn & D. Kraft-Krumm (1980), *Gesundheitsverhalten und Krankheitsgewinn*. Zur Methode einer Studie über Widerstand gegen Gesundheitsaufklärung. (Europäische Monographien zur Forschung in Gesundheitserziehung, Vol. 2). Köln: Bundeszentrale für gesundheitliche Aufklärung, 59-100

Berding, H. (1988), *Moderner Antisemitismus in Deutschland*. Frankfurt a.M.: Suhrkamp

Berens, C. (1996), International Study Group for Trauma, Violence, and Genocide. Internationale Erforschung von Trauma, Gewalt und Genozid. *Mittelweg 36*, Vol. 5, No. 6, 38-40

Bergmann, M.S. & M.E. Jucovy (eds.) (1982), *Generations of the Holocaust*. New York: Basic Books

Bergmann, M.S. (1982), Recurrent problems in the treatment of survivors and their children. In: M.S. Bergmann & M.E. Jucovy (eds.), *Generations of the Holocaust*. New York: Basic Books, 247-266

Bergmann, M.S. (1996), Fünf Stadien in der Entwicklung der psychoanalytischen Trauma-Konzeption. *Mittelweg 36*, Vol. 5, No. 2, 12-22

Bergmann, M.V. (1982), Thoughts on superego pathology of survivors and their children. In: M.S. Bergmann & M.E. Jucovy (eds.), *Generations of the Holocaust*. New York: Basic Books, 287-309

Bergmann, W. & R. Erb (1991), *Antisemitismus in der Bundesrepublik Deutschland*. Ergebnisse der empirischen Forschung von 1946-1989. Opladen: Leske und Budrich

Best, M. (ed.) (1988), *Der Frankfurter Börneplatz*. Zur Archäologie eines politischen Konflikts. Frankfurt a.M.: Fischer Taschenbuch Verlag

Blanck, R. & G. Blanck (1968), *Marriage and personal development*. New York: Columbia University Press

Blumenberg, Y. (1995), Rezension: A. Dührssen, Ein Jahrhundert Psychoanalytische Bewegung in Deutschland. Göttingen 1994. *Luzifer-Amor 8*, No. 15, 153-175

Blumenberg, Y. (1997), »Die Crux mit dem Antisemitismus«. Zur Gegenbesetzung von Erinnerung, Herkommen und Tradition. *Psyche* 51, 1115-1160

Bohleber, W. & J.S. Kafka (eds.) (1992), *Antisemitismus*. Bielefeld: Aisthesis Verlag

Bohleber, W. (1998), Transgenerationelles Trauma, Identifizierung und Geschichtsbewußtsein. In: J. Rüsen & J. Straub (eds.), *Die dunkle Spur der Vergangenheit*. Psychoanalytische Zugänge zum Geschichtsbewußtsein. Erinnerung, Geschichte, Identität 2. Frankfurt a.M.: Suhrkamp, 256-274

Borries, A.v. (ed.) (1962), *Selbstzeugnisse des deutschen Judentums 1861-1945*. Frankfurt a.M.: Fischer Taschenbuch Verlag, 1988

Bortz, J. & N. Döring (1984), *Forschungsmethoden und Evaluation für Sozialwissenschaftler*. 2nd. ed. Berlin/Heidelberg/New York: Springer, 1995

Bortz, J. (1977), *Statistik für Sozialwissenschaftler*. 4th ed. Berlin/Heidelberg/New York: Springer, 1993

Brainin, E., V. Ligeti & S. Teicher (1993), *Vom Gedanken zur Tat*. Zur Psychoanalyse des Antisemitismus. Frankfurt a.M.: Brandes und Apsel

Brecht, K., V. Friedrich, L.M. Hermanns, I. Kaminer & D. Juelich (eds.) (1985), »*Here life goes on in a most peculiar way* ...« Psychoanalysis before and after 1933. Hamburg: Kellner

Brede, K. (2000), Die Walser-Bubis-Debatte. Aggression als Element öffentlicher Auseinandersetzung. *Psyche* 54, 203-233

Broder, H.M. & M.R. Lang (eds.) (1979), *Fremd im eigenen Land*. Juden in der Bundesrepublik. Frankfurt a.M.: Fischer Taschenbuch Verlag

Broder, H.M. (1979), Warum ich lieber kein Jude wäre; und wenn schon unbedingt – dann lieber nicht in Deutschland. In: H.M. Broder & M.R. Lang (eds.), *Fremd im eigenen Land*. Juden in der Bundesrepublik. Frankfurt a.M.: Fischer Taschenbuch Verlag, 82-102

Broder, H.M. (1981a), Ihr bleibt die Kinder Eurer Eltern. *Die Zeit*, No. 10 of February 2nd 1981, 9-11

Broder, H.M. (1981b), »Spiegel-Gespräch«: »Für Juden gibt es hier keine Normalität«. *Der Spiegel*, No. 17

Broder, H.M. (1986), *Der ewige Antisemit*. Über Sinn und Funktion eines beständigen Gefühls. Frankfurt a.M.: Fischer Taschenbuch Verlag

Broder, H.M. (n.d.), *Danke schön*. Bis hierher und nicht weiter. Hamburg: Konkret Literaturverlag [1980]

Browning, C. (1992), *Ordinary men. Reserve Police Battalion 101 and the final solution in Poland.* New York: Aaron Asher Books

Brumlik, M. (1980), Krise der jüdischen Identität? In: *Cheschbon.* Ed. by Bundesverband Jüdischer Studenten in Deutschland. München, 4-11

Brumlik, M. (1982), Bewältigung oder Verdrängung? Juden in der BRD. *links* 1, 15-17

Brumlik, M. (1983a), Begin und Schmidt – oder: Die Unfähigkeit zu trauern. In: D. Wetzel (ed.), *Die Verlängerung von Geschichte. Deutsche, Juden und der Palästinakonflikt.* Frankfurt a.M.: Verlag Neue Kritik, 93-102

Brumlik, M. (1983b), Sabra und Schatila. In: D. Wetzel (ed.), *Die Verlängerung von Geschichte. Deutsche, Juden und der Palästinakonflikt.* Frankfurt a.M.: Verlag Neue Kritik, 15-24

Brumlik, M. (1985), Warum ich mit Ignatz Bubis solidarisch bin. Ein Bekenntnis. In: E. Kiderlen (ed.), *Pflasterstrand Flugschrift – 1. Deutsch-jüdische Normalität ... Fassbinders Sprengsätze.* Frankfurt a.M.: Pflasterstrand, 74-80

Bubis, I. (1993), *Ich bin ein deutscher Staatsbürger jüdischen Glaubens. Ein autobiographisches Gespräch mit Edith Kohn.* Köln: Kiepenheuer und Witsch

Bubis, I. (1999), Interview. *Stern,* No. 31 of July 7th 1999, 56-59

Buchner, A., E. Erdfelder & F. Faul (1996), Teststärkeanalysen. In: E. Erdfelder, R. Mausfeld, T. Meiser & G. Rudinger (eds.), *Handbuch Quantitative Methoden.* Weinheim: Psychologie Verlags Union, 123-134

Bühl, A. & P. Zöfel (1998), *SPSS Version 8. Einführung in die moderne Datenanalyse unter Windows.* Bonn: Addison-Wesley

Büssing, A. & B. Jansen (1988), Exact tests of two-dimensional contingency tables. Procedures and problems. *Methodika* 2, 27-39

Bunzl, J. (1983), Was Israelis in den Palästinensern sehen. In: D. Wetzel (ed.), *Die Verlängerung von Geschichte. Deutsche, Juden und der Palästinakonflikt.* Frankfurt a.M.: Verlag Neue Kritik, 43-58

Chaussy, U. (1992), »*Ritual oder Erinnerung?*« Kultur aktuell am Morgen, Radio programme of January 16th 1992, Bayern 2

Claussen, D. (1983), Im Hause des Henkers. In: D. Wetzel (ed.), *Die Verlängerung von Geschichte. Deutsche, Juden und der Palästinakonflikt.* Frankfurt a.M.: Verlag Neue Kritik, 113-125

Claussen, D. (1986), Ein neuer kategorischer Imperativ. Die politische Linke und ihr Verhältnis zum Staat Israel. In: M. Brumlik, D. Kiesel, C. Kugelmann & J.H. Schoeps (eds.), *Jüdisches Leben in Deutschland seit 1945.* Frankfurt a.M.: Athenäum, 230-242

Claussen, D. (1987), *Vom Judenhaß zum Antisemitismus. Materialien einer verleugneten Geschichte.* Darmstadt/Neuwied: Luchterhand

Cohen, J. (1977), *Statistical power analysis for the behavioral sciences*. First revised edition. Hillsdale: Erlbaum

Cohen, J. (1988), *Statistical power analysis for the behavioral sciences*. Second edition. Hillsdale: Erlbaum

Cohen, J. (1992), A power primer. *Psychological Bulletin* 112, 155-159

Cohen, J. (1994), The earth is round ($p < .05$). *American Psychologist* 49, 997-1003

Cook, T.D. & D.T. Campbell (1979), *Quasi-experimentation*. Design and analysis issues for field settings. Boston: Houghton Mifflin

Davidson, S. (1980), Transgenerational transmission in the families of Holocaust survivors. *International Journal of Family Psychiatry* 1, 95-112

Davidson, S. (1987), Trauma in the life cycle of the individual and the collective consciousness in relation to war and persecution. In: H. Dasberg et al., *Society and trauma of war*. Assen/Maastricht/Wolfeboro: Van Gorcum, 14-32

de Winter, L. (1991), *SuperTex*. Zürich: Diogenes, 1996

de Winter, L. (1995), *Serenade*. Zürich: Diogenes, 1996

de Winter, L. (1995), *Zionoco*. Zürich: Diogenes, 1997

Denzin, N.K. (1970), *The research act*. A theoretical introduction to sociological methods. New York: McGraw-Hill

Der Spiegel (1976), No. 28, Das Geiseldrama: »Professionell, eingeübt«, 84-88

Deutscher, I. (1977), *Die ungelöste Judenfrage*. Zur Dialektik von Antisemitismus und Zionismus. Berlin: Rotbuch Verlag

Dimsdale, J.E. (ed.) (1980), *Survivors, victims, and perpetrators*. Essays on the Nazi Holocaust. Washington/New York/London: Hemisphere Publishing

Diner, D. (1982), »Keine Zukunft auf den Gräbern der Palästinenser«. Eine historisch-politische Bilanz der Palästinafrage. Hamburg: VSA-Verlag

Diner, D. (1983a), Israel und das Trauma der Massenvernichtung. In: D. Wetzel (ed.), *Die Verlängerung von Geschichte*. Deutsche, Juden und der Palästinakonflikt. Frankfurt a.M.: Verlag Neue Kritik, 25-42

Diner, D. (1983b), Fragmente von unterwegs. Über jüdische und politische Identität in Deutschland. *Ästhetik und Kommunikation*, No. 51, 5-15

Diner, D. (1986), Negative Symbiose. Deutsche und Juden nach Auschwitz. *Babylon*. Beiträge zur jüdischen Gegenwart, No. 1, 9-20

Diner, D. (ed.) (1987), *Ist der Nationalsozialismus Geschichte?* Zu Historisierung und Historikerstreit. Frankfurt a.M.: Fischer Taschenbuch Verlag

Diner, D. (ed.) (1988), *Zivilisationsbruch*. Denken nach Auschwitz. Frankfurt a.M.: Fischer Taschenbuch Verlag

Dominik, M. & A. Teutsch (1978), Neurosen bei der Nachkommenschaft ehemaliger Konzentrationslagerhäftlinge. *Mitteilungen der internationa-*

len Föderation der Widerstandskämpfer (FJR) zu medizinischen, sozialen, und Rechtsfragen, No. 15, 9-18
Dreher, K. (1998), Helmut Kohl. Leben mit Macht. Stuttgart: Deutsche Verlags-Anstalt
Dührssen, A. (1994), Ein Jahrhundert Psychoanalytische Bewegung in Deutschland. Die Psychotherapie unter dem Einfluß Freuds. Göttingen: Vandenhoeck und Ruprecht
Durst, N. (1994), Über die Einsamkeit und das unendliche Trauern von alternden Überlebenden des Holocaust. In: H. Stoffels (ed.), *Terrorlandschaften der Seele*. Beiträge zur Theorie und Therapie von Extremsituationen. Regensburg: Roderer, 44-52
Durst, N. (1995), Die Einsamkeit im Alter. In: L.M. Tas & J. Wiesse (eds.), *Ererbte Traumata*. (Psychoanalytische Blätter, 2). Göttingen/Zürich: Vandenhoeck und Ruprecht, 13-30
Ebel, R. (1983), Zwischenbericht. Auf der Suche nach Unbefangenheit. *Ästhetik und Kommunikation* 51, 17-23
Eckstaedt, A. (1989), *Nationalsozialismus in der »zweiten Generation«*. Psychoanalyse von Hörigkeitsverhältnissen. Frankfurt a.M.: Suhrkamp
Ehebald, U. (1993a), Brief von Ulrich Ehebald an den Vorstand der Hamburger Arbeitsgemeinschaft vom 30.12.1992. *DPV-Informationen*, No. 14, 10
Ehebald, U. (1993b), Brief von Ulrich Ehebald vom 13.05.1993. *DPV-Informationen*, No. 14, 12-13
Eissler, K.R. (1963), Die Ermordung von wie vielen seiner Kinder muß ein Mensch symptomfrei ertragen können, um eine normale Konstitution zu haben? *Psyche* 17, 241-291
Eitinger, L. (1980), The concentration camp syndrome and its late sequelae. In: J.E. Dimsdale (ed.), *Survivors, victims, and perpetrators*. Essays on the Nazi Holocaust. Washington/New York/London: Hemisphere Publishing, 127-162
Elbogen, I. & E. Sterling (1966), *Die Geschichte der Juden in Deutschland*. Wiesbaden: Fourier Verlag, 1982
Engler, S. (1997), Zur Kombination von qualitativen und quantitativen Methoden. In: B. Friebertshäuser & A. Prengel (eds.), *Handbuch Qualitative Forschungsmethoden in der Erziehungswissenschaft*. Weinheim/München: Juventa, 118-130
Epstein, H. (1977), The heirs of the Holocaust. *The New York Times Magazine* of June 19th, 12-14 and 74-77
Epstein, H. (1979), *Children of the Holocaust*. Conversations with sons and daughters of survivors. New York: Bantam Books

Erdfelder, E., F. Faul & A. Buchner (1996), GPOWER. A general power analysis program. *Behavior Research Methods, Instruments, & Computers* 28, 1-11

Erikson, E.H. (1959), *Identity and the life cycle*. New York: International Universities Press

Ermann, M. (1996), *Verstrickung und Einsicht*. Nachdenken über die Psychoanalyse in Deutschland. Tübingen: Edition diskord

Esser, H. (1987), Zum Verhältnis von qualitativen und quantitativen Methoden in der Sozialforschung, oder: Über den Nutzen methodologischer Regeln bei der Diskussion von Scheinkontroversen. In: W. Voges (ed.), *Methoden der Biographie- und Lebenslaufforschung*. Opladen: Leske und Budrich, 87-100

Etty, P. & S. Gingold (1979), Die Antwort heißt Assimilation. In: H.M. Broder & M.R. Lang (eds.), *Fremd im eigenen Land*. Juden in der Bundesrepublik. Frankfurt a.M.: Fischer Taschenbuch Verlag, 157-167

Fahrenberg, J., R. Hampel & H. Selg (1970a), *Das Freiburger Persönlichkeitsinventar FPI*. Revidierte Fassung FPI-R. Handanweisung. 4th rev. ed. Göttingen/Toronto/Zürich: Verlag für Psychologie, Hogrefe, 1984

Fahrenberg, J., R. Hampel & H. Selg (1970b), *Das Freiburger Persönlichkeitsinventar FPI*. Revidierte Fassung FPI-R und teilweise geänderte Fassung FPI-A1. Handanweisung. 6th ed. Göttingen/Bern/Toronto/Seattle: Verlag für Psychologie, Hogrefe, 1994

Fahrenberg, J., R. Hampel & H. Selg (1985), Die revidierte Form des Freiburger Persönlichkeitsinventars FPI-R. *Diagnostica* 31, 1-21

Faimberg, H. (1987), The telescoping of generations: Genealogy of certain identifications. *Contemporary Psychoanalysis* 24, 1988, 99-118

Fassbinder, R.W. (1981), Der Müll, die Stadt und der Tod. In: R.W. Fassbinder, *Die bitteren Tränen der Petra von Kant*. Der Müll, die Stadt und der Tod. 2 Stücke. Frankfurt a.M.: Verlag der Autoren, 1984, 57-105

Fischer, G. & P. Riedesser (1998), *Lehrbuch der Psychotraumatologie*. München/Basel: Ernst Reinhardt

Fischer, P.M. (1982), Inhaltsanalytische Auswertung von Verbaldaten. In: G.L. Huber & H. Manol (eds.), *Verbale Daten*. Eine Einführung in die Grundlagen und Methoden der Erhebung und Auswertung. Weinheim/Basel: Beltz Verlag, 179-196

Fleischmann, L. (1979), Warum ich gehe. In: H.M. Broder & M.R. Lang (eds.), *Fremd im eigenen Land*. Juden in der Bundesrepublik. Frankfurt a.M.: Fischer Taschenbuch Verlag, 138-143

Fleischmann, L. (1980), *Dies ist nicht mein Land*. Eine Jüdin verläßt die Bundesrepublik. Hamburg: Hoffmann und Campe

Fleischmann, L. (1982), *Ich bin Israelin*. Erfahrungen in einem orientalischen Land. Hamburg: Hoffmann und Campe

Flick, U. (1991), Triangulation. In: U. Flick, E. v. Kardorff, H. Keupp, L. v. Rosenstiel & S. Wolff (eds.), *Handbuch Qualitative Sozialforschung*. Weinheim: Psychologie Verlags Union, 432-434

Fogelman, E. & B. Savran (1979), Therapeutic groups for children of Holocaust survivors. *International Journal of Group Psychotherapy* 29, 211-235

Fogelman, E. (1998), Group belonging and mourning as factors in resilience in second generation of Holocaust survivors. *Psychoanalytic Review* 85, 537-549

Francesconi, H. (1983), *Extremtraumatisierung und ihre Folgen für die nächste Generation. Die psychischen Störungen der Nachkommen ehemaliger KZ-Häftlinge*. Wien: Sensen-Verlag

Freud, S. (1923), The ego and the id. *SE* 19, 12-59

Freyberg, J.T. (1980), Difficulties in seperation-individuation as experienced by offspring of Nazi Holocaust survivors. *American Journal of Orthopsychiatry* 50, 87-95

Friedrichs, J. (1973), *Methoden empirischer Sozialforschung*. Opladen: Westdeutscher Verlag, 1982

Fromm, M. (1990), Zur Verbindung quantitativer und qualitativer Methoden. *Pädagogische Rundschau* 44, 469-481

Früh, W. (1992), Analyse sprachlicher Daten. Zur konvergenten Entwicklung »quantitativer« und »qualitativer« Methoden. In: J.H.P. Hoffmeyer-Zlotnik (ed.), *Analyse verbaler Daten. Über den Umgang mit qualitativen Daten*. Opladen: Westdeutscher Verlag, 59-89

Funke, H. (1983), Einige persönliche Notizen. *Ästhetik und Kommunikation* 51, 90-93

Funke, H. (ed.) (1988), *Von der Gnade der geschenkten Nation. Zur politischen Moral der Bonner Republik*. Berlin: Rotbuch Verlag

Gampel, Y. (1998), Reflections on countertransference in psychoanalytic work with child survivors of the Shoah. *Journal of the American Academy of Psychoanalysis* 26, 343-368

Gidal, N.T. (1988), *Die Juden in Deutschland von der Römerzeit bis zur Weimarer Republik*. Gütersloh: Bertelsmann Lexikon Verlag

Giegler, H. (1992), Zur computerunterstützten Analyse sozialwissenschaftlicher Textdaten. Quantitative und qualitative Strategien. In: J.H.P. Hoffmeyer-Zlotnik (ed.), *Analyse verbaler Daten. Über den Umgang mit qualitativen Daten*. Opladen: Westdeutscher Verlag, 335-388

Gingold, E., P. Gingold & S. Gingold (1979), Die Antwort heißt Assimilation. In: H.M. Broder & M.R. Lang (eds.), *Fremd im eigenen Land. Juden in der Bundesrepublik*. Frankfurt a.M.: Fischer Taschenbuch Verlag, 157-167

Ginzel, G.B. (ed.) (1991), *Antisemitismus. Erscheinungsformen der Judenfeindschaft gestern und heute*. Köln: Verlag Wissenschaft und Politik

Giordano, R. (1987), *Die zweite Schuld oder Von der Last Deutscher zu sein.* Hamburg/Zürich: Rasch und Röhring

Goldhagen, D.J. (1996a), Täter aus freien Stücken. Warum die Deutschen als Kollektiv schuldig wurden. *Die Zeit,* No. 16 of April 12th 1996

Goldhagen, D.J. (1996b), *Hitlers willige Vollstrecker.* Ganz gewöhnliche Deutsche und der Holocaust. Berlin: Siedler. [orig.: *Hitler's willing executioners.* New York: Knopf]

Greive, H. (1983), *Geschichte des modernen Antisemitismus in Deutschland.* Darmstadt: Wissenschaftliche Buchgesellschaft

Groeben, N. & R. Rustemeyer (1995), Inhaltsanalyse. In: E. König & P. Zedler (eds.), *Bilanz qualitativer Forschung,* Vol. 2: Methoden. Weinheim: Deutscher Studien Verlag, 523-554

Groeben, N. (1987), Möglichkeiten und Grenzen der Kognitionskritik durch Inhaltsanalyse von Texten. In: P. Vorderer & N. Groeben (eds.), *Textanalyse als Kognitionskritik?* Möglichkeiten und Grenzen ideologiekritischer Inhaltsanalyse. Tübingen: Narr, 1-21

Grözinger, K.E. (1992): Gedenken, Erinnern und Fest als Wege zur Erlösung des Menschen und zur Transzendenzerfahrung im Judentum. In: B. Casper & W. Sparn (eds.), *Alltag und Transzendenz.* Studien zur religiösen Erfahrung in der gegenwärtigen Gesellschaft. Freiburg/München: Albes, 19-49

Grubrich-Simitis, I. (1979), Extreme traumatization as cumulative trauma – psychoanalytic investigations of the effects of concentration camps experiences on survivors and their children. *Psychoanalytic Study of the Child* 36, 1981, 415-450

Grünberg, K. (1983), Folgen nationalsozialistischer Verfolgung bei Kindern von Überlebenden/Juden in der BRD. Marburg, Universität, Fachbereich Psychologie, diploma thesis

Grünberg, K. (1986), Jüdische Überlebende der nationalsozialistischen Verfolgung und deren Nachkommen. *Babylon.* Beiträge zur jüdischen Gegenwart, No. 1, 127-136

Grünberg, K. (1987), Folgen nationalsozialistischer Verfolgung bei jüdischen Nachkommen Überlebender in der Bundesrepublik Deutschland. *Psyche* 41, 492-507

Grünberg, K. (1990).»Psychoanalyse des Nazi-Faschismus« – Stellungnahme eines Ungebildeten. Unveröffentlichtes Manuskript

Grünberg, K. (1991), Die Generation nach der Shoah. Eine psychologische Untersuchung über Nachkommen von Überlebenden der nationalsozialistischen Judenverfolgung. In: H. Stoffels (ed.), *Schicksale der Verfolgten.* Psychische und somatische Auswirkungen von Terrorherrschaft. Berlin/Heidelberg: Springer, 173-189

Grünberg, K. (1993), Versöhnung über Auschwitz? Von der Differenz der Deutschen und Juden im Leben nach der Shoah. Umpublished lecture, B'nai B'rith Menorah Loge Munich, Juni 15th 1993

Grünberg, K. (1995), Vermitteltes Trauma an die Zweite Generation von Holocaust-Überlebenden. In: W. Fischer-Rosenthal & P. Alheit (eds.), *Biographien in Deutschland*. Soziologische Rekonstruktionen gelebter Gesellschaftsgeschichte. Opladen: Westdeutscher Verlag, 372-397

Grünberg, K. (1997), Schweigen und Ver-Schweigen. NS-Vergangenheit in Familien von Opfern und von Tätern oder Mitläufern. Psychosozial 20, No. 2, Nr. 68, 9-22

Grünberg, K. (1998a), Versöhnung über Auschwitz? In: T. Haland-Wirth, N. Spangenberg & H.-J. Wirth (eds.), *Unbequem und engagiert*. Horst-Eberhard Richter zum 75. Geburtstag. Gießen: Psychosozial-Verlag, 148-158

Grünberg, K. (1998b), Zur Weitergabe des Traumas der NS-Verfolgung an die Zweite Generation. Eine Falldarstellung. *Analytische Kinder- und Jugendlichen-Psychotherapie* 29, No. 100, 493-530

Grünberg, K. (2002), Schweigen, Ver-Schweigen, Verwirren. Juden und Deutsche nach der Shoah. In: K. Platt (ed.), *Reden von Gewalt*. Genozid und Gedächtnis. München: Fink, 303-326

Habermas, J. (1986), Eine Art Schadensabwicklung. Die apologetischen Tendenzen in der deutschen Zeitgeschichtsschreibung. In: R. Augstein et al., »*Historikerstreit*«. München/Zürich: Piper, 62-76

Hadar, Y. (1991), Existentielle Erfahrung oder Krankheitssyndrom? Überlegungen zum Begriff der »Zweiten Generation«. In: H. Stoffels (ed.), *Schicksale der Verfolgten*. Psychische und somatische Auswirkungen von Terrorherrschaft. Berlin/Heidelberg: Springer, 160-172

Hahlweg, K. (1979), Konstruktion und Validierung des Partnerschaftsfragebogens PFB. *Zeitschrift für Klinische Psychologie* 8, 17-40

Hahlweg, K. (1996), *Fragebogen zur Partnerschaftsdiagnostik (FPD)*. Handanweisung. Göttingen/Bern/Toronto/Seattle: Verlag für Psychologie, Hogrefe

Hahn, A. (1994), *Erfahrung und Begriff*. Zur Konzeption einer soziologischen Erfahrungswissenschaft als Beispielhermeneutik. Frankfurt a.M.: Suhrkamp

Hampel, C. (1995), Ein hundertjähriges Mißverständnis und seine Folgen. Einige Bemerkungen zu Annemarie Dührssen: Ein Jahrhundert Psychoanalytische Bewegung in Deutschland. Die Psychotherapie unter dem Einfluß Freuds. In: W. Burian (ed.), *Die Zukunft der Psychoanalyse*. (Psychoanalytische Blätter, 3). Göttingen/Zürich: Vandenhoeck und Ruprecht, 147-155

Hardtmann, G. (ed.) (1992), *Spuren der Verfolgung.* Seelische Auswirkungen des Holocaust auf die Opfer und ihre Kinder. Gerlingen: Bleicher
Hartmann, E. (1991), *Boundaries in the mind.* A new psychology of personality. New York: Basic Books
Hass, A. (1990), *In the shadow of the Holocaust.* The second generation. Ithaca/London: Cornell University Press
Haug, W.F. (1987), *Vom hilflosen Antifaschismus zur Gnade der späten Geburt.* Hamburg/Berlin: Argument Verlag
Heenen, S. (1983), Deutsche Linke, linke Juden und der Zionismus. In: D. Wetzel (ed.), *Die Verlängerung von Geschichte.* Deutsche, Juden und der Palästinakonflikt. Frankfurt a.M.: Verlag Neue Kritik, 103-112
Heenen-Wolff, S. (1992), *Im Haus des Henkers.* Gespräche in Deutschland. Frankfurt a.M.: Dvora Verlag im Alibaba Verlag
Heer, H. (1997), Von der Schwierigkeit, einen Krieg zu beenden. *Mittelweg 36*, Vol. 6, No. 6, 65-79
Heinsohn, G. (1988a), »Auschwitz werden uns die Deutschen niemals verzeihen«. Was ist Antizionismus? – Über die unstillbare Gier nach Missetaten, die den Juden angehängt werden können. *Frankfurter Rundschau* of November 7th 1988
Heinsohn, G. (1988b), *Was ist Antisemitismus?* Der Ursprung von Monotheismus und Judenhaß – Warum Antizionismus? Frankfurt a.M.: Eichborn
Herrmann, T. & K.H. Stäcker (1969), Sprachpsychologische Beiträge zur Sozialpsychologie. In: C.F. Graumann (ed.), *Handbuch der Psychologie,* Vol. 7 (Sozialpsychologie), 1. Halbband: Theorien und Methoden. Göttingen: Verlag für Psychologie, Hogrefe, 398-474
Herzka, H.S., A. v. Schumacher & S. Tyrangiel (1989), *Die Kinder der Verfolgten.* Die Nachkommen der Naziopfer und Flüchtlingskinder heute. Göttingen: Verlag für Medizinische Psychologie im Verlag Vandenhoeck und Ruprecht
Hilberg, R. (1961), *The destruction of the European Jews.* New York: Octagon Books, 1978
Hilberg, R. (1992), *Täter, Opfer, Zuschauer.* Die Vernichtung der Juden 1933-1945. Frankfurt a.M.: S. Fischer. [orig.: *Perpetrators, victims, bystanders.* New York: Asher]
Hoffmann-Axthelm, D. (1983), Ins Unreine geschrieben. *Ästhetik und Kommunikation,* No. 51, 27-32
Hogman, F. (1998), Trauma and identity through two generations of the Holocaust. *Psychoanalytic Review* 85, 551-578
Iden, P. (1985), Das muß jetzt sichtbar werden für alle. Rainer Werner Fassbinders Stück »Der Müll, die Stadt und der Tod« uraufgeführt. *Frankfurter Rundschau* of November 5th 1985

Jacobs, B. (1990), Produktive Arbeit für die Zukunft. Ratstagung befaßte sich mit der »Affäre Nachmann« und der Lage in der DDR. *Jüdische Allgemeine Wochenzeitung,* No. 45/1 of January 4th 1990

Juelich, D. (ed.) (1991), *Geschichte als Trauma.* Festschrift für Hans Keilson zu seinem 80. Geburtstag. Frankfurt a.M.: Nexus Verlag

Kaminer, I. (1997), Normalität und Nationalsozialismus. *Psyche* 51, 385-409

Kampmann, W. (1963), *Deutsche und Juden.* Die Geschichte der Juden in Deutschland vom Mittelalter bis zum Beginn des Ersten Weltkrieges. Frankfurt a.M.: Fischer Taschenbuch Verlag, 1981

Karpf, A. (1996), *The war after.* Living with the Holocaust. London: Heinemann

Katz, J. (1973), *Erinnerungen eines Überlebenden.* Kiel: Neuer Malik Verlag, 1988

Keilson, H. (1979), *Sequential traumatization in children:* A study on the fate of the Jewish war orphans in the Netherlands. Jersualem: Magnes Press, 1992

Keilson, H. (1986), *Sprachwurzellos.* Gedichte. Gießen: Edition Literarischer Salon

Keilson, H. (1988), Linker Antisemitismus? *Psyche* 42, 769-794

Kenning, J. (1993), Brief an Carl Nedelmann vom 14.05.1993. *DPV-Informationen,* No. 14, 4-6

Kestenberg, J.S. (1980), Psychoanalyses of children of survivors from the Holocaust. Case presentations and assessment. *Journal of the American Psychoanalytic Association* 28, 775-804

Kestenberg, J.S. (1982a), Survivor-parents and their children. In: M.S. Bergmann & M.E. Jucovy (eds.), *Generations of the Holocaust.* New York: Basic Books, 83-102

Kestenberg, J.S. (1982b), A metapsychological assessment based on an analysis of a survivor's child. In: M.S. Bergmann & M.E. Jucovy (eds.), *Generations of the Holocaust.* New York: Basic Books, 137-158

Kestenberg, M. (1982), Discriminatory aspects of the German indemnification policy. A continuation of persecution. In: M.S. Bergmann & M.E. Jucovy (eds.), *Generations of the Holocaust.* New York: Basic Books, 62-79

Keval, S. (1983), Jüdische Identität in der Bundesrepublik Deutschland am Beispiel autobiographischer Literatur. Frankfurt a.M., Universität, Institut für Kulturanthropologie und Europäische Ethnologie, thesis

Klein, H. (1973), Children of the Holocaust. Mourning and bereavement. In: E.J. Anthony & C. Koupernik (eds.), *The child in his family.* (The impact of disease and death, 2). New York/London/Sydney/Toronto: Wiley, 393-409

Klüger, R. (1992), *Still alive.* A Holocaust girlhood remembered. New York: Feminist Press, 2001

Knödler-Bunte, E. (1983), Verlängerung des Schweigens. *Ästhetik und Kommunikation*, No. 51, 33-47

Kogan, I. (1995), *The cry of mute children*. A psychoanalytic perspective of the second generation of the Holocaust. London/New York: Free Association Books

König, R. (ed.) (1952), *Das Interview*. Formen. Technik. Auswertung. 3rd. ed. Köln/Berlin: Kiepenheuer und Witsch, 1962

Körner, J. (1998), Eine Entgegnung auf Judith Kraus. *Psyche* 52, 1101-1105

Kraft-Sullivan, G. (1979), Ich habe mich daran gewöhnt, hier wie selbstverständlich zu leben. In: H.M. Broder & M.R. Lang (eds.), *Fremd im eigenen Land*. Juden in der Bundesrepublik. Frankfurt a.M.: Fischer Taschenbuch Verlag, 233-241

Kraus, J. (1998), Psychoanalyse im Exil – Schicksal? *Psyche* 52, 1093-1101

Krell, R. (1979), Holocaust families. The survivors and their children. *Comprehensive Psychiatry* 20, 560-568

Krell, R. (1984), Holocaust survivors and their children. Comments on psychiatric terminology. *Comprehensive Psychiatry* 25, 521-528

Kriz, J. (1978), Methodologische Grundlagen der Inhaltsanalyse. In: R. Lisch & J. Kriz, *Grundlagen und Modelle der Inhaltsanalyse*. Bestandsaufnahme und Kritik. Reinbek bei Hamburg: Rowohlt Taschenbuch Verlag, 29-55

Kruskal, W. & F. Mosteller (1979), Representative sampling, II. Scientific literature, excluding statistics. *International Statistical Review* 47, 111-127

Krystal, H. & W.G. Niederland (eds.) (1971), *Psychic traumatization*. Aftereffects in individuals and communities. Boston: Little, Brown and Company

Krystal, H. (ed.) (1968), *Massive psychic trauma*. New York: International Universities Press

Kugelmann, C. (1981), Was heißt jüdische Identität? (II). *alternative* 24, No. 140/141, 234-240

Kuperstein, E. (1981), Adolescents of parent survivors of concentration camps. A review of the literature. *Journal of Psychology and Judaism* 6, 7-22

Kuschner, D. (1977), Die jüdische Minderheit in der Bundesrepublik Deutschland. Eine Analyse. Köln, Universität, dissertation

Lamnek, S. (1988), *Qualitative Sozialforschung*, Vol. 1: Methodologie. 3rd, rev. ed. Weinheim: Psychologie Verlags Union, 1995

Langer, L.L. (1991), *Holocaust testimonies*. The ruins of memory. New Haven/London: Yale University Press

Laub, D. (1998), The empty circle. Children of survivors and the limits of reconstruction. *Journal of the American Psychoanalytic Association* 46, 507-529

Laufner, R. (1990), Die ausweglose Spiegelung. Eklat im Seminar »Psychoanalyse des Nazi-Faschismus«. *Marburger Magazin Express* 8, No. 6, 8-9; reprint in: Fachschaft Medizin (ed.), *Curare*, No. 17, Juni 1990, 16-17

Leiser, E. (1982), *Leben nach dem Überleben*. Dem Holocaust entronnen – Begegnungen und Schicksale. Königstein/Ts.: Athenäum Verlag

Lempp, R. (1979), *Extrembelastung im Kindes- und Jugendalter*. Über psychosoziale Spätfolgen nach nationalsozialistischer Verfolgung im Kindes- und Jugendalter anhand von Aktengutachten. Bern/Stuttgart/Wien: Huber

Leuzinger-Bohleber, M. (1995), Die Einzelfallstudie als psychoanalytisches Forschungsinstrument. *Psyche* 49, 434-480

Leuzinger-Bohleber, M. (1998), Pathogenes Leiden an der Schuld der Väter – eine Fallskizze. In: M. Leuzinger-Bohleber et al. (eds.), *Psychoanalyse im Spannungsfeld zwischen Klinik und Kulturtheorie*. Festschrift zur Eröffnung des Instituts für Psychoanalyse der Fachbereiche Erziehungswissenschaft, Humanwissenschaften und Sozialwesen der Universität/Gesamthochschule Kassel. Kassel: Institut für Psychoanalyse, 79-98

Leuzinger-Bohleber, M., H. Schneider und R. Pfeifer (eds.) (1992), *»Two butterflies on my head...«* Psychoanalysis in the interdisciplinary scientific dialogue. Berlin/Heidelberg: Springer

Levi, P. (1990), *Die Untergegangenen und die Geretteten*. München/Wien: Hanser

Levkov, I. (ed.) (1987), *Bitburg and beyond*. Encounters in American, German and Jewish history. New York: Shapolsky Publishers

Lewin, M. (1986), *Psychologische Forschung im Umriß*. Berlin/Heidelberg/New York/Tokyo: Springer

Lifton, R.J. (1980), The concept of the survivor. In: J.E. Dimsdale (ed.), *Survivors, victims, and perpetrators*. Essays on the Nazi Holocaust. Washington/New York/London: Hemisphere Publishing, 113-126

Lisch, R. (1978), Kategorien. In: R. Lisch & J. Kriz (1978), *Grundlagen und Modelle der Inhaltsanalyse*. Bestandsaufnahme und Kritik. Reinbek bei Hamburg: Rowohlt Taschenbuch Verlag, 69-83

Lockot, R. (1994), *Die Reinigung der Psychoanalyse*. Die Deutsche Psychoanalytische Gesellschaft im Spiegel von Dokumenten und Zeitzeugen (1933-1951). Tübingen: Edition diskord

Loewenstein, R.M. (1952), *Psychoanalyse des Antisemitismus*. Frankfurt a.M.: Suhrkamp, 1971

Lorenzer, A. (1981), Möglichkeiten qualitativer Inhaltsanalyse. Tiefenhermeneutische Interpretation zwischen Ideologiekritik und Psychoanalyse. *Das Argument* 23, 170-180

Luel, S.A. & P. Marcus (eds.) (1984), *Psychoanalytic reflections on the Holocaust*. Selected essays. New York: Ktav Publishing House

Magistrat der Stadt Stadtallendorf & Förderverein für Stadt- und Regionalgeschichte Stadtallendorfs 1933 – 1945 e.V. (eds.) (1991), *Dokumentation der Internationalen Tage der Begegnung in Stadtallendorf,* KZ-Außenlager Münchmühle/Nobel vom 21. bis 26.10.1990. »Das Geheimnis der Versöhnung heißt Erinnerung«. Fuldaer Verlagsanstalt

Mahler, E. (1995), Die Liebe zur radikalen Vernunft. Anmerkungen zur Krise und zur Chance der DPV. *Psyche* 49, 373-391

Mahler, M.S., F. Pine & A. Bergman (1975), *The psychological birth of the human infant.* New York: Basic Books

Marcus, P. & A. Rosenberg (eds.) (1989), *Healing their wounds.* Psychotherapy with Holocaust survivors and their families. New York/Westport/London: Praeger

Markovits, A.S. & S. Reich (1997), *Das deutsche Dilemma.* Die Berliner Republik zwischen Macht und Machtverzicht. Berlin: Alexander Fest Verlag, 1998. [orig.: *The German predicament.* Ithaca: Cornell University Press]

Mathes, R. (1992), Hermeneutisch-klassifikatorische Inhaltsanalyse von Leitfadengesprächen. Über das Verhältnis von quantitativen und qualitativen Verfahren der Textanalyse und die Möglichkeit ihrer Kombination. In: J.H.P. Hoffmeyer-Zlotnik (ed.), *Analyse verbaler Daten.* Über den Umgang mit qualitativen Daten. Opladen: Westdeutscher Verlag, 402-424

Mayring, P. (1988), *Qualitative Inhaltsanalyse.* Grundlagen und Techniken. Weinheim: Deutscher Studien Verlag

Mayring, P. (1991), Qualitative Inhaltsanalyse. In: U. Flick, E. v. Kardorff, H. Keupp, L. v. Rosenstiel & S. Wolff (eds.), *Handbuch Qualitative Sozialforschung.* München: Psychologie Verlags Union, 209-213

Medico international (ed.) (1997), *Schnelle Eingreiftruppe »Seele«.* Auf dem Weg in die therapeutische Weltgesellschaft. Frankfurt a.M.: Verlag medico international

Medizinische Kommission der Fédération Internationale Résistants (FIR) (ed.) (1973), *Ermüdung und vorzeitiges Altern.* Folge von Extrembelastungen. Leipzig: Kommissionsverlag Johann Ambrosius Barth

Meehl, P.E. (1990), Why summaries of research on psychological theories are often uninterpretable. *Psychological Reports* 66 (Monograph Suppl., 1), 195-244

Menke, J. (1960), Die soziale Integration jüdischer Flüchtlinge des ehemaligen Regierungslagers »Föhrenwald« in den westdeutschen Großstädten Düsseldorf, Frankfurt und München. In: H. Harmsen (ed.), *Sozialhygienische Forschungen,* Vol. 2. Bielefeld: W. Bertelsmann Verlag

Métraux, A. (1998), Authentizität und Autorität. Über die Darstellung der Shoah. In: J. Straub (ed.), *Erzählung, Identität und historisches Bewußtsein.*

Die psychologische Konstruktion von Zeit und Geschichte. Erinnerung, Geschichte, Identität 1. Frankfurt a.M.: Suhrkamp, 362-388

Minuchin, S. (1974), *Familie und Familientherapie*. Theorie und Praxis struktureller Familientherapie. Freiburg i.Br.: Lambertus Verlag, 1977. [orig.: *Families and family therapy*. Cambridge: Harvard University Press, 1976]

Mitscherlich, A. & L. Rosenkötter (1975), Hans Jürgen Eysenck oder die Fiktion der reinen Wissenschaft. *Psyche* 36, 1982, 1144-1163

Mohler, P.P. (1992), Cui bono – Computerunterstützte Inhaltsanalyse für die qualitative empirische Sozialforschung. In: J.H.P. Hoffmeyer-Zlotnik (ed.), *Analyse verbaler Daten*. Über den Umgang mit qualitativen Daten. Opladen: Westdeutscher Verlag, 389-401

Moser, T. (1993), *Politik und seelischer Untergrund*. Aufsätze und Vorträge. Frankfurt a.M.: Suhrkamp

Moser, T. (1995), Psychoanalyse und Holocaust. Die Kinder der Opfer und Täter. *Süddeutsche Zeitung* of July 11th 1995

Moser, T. (1996), *Dämonische Figuren*. Die Wiederkehr des Dritten Reiches in der Psychotherapie. Frankfurt a.M.: Suhrkamp

Müller-Hohagen, J. (1988), *Verleugnet, verdrängt, verschwiegen*. Die seelischen Auswirkungen der Nazizeit. München: Kösel

Münzberg, O. (1983), Wovon berührt? Vom jüdischen Trauma? Von den Traumata der Eltern? *Ästhetik und Kommunikation*, No. 51, 24-26

Nadler, A., S. Kav-Venaki & B. Gleitman (1985), Transgenerational effects of the Holocaust. Externalization of aggression in second generation of Holocaust survivors. *Journal of Consulting and Clinical Psychology* 53, 365-369

Nathan, T.S., L. Eitinger & H.Z. Winnik (1964), A psychiatric study of survivors of the Nazi Holocaust. A study in hospitalized patients. *Israel Annals of Psychiatry and Related Disciplines* 2, 47-80

Newman, L. (1979), Emotional disturbance in children of Holocaust survivors. Social casework. *The Journal of Contemporary Social Work* 60, 43-50

Niederland, W.G. (1961), The problem of the survivor. Part I: Some remarks on the psychiatric evaluation of emotional disorders in survivors of Nazi persecution. *Journal of the Hillside Hospital* 10, 233-247

Niederland, W.G. (1980), *Folgen der Verfolgung*. Das Überlebenden-Syndrom. Seelenmord. Frankfurt a.M.: Suhrkamp

Nolte, E. (1987), Zwischen Geschichtslegende und Revisionismus? Das Dritte Reich im Blickwinkel des Jahres 1980. In: R. Augstein et al., »*Historikerstreit*«. Die Dokumentation der Kontroverse um die Einzigartigkeit der nationalsozialistischen Judenvernichtung. München/Zürich: Piper, 13-35

Nolte, J. (1996), Sisyphos ist Deutscher. *Die Welt* of April 16th 1996

Oakes, M. (1986), *Statistical inference*. A commentary for the social and behavioural sciences. Chichester/New York/Brisbane/Toronto/Singapore: Wiley

Oliner, M.M. (1982), Hysterical features among children of survivors. In: M.S. Bergmann & M.E. Jucovy (eds.), *Generations of the Holocaust*. New York: Basic Books, 267-286

Pant, A. (1998), HIV-Infektionen bei iv Drogenkonsumenten – sozialepidemiologische Befunde zur Ätiologie durch Metaanalysen und Primärdatenanalysen. Berlin, Freie Universität, dissertation

Pavel, F.-G. (1975), Die Entwicklung der klientenzentrierten Psychotherapie in den USA von 1942-1973. In: Gesellschaft für wissenschaftliche Gesprächspsychotherapie (ed.), *Die klientenzentrierte Gesprächspsychotherapie*. Frankfurt a.M.: Fischer Taschenbuch Verlag, 1983, 25-41

Pehle, W.H. (ed.) (1990), *Der historische Ort des Nationalsozialismus*. Annäherungen. Frankfurt a.M.: Fischer Taschenbuch Verlag

Phillips, R.E. (1978), Impact of Nazi Holocaust on children of survivors. *American Journal of Psychotherapy* 32, 370-378

Philo-Lexikon (1982), *Handbuch des jüdischen Wissens*. Reprint of the 3rd ed. 1936. Königstein/Ts.: Jüdischer Verlag im Athenäum-Verlag

Poliakov, L. (1977), *Geschichte des Antisemitismus*. Bd. I-VIII. Worms: Heintz; Frankfurt a.M.: Athenäum Verlag, 1977-1988

Postone, M. (1981), Antisemitismus und Nationalsozialismus. *alternative* 24, No. 140/141, 241-258

Prince, R.M. (1975), Psychohistorical themes in the lives of young adult children of concentration camp survivors. New York, Columbia University, dissertation

Quindeau, I. (1995), *Trauma und Geschichte*. Interpretationen autobiographischer Erzählungen von Überlebenden des Holocaust. Frankfurt a.M.: Brandes und Apsel

Rakoff, V., J.J. Sigal & N.E. Epstein (1966), Children and families of concentration camp survivors. *Canada's Mental Health* 14, 24-26

Reich, G. (1987), *Partnerwahl und Ehekrisen*. Eine familiendynamische Studie. Heidelberg: Asanger, 1988

Reichmann, E.G. (1974), *Größe und Verhängnis deutsch-jüdischer Existenz*. Zeugnisse einer tragischen Begegnung. Heidelberg: Lambert Schneider

Richter, H.-E. (1986), *Die Chance des Gewissens*. Erinnerungen und Assoziationen. Hamburg: Hoffmann und Campe

Riedl, J. (1988), Herrenloses Geld. Das Millionenkarussell des Werner Nachmann. *Die Zeit*, No. 22 of May 27th 1988

Ritsert, J. (1972), *Inhaltsanalyse und Ideologiekritik*. Ein Versuch über kritische Sozialforschung. Frankfurt a.M.: Athenäum Fischer Taschenbuch Verlag

Rogers, C.R. (1951), *Die klientenzentrierte Gesprächspsychotherapie*. Client-centered therapy. München: Kindler, 1981. [orig.: *Client-centered therapy*. Boston: Mifflin]

Rosenstrauch, H. (1979), Verwurzelt im Nirgendwo. In: H.M. Broder & M.R. Lang (eds.), *Fremd im eigenen Land*. Juden in der Bundesrepublik. Frankfurt a.M.: Fischer Taschenbuch Verlag, 339-350

Rosenthal, G. (1995), Familienbiographien. Nationalsozialismus und Antisemitismus im intergenerationellen Dialog. In: I. Attia, M. Basqué, U. Kornfeld, G. Magiriba Lwanga, B. Rommelspacher, P. Teimoori, S. Vogelmann & U. Wachendorfer (eds.), *Multikulturelle Gesellschaft – monokulturelle Psychologie?* Antisemitismus und Rassismus in der psychosozialen Arbeit. Tübingen: dgvt-Verlag, 30-51

Rosenthal, G. (ed.) (1997), *Der Holocaust im Leben von drei Generationen*. Familien von Überlebenden der Shoah und von Nazi-Tätern. Gießen: Psychosozial-Verlag

Rüsen, J. & J. Straub (eds.) (1998), *Die dunkle Spur der Vergangenheit*. Psychoanalytische Zugänge zum Geschichtsbewußtsein. Erinnerung, Geschichte, Identität 2. Frankfurt a.M.: Suhrkamp

Russell, A. (1974), Late psychosocial consequences in concentration camp survivor families. *American Journal of Orthopsychiatry* 44, 611-619

Rustin, S.L. & F.S. Lipsig (1972), Psychotherapy with the adolescent children of concentration camp survivors. *Journal of Contemporary Psychotherapy* 4, 87-94

Saldern, M. v. (1995), Zum Verhältnis von qualitativen und quantitativen Methoden. In: E. König & P. Zedler (eds.), *Bilanz qualitativer Forschung*, Vol. 1: Grundlagen qualitativer Forschung. Weinheim: Deutscher Studien Verlag, 331-371

Savran, B. & E. Fogelman (1976), Psychological issues in the lives of children of survivors. An update, the children as adults. In: L.Y. Steinitz & D.M. Szonyi (eds.), *Living after the Holocaust*. Reflections by children of survivors in America. Revised second edition. New York: Bloch, 1979, 147-156

Scheffer, C. (1988), »Der Jude« als Symbol. Antisemitische Vorurteile im Kontext von Einstellungen zu Ökonomie und Politik. Marburg, Universität, Fachbereich Psychologie, diploma thesis

Schirrmacher, F. (1999), *Die Walser-Bubis-Debatte*. Eine Dokumentation. Frankfurt a.M.: Suhrkamp

Schlösser, A.-M. & K. Höhfeld (eds.) (1998), *Trauma und Konflikt*. Gießen: Psychosozial-Verlag

Schmidt, C. (1997), »Am Material«: Auswertungstechniken für Leitfadeninterviews. In: B. Friebertshäuser & A. Prengel (eds.), *Handbuch Qualita-*

tive Forschungsmethoden in der Erziehungswissenschaft. Weinheim/München: Juventa, 544-568

Schmidt, F.L. (1992), What do data really mean? Research findings, meta-analysis, and cumulative knowledge in psychology. *American Psychologist* 47, 1173-1181

Schmidt, J.U. & F. König (1986), Untersuchungen zur Validität der revidierten Form des Freiburger Persönlichkeitsinventars FPI-R. *Diagnostica* 32, 197-208

Schneider, C., C. Stillke & B. Leineweber (1996), *Das Erbe der Napola. Versuch einer Generationengeschichte des Nationalsozialismus.* Hamburg: Hamburger Edition

Schneider, R.C. (1989), Unter der Decke. *Die Zeit*, No. 1 of December 29th 1989

Schneider, S. (1981), A proposal for treating adolescent offspring of Holocaust survivors. *Journal of Psychology and Judaism* 6, 68-76

Schnell, R., P.B. Hill & E. Esser (1995), *Methoden der empirischen Sozialforschung.* München/Wien: Oldenbourg Verlag

Schölch, A. (1983), Das Dritte Reich, die zionistische Bewegung und der Palästinakonflikt. In: D. Wetzel (ed.), *Die Verlängerung von Geschichte. Deutsche, Juden und der Palästinakonflikt.* Frankfurt a.M.: Verlag Neue Kritik, 65-92

Schönhuber F. (1989), *»Ich war dabei«.* München: Herbig Verlag

Schründer-Lenzen, A. (1997), Triangulation und idealtypisches Verstehen in der (Re-) Konstruktion subjektiver Theorien. In: B. Friebertshäuser & A. Prengel (eds.), *Handbuch Qualitative Forschungsmethoden in der Erziehungswissenschaft.* Weinheim/München: Juventa, 107-117

Schultz-Venrath, U. (1995), Der Mißbrauch von Geschichte als transgenerationelles Traumatisierungsphänomen. *Psyche* 49, 392-403

Schütze, F. (1977), Die Technik des narrativen Interviews in Interaktionsfeldstudien – dargestellt an einem Projekt zur Erforschung von kommunalen Machtstrukturen. Arbeitsberichte und Forschungsmaterialien der Universität Bielefeld, Fakultät für Soziologie

Sichrovsky, P. (1985), *Wir wissen nicht was morgen wird, wir wissen wohl was gestern war. Junge Juden in Deutschland und Österreich.* Köln: Kiepenheuer und Witsch

Sichrovsky, P. (1987), *Schuldig geboren. Kinder aus Nazifamilien.* Köln: Kiepenheuer und Witsch

Sigal, J.J. & M. Weinfeld (1989), *Trauma and rebirth.* Intergenerational effects of the Holocaust. New York: Praeger

Sigal, J.J., D. Silver, V. Rakoff & B. Ellin (1973), Some Second-Generation effects of survival of the Nazi persecution. *American Journal of Orthopsychiatry* 43, 320-327

Silbermann, A. & J.H. Schoeps (eds.) (1986), *Antisemitismus nach dem Holocaust.* Bestandsaufnahme und Erscheinungsformen in deutschsprachigen Ländern. Köln: Verlag Wissenschaft und Politik

Slipp, S. (1979), The children of survivors of Nazi concentration camps. A pilot study of the intergenerational transmission of psychic trauma. *Group Therapy* 9, 197-204

Speier, S. (1987), Der ges(ch)ichtslose Psychoanalytiker – die ges(ch)ichtslose Psychoanalyse. *Psyche* 41, 481-491

Spiegelman, A. (1986), *Maus.* Die Geschichte eines Überlebenden. Reinbek bei Hamburg: Rowohlt, 1989

SPSS for Windows (1998), Release 8.0.2. Chicago: SPSS Inc.

Statistisches Bundesamt (ed.) (1991), *Statistisches Jahrbuch 1992 für die Bundesrepublik Deutschland.* Stuttgart: Metzler-Poeschel

Steinitz, L.Y. & D.M. Szonyi (eds.) (1976), *Living after the Holocaust.* Reflections by children of survivors in America. Revised second edition. New York: Bloch, 1979

Sterling, E. (1966). Vorwort. In: I. Elbogen & E. Sterling, *Die Geschichte der Juden in Deutschland.* Wiesbaden: Fourier Verlag, 1982, 5-10

Stierlin, H. (1978), *Delegation und Familie.* Beiträge zum Heidelberger familiendynamischen Konzept. Frankfurt a.M.: Suhrkamp, 1982

Stoffels, H. (ed.) (1991), *Schicksale der Verfolgten.* Psychische und somatische Auswirkungen von Terrorherrschaft. Berlin/Heidelberg: Springer

Strauss, H.A. & N. Kampe (eds.) (1985), *Antisemitismus.* Von der Judenfeindschaft zum Holocaust. Frankfurt a.M./New York: Campus

Streeck-Fischer, A. (ed.) (1998), *Adoleszenz und Trauma.* Göttingen: Vandenhoeck und Ruprecht

Tausch, R. & A.-M. Tausch (1960), *Gesprächspsychotherapie.* Einfühlsame hilfreiche Gruppen- und Einzelgespräche in Psychotherapie und alltäglichem Leben. 7th, rev. ed. Göttingen/Toronto/Zürich: Verlag für Psychologie, Hogrefe, 1979

Terman, L.M. (1938), *Psychological factors in marital happiness.* New York: McGraw-Hill

Torberg, F. (1968), *Mein ist die Rache.* Erzählungen. Frankfurt a.M./Berlin: Ullstein, 1986

Trossman, B. (1968), Adolescent children of concentration camp survivors. *Canadian Psychiatric Association Journal* 12, 121-123

Valent, P. (1998), Auswirkungen des Holocaust auf überlebende jüdische Kinder. Traumen und Spätfolgen nach 50 Jahren. *Psyche* 52, 751-771

van der Kolk, B.A. (1998), Zur Psychologie und Psychobiologie von Kindheitstrauma (Developmental Trauma). In: A. Streek-Fischer (ed.), *Adoleszenz und Trauma.* Göttingen: Vandenhoeck und Ruprecht, 32-56 van der Kolk, B.A., A.C. McFarlane und L. Weisaeth (1996), *Traumatic stress*. The effects of overwhelming experience on mind, body, and society. New York/London: Guilford Press

van der Kolk, B.A., J.A. Burbridge & J. Suzuki (1998), Die Psychobiologie traumatischer Erinnerungen. Klinische Folgerungen aus Untersuchungen mit bildgebenden Verfahren bei Patienten mit Posttraumatischer Belastungsstörung. In: A. Streek-Fischer (ed.), *Adoleszenz und Trauma*. Göttingen: Vandenhoeck und Ruprecht, 57-78

Vogt, R. (1995), Rainer Werner Fassbinders »Der Müll, die Stadt und der Tod« – eine deutsche Seelenlandschaft. *Psyche* 49, 309-372

Wallmann, W. (n.d.), Grußwort. In: Magistrat der Stadt Stadtallendorf & Förderverein für Stadt- und Regionalgeschichte Stadtallendorfs 1933-1945 e.V. (eds.), *Internationale Tage der Begegnung in Stadtallendorf*, KZ-Außenlager Münchmühle 21.-26.10.1990. »Das Geheimnis der Versöhnung heißt Erinnerung«, Marburg. Alp-Druck, 9-11

Wardi, D. (1990), *Memorial candles*. Children of the Holocaust. London/ New York: Tavistock/Routledge, 1992

Wehler, H.U. (1988), *Entsorgung der deutschen Vergangenheit?* Ein polemischer Essay zum »Historikerstreit«. Frankfurt a.M.: Büchergilde Gutenberg

Werthmann, H.V. (1997), Stellungnahme zur »Erklärung von Frankfurter DPV-Mitgliedern zum Konflikt zwischen Herrn Werthmann und Herrn Hilbert«. *FPI-Forum*. Zeitschrift der Mitglieder des Frankfurter Psychoanalytischen Instituts e.V., No. 5 of December 10th 1997

Westernhagen, D. v. (1987), *Die Kinder der Täter*. Das Dritte Reich und die Generation danach. München: Kösel, 1988

Westhoff, G. (1993), *Handbuch psychosozialer Meßinstrumente*. Ein Kompendium für epidemiologische und klinische Forschung zu chronischer Krankheit. Göttingen: Verlag für Psychologie, Hogrefe

Wetzel, D. (1983), »Die Verlängerung von Geschichte«. Anstatt einer Einleitung. In: D. Wetzel (ed.), *Die Verlängerung von Geschichte*. Deutsche, Juden und der Palästinakonflikt. Frankfurt a.M.: Verlag Neue Kritik, 7-14

Winnicott, D.W. (1965), *The family and individual development*. London: Tavistock Publ.

Wolffsohn, M. (1983), Leben im Land der Mörder. Deutschlands Juden im Spannungsfeld zwischen Israel und Diaspora. *Die Zeit*, No. 22 of May 5th 1983

Wolffsohn, M. (1993), *Verwirrtes Deutschland?* Provokative Zwischenrufe eines deutschjüdischen Patrioten. München: Ed. Ferenczy bei Bruckmann

Young, J.E. (1988), *Beschreiben des Holocaust. Darstellung und Folgen der Interpretation*. Frankfurt a.M.: Suhrkamp, 1997. [orig.: *Writing and rewriting the Holocaust*. Bloomington: Indiana University Press]
Zentralwohlfahrtsstelle der Juden in Deutschland (ed.) (1998), Mitgliederstatistik der einzelnen Jüdischen Gemeinden und Landesverbände per 1. Januar 1998. Frankfurt a.M.
Zollinger, P. (1985), Der Normalbürger spricht. Eine Schnellumfrage zum Theaterstreit. In: E. Kiderlen (Hrsg.), *Pflasterstrand Flugschrift – 1. Deutsch-jüdische Normalität ... Fassbinders Sprengsätze*. Frankfurt a.M.: Pflasterstrand, 52-56
Zwerenz, G. (1973), *Die Erde ist unbewohnbar wie der Mond*. Frankfurt a.M.: S. Fischer

On the Myth of Objective Research after Auschwitz

Unconscious Entanglements with the National Socialist Past in the Investigation of Long-term Psychosocial Consequences of the Shoah in the Federal Republic of Germany[1]

"A hotel owner named Adam, before the eyes of a child that liked him, killed with a cudgel the rats that poured out of holes in the courtyard; the child created in his image its image of the first human being. That this is being forgotten; that one no longer understands what one once felt next to the cart of the dog catcher, that is the triumph of culture and its failure. It cannot bear the memory of that zone, because it always does as old Adam did, and precisely that is incompatible with its conception of itself. It abhors the stench because it stinks; because its palace, as Brecht put it in a brilliant passage, is built from dog shit. Years after that passage was written, Auschwitz irrevocably proved the failure of culture. That this could happen amidst the traditions of philosophy, art and the enlightening sciences, says more than that these, that the spirit, were unable to touch people and to change them. These disciplines themselves, their emphatic claim of autarky, harbours untruth. All culture after Auschwitz, including its specific critique, is junk. [...] Whoever pleads for the preservation of the radically guilty and miserable culture, is an accomplice, while one who rejects culture directly promotes the barbarism that culture revealed itself to be. Not even silence can escape this circle; it merely serves to rationalise one's own subjective impotence using

---

1 | Published in: Leuzinger-Bohleber, M., H. Deserno & S. Hau (eds.) (2004), *Psychoanalyse als Profession und Wissenschaft* (Psychoanalysis as profession and science). Stuttgart; Berlin; Cologne: Kohlhammer. English publication in Rüsen, J. & Straub, J. (eds) (in press), *Dark Traces of the Past*. Oxford/New York: Berghahn Books

the state of objective truth, thus once again degrading truth into a lie." (Theodor W. Adorno 1966, 359f.; transl. by N.R.)

These words by Theodor W. Adorno from his *Meditationen zur Metaphysik* (Meditations on Metaphysics) provide an inkling of the personal and collective abysses that may open when, albeit many years after 'the deed', but in the very country of the murderers, one undertakes to examine the legacy of the National Socialist extermination of the Jews, when one gets involved with the Lebenswelt (lifeworld) of Jews – survivors and their sons and daughters born after the Shoah, and in the non-Jewish German world of Nazi perpetrators, Nazi sympathizers and observers and *their* children. About sixty years after Auschwitz, these Second Generation individuals meet in their day-to-day dealings at work, in politics and in cultural life. They achieve various degrees of closeness, and sometimes get in each other's way. A love relationship probably represents the most intimate contact between the side of the former victims and the side of the perpetrators, or their sympathizers. In my doctoral dissertation (Grünberg 2000) I explored such second-generation relationships in post-National-Socialist Germany in order to gain deeper insights into the "culture after Auschwitz". The true extent and significance of the abyss that did indeed emerge during the course of this endeavour only became apparent in hindsight.

A doctoral dissertation is evaluated in terms of various criteria: some good, some less useful, and some downright bad. The assessment always depends on the values attached to a given type of research. There are no *generally* applicable criteria. For instance, if one were to focus on the length of a thesis, or the time it took to complete it, one would soon conclude that the number of words or the number of years to completion do not necessarily correspond to its scientific import. It would seem that the scientific and social significance of a problem, the complexity of the subject matter, unexpected results or the originality of a scientific study are more suitable criteria. At times, the evaluation of a piece of research may be based on something entirely different, for example, on what was *not* said and *not* reported. Presumably, the very aspects of a study that have fallen victim to the researcher's censorship, in a manner of speaking, can themselves lead to fundamental insights into the topic under investigation. One may object that outsiders do not have access to this domain, and – this is undoubtedly true. But is it not always the case that the reader of a study is reliant on the author to grant him insight into his or her work? In any event, especially if some time has passed since the completion of the study, the author *himself* has the option of taking a second look at his own study.

I will pursue some of these considerations as I address certain thoughts and feelings I experienced when I submitted my dissertation in 1999, but chose not to make public at the time. I posit that certain experiences that occurred with increasing frequency while I was working on my thesis, as well as during the many years of in-depth engagement with the subject matter, did, at least latently, encroach upon the study and are therefore of considerable significance to its content. A number of factors encourage me to disclose some of my thoughts and experiences regarding certain entanglements and conflicts that arose during my investigation of the psychosocial consequences of the Shoah: the length of time that has passed since completing my dissertation, my own work and life experience and increased freedom, i.e. *not* being subject to specific evaluation upon which academic qualification and promotion were contingent. I hope to shed light on the fact that, when investigating the consequences of the National Socialist crimes against humanity in particular, striving for *purely objective scientific research* must necessarily be a myth. This is the case because the individual, familial and social NS entanglements of everybody involved do not permit a position of non-involvement. At best, the endeavour to objectively study the Nazi legacy may be viewed as a *naïve* attempt to assume a quasi-objective perspective to avoid becoming infected with the Nazi horror. More likely, however, such an approach will lead to serious distortions and misrepresentation. Relative to the far-reaching significance for the life "afterwards", of the break with civilisation that occurred at Auschwitz, this stance will merely scratch the surface. It will not meet Adorno's challenge to allow a genuine engagement with "culture after Auschwitz" (Adorno 1966, 359) and the "terror without end" (cf. Adorno 1951, 316 [German edition]), a manifestation of the horrific facet of an epoch, which, through the millionfold systematic murder of a people by means of a type of hydrocyanic acid originally produced for pest control, most profoundly marked the past century.

I shall begin by addressing questions of the design of my studies of the psychosocial consequences of the Shoah. I shall then focus on the "independent third-party rating" procedure employed and on the conflicts that arose within the group of researchers, which eventually caused our collaboration to fail. These conflicts are understood as a confrontation of two partially subconscious lines of tradition, which ultimately underlie the German-Jewish relationship in post-National-Socialist Germany: the transmission of the trauma of Nazi persecution in the Second Generation on one side, versus the transmission of Nazi support by non-Jewish Germans on the other. Finally, I shall describe a dispute that arose with a university lecturer who declared that the Jews who were persecuted under National Socialism were "unconscious accomplices". I shall explain this scenario in terms of the social generation of anti-Semitism. Here, too, dissociated fragments of the National Socialist legacy become evident. Both these controversies must be viewed as part of Adorno's "culture after Auschwitz".

Issues of Study Design

When I began my investigations of *Liebesbeziehungen der Zweiten Generation in der Bundesrepublik Deutschland* (Intimate relationships of the Second Generation in the Federal Republic of Germany) in 1986, I soon realised how difficult it was to find interviewees who were prepared to participate in my study, namely Jews, daughters and sons of concentration camp survivors who were born, or at least raised, in Germany, and a comparison group of non-Jewish Germans matched for gender, age and occupation. This alone disrupted my original time frame, since it took me more than a year to recruit the control sample. My first supervisor had become somewhat impatient and thought that I should content myself with what I had. I had planned to interview at least twenty Jews and the same number of non-Jewish Germans. Some prospective interviewees initially confirmed their participation in the study only to withdraw from it just before the interview. Neither was I deterred from pursuing my original goal by the discovery in the course of seven interviews that the individuals did not meet the criteria for participation in the study, as I had been previously led to believe. For example, one individual who had been introduced to me as a Second Generation Jew was not even Jewish. The parents of other interviewees were not concentration camp survivors etc.

Apart from my own stubbornness, however, there were other reasons for holding on to the original plan of study. I remembered all too well the reaction of the chairman of the graduate seminar in the psychology department at Marburg University, where in the early eighties, I presented my diploma thesis *Folgen nationalsozialistischer Verfolgung bei Kindern von Überlebenden/Juden in der BRD* (Consequences of National Socialist persecution in children of survivors/Jews in the Federal Republic of Germany) (Grünberg 1983). To my knowledge, my thesis was one of the first to use a *qualitative* approach in the department in Marburg, which adheres to "academic psychology". The head of the graduate seminar simply refused to accept a diploma thesis that did not conform to the standards of 'proper' study design, involving an experimental and a control group. He was outraged that I even seriously considered this. The expert assessor of a foundation where I applied for a doctoral grant was similarly disparaging. His statement, "No doctorate in this area of research without a control group", still resounds in my ears today.

These experiences left me feeling unable to do right by anyone. Some critics were extremely sceptical of a research approach they considered entirely speculative with many confounding factors and with variables that could not be properly operationalised. Others criticised what they considered a nitpicking approach; did I imagine that I could arrive at important insights that way? Years later, a famous psychoanalyst was full of praise for my work – the statistical part, however, apparently meant "nothing at all" to her. I, on the other hand, wanted to create a dialogue of opposing study procedures. I had hoped to combine qualitative and quantitative approaches, because I believed that proceeding *multi*-methodologically would lead to deeper insights into my chosen research topic. I was also of the opinion that empirical proof and mere assertion were two different things. Whether the above critical objections represented attempts at avoiding confrontation with a bothersome research topic, will not be addressed at this point. Sometimes, methodological inquiries are part and parcel of a process of collective resistance, a means to avoid getting involved with uncomfortable and tormenting questions. After all, engagement with the Shoah in Germany entails not only confrontation with the painful and unbearable reality of the experience of persecution by the victims. It also involves confrontation with one's own family's direct and indirect *entanglement* in the process of marginalisation, persecution and extermination of people, a crime against humanity committed by Nazi perpetrators, Nazi sympathizers and onlookers – who *wanted* what they did (cf. Goldhagen 1996).

"Independent" Third-Party Rating?

In this section I shall discuss a controversy that arose *within* the research team during the stage of data analysis. This conflict is part of what I later called the "Marburg chapter". In the end, there was a rather unpleasant hearing before the district court, which ended with a settlement. Certainly, the most important insights did not pertain to the outcome of these proceedings, but to a deeper understanding of the significance of the conflict in the context of the relationship between Jewish and non-Jewish researchers in a study on the psychosocial consequences of the Shoah in Germany. In order to elucidate these problems, I shall first deal with the methodological issues of combining qualitative and quantitative research approaches within this study.

In order to match the complexity of the issues to be examined the methodology employed was conceptualized as requiring continuous changes in perspective. First, this concerns the question of interdisciplinarity: in order to arrive at a comprehensive picture of the topic under investigation, insights into National Socialism and the continuing effect of Nazi persecution were to be derived from various scientific disciplines such as psychology, psychoanalysis, sociology, political science as well as historical and literary studies. Second, the imperative of a multi-methodological research strategy was to be reflected in the use of diverse methodologies. In addition to publicly accessible reports from specialised literature and the daily press, subjective impressions and experiences from the perspective of the Second Generation also played an important role in the conceptualisation of the life experience (*Lebenswelt*) of Jews in Germany today. In addition to employing standardised surveys that assess personality traits (Freiburg Personality Inventory-Revised FPI-R) and analyse relationship behaviour in current intimate relationships (partnership questionnaire PFB), I also designed and employed rating scales to evaluate relationships with parents and the autonomy of intimate relationships. The qualitative evaluation of the semi-structured in-depth interviews was based on verbatim transcripts of the three to nine hour long conversations, which produced about four thousand pages of material. In the final part of the interviews we used a projective sentence completion test. The only limitations placed on two detailed single case analyses (cf. Leuzinger-Bohleber 1995) were that all insights and interpretations had to be related to specific passages in the text.

The content analysis and evaluation of the interview transcripts using independent third-party raters served to render the study more objective. Three advanced psychology students who were employed as student assistants functioned as third-party raters. Like the interviewees, the third-party raters were not informed about any details of the study and its hypotheses. At the beginning of the interview, the interviewees were told the following: "I am conducting an investigation of intimate relationships at the department of psychology at Philipps University Marburg. [...] A further component of the study is an examination of family of origin. This also includes parents' life experiences." At a later stage of the interview, interviewees were asked about parents' life experiences "in the 30s and 40s". National Socialism was *not* explicitly mentioned because it was important not to place interviewees, especially non-Jewish Germans, in a position of defensiveness or resistance. The "30s and 40s" could be understood in terms of whatever significance the various families attributed to it.

Presumably, it was more important for the Jewish participants to see the interviewer as "one of their own", in order to be able to be open about extremely difficult or intimate topics, and to feel understood. However, I did not explicitly mention my own background even to the Jewish interviewees. The Jewish participants probably knew implicitly that I myself was Jewish and part of the Second Generation. I was hoping that both the experimental and the comparison group would express their views, based on trust. The offer to conduct the interviews in people's homes, which was taken up by most interviewees, further helped to build trust. The third-party raters met in my flat, where they were offered food and drink and were free to ask me any questions.

The underlying idea about independent third-party rating was not to determine inter-rater reliabilities or other comparative data, but rather to bring about a consensus between the three students. The third-party raters were supposed to discuss matters, learn from each other and, in case of doubt, discuss and agree on category assignments. Some interviews were analysed separately by the three students and discussed later. Some interviews were only rated by one student, and later, analysed together again etc. Specifically, the analysis of interview transcripts by the third-party raters proceeded as follows:

Initially, all third-party coders read the same transcripts from the test and control group (the third-party raters did not know how the groups were divided). Following the *coding guideline*, they were asked to mark passages of the interview that were relevant to the four central questions in different colours. They then discussed the results. The aim of this discussion was to arrive at an agreement about the colour coding of the passages.

The third-party coders familiarised themselves with Mayring's concept of a "summarising content analysis" (1988; 1991), according to which the chosen passages are first *paraphrased* and presented in pre-designed tables. Then the statements are *generalised*. Finally, the generalisations are *reduced* and assigned to various numbered categories. The third-party raters then discussed their various paraphrases, generalisations and reductions with the aim of arriving at consensually generated category.

The same procedure was followed with one further interview transcript. Then the students were presented with *different* transcripts, which the students analysed independently. Later, the third-party raters received another identical interview for analysis and then again different ones. We proceeded this way until all interviews were analysed, i.e., some identical interviews were analysed separately with a view to arriving at a consensus afterwards, but most interviews were analysed by only one third-party coder.

In the end, the overall results of the third-party coding were summarised by the group. *All extracted categories* were listed in a table according to a central question. An attempt was made to assign each category to a superordinate category (e.g. *entangled* or *not entangled attention or inattention*; *open* or *hidden pressure* etc.). The table's column contained the frequency with which the various categories appeared in the individual interviews.

After that, the compilation of categories was to be compared with the deductive categories derived from the theory (cf. Groeben 1987; Groeben & Rustemeyer 1995). This comparison was to be made by assigning inductively derived categories to the deductively obtained categories. The hypotheses were to be tested via quantitative analyses.

Conflict with the Third-Party Raters

Conflict with the three students arose when the various extracted categories were to be assigned to certain superordinate categories, a prerequisite for group comparison. I will illustrate this via a specific example.

The interview contained the following question: "Which experiences in the 30s and 40s had the most lasting impact on the life of your parents?" The answers were then discussed in detail. Once the interviews had been completed, the third-party raters were presented with four "central questions for third-party rating", designed to assist categorisation. In "Central question 2" the term National Socialism was mentioned for the first time, an indication for the students that "dealing with" the time of National Socialism was to be the focus of the analysis. Verbatim, the second question read as follows: "What did the interviewee say directly about how and to what extent his/her parents passed on information about their experiences during National Socialism? What did they pass on, how did they do that and what were their motivations for doing so? Parents may confront their descendants with their main, actual NS experiences, but they may also confront them with experiences that obscure events. They may also remain silent about their main experiences while being clear or they may hide their main experiences through silence."

The third-party raters were presented with an example for each superordinate category:

1) *Confrontation with main NS experiences:*
   "My mother always talked about her arrest and how she got separated from her family."
2) *Confrontation with covering experiences:*
   "My father frequently talked about the technological innovations in the company were he was employed as an engineer at the time, but he never mentioned the forced labourers that worked there."
3) *Silence while being clear about the main NS experiences:*
   "My father hardly ever talked about his experiences of that time. I always knew what it was that he experienced, but the memories seem to be too painful to talk about. Maybe he wanted to spare me that."
4) *Silence while hiding the main NS experiences:*
   "My mother never talked about her experiences of that time. She said that it was not that important. So, I don't really know what she really experienced."

The third-party raters did fulfil their task up to a point. Their categories and their assignment to superordinate categories for "central question 2. Parent's experiences of National Socialism" looked like this:

2.1 *Confrontation with major experiences during National Socialism:*
 – Supporting Jews
 – Stories about parent's sufferings under Nazi crimes
 – Reports about experiences during the war as soldiers and, about the post-war period as prisoners of war[2]
2.2 *Confrontation with hidden experiences:*
 – (no assignments)
2.3 *Silence while being clear about the main NS experiences:*
 – Hesitant and incomplete reports about experiences of persecution
2.4 *Silence while hiding main NS experiences:*
 – Incomplete reports about experiences under National Socialism
 – Parents refuse to talk about experiences under National Socialism

When it came to classifying another of their own categories, "Private experiences with family, job etc." according to the above pattern, the third-party raters refused to continue their work. At this point, they suddenly and unexpectedly accused me of conducting my study "completely unscientifically". They claimed that the results of the study had been predictable, and that the procedure forced them to make assumptions about the non-Jewish interviewees and their parents. They did not want to be used by me and be part of something that ought to be rejected as unscientific. The only aim of the study, so they claimed, was "to condemn Germans". The fact that many people in Germany know little about what their parents had experienced or done during the time of National Socialism was "not something they could be reproached for just like that". The raters maintained that one ought not to conduct a scientific investigation in which the participants were deceived this way. It was only supposed to seem as if they – the third-party raters – had really worked independently of me – the interviewer and author of the study.

Initially, I was very surprised by the students' sudden and vehement

---

2 | With regard to superordinate category *Confrontation with main experiences during National Socialism,* the students cited Jewish people's experiences of suffering side by side with war and prisoner of war experiences. I found this remarkable, since it demonstrates that the students were free to combine the categories extracted by them as they deemed appropriate. As far as my statistical calculations are concerned, this means that parents' reports about their experiences as soldiers or as prisoners of war counted as much as parental reports about Nazi persecution regarding the *clarity* of the major experiences of parents' experiences under National Socialism.

accusations after many months of constructive efforts and collaboration. I tried to remain calm and asked them for the reasons for their dissatisfaction. I explained that as independent third-party coders they did not have to adopt the specified superordinate categories. If they thought that certain categories did not fit the pattern, they were free to advance different suggestions. They did, however, have to assign their categories to certain superordinate categories in order to allow statistical analysis regarding group differences. Without that, it would be impossible to evaluate this important part of the study.

Because I was beginning to lose my composure – my entire thesis was falling apart – I withdrew in order to seek advice from a friend and university lecturer who knew my work very well. His advice was to have another 'sensible' conversation with the students. I was to explain that my method was not at all unscientific even if some of the results might perhaps have been expected. Perhaps, he thought, it would be better for all involved to meet at a later date rather than making any rash decisions.

At our next meeting I once again tried to persuade the students to complete their third-party rating task – to no avail. I asked them whether they felt personally attacked, or whether they found themselves confronted with their own family histories. Perhaps we could come to an agreement that way. "That has nothing at all to do with it", they said. The only problem was that the design of my study was "unscientific". My request that the students complete their work for *my* sake, so that the project, which I had been working on for many years, would not fail, was also in vain. Neither did it make any difference that I threatened to not pay outstanding invoices if the third-party raters did not complete their work. The students discontinued their participation. They were not prepared to make any concessions.

A little later, two of the students sent me a demand for payment via a solicitor, which I ignored. First, I explained that I had entered into a contract with the student assistants, which they did not fulfil. Second, I pointed out that I would have to train new assistants, which would involve further expenses. I still had a glimmer of hope that the three students might change their minds and complete their third-party rating task after all.

As mentioned above, the legal proceedings ended with a settlement. After the hearing, the judge pointed out to me that jurisdiction does not necessarily go hand in hand with justice. A civil law suit is merely an attempt to bring about an agreement between two parties in order to settle a conflict. Out of court, the conflict was never settled, however. To this day, I have not even spoken to the two students who initiated proceedings. In summary, I was not able to reach an agreement on this far-reaching and, for the topic under investigation, very significant issue, neither through my own efforts, nor with the help of any trusted third parties available to me.

Did the third-party raters, in their own way and provoked by me and my procedure, come into contact with Adorno's "terror without end" *after all*?

Clarity Regarding Parents' main Experiences during National Socialism

Another psychology student finally finished the "independent third-party rating". With respect to the assignment of the category "Private experiences with family, job etc.", she chose none of the existing superordinate categories and instead introduced a new category (2.5) without a title for this purpose. For statistical purposes, categories 2.1 *Confrontation with main experiences during National Socialism* and 2.3 *Silence while being clear about main experiences during National Socialism* of subsection 2 (parents' experiences of National Socialism) were combined. In this context, whether or not parents kept silent about their main experiences during National Socialism, was not regarded as a relevant differentiation. This occurred because the issue concerned whether daughters and sons, i.e. the interviewees, knew what their parents' main experiences under National Socialism had been – irrespective of whether the parents spoke about those.

As shown in figure 1, the difference between the two groups in the *parents' important experiences under National Socialism* category was very pronounced. In the Jewish group, on average nine of ten statements in this area expressed clarity regarding parents' experiences under National Social-

Figure 1: Average percentage of superordinate categories of the sub-section "parents' important experiences under National Socialism" in both groups

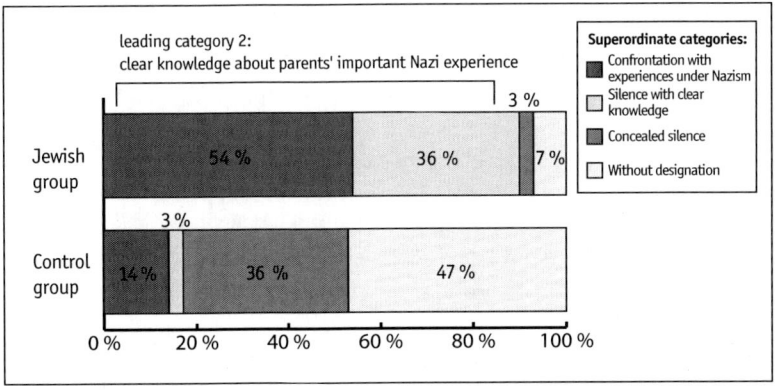

ism, while in the comparison group this was the case for an average of 17 per cent of the categorised statements.

Researchers' Entanglement with National Socialism

Why did the third-party raters discontinue their work? Might the conflict have been avoided? A scientific investigation of the psychosocial consequences of the National Socialist extermination of Jews in Germany, necessarily entails conflicts related to the relationship of Jews and non-Jews in Germany, especially when researchers from both groups collaborate. In the present case, the subject of investigation itself became the cause of an irresolvable conflict that can only be understood when both sides' entanglement with the history of National Socialism is examined.

When the students discontinued their work, my emotional entanglement consisted of my feeling abandoned and let down. Although I myself never experienced it, I imagined myself back in the time of National Socialism. I felt that my efforts to gain insight into the continuing effects of the extreme trauma caused by the National Socialist extermination of the Jews in Germany had failed. I felt as if I was experiencing something Jews had suffered during the early phase of National Socialism, when they lost their jobs, their friends and their partners. In the end I felt I had to do what I had already gone through passively, namely to leave Marburg and start over elsewhere.

Although they explicitly denied it, I believed that the three students *also* saw themselves confronted with their own origins and with the history of their own families. They were probably afraid to accuse their own parents or, as a result of their own ignorance, to find that they were the accused themselves. They did not want to be reproached for 'not having asked' their parents. Had they accepted the reproach, they might have found themselves on par with the unthinking silent sympathizers. They would no longer have been able to regard their own position as a good one. Awareness of such unease may either lead to feelings of hurt or shame, or it may lead to *rejection* of guilt. This is not, however, the rejection of guilt by Nazi perpetrators or silent sympathizers. Rather, this is what Ralph Giordano called the Germans' "second guilt" (Giordano 1987): being part of the denial of the crimes of the Nazis and to maintain this, without the threat of Nazi persecution, contrary to people's own experience, contrary to their knowledge and understanding.

The third-party raters thoughts of my work and my person must also be taken into consideration. In this context I should mention that the argument occurred very soon after the dispute with Pohlen, head of the Marburg clinic, which is outlined below. The first letter from the two students' solicitor was dated March 27, 1990, the same month during which the article *Eklat im Psychoanalyse-Seminar*[3] (scandal in the psychoanalysis seminar) appeared. The incident was much discussed in psychology circles, which suggests that the students were probably aware of it. This is significant because the students regarded me as someone who provoked conflict, who would not let go and who therefore needed to be reprimanded. But who likes to surround himself with victims? Are such situations not more likely to give rise to the need to break away, or even to 'throw another punch'? Is it not possible that the third-party raters felt the need to punish, which they did by discontinuing their work? It is likely that they regarded me as provocative, as someone who must become a victim, as someone who must be prevented from making Germans feel guilty. They also took offence at the fact that I did not inform the non-Jewish interviewees at the outset about the objective of my study – they may have thought, or rather hoped, that if I had, the research results would have been much more favourable for their group. The third-party raters probably saw me as a troublemaker. But how to silence a troublemaker?

One significant aspect must be emphasized as it does not require conjectures about hidden motivation and unconscious entanglements. The timing of the students' "protest campaign" that ultimately led to the discontinuation of their work is also of special significance. After all, the students did not voice their critical reservations when they initially encountered the methodology of the empirical investigation. Rather, they raised their objections when certain *results* of their analysis became apparent. The third-party raters discontinued their work when it became apparent that the Second Generation Jews were confronted with their parents' main experiences during National Socialism in a much clearer and more authentic way than the non-Jewish German comparison group. Obviously the third-party raters had problems with the *results* of the analysis, something they were not able to mention within the context of our collaboration. As long as they regarded the non-Jewish interviewees simply as a control group – which in all likelihood was the case until the results were collated –, the study design did not appear problematic to them. The conflict arose once the comparison group was examined more closely, when provocative results emerged from the comparison of the two groups.

The students began looking for a different explanation for their feelings, finding fault with other aspects of the study, not with the results part. The way they harmed me was perhaps an unconscious continuation of a tradi-

---

3 | These were the words used on the cover page of the Marburg magazine *Express* (Volume 8, No. 6, 1990) to refer to the article.

tion, which would need to be investigated in detail in subsequent studies. It is a legacy that entangles non-Jewish Germans with their parents who went along with the National Socialist regime: the *transmission of being a bystander* in post-National-Socialist Germany. The students *knew* that their actions caused me a great deal of distress. Nonetheless, they thought that this was appropriate and just.

When the *practical* aspect of research brings about a (partly unconscious) conflict such that the progress of the study is jeopardized, psychoanalytic interpretation seems appropriate. We obviously did not have any suitable means for settling the issue at the time. However in retrospect I am inclined to reproach myself for the naivety with which I assumed I would be able to carry out a study without taking into appropriate consideration the "loyalties" (Müller-Hohagen 2001) that prevail on all sides. A truly independent third-party rating was and probably is impossible, at least given the topic under investigation. Recognition of the *entanglements* and *loyalties* related to National Socialism may always remain highly difficult. However, such recognition constitutes a necessary condition for the resolution of conflicts that almost necessarily arise in the context of this complex and distressing topic, thus jeopardizing the scientific process of inquiry.

Complicity between Perpetrators and Victims?

> "I learned that Mr Grünberg is Jewish; Relatives of his were murdered by the Nazis. This has evidently obscured pure understanding and comprehension."
>
> (Solicitor Peter Becker, 22nd February, 1990)

Elsewhere I have described in greater detail the various strategies that exist for denying and rationalising the Shoah (Grünberg 2001). I also want to mention a few experiences, some very personal, that are related to my discussion of the psychosocial consequences of the Shoah in the context of my investigations, to the strategies of denial of Nazi persecution in the name of science and last but not least to my feelings of loneliness. The particular significance of these factors can only be understood in the context of the collision of the consequences of Nazi persecution on the descendants of survivors in Germany on the one hand, and the transmission of Nazi perpetration and silent support in the next generation of non-Jewish Germans on the other. As became apparent in the context of the so-called independent third-party rating described above, the perception and conceptualisation of the *entanglement* with people's family history under National Socialism and its effects on both sides regarding relationships, work contexts and political and cultural relations is of great significance to the topic under discussion. For that reason, the personal experiences described here are not to be understood merely as *private* experiences. Rather, they should be regarded as having social significance and as being socially determined. My research targets the *distributively organised social production of anti-Semitism* (cf. Grünberg 2002), the *dissociated fragments* of the National Socialist heritage in the "culture after Auschwitz", which must be expounded in people's interpersonal relationships and within their culture. Scientific striving for 'pure' understanding and comprehension, however, is almost certainly destined to miss these determining characteristics of the German-Jewish *Lebenswelt* after the Shoah. It is no coincidence that "academic psychology" uses the term *confounding* variable. It is precisely these "confounding" variables that grant a deeper understanding of the subject under investigation.

In early 1990 I was involved in a serious conflict with a professor at the university of Marburg. The conflict was not limited to my research, but also affected my participation in a seminar and my dissertation at Marburg University. In short, my life in Marburg was seriously thrown into question. I will analyze this controversy by examining unconscious *entanglements* of the people or groups involved with the history of National Socialism, which in turn will be invoked as a possible explanation for the disagreement.

What happened? Pohlen, at that time head of the clinic for psychotherapy at the Centre for Neurology, conducted a seminar entitled *Psychoanalysis of Nazi Fascism* (Psychoanalyse des Nazi-Faschismus). In view of the often rather tedious process at the university, I thought it remarkable for someone to tackle this important as well as altogether difficult topic in such a setting. Furthermore, Professor Pohlen was regarded as unconventional and opinionated, rhetorically adept, and not as readily conforming to the scientific mainstream. However, my initially positive assessment soon gave way to a more critical attitude when the ostensibly progressive but in reality authoritarian director of the clinic spoke about what seemed to be his real concern: Pohlen declared the persecuted Jews "unconscious accomplices". He spoke of "parallel perpetrator-victim structures" and of "dizzying mirror effects". The seminar's central concept was "complicity". Subsequent to my criticism of him (Grünberg 1990), the head of the clinic announced that he would initiate legal action against me. He threatened me with large fines and with his intention to prevent me from completing my dissertation. In a move that reversed the actual events, Pohlen declared me, his critic, a perpetrator, precisely the role he wanted me to fit. And so Pohlen – quite consistent with and confirming his "complicity" thesis – accused me of "perfidious denunciation" (Pohlen 1990, 21), and of employing "Nazi methods" (ibid., 25), "Gestapo-style slander" (ibid., 20) and "Stürmer style" (ibid., 25).[4] He sought to hide his own responsibility and – if applicable here – *his* complicity with the Nazis by creating terminological confusion. His use of language suggested that ultimately there was a degree of arbitrariness and interchangeability with respect to the terms perpetrator and victim. Such de-differentiation of concepts must have been confusing for many, if not most, of the students. Furthermore, it must have had a liberating effect and generated relief from guilt, since presumably most members of the seminar were not members of persecuted families or families of resistance fighters. If the victims were unconscious accomplices, was it not also the case that the perpetrators were victims?

At the time I was certain that I had personally experienced, recognised and reasonably clearly labelled one of the defence strategies and rationalisations of the Shoah, namely the *construction of "complicity" between perpetrators and victims*. I also felt extremely threatened. In the presence of about forty seminar participants the university professor presented a detailed charge against "the informant" who, so he claimed, wanted to bring about Pohlen's "social death, social destruction" (Pohlen 1990, 28). Shortly prior to the end of the seminar, he banished me from the room. None of the students present made even the slightest attempt to interrupt him during his one and a half hour long indictment, let alone challenge him. Only one person, a good friend of mine, timidly asked the professor at the end of the seminar whether it was possible that he Pohlen, himself, might be misguided rather than just recognising this in others. Later, after the Pohlen showdown (Laufner 1990), there *were* reactions: the medical department reprinted an article by a journalist who had snuck into Pohlen's seminar (Richard Laufner of the magazine *Express* in Marburg) and in conjunction with the Marburg "history workshop", organised a public event in the summer of 1990. I received telephone calls of support and expressions of solidarity. People were worried about me, they said.

Perhaps they were right. After all, at the very beginning of the seminar meeting, Pohlen, referring to me, spoke of a "psychopathological incident" "of what I want to *finish off* in the abstract" (Pohlen 1990, 4; my emphasis) His charge included what he had learned from Carlo Schmidt during SDS times: "Beat them up, boys. What could kill you, you must kill first." (ibid., 28) Pohlen should "beat me like he would a fascist. You should know that. I

---

4 | There has been a structurally similar controversy concerning the National Socialist past of the late founding member, training analyst, former head and honorary member of the Deutsche Psychoanalytische Vereinigung (German Psychoanalytic Association), Gerhart Scheunert, in Frankfurt/Main (cf. Grünberg 2000, 84-86).

know no mercy in this regard. Even if you confirm in writing before a court that you are a Second Generation Jew, this makes you in my eyes a Fascist whom I persecute like I would persecute Fascists. I say it again, Carlo Schmidt was completely right." (ibid.)

I probably was frightened at the time. Since I did not comply with Pohlen's demand for a "thorough and detailed apology" despite his solicitor repeatedly threatening serious fines and that I would be prevented from completing my dissertation at Marburg University, I did not feel safe. I was initially pleased about a telephone call I received at my home from the university's president reassuring me that no attempts were being made to prevent me from completing my doctoral studies at the Philipps University. He stated that he was very sorry about controversies being forcibly conducted that way at *our* university. I later questioned the value of this private telephone call. After all, it left no tangible trace that I could have referred to at a later date. I had nothing definitive to resort to.

My subsequent application to Frankfurt/Main was accompanied by some degree of worry. Was it possible that the conflict with a psychoanalyst was going to hinder my application at a psychoanalytic research institute? The above mentioned publication in the *Express* (Laufner 1990) and a radio interview on Hessischer Rundfunk radio station had generated a certain amount of publicity. It was increasingly important to me to conclude the "Marburg chapter".

In contrast to the conflict with the third-party raters, a lawsuit "Pohlen vs. Grünberg" never occurred. My solicitor in Marburg closed her offices a few months later, and I never heard from Pohlen's solicitor again either. I remember my Marburg experiences to this day, even though I have written and talked about them numerous times in order to put the matter behind me. Only much later did I realise why it was so important for Pohlen to push me into this supposed role of persecutor. His aim was to validate – for everybody to see – his thesis of the "dizzying mirror effects" between perpetrator and victim. Pohlen was fascinated by himself and by the possibility of being able to oscillate between Nazi perpetrators and the victims of Nazi persecution. Such equalisation of perpetrators and victims is a central element not only in the so-called *Historikerstreit* (historians' conflict). To this day, it is a frequently employed defence strategy to deny or rationalise the Shoah. It is often the case that German intellectuals, claiming to act on the basis of a socio-critical approach, are in actual fact embedded in the intellectual mainstream.

In his *Minima Moralia*, Theodor W. Adorno addressed in-depth the question of the particular significance of the National Socialist extermination of Jews with respect to historical comparison. He pointed out that an examination of history can only result in valuable insight if the researcher –

based on his current experience – deals with his own emotions regarding the topic under investigation. Such emotions may disturb the researcher's peace of mind so that a purely detached analysis is not possible.[5] In the case of the Shoah, the "observer" is drawn into an extreme state of emotional tension – Adorno speaks of "terror without end" – which must, at the same time, be understood as an indication of the uniqueness of the National Socialist extermination of the Jews. In its content, the thus emerging terror without end is connected to the Nazis' crimes against humanity. Any attempts to loosen this connection or to dissolve it constitute a serious relapse, a disregard of that which Adorno so strikingly explored. Adorno states:

"Auschwitz cannot be brought into analogy with the destruction of the Greek city-states as a mere gradual increase in horror, before which one can preserve tranquility of mind. Certainly, the unprecedented torture and humiliation of those abducted in cattle-trucks does shed a deathly-livid light on the most distant past, in whose mindless, planless violence the scientifically confected was already teleologically latent. The identity lies in the non-identity, in what, not having yet come to pass, denounces what has. The statement that things are always the same is false in its immediateness, and true only when introduced into the dynamics of totality. He who relinquishes awareness of the growth of horror not merely succumbs to cold-hearted contemplation, but fails to perceive, together with the specific difference between the newest and that preceding it, the true identity of the whole, of terror without end." (Adorno 1951, 234f.)

According to Adorno, after Auschwitz people had to recognise "together with the specific difference between the newest and that preceding it, the true identity of the whole" (ibid., 316 [German edition]). This is precisely what Pohlen obscured, by deliberately refraining from making important distinctions. Similarly, he was critical of Habermas' position regarding the *Historikerstreit*: "Just think of Habermas and the *Historikerstreit*. They Habermas and others; K.G.] have settled the indescribable simply by declaring it a singular occurrence – and nothing has been explained" (Pohlen 1990, 29). Interestingly, here, too, Pohlen turns the attacked into the perpetrator. In the aftermath of Pohlen's actions, a *dissociated fragment*

---

5 | Similarly Jean Améry (1977) in his preface to his book *Jenseits von Schuld und Sühne* (Beyond guilt and atonement) states: "Soon, the method forced itself upon me. While during the first few lines of the Auschwitz essay I thought that I would be able to remain cautious and detached and face the reader with distinguished objectivity, I soon realised that *this* was simply not possible. Where the 'I' should have been avoided, was the only viable starting point." (p. 15f., transl. by N.R.)

that had previously been separate became evident in the seminar: the "terror without end", which Adorno referred to in the passage cited above. During the trial situation staged by Pohlen, the accused – but perhaps also 'the people' – felt some of this terror, pointing towards the "dark traces of the past" (Rüsen and Straub 1998), towards that which Pohlen had to dilute because it is so difficult to bear. Because I was not prepared to submit to this interpretation of the past, Pohlen wanted to punish me: "There must be atonement for guilt", Pohlen said (1990, 26).

translated by Nadja Rosental

Bibliography

Adorno, T.W. (1951), *Minima moralia*. Reflections from damaged life. Translated from the German by E.F.N. Jephcott. London: Verso, 1999 [German edition: *Minima Moralia. Reflexionen aus dem beschädigten Leben*. Frankfurt a.M.: Suhrkamp, 1984]

Adorno, T.W. (1966), *Negative Dialektik*. (Gesammelte Schriften, Vol. 6). Frankfurt a.M.: Suhrkamp, 1997

Améry, J. (1977), *Jenseits von Schuld und Sühne. Bewältigungsversuche eines Überwältigten*. Stuttgart: Klett, 1980

Giordano, R. (1987), *Die zweite Schuld oder Von der Last Deutscher zu sein*. Hamburg/Zürich: Rasch und Röhring

Goldhagen, D.J. (1996), *Hitler's willing executioners*. New York: Knopf

Groeben, N. & R. Rustemeyer (1995), Inhaltsanalyse. In: E. König & P. Zedler (eds.), *Bilanz qualitativer Forschung*. Vol. 2: Methoden. Weinheim: Deutscher Studien Verlag, 523-554

Groeben, N. (1987), Möglichkeiten und Grenzen der Kognitionskritik durch Inhaltsanalyse von Texten. In: P. Vorderer & N. Groeben (eds.), *Textanalyse als Kognitionskritik? Möglichkeiten und Grenzen ideologiekritischer Inhaltsanalyse*. Tübingen: Narr, 1-21

Grünberg, K. (1983), *Folgen nationalsozialistischer Verfolgung bei Kindern von Überlebenden/Juden in der BRD*. Marburg, Universität, Fachbereich Psychologie, diploma thesis

Grünberg, K. (1990), "Psychoanalyse des Nazi-Faschismus" – Stellungnahme eines Ungebildeten. Unpublished manuscript

Grünberg, K. (2000), *Love after Auschwitz*. The Second Generation in Germany, Bielefeld: transcript – New Brunswick/London: Transaction Publishers, 2006

Grünberg, K. (2001), Vom Banalisieren des Traumas in Deutschland. Ein Bericht über die Tradierung des Traumas der nationalsozialistischen

Judenvernichtung und über Strategien der Verleugnung und Rationalisierung der Shoah im Land der Täter. In: K. Grünberg & J. Straub (eds.) *Unverlierbare Zeit*. Psychosoziale Spätfolgen des Nationalsozialismus bei Nachkommen von Opfern und Tätern. Tübingen: Edition diskord, 181-221

Grünberg, K. (2002), Zur "Rehabilitierung" des Antisemitismus in Deutschland durch Walser, Möllemann u.a. oder Ich weiß wohl, was es bedeutet. Über das allmähliche Verfertigen des Ressentiments beim Reden: Eine psychoanalytische Betrachtung des Antisemitismus. In: M. Naumann (ed.), *"Es muß doch in diesem Lande wieder möglich sein...". Der neue Antisemitismus-Streit*. München: Ullstein, 224-229

Laufner, R. (1990), Die ausweglose Spiegelung. Eklat im Seminar "Psychoanalyse des Nazi-Faschismus". *Marburger Magazin Express 8*, No. 6, 8-9; reprint in: Fachschaft Medizin (ed.), *Curare*, No. June, 17, 1990, 16-17

Leuzinger-Bohleber, M. (1995), Die Einzelfallstudie als psychoanalytisches Forschungsinstrument. *Psyche 49*, 434-480

Mayring, P. (1988), *Qualitative Inhaltsanalyse*. Grundlagen und Techniken. Weinheim: Deutscher Studien Verlag

Mayring, P. (1991), Qualitative Inhaltsanalyse. In: U. Flick, E. v. Kardorff, H. Keupp, L. v. Rosenstiel & S. Wolff (eds.), *Handbuch Qualitative Sozialforschung*. München: Psychologie Verlags Union, 209-213

Müller-Hohagen, J. (2001), Seelische Weiterwirkungen aus der Zeit des Nationalsozialismus zum Widerstreit der Loyalitäten. In: K. Grünberg & J. Straub (eds.), *Unverlierbare Zeit*. Psychosoziale Spätfolgen des Nationalsozialismus bei Nachkommen von Opfern und Tätern. Tübingen: Edition diskord, 83-118

Pohlen, M. (1990), Theorieseminar Psychoanalyse des Nazifaschismus vom 19.2.1990. Universität Marburg, unpublished manuscript

Rüsen, J. & J. Straub (eds.) (1998), *Die dunkle Spur der Vergangenheit*. Psychoanalytische Zugänge zum Geschichtsbewußtsein. Frankfurt a.M.: Suhrkamp